Guide to Wireless Communications

Fourth Edition

Jorge L. Olenewa

CENGAGE
Learning·

Australia • Brazil • Mexico • Singapore • United Kingdom • United States

CENGAGE
Learning·

Guide to Wireless Communications, Fourth Edition

Jorge L. Olenewa

SVP, GM Science, Technology & Math: Balraj S. Kalsi

Senior Product Director: Kathleen McMahon

Product Team Manager: Kristin McNary

Associate Product Manager: Amy Savino

Senior Director, Development: Julia Caballero

Senior Content Development Manager: Leigh Hefferon

Senior Content Developer: Michelle Ruelos Cannistraci

Product Assistant: Abigail Pufpaff

Marketing Director: Michelle McTighe

Production Director: Patty Stephan

Senior Content Project Manager: Brooke Baker

Art Director: Jack Pendleton

Cover Image(s): iStockphoto.com/agsandrew

For product information and technology assistance, contact us at **Cengage Learning Customer & Sales Support, 1-800-354-9706**

For permission to use material from this text or product, submit all requests online at **www.cengage.com/permissions**. Further permissions questions can be e-mailed to **permissionrequest@cengage.com**

Library of Congress Control Number: 2016952388

ISBN: 978-1-305-95853-1

Cengage Learning
20 Channel Center Street
Boston, MA 02210
USA

Cengage Learning is a leading provider of customized learning solutions with employees residing in nearly 40 different countries and sales in more than 125 countries around the world. Find your local representative at **www.cengage.com**.

Cengage Learning products are represented in Canada by Nelson Education, Ltd.

To learn more about Cengage Learning, visit **www.cengage.com**

Purchase any of our products at your local college store or at our preferred online store **www.cengagebrain.com**

Notice to the Reader

Publisher does not warrant or guarantee any of the products described herein or perform any independent analysis in connection with any of the product information contained herein. Publisher does not assume, and expressly disclaims, any obligation to obtain and include information other than that provided to it by the manufacturer. The reader is expressly warned to consider and adopt all safety precautions that might be indicated by the activities described herein and to avoid all potential hazards. By following the instructions contained herein, the reader willingly assumes all risks in connection with such instructions. The publisher makes no representations or warranties of any kind, including but not limited to, the warranties of fitness for particular purpose or merchantability, nor are any such representations implied with respect to the material set forth herein, and the publisher takes no responsibility with respect to such material. The publisher shall not be liable for any special, consequential, or exemplary damages resulting, in whole or part, from the readers' use of, or reliance upon, this material.

Some of the product names and company names used in this book have been used for identification purposes only and may be trademarks or registered trademarks of their respective manufacturers and sellers.

Printed in the United States of America
Print Number: 01   Print Year: 2016

Brief Contents

ch 1, 5, 6, 7, 8, 12, 10

Table of Contents

CHAPTER 7
Enhancing WLAN Performance **233**

CHAPTER 8
Expanding WLANs and WLAN Security **271**

Introduction

We live in a wireless world! All the technologies and standards that have been released in the past five years, along with the ones that will be released between now and 2020, means that almost everything we do—every aspect of our lives—has a wireless component. In fact, wireless data communication is omnipresent today—in the cordless phones we use in our homes and offices, in the over 6 billion cellular phones that roam the world, even in warehouses, where wireless is used to keep track of inventory. Today, we can purchase nearly all types of products or board a flight with our cellular phones and tablets, thanks to wireless. Furthermore, homes, businesses, and even whole towns are now equipped with wireless networks that allow residents, employees, and visitors to access the Internet from anywhere using laptop computers, mobile phones, and tablets.

Whether you are a manager who needs a better understanding of the impact of wireless communication devices, an IT professional looking to enhance your understanding of the field by learning more about wireless data communications, or a student taking an introductory course in this topic, *Guide to Wireless Communications*, Fourth Edition, will help you in that journey and prepare you for more in-depth learning.

Approach

Since the introduction, in mid-1995, of infrared data interfaces in laptop computers, which allowed two computers to communicate without wires, along with the publication, in 1997, of the first IEEE 802.11 wireless local area network standards, the field of wireless data communications has continued to expand at a dramatic pace. This book provides the reader with an in-depth introduction to wireless data communication technologies that are based on standards, along with others that are important components of today's wireless world. The text covers the basics of radio frequency transmissions, transmitters, receivers, antennas, IEEE 802.15.1 and Bluetooth, IEEE 802.15.4 and ZigBee standards for low-rate wireless personal area networks, IEEE 802.11a/b/g/n/ac/ad and the upcoming /ax and /ay standards for wireless local area networking (Wi-Fi), IEEE 802.16 (WiMAX) and Free Space Optics (infrared) wireless metropolitan area networks, the evolution of cellular technology all the way to 5G and satellite wireless wide area networks, and, finally, radio frequency identification (RFID) and near field communication (NFC). Many aspects of coexistence (the ability of two or more of these technologies to work in the same physical space) are also discussed, as are the basics of implementation and security issues for each of the mentioned technologies, along with a comprehensive tour of the various business and residential applications of wireless technologies in Chapter 12.

Using straightforward language, this text introduces the most important technical aspects of each technology and can be used in classroom settings in technical colleges, early year university courses, or for distance education. It features extensive linking to websites where the reader can find additional materials. Please note, however, that although the URLs for some of these sites were accurate at the time this book was printed, these web resources can change frequently.

This text's pedagogical materials include Real-World Exercises, which further your learning outside the classroom setting, and Hands-On Projects, which take you through the often step-by-step process of performing tasks relevant to working in wireless communications. The Hands-On Projects, which can be performed in the lab or at home, use inexpensive, consumer-class equipment as well as freeware and demo versions of popular software. Finally, there are Challenge Case Projects, team-based research projects that help expand the students' knowledge of the technologies discussed and direct them to additional learning resources.

Intended Audience

Guide to Wireless Communications, Fourth Edition, is designed to meet the needs of students and professionals who want to gain a better understanding of the fundamental concepts, scope, and issues surrounding the implementation of wireless data communications technologies. The text assumes a basic knowledge of computers and networks at CompTIA A+ and Network+ levels. The pedagogical features provide a realistic, interactive learning experience to help prepare students for the challenges of working in the field of wireless data communications.

Chapter Descriptions

Here is a summary of the topics covered in each chapter of this book:

Chapter 1, Introduction to Wireless Communications, provides an overview of a range of applications of wireless data communications in personal, local, metropolitan, and wide area networks. This chapter also looks at some of the advantages and challenges of wireless data communications.

Chapter 2, Wireless Data Transmission, introduces you to wireless data transmission techniques by discussing various techniques used with infrared light and radio waves to transmit data without wires.

Chapter 3, Radio Frequency Communications, looks at the individual component blocks used in the design of radio systems and how they are used to transmit data. It also provides an overview of standards and their role in the wireless data communications industry, which is important knowledge for anyone working in the industry.

Chapter 4, How AntennasWork, takes a simplified but in-depth look at antennas and the important role they have in the successful implementation of a wireless data communications system.

Chapter 5, Wireless Personal Area Networks, looks at the first two technologies developed for short-range wireless data communications, Bluetooth and ZigBee (IEEE 802.15.4).

Chapter 6, Introduction to Wi-Fi WLANs, provides essential knowledge of the basics of Wi-Fi LANs by taking an in-depth look at the early design and implementation of IEEE 802.11, Wi-Fi, and prepares the reader to learn about the more complex enhancements to the standard covered in later chapters.

Chapter 7, Enhancing WLAN Performance, details all of the IEEE 802.11 amendments that have helped make WLAN performance competitive with wired LANs, from 802.11a/g to 802.11ac and introduces 802.11ax and ay.

Chapter 8, Expanding WLANs and WLAN Security, covers implementation enhancements that have been created to expand WLANs and make them easier to manage. It also introduces core WLAN security concepts.

Chapter 9, Wireless Metropolitan Area Networks, is an introduction to Free Space Optics, microwave, and WiMAX, wireless technologies that can interconnect LANs, provide last-mile connectivity, and also make it possible to deploy data networks in remote areas, across and in between cities and even covering entire continents.

Chapter 10, Wireless Wide Area Networks, takes a look at the evolution, design, and the basics of implementation of cellular networks, as well as satellite technologies and how these are used to extend the reach of wireless data communications networks across the entire world.

Chapter 11, Radio Frequency Identification and Near Field Communication, describes the RFID technology that is being used today to help identify, count, and track everything from small packaged products to the entire contents of large warehouses automatically and without wires. It then introduces NFC, the technology that enables wireless payments such as Apple Pay, enables tap-to-pay using credit and debit cards, and can simplify the establishment of connections between devices like cellular phones, tablets, wireless speakers, cameras, and other devices.

Chapter 12, Wireless Communications Everywhere, takes learners on a comprehensive tour of how wireless data communication technologies are being used today and introduces some potential future applications.

Appendix A, Completing Hands-On Projects Using Windows 10, outlines some of the differences between the text's Hands-On Projects in Microsoft Windows 7 and completing them using Windows 10 to guide users who might be using the latest version of the operating system.

Features

This book includes many features designed to enhance your understanding of wireless data communications technology:

- **Chapter Objectives**—Each chapter begins with a detailed list of the concepts to be mastered within that chapter. This list provides you with both a quick reference to the chapter's contents and a useful study aid.

- **Illustrations and Tables**—Numerous illustrations of wireless LAN concepts and technologies help you visualize theories and concepts. In addition, the tables provide details and comparisons of practical and theoretical information.

- **Chapter Summaries**—Each chapter's text is followed by a summary of the concepts introduced in that chapter. These summaries provide a helpful way to review the ideas covered in each chapter.

- **Key Terms**—The important terminology introduced in each chapter is summarized in a list at the end of each chapter. The Key Term list includes definitions for each term.

- **Review Questions**—The end-of-chapter assessment begins with a set of review questions (including multiple choice, fill-in-the-blank, and true/false) that reinforces the ideas introduced in each chapter. These questions help you evaluate and apply the material you have learned. Answering these questions will ensure that you have mastered the important concepts.

- **Hands-On Projects**—Although it is important to understand the theory behind wireless networking technology, nothing can improve on real-world experience. Toward this end, each chapter provides several Hands-On Projects that provide you with a practical wireless network experience. Some of these projects require Internet and library research to investigate concepts covered in the chapter; others let you put into practice the chapter's content using Linksys and D-Link equipment and the Windows operating system as well as software downloaded from the Internet.

- **Real-World Exercises**—In these exercises, students implement the skills and knowledge gained in the chapter by doing research and working on real design and implementation scenarios.

- **Challenge Case Projects**—These group exercises take students even further, posing questions that emulate real-life situations, thereby helping students apply their knowledge, initiative, and in-depth research.

New To This Edition

This edition covers a number of standards and technologies that were not yet approved when the third edition was published. It also covers several new topics and provides enhanced coverage of ongoing topics. New areas include:

- IEEE 802.11ac and IEEE 802.11ad/ax/ay

- LoRa (Long Range Wide Area Network)

- Microwave

- Expanded coverage of cellular technologies with LTE Advanced and 5G

- A chapter dedicated to current and future wireless data communication applications

Text and Graphic Conventions

Wherever appropriate, additional information has been added to help you better understand the topic at hand. The following icons are used throughout the text to alert you to additional materials:

The Note icon indicates helpful material related to the subject being described.

The Tip icon indicates helpful pointers on completing particular tasks.

The Hands-On Project icon indicates lab-setting projects that provide practical wireless network experience.

The Challenge Case Projects icon indicates group exercises that promote further learning by emulating real-life scenarios.

Instructor's Materials

Everything you need for your course is in one place! The following supplemental materials are available for use in a classroom setting. All the supplements available with this book are provided to the instructor online. Please visit *login.cengage.com* and log in to access instructor-specific resources on the Instructor's Companion Site.

Instructor's Manual. The Instructor's Manual that accompanies this textbook includes the following items: additional instructional material to assist in class preparation, including suggestions for lecture topics, tips on setting up a lab for the Hands-On Projects, and solutions to all end-of-chapter materials.

Cengage Learning Testing Powered by Cognero. This flexible, online system allows you to do the following:

- Author, edit, and manage test bank content from multiple Cengage Learning solutions.
- Create multiple test versions in an instant.
- Deliver tests from your LMS, your classroom, or wherever you want.

PowerPoint Presentations. This book comes with a set of Microsoft PowerPoint slides for each chapter. These slides are meant to be used as a teaching aid for classroom presentations, to be made available to students on the network for chapter review, or to be printed for classroom distribution. Instructors are also at liberty to add their own slides for other topics introduced.

Figure Files. All the figures in the book are reproduced. Similar to the PowerPoint presentations, these are included as a teaching aid for classroom presentation, to make available to students for review, or to be printed for classroom distribution.

Solutions. Answers to the end-of-chapter material are provided. These include the answers to the Review Questions and to the Hands-On Projects (when applicable).

Syllabus. To help prepare for class, a sample syllabus is provided.

About the Author

Jorge L. Olenewa has been working in and teaching data communications since 1970. With a passion for learning and teaching, Jorge has spent the past 16 years developing and teaching courses in wireless data communications at George Brown College in Toronto, Ontario, Canada. Prior to this, he worked for several large and small IT organizations, beginning with Burroughs (today Unisys), in Brazil, where he supported and trained data communications technologists throughout South and Central America. Jorge L. Olenewa is also the author of the second and third editions of *Guide to Wireless Communications*. In addition, he is actively involved in applied research at George Brown College, working on building automation and is also involved in teaching courses related to the Internet of Things, helping industry adopt and develop new wired and wireless data communications products for building and residential control systems.

Acknowledgments

Writing a textbook, especially one covering so many different technologies, is a huge undertaking that requires the involvement of a large team of people. The folks at Cengage Learning are undoubtedly one of the very best teams I have ever worked with. A special thank you is due to Product Team Manager Kristin McNary and Associate Product Manager Amy Savino, for supporting the creation of this edition. Product Manager Michelle Ruelos Cannistraci was wonderful in helping to keep this project on track and was always helpful and supportive. Developmental Editor Deb Kaufmann provided wonderful insight into my writing but also wonderful suggestions to improve the readability of the book. Content Project Manager Brooke Baker worked tirelessly behind the scenes to ensure that this edition would be released to readers as soon as possible. Technical Editor Danielle Shaw's sharp skills and knowledge helped me correct many oversights, mistakes, and inconsistencies in the text. She caught many of my "slips" and made excellent suggestions to improve the technical content. I hope to get a chance to work with this team again in a future edition of this book. A very special thank you is also due to Albert Danison, Chair of the School of Computer Technology at George Brown College in Toronto, Ontario, Canada, for his support; Hisham Alasady for sharing his in-depth knowledge of Microwave systems and LTE technology; Lei Li and Wilson Liu from Huawei in Canada for their contributions on LTE and 5G cellular technology; and James West from the University of Washington, who has been in touch with me several times since the second edition of this book with excellent questions and suggestions based on courses that he teaches and who also participated as a reviewer, for a few of the chapters. Carolyn

Duarte, from Nelson Canada, our Cengage Learning representative in Canada, also deserves a special mention here for caring and being supportive of this project. In addition, I would like to thank our team of peer reviewers, many of whom use the text in their courses and who also evaluated each chapter and provided extremely helpful suggestions and comments:

Feng Li—Indiana University Purdue University Indianapolis

Donna M. Lohn—Lakeland Community College

Babak Shoraka—Northeastern University

Sammy J. Van Hoose—Wayland Baptist University

Garrett C. Whelan—Long Beach City College

The entire Cengage Learning staff was always helpful and worked very hard to create this finished product. I feel privileged and honored to be part of such an outstanding group of professionals, and to these people and everyone on the team I extend a very sincere thank you.

Writing about such a diverse range of wireless data communications technologies also demands many hours of reading, research, and experimentation. Translating the technical language and standards into text that can be read by virtually anyone with an interest in the field is made far easier when you can count on the assistance of people who work with the various technologies every day and who can provide invaluable help with examples, equipment, and many of the pictures used to illustrate this edition.

Lab Requirements

To the User

This book is intended to be read in sequence, from beginning to end. Each chapter builds on preceding chapters to provide a solid understanding of wireless data communications. However, you may find it useful to follow Chapter 1 with Chapter 12 as a means of sparking additional interest in learning about all the technologies mentioned throughout the book. For additional information on hardware, software, and specialized requirements, as well as extra labs, or to exchange ideas and suggestions for lab exercises, please visit the author's website at *http://faculty.georgebrown.ca/~jolenewa*.

Hardware and Software Requirements

Here are the hardware and software requirements needed to perform the end-of-chapter Hands-On Projects:

- Built-in or USB Bluetooth 2.1 or 4.X adapter (supported by Windows 7 or Windows 10)
- Any consumer-class wireless residential gateway or access point, such as Linksys or DLink, and preferably a dual-band router compatible with 802.11ac. If possible, try to acquire a few new or used enterprise-class access points (APs) to provide learners with a higher-end perspective on the available configuration options. In my opinion, the standards supported by the AP are not as important as the differences between configuring a home wireless router and an enterprise AP.

- Wi-Fi-certified IEEE 802.11a/b/g/n/ac and, if possible, /ad wireless network adapter
- Windows 7 Professional or Windows 10 Professional
- An Internet connection and the most current version of a web browser such as Google Chrome or Firefox

Specialized Requirements

Whenever possible, the need for specialized equipment was kept to a minimum. However, Chapters 5, 6, 7, and 8 require the following specialized hardware:

- Laptop or desktop computers with USB version 2.0+ ports, a dual-band Wi-Fi adapter that supports 802.11n/ac, and Bluetooth (USB Bluetooth is acceptable)
- Dual- or tri-band wireless router that supports the same standards as the wireless adapter mentioned above
- One or more enterprise-class wireless access points (APs) if possible

Free downloadable software is required for some of the Hands-On Projects. Instructions for downloading the software are given in each chapter, as required. Although not mentioned specifically in the text, an Android smartphone with a Wi-Fi scanner application can prove very useful for scanning the RF Wi-Fi environment in the classroom as well as for around the campus.

This book is dedicated to the memory of my best friend ever, our toy poodle, who was my most loyal companion for just over 12 years. I will always love and remember you Charlie, and in my heart, you will live forever.

chapter 1

Introduction to Wireless Communications

After reading this chapter and completing the exercises, you will be able to:

- Describe the various types of wireless communications technologies used today
- Discuss some trends in wireless data communications
- Outline the advantages and challenges of wireless communications technology

We all know that wireless communications technologies have had a huge impact around the world. Today, wireless communications affects almost everything we do, from using our ever-present smartphones to make voice calls, to access information on the Internet, shop, keep up with friends and family, watch videos and play games, listen to music, buy movie and event tickets, and thousands of other applications, to business uses such as counting inventory using handheld wireless scanners and using portable credit or debit card readers that communicate over the cellular phone network and can also read the cards simply by having them placed near the device. There should be no question that the use of wireless devices will continue to expand into virtually every aspect of our lives.

Wireless communications has completely revolutionized the way we live, just as personal computers forever altered how we worked in the 1980s and the Internet dramatically changed how we obtained and accessed information in the 1990s. The Internet has also changed how we communicate around the world. Using wireless devices to send and receive messages through a variety of apps, as well as to connect to the Internet and access corporate applications and databases from any location in the world is now an integral part of our daily lives. And numerous devices—laptop computers, tablets, digital still picture and video cameras, printers, portable digital music players, even refrigerators, washers and dryers, watches, and electricity meters—are equipped with the ability to communicate without wires.

Today, we can all be in touch with the digital resources we need, no matter where we may find ourselves. Nearly everyone has experienced dramatic changes based on wireless technologies, to the extent that, without even thinking about it, we expect devices to be connected at all times, without using wires or cables.

Wireless Communications Technologies

Before we continue, let's define precisely what we mean by wireless communications. The term *wireless* is often used to describe all types of electronic devices and technologies not connected by a wire. A garage door opener and a television remote control can be called "wireless devices," and although they do transmit data, they have little in common with the technologies discussed in this book. Because the term *wireless* is sometimes used to refer to any device that has no wires, people can sometimes be puzzled about the exact meaning of wireless communications. A home or office cordless phone can also be considered a wireless communications device —for communicating with the human voice, that is. But for the purposes of this book, **wireless communications** is defined as the transmission of digital data while connected to some type of data network, without the use of wires. **Smartphones**, for example, can be used to make a simple voice call, but these devices have capabilities that extend far beyond that, and are also able to connect to data networks. Digital data in this case may include email messages, spreadsheets, and short messages transmitted to or from a digital cellular phone.

The next sections discuss the various forms that wireless data communications can take. You will read about Wi-Fi-based wireless LANs, Bluetooth, ZigBee, WiGig, radio frequency identification (RFID) and near field communication (NFC), as well as satellite, cellular, and fixed broadband wireless communications technologies. The specific details of each of these technologies are covered in later chapters. Let's first take a look at a few examples of technologies and what it is like to use a variety of wireless data devices.

Wi-Fi (Wireless LAN)

We begin with Wi-Fi, because it is the most common and most recognizable of all the different technologies discussed in this book. Imagine that you are getting ready to leave home for a busy workday. While you are getting ready, using your smartphone's connection to the **Wi-Fi** network or **wireless local area network** (**WLAN**), which enables you to access all the digital-data-enabled devices in the house, you play music from your smartphone through wireless speakers. These Wi-Fi-enabled speakers can play music from any of the devices connected to the Wi-Fi network and can be installed anywhere in the house without the need for wires, except for power cords. You then open your tablet and print a spreadsheet on your Wi-Fi printer to take to work, and place a call to your office to pick up your messages using your smartphone with a **Voice over Internet Protocol** (**VoIP**) app, which allows you to make calls over the Internet.

Figure 1-1 illustrates a home wireless network.

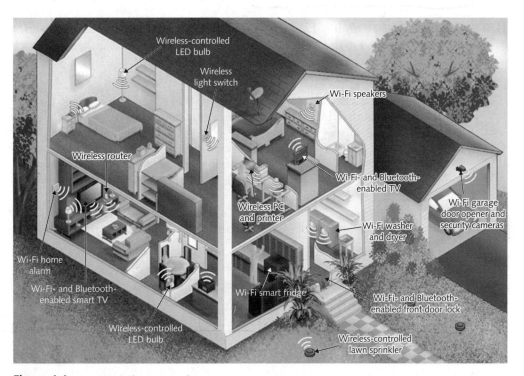

Figure 1-1   Home wireless network

Because you are inside your home using the Wi-Fi network, your smartphone can automatically connect and access the Internet. Using VoIP over your wireless network and the Internet instead of your cellular provider can help you save money on your bills. In fact, many people no longer have or use traditional telephone lines, preferring to have only a mobile phone. Some carriers offer a service that makes the phone automatically switch the call between your wireless network and the cellular network when you are out of range and not connected to a Wi-Fi network. This also helps the cellular carriers by reducing the amount of voice call traffic on their expensive cellular networks.

While you are having breakfast, a short beep sounds and you notice that a shopping list has been emailed to your smartphone from the refrigerator. A computer system installed in the refrigerator door lets you share a family schedule, make shopping lists, as well as exchange information through text messages or email with your computers, smartphones, and tablets. Because the refrigerator is also connected to the Internet through your Wi-Fi network, you can access this information even when you are not at home.

To watch a video demonstration of a smart refrigerator in action, search the web or YouTube using the keywords "Samsung Internet fridge."

Now let's take a look at some of the technology behind using your home WLAN.

A WLAN is an extension of a wired LAN. Wireless devices connect to it through a **wireless access point (wireless AP or just AP)**. The AP relays data signals between all the devices on the wired network, including file servers, printers, and even other access points and the wireless devices connected to the AP itself. The AP is fixed in one place, although it can be moved when necessary, whereas the devices that connect to an AP are usually portable and have the freedom to move around the office area or sometimes an entire business or school campus.

In your home, each device that is connected to the Wi-Fi WLAN is equipped with a **wireless network interface card (wireless NIC)**, which communicates with your **wireless residential gateway** (often called a **wireless router**), and some have more than one NIC, to allow connection to different types of wireless networks. A wireless NIC performs the same function as a wired NIC and looks very similar, except that it has one or more antennas instead of a socket for a cable connection. The gateway includes an AP that enables every Wi-Fi-capable device in your home to be interconnected without the trouble and expense of installing cables; this wireless network also enables these devices to share any kind of data that they can process and also allows devices to share an Internet connection.

The devices that can be part of your home or office wireless network include not only computers but also VoIP cordless telephones, home entertainment systems, game consoles, portable digital music players, tablet computers, printers, the home security system, lighting and environment (HVAC) controls, and many other devices.

WLANs operate based on networking standards established by the **Institute of Electrical and Electronics Engineers (IEEE)**. The IEEE has published and is continuing to work on a series of standards used in WLANs. One of the latest standards provides for data transmission speeds of over 1 Gigabit per second or Gbps, that is, over 1,000,000,000 (1 billion) bits per second at distances of up to 375 feet (114 meters). The maximum transmission speeds that can be achieved in WLANs is dependent on the number of radios used simultaneously as well as on the maximum distance. You will learn more about this in the chapters that cover WLANs.

Throughout this book, "IEEE 802.11," "802.11," and "Wi-Fi" are used interchangeably, with or without a letter after the standard number, IEEE 802.11. If there is a letter after the number, it indicates an amendment to the standard.

To get a better idea of the data transmission speed of a Wi-Fi network, consider that each alphanumeric character transmitted typically uses 16 bits of data. This means that at only 300 Mbps, which is the speed of a typical home wireless network today, a computer can transmit about 9,000 letter-sized pages per second, with approximately 2,000 letters and spaces in each. Can you read that fast?

Virtually all smartphones, tablets, and laptop computers today are able to connect to a Wi-Fi network, and most of the latest home security, environmental control systems (heating and air conditioning), a few of the newer home appliances like refrigerators, washers and dryers, door locks, and garage doors now include the ability to connect to the Internet. This enables you to control an ever-growing number of devices in your home from wherever you may be. You can also add wireless NICs to desktop computers that may not be equipped with Wi-Fi when you purchase them and eliminate the need for network wires.

Bluetooth

Bluetooth is a wireless technology that is part of standards designed to transmit data at typically very short ranges, from a few inches to 33 feet (10 meters). The main purpose of technologies, such as Bluetooth, is to eliminate the cables between devices such as smartphones and computers, which allows data to be transmitted wirelessly between, say, a computer and a printer, as well as to synchronize your smartphone and computer. Bluetooth communicates using small, low-power transceivers called **radio modules**, which are built into tiny circuit boards and contain very small microprocessors. Bluetooth devices use a **link manager**, which is a software that helps it identify other Bluetooth devices, create a link between them, and send and receive digital data, including music and voice. Bluetooth can also be used to share many other types of data.

Bluetooth headphones and headsets are popular because they avoid annoying wires that can get caught on clothing, door handles, other people, etc., and can easily be damaged. There are also portable speakers that use Bluetooth to connect to your smartphone or tablet so you can play and share music, and some of these wireless speakers are equipped with a microphone, which allows you to use them to make hands-free phone calls.

Bluetooth is now also common in many other devices, such as smart TVs, which have web browsers and can be connected to the Internet. For example, you could connect a Bluetooth keyboard to a smart TV set and enter a web addresses from the comfort of your couch. Bluetooth is also used for connecting many other types of devices, such as a keyboard and mouse to your computer, which eliminates cables and the need to use **USB** interfaces for these devices. Tablets running on the Google Android operating system can also use Bluetooth to transfer pictures and files and you can use Bluetooth to transfer other types of files between two computers. Bluetooth is also extensively used to connect smartphones to car audio systems. This provides support for hands-free cellular phone calls as well as for playing and controlling music stored in Bluetooth-equipped smartphones and other types of music players.

Bluetooth is named after the tenth-century Danish King Harald Blåtand (or in Old Norse *Blåotnn*, which means Bluetooth) who was responsible for unifying Scandinavia. You can read more of his story on the web by searching for the king's name.

Among other technologies that use Bluetooth is iBeacon. Originally developed by Apple, iBeacon-enabled apps can not only be used in shopping malls and stores to deliver coupons and direct regular customers of a store to sale items, but it can also be used to help visually impaired persons to more easily find their way around a subway station. iBeacon uses small, inconspicuous, usually battery-powered Bluetooth transmitters that can be installed on walls and issue voice instructions from an app. Most Bluetooth devices can transfer a maximum of between 1 and 3 Mbps at distances of up to 33 feet (10 meters), but one of the latest versions of this technology is capable of transmitting data at rates of 20+ Mbps. Bluetooth is also used to connect **smartwatches** to smartphones and laptops. Most smartwatches can display notifications, who is calling, and email messages right on your wrist, so you do not have to always take your smartphone out of your pocket or purse to check it. Wearable fitness and sleep tracking devices also connect to smartphones via Bluetooth.

Take a look at some iBeacon applications at *www.iBeacon*.com or by searching for "iBeacon" on the web.

Search the web for more information on smartwatches such as those from Pebble, Apple, Motorola, Samsung, and Asus. Even a few of the traditional watch manufacturers such as Breitling are now producing smart versions that can give you notifications via your smartphone over a Bluetooth connection.

The automatic connection between various Bluetooth devices creates a **piconet**, also called a **wireless personal area network (WPAN)**. A piconet consists of two or more Bluetooth devices that are exchanging data with each other. Up to seven devices can belong to a single Bluetooth WPAN. Although Bluetooth can send data through physical barriers like walls, its limited range is more suitable for replacing cables and wires at short ranges. More than 15,000 different computer, smartphone, peripheral, and other equipment vendors today create products based on the Bluetooth standard.

The IEEE standards with the numbering beginning with 802.15 cover WPAN technologies.

ZigBee

Over the past few decades, several home automation or "smarthome" technologies have appeared on the market. Most of them were implemented as systems that depended on house electrical wiring. Later, wireless capabilities were added in the form of devices that bridged between wireless and the house's power wires. Practically none of these legacy systems are based on standards ratified by organizations like the IEEE, and although there are many compatible devices on the market that support these technologies, they will not be covered in this text.

A notable exception is **ZigBee,** a wireless communications specification based on IEEE standard 802.15.4, which is also intended for short-range transmissions. The ZigBee Alliance is the organization that creates and maintains the specification covering the upper protocol communication layers. The ZigBee Alliance also certifies compatible products.

The ZigBee specification is designed for applications that require devices with long battery life and can transmit data at distances of between 33 and 50 feet (10 to 15 meters). To pass certification, the battery life on ZigBee devices must be at least 2 years. Devices can reach others that are located farther than the maximum 50 feet (15 meters) by making use of a mesh network where devices can pass or "route" data through other devices, similar to how a router in a TCP/IP network can pass data to other routers. The maximum data rate for ZigBee is 250 Kbps (kilobits per second).

When ZigBee-enabled devices are not being used (e.g., think of a typical house light switch), they can save power by turning off their transmitters for long periods of time and only wake up periodically to check the status of the network.

Most smart LED light bulbs being produced today by large manufacturers like General Electric, Philips, and others support the ZigBee protocol and can be controlled by central hub (a kind of wireless AP), which is accessed from a smartphone app.

In addition to home automation, ZigBee is used for automating entire commercial buildings, dramatically reducing the need for control wires from every office to a central control room on the ground level or basement. This can represent major cost reductions for builders and lower maintenance expenses for the building management or owners, in addition to the potential energy savings that can be realized by making it easier for lights to be turned off at night and during holidays and weekends.

The ZigBee specification covers several other applications in addition to home and building automation. Among these are environmental sensors, medical data collection devices, smoke detectors, and security systems as well as controlling industrial equipment.

Find out more about ZigBee products by visiting the Alliance website at *www.zigbee.org* and selecting ZigBee Products. You can also learn more about smart LED lighting that works with ZigBee networks by visiting *lighting.cree.com* (search for ZigBee), *www2.meethue.com* (Philips), or *www.gelinkbulbs.com* (GE). To learn more about home automation, visit *www.wink.com* or search the web for "home automation."

WiGig

WiGig is another short-range wireless technology designed for use primarily in the home; it can transmit larger quantities of data at much higher speeds. WiGig can send and receive CD- and DVD-quality audio and video as well as Blu-ray high-definition movies from entertainment equipment, computers, or mobile devices to a TV, for example. WiGig can transfer video and sound at speeds of up to 7 Gbps (much slower from mobile devices that need to conserve battery power), using a technology called **Ultra Wide Band (UWB).** However, WiGig can transmit up to a distance of only 2 meters at these high speeds. Thus, its use is confined to the space within a room with few or no obstacles between transmitter and receiver devices, which is similar to using a TV remote control that uses infrared light, and cannot be used from a different room than the TV because light does not go through walls. In addition, the more obstacles, including people, that there are in a room, the shorter the transmission range of WiGig.

WiGig products are just beginning to be introduced into the home entertainment market. Wireless routers that support WiGig also include Wi-Fi and are able to switch automatically between the two types of connection when the devices are out of the 2-meter range of each other. You will learn more about radio frequency and WiGig in later chapters.

 WiGig was originally created by the WiGig Alliance. In 2013, this organization merged with the Wi-Fi Alliance. You can visit the Wi-Fi Alliance website to search for the latest information about WiGig and compatible products at *www.wi-fi.org*.

RFID and NFC

Radio frequency identification (RFID) is another short-distance wireless technology, developed primarily to replace the barcodes you see on nearly every product sold today. Barcodes can only store a limited amount of information, the long numbers, and sometimes letters, that are usually printed below the black and white vertical bars of the code. A key advantage of RFID over barcodes is that the information can be read from the tag regardless of whether it is visible, unlike barcodes, which require the vertical bars to be exposed to a laser beam to be read. **RFID tags** are small chips containing a CPU, memory, and other electronic circuitry plus an antenna. RFID tags offer a way to store and access additional information right on the product or the packaging, which makes it easier to identify the product type, serial number, where it was manufactured and when, as well as other information. An **RFID reader** or **RFID interrogator** emits electromagnetic waves that produce a small amount of current in the tag antenna. This current powers the chip in the tag, which in turn transmits the information stored in the tag's memory back to the reader. You will learn more about RFID technology in Chapter 11.

RFID tags are available in a large variety of types and sizes, from self-adhesive labels to key fobs, in plastic nails that can be driven into trees to help identify and track them during their lifetime, in buttons that can be sewn on clothes, and in many other forms. Automobiles that can be started by simply pressing a button on the dashboard incorporate an RFID tag in the key fob and only require the key to be inside the car for the engine to start. Some RFID tags, called active tags, are battery-powered and have a longer range. These tags can include sensors that measure and record environmental parameters that can be used to track if perishable products have been exposed to damaging temperatures or humidity, for example.

Some airports use RFID to identify luggage, a system that vastly reduces the possibility of bags being lost or redirected. As shipments are unloaded from a truck and carried into a warehouse, boxes that include an RFID tag can be read right at the loading dock, updating inventory and also directing the forklift operator where to place the products. It is also possible to tag each individual product and have inventory counted automatically.

One of the most common uses for RFID today is for inventory control. Instead of employees counting inventory manually, an extremely time-consuming and often inaccurate task, RFID readers can be installed throughout the building and inventory can be counted automatically by a computer operator located in an office, as frequently as desired.

Tags can be read at varying distances depending on the type of tag and reader, from less than 1 inch (2.54 centimeters) up to about 330 feet (100 meters). Data rates are usually only few kilobits per second, but this is more than enough for the small amount of data contained in the typical tag.

Near field communication (NFC) is very similar to RFID and, in fact, some RFID equipment is also able to read NFC tags. NFC is intended to work at an average distance of about 2 to 4 inches (about 5 to 10 centimeters) between a single tag and a device or between two capable devices. The transmission speed is approximately 250 Kbps, so it is suitable for reading items like credit or debit cards and for some types of wireless communications between two NFC-enabled devices. The NFC communication protocols allow battery-powered devices to exchange information and, if authorized, both read and write data to each other using secure, encrypted communications. While most RFID tags are passive and designed to store fixed numbers in a predetermined format, NFC tags can include more flexible information like web addresses, commands, or instructions. This technology has been incorporated in many smartphones and tablets today. When two NFC-equipped devices are brought close to each other, they can read data containing instructions, like how to automatically configure a Bluetooth connection between them or set up a peer-to-peer Wi-Fi network to transfer larger amounts of data.

Search the web for "NFC enabled Bluetooth speakers" to view an example of devices that use NFC to configure a connection.

Smartphones and tablets equipped with NFC are sometimes able to write on the tags. For example, you could configure an NFC tag to open your email app on your tablet, so that you would not have to search for the tag icon on the screen and tap it to access your email account. Payment systems like Google Wallet and Apple Pay use NFC to read information from an app on your phone that allows you to pay for purchases without needing to access your wallet and use a credit or debit card. Tap-to-pay debit and credit cards also use NFC to enable you to pay for purchases, usually up to a small value, often without needing to insert a card or swipe the magnetic strip, and enter your PIN code on a keypad, which helps speed the transaction.

As early as 2004, runners in the Boston Marathon covered the 26.2-mile course with tiny wireless chips clipped to their shoelaces. The chips transmit an identification code that is detected at several stations along the marathon course, and the code is used to track the runners' times as well as to email updates to the runners' friends and relatives regarding their locations and progress. For a full description of the technology employed, search the web using the keywords "Boston marathon wireless."

Wireless Metropolitan Area and Wide Area Networks

The technologies in this section are used for communications over a much wider area than the ones discussed so far. These wireless technologies can cover areas ranging from an entire city all the way to the entire planet. We begin with a look at satellite networks and also cover cellular and microwave links.

Satellite Networks Companies that have offices and stores in locations where a wired connection to the Internet is not easily available can use satellite communications to connect to the Internet. Isolated communities, away from the major cities in many countries, frequently make use of satellite communications for Internet access. International airlines offer Wi-Fi connections in flight and use a satellite connection to enable travelers to access the Internet. Passengers can use this connection to connect to corporate networks, especially during long overseas flights. Courier companies making deliveries in remote locations can use satellite-based Internet and phone connections to track and update deliveries and pick-ups, as well as update truck routes and track the location and status of their delivery vehicles in real-time. News organizations use satellite phones to establish a private connection to their data networks in remote and disaster areas, as well as in war-torn locations that lack a reliable cellular phone or other type of Internet connection. This enables news to be delivered live from virtually any place on the planet via a data connection. Scientists and people working in remote areas such as the Arctic or Antarctic, for example, use portable satellite antennas for Internet connectivity.

Figure 1-2 shows a how a satellite retransmits the signal between points on the surface of the planet.

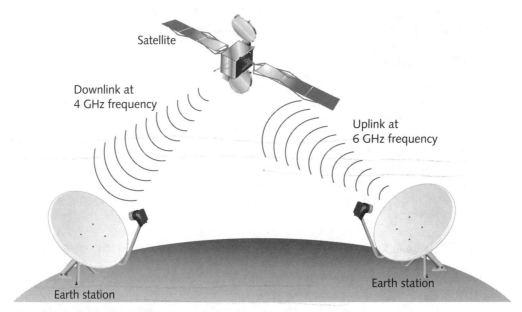

Figure 1-2   Satellite repeating a signal from one Earth station to another

In satellite communications, a device called a **repeater** is located in the satellite itself. An Earth station transmits to the satellite on one frequency band, and the satellite regenerates and retransmits (repeats) the signal back to Earth on a different frequency. The transmission time needed to repeat a signal from one Earth station to another can be up to 250 milliseconds, depending on the type of satellite used and its distance from the surface of the planet.

Satellite communications are often handled through third-party, dedicated providers, instead of the usual land-based communications companies.

The first satellite to orbit Earth successfully, called Sputnik, was launched by the Soviet Union in 1957. Today, there are more than 900 operational satellites in orbit around the planet and reportedly over 5,000 that are no longer functional. It's only due to some truly amazing mathematical calculations that they don't crash into one another, but on February 10, 2009, a nonoperational Russian satellite did crash into the Iridium 33 communications satellite, which is used for satellite phones.

Global Positioning System (GPS), used for determining the location of GPS receivers on the surface of the Earth, is also based on satellite technology. Dedicated satellites containing an atomic clock send timing signals to both GPS devices and Earth-based receivers, which use the timing information from multiple satellites to triangulate their position on the surface, with reference to the position of the satellites in orbit. GPS receivers can also provide traffic information to moving vehicles. The traffic information is transmitted from Earth stations, not the satellites, usually via the same type of signal that is transmitted by FM radio stations. GPS is not strictly a data communications technology, in the sense that GPS receivers are similar to in-car audio and do not communicate back to the satellites. Some after-market GPS receivers are also equipped with Bluetooth technology and use this to transmit turn-by-turn directions through the vehicle's audio system, instead of tiny speakers in the GPS device itself.

Satellite radio, such as SiriusXM in North America or Astra in Europe, is another example of a technology that is not strictly data communications. Satellite receivers do not communicate back to the satellites. Detailed coverage of GPS and satellite radio is beyond the scope of this text.

Cellular Networks Cellular digital technology is widely used today to maintain connectivity while out of range of a Wi-Fi network. Cellular communications today spans not only cities but can cover an entire country, as well as a continent, enabling users to travel very long distances while being able to make voice calls and access the Internet. A modern cellular telephone network is built around the concept of low-power transmitters, with each "cell" handling a number of users. How many users can connect to a cell depends on the type of cellular technology. With transmission towers spread throughout a city, as well as along major highways, the same radio frequency channel can be used by towers located a few miles from each other, thereby avoiding interference. The issue is that there is only a limited range of radio frequencies available. The concept of cells maximizes the use of the available frequency channels by reusing the same frequency two or more antenna towers away from each other. This is also made possible within major urban centers by using low-power digital transmission technology, which permits another transmitter to use the same frequency a relatively short distance away without causing interference problems. This topic is discussed in greater detail in Chapter 10.

Tablet computers can also be equipped with cellular technology, which can be used to keep a user connected regardless of the location, so long as you can connect to a carrier's network. Most smartphones also allow wireless tethering, meaning that you can use them to create a **Wi-Fi hotspot** and wirelessly connect a tablet or laptop computer to the smartphone, which then lets you access the Internet. People who work in the field, such as in heating and ventilation service, computer service, and many other types of service, often carry tablets or other dedicated data terminal equipment that enables them to connect to the main office, download and edit service orders, view schematic diagrams, send and receive email messages, access maps and get directions via the Internet, and connect to wireless printers so they can provide receipts to customers. Many restaurants are now equipped with portable terminals that enable you to use a credit card to pay and get your receipt right at your table.

Courier companies were one of the first types of business to use dedicated terminals to read the barcode information on package labels, allow the customer to electronically sign on an LCD screen, and transmit this information immediately to the main office via the cellular network. Many passenger cars today offer connectivity to the Internet via the cellular network and some cars even offer Wi-Fi so that all passengers (but hopefully not the driver, for safety reasons) can connect and access the Internet. Public transportation such as buses and trains also offer Wi-Fi capability, even on some intercity routes frequently used by commuters and businesspeople.

The data is actually transmitted to a cellular tower, which retransmits it to the destination via the cellular carrier's central office. This cellular technology is based on a standard commonly known as **4G (fourth generation)** technology, which uses 100 percent digital transmission for data and, in the most advanced versions, voice calls are also transmitted through the same data network that is used for Internet access. Using a 4G cellular phone, dedicated mobile data terminal, tablet computer, or laptop, cellular technology allows the user to make a voice call at the same time as data is being transmitted or received.

 The range of cellular-enabled data terminal equipment that can be connected to the Internet using cellular technology is always expanding. You can get an idea about what is available today by searching the web for "Mobile Data Terminal (MDT)."

Fourth generation or 4G sends data to mobile devices at rates that can theoretically reach well over 100 Mbps when the devices are not moving and located in an area with few concurrent users, 50 Mbps for slow-moving pedestrians, and over 20 Mbps in a fast-moving vehicle. LTE Advanced, a newer version, has theoretical downstream speeds of 1 Gbps and upstream speeds of up to 500 Mbps. 4G technologies are today being deployed worldwide and are expected to eventually harmonize all the different digital cellular specifications around the world into a single standard. In most cases, when you are outside of the reach of a 4G cellular network, a mobile device can switch to **3G** **(third generation)** cellular technology. The 3G or third generation data speeds will be much lower, but should be able to maintain a data connection at speeds between 3 and 11 Mbps.

Many Wi-Fi home routers and even some enterprise-class APs can have cellular capability added. Should the wired Internet connection fail, the devices can switch to a cellular data connection automatically. A digital cellular network is illustrated in Figure 1-3.

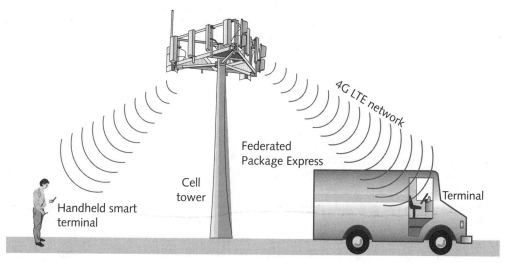

Figure 1-3 Digital cellular network

NOTE One of the most recent and innovative uses of cellular technology combined with Bluetooth is luggage tracking. Because of the large volume of lost luggage by airline customers, a few companies have introduced small, battery-powered devices that you can simply turn on and throw inside bags that will be checked in. If your bag is misdirected, the devices will attempt to connect over the cellular network available at airports. Upon arriving at your destination, if your luggage does not arrive, you can use an app on your mobile phone to find its location and inform the airline, which should then be able to retrieve it. The devices also use Bluetooth technology to send a message via the app to your smartphone when your luggage has arrived at the carousel, assuming, of course, that it made it to same destination as you and on the same flight. This device can reduce your time and frustration in tracking your luggage. Search the web for "luggage tracking" to find a range of products.

Using cellular technologies, companies can create a **wireless wide area network (WWAN)** that enables their employees to access corporate data and applications from virtually anywhere—across the country, an entire continent, and from anywhere around the world.

Fixed Broadband Wireless In areas where wired Internet connectivity may not be available and where the installation of cables may be difficult, the solution often is to deploy wireless links based on microwave data equipment or WiMAX. These technologies are commonly called **fixed broadband wireless**, because they were originally intended for communications between fixed points like buildings or towers, although the WiMAX specification and the related IEEE 802.16 standard include an amendment for mobile communications as well. Even in cities, traditional high-speed land-based digital phone lines such as **T1** or faster, or the more modern **optical fiber** cables, can be very expensive to rent and cost far too much to install and maintain. These types of wired connections are usually installed by and leased from telephone and other utility companies, who already own most of the communication infrastructure. Technologies such as **cable modems**, which 1use a television cable connection to provide Internet access, are generally available only in or near residential areas. **Digital subscriber line** (DSL), which uses either regular or special telephone lines, is sometimes available, but the speed is dependent on the distance between a company's office and the nearest telephone switching office (CO, for "central office").

The best and lowest-cost way for companies to link their office locations is to use a **wireless metropolitan area network (WMAN)**. A single WMAN link can cover an area of about 25 square miles (40 square kilometers), and it can be used to carry data, voice, and video signals. Some WMANs today are based on the IEEE **802.16 (WiMAX)** fixed broadband wireless standard and use radio waves for data communications. Longer distance links of 35 miles (56 kilometers) are usually installed by carriers and similar types of service providers using microwave data transceivers that can transmit at 400+ Mbps. Some companies, such as those in the petroleum drilling and extraction industry, install their own dedicated networks in remote areas to ensure the data they collect is made available at their central offices as quickly as possible. For shorter distances, fixed broadband networks use small antennas on the roof of each building in urban centers to create a dedicated WMAN.

WiMAX can transmit at speeds as high as 75 Mbps at distances of up to 4 miles (6.4 kilometers) and 17 to 50 Mbps (depending on link quality) at distances over 6 miles (10 kilometers) in a straight line. A recent amendment to WiMAX (IEEE 802.16m) can achieve speeds of up to 100 Mbps and up to 1 Gbps in a point-to-point link. The use of antennas substantially reduces the cost of WiMAX when compared to traditional wired connections, which require installation under city roads, are more prone to damage, and are more expensive to repair and maintain.

Ironman triathlons, which can encompass a wide geographical area, can now be viewed live online using an IEEE 802.16 WMAN to connect cameras along the race route to the event's website. Several channels of video are sent out, allowing enthusiasts to check what is happening at different race checkpoints simultaneously.

The Wireless Landscape

Most of what we do in terms of data access in a typical day could not be attempted—much less completed—without wireless technology. As new wireless communications technologies are introduced, they will continue to be a part of our lifestyle and will continue to change how we live. Figure 1-4 provides a visual comparison of the range of different wireless data technologies discussed in this chapter.

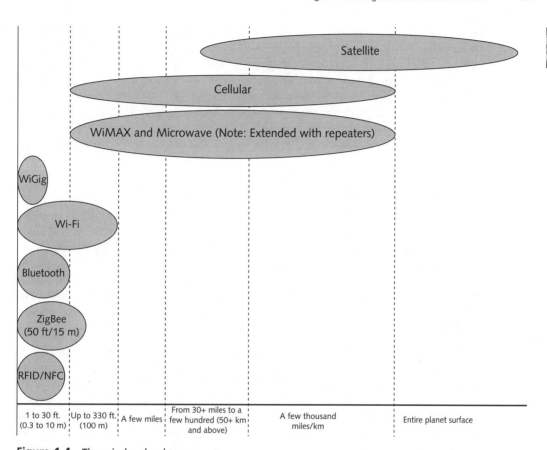

Figure 1-4   The wireless landscape

The speed of wireless networks varies greatly, depending on the number of users connected, the amount of data traffic, the amount of interference present at the time, and many other factors that will be discussed in later chapters.

Just as the number of wireless devices will dramatically increase, so will the number of job opportunities to support these new technologies. The demand for professionals such as wireless engineers, wireless network managers, and wireless technical support personnel, the people who build and maintain the networks, will continue to grow for many years to come.

Digital Convergence and Future Trends

Users are constantly demanding more functionality from their computers, and as a result, wireless devices such as cellular phones and tablets are being combined into single devices, what we today call smartphones or phablets. These devices have also continued to add capabilities. Whereas they were initially used only as appointment calendars, contact lists, and phones, today they can play computer games with sophisticated graphics, play short- and full-length movies, and play music as well as provide web access and run business and utility software while connecting via the cellular network or WLAN. Some carriers even provide users with the ability to watch live television programs and full-length movies on their smartphones.

Digital convergence refers to the power of digital devices—such as desk and laptop computers and wireless handhelds like smartphones—to combine voice, video, and text-processing capabilities as well as to be connected to business and home networks and to the Internet. The same concept applies to the development of VoIP networks, which use the same protocols and media (both wired and wireless) that once carried only data to carry two-way voice conversations. Wireless networks in general play an important part in digital convergence as users demand to be connected to their data and voice networks at all times, wherever they may be. Cellular providers worldwide are making it possible to watch TV programming and even access on-demand movies and Internet radio. Video calls, using Apple's FaceTime app and many others, are also commonplace today, finally realizing a long-standing ambition of major telephone companies worldwide to provide this capability.

The recent and upcoming advances in wireless technology and standards discussed in this book will enable an ever-wider range of applications for wireless devices. There are now smartphones that incorporate all voice and data communications in addition to providing entertainment functions and allowing the user to make payments and debits directly from a bank or prepaid account, and many more devices with these same capacities will be introduced in the near future. Today, people in many parts of the world can book a hotel, pay for a bus or streetcar ride, buy a snack from a vending machine, order movie tickets, and so forth just using their smartphones. They don't need to carry a wallet.

Digital wireless communications has expanded almost beyond human imagination and this trend is likely to continue at a very fast pace. Wireless networks have overcome most of the speed limitations since the original WLAN and other standards were approved. At one time, paperless tablet devices like the ones you may have seen in old Star Trek movies were practically unthinkable. Today, they are commonplace in homes and offices and are being used for a very wide range of applications. Patients can swallow tiny wireless cameras installed in capsules that enable doctors to conduct examinations inside a person's body without the need for exploratory surgery. It is virtually impossible to make predictions or to cover every single application here. Every day, a new application for wireless data transmission is thought of or implemented.

Wireless Advantages and Challenges

As with any technology, wireless communications offers both advantages and challenges.

Advantages of Wireless Networking

There are many advantages to using wireless technology compared to wired networks. These include mobility, easier and lower-cost installation, increased reliability, and more rapid disaster recovery.

Mobility The freedom to move about without being tethered by wires is certainly the principal advantage of a wireless network. Mobility enables users to stay connected to the network no matter where they roam within the network's range. Many workers who can't stay tied to a desk—such as police officers who need to access vehicle registration and infraction records or inventory clerks who work in large stores or warehouses—are finding that wireless data communications has become vital to the performance of their jobs.

Wireless technology also enables many industries to shift toward an increasingly mobile workforce. Many employees spend large portions of their time away from a desk—whether they are in meetings, working on a hospital floor, or conducting research. Laptop computers—and, more recently, tablet computers, smartphones, and other portable devices—allow these employees to enjoy added convenience, including access to the company network and business applications.

One characteristic of today's business world is "flatter" organizations, meaning there are fewer management levels between top executives and regular employees. Much of the work is done in teams that cross both functional and organizational boundaries, requiring many team meetings away from the employees' desks. The need for immediate access to network resources exists while these meetings are taking place and video conferencing is a popular way for staff in different locations around the world to get together, watch presentations, and view different types of information via screen sharing. Instead of sending staff on long trips, companies can save time and travel expense with video conferencing, which also helps reduce their carbon footprint. WLANs are again here the solution to the problem. They give team-based workers the ability to access the network resources they need while collaborating in a team environment from their home offices or virtually anywhere.

Easier and Less Expensive Installation

Installing network cabling can be a difficult, slow, and costly task, especially in older buildings. Facilities constructed prior to the mid-1980s were built without any thought given to running computer wiring in each room. Thick masonry walls and plaster ceilings are difficult, messy, and loud to drill holes through and snake cabling around. Some older buildings have asbestos—a potentially cancer-causing insulation material—that has to be completely removed before cabling can be installed. And there are often restrictions on modifying older buildings that have historical value.

In all these instances, a WLAN is the ideal solution. Historical buildings can be preserved, dangerous asbestos doesn't need to be disturbed, and difficult drilling can be avoided by using a wireless system. And, of course, eliminating the need to install and reinstall cabling can result in significant cost savings for companies.

WLANs also make it easier for any office to be modified with new cubicles or furniture. No longer does the design for a remodeled office first have to consider the location of the computer jack in the wall when relocating furniture. Instead, the focus can be on creating the most effective work environment for the employees.

The amount of time required to install network cabling is generally significant. Although the cable itself is not very expensive, installers must pull wires through the ceiling and then drop cables down walls to network outlets. This can usually take days or even weeks to complete, and in countries where labor costs are high, this can make it very expensive. And except in the case of brand-new buildings, employees must somehow continue their work in the midst of the construction zone, which is often difficult to do. Using a WLAN eliminates any such disruption.

To find interesting articles about installing data networks in very old buildings, search the web for "installing wireless in a castle."

Increased Reliability Network cable failures may be the most common source of network problems. Moisture in the air, a leak during a stormy season, or something as simple as a coffee spill can erode metallic conductors. A user who shifts the computer on her desk might break the network connection. When cables are installed in the ceiling or behind walls, a cable splice that is done incorrectly can result in unexplainable errors that are very difficult to locate and troubleshoot. Using wireless technology eliminates these types of cable failures and increases the overall reliability of the network.

Disaster Recovery Accidents happen every day. Fires, tornados, and floods can occur with little, if any, warning. Any organization that is not prepared to recover from such disasters will find itself quickly out of business. A documented disaster recovery plan is vital to every business if it is to get back to work quickly after a calamity.

Because the computer network is such a vital part of the daily operation of a business, the ability to have the network up and working after a disaster is critical. Many businesses are turning to WLANs as a major piece of their disaster recovery plans, in addition to using IEEE 802.11n or IEEE 802.11ac wireless networking as the main connectivity solution. Savvy planners keep laptop computers with wireless NICs and access points in reserve along with backup network servers. Then, in the event that an unfortunate disaster such as a flood, fire, hurricane or tornado destroys the facilities, managers can quickly relocate the office without needing to install new network wiring. Instead, the network servers are installed in the building along with the access points, and the laptop computers are distributed to the resettled employees.

Challenges of Wireless Networking

Along with the many advantages of wireless technology, there are challenges and concerns, including radio signal interference, security issues, and possible health risks.

Radio Signal Interference Because wireless devices operate using radio signals, the potential for two signals to interfere with each other exists. Virtually any wireless device can be a source of interference for other devices.

Several common office devices emit signals that may interfere with the receivers in a WLAN. These devices include microwave ovens, elevator motors, and other heavy electrical equipment, such as manufacturing machines, photocopiers, certain types of outdoor lighting systems, theft protection systems, and cordless telephones. These may cause errors to occur in the transmission between a wireless device and an access point. In addition, Bluetooth, WLAN 802.11b/g/n, and ZigBee devices can all operate in the same radio frequency, potentially resulting in interference between such devices in spite of efforts to design these radios to automatically avoid interference.

Interference is nothing new for a computer data network. Even when using cables to connect network devices, interference from fluorescent light fixtures and electric motors can sometimes disrupt the transmission of data. The solution for wireless devices is the same as that for standard cabled network devices: locate the source of the interference and eliminate it. This can usually be resolved by moving a photocopier or microwave oven across the room or to another room. Most wireless devices can identify that an error has occurred in the transmission and retransmit the data as necessary.

Outside interference from AM or FM radio stations, TV broadcast stations, or other large-scale transmitters is not an issue because they operate on vastly different frequencies and power levels. However, global positioning system (GPS) and satellite transmissions can sometimes affect Bluetooth and WLAN transmissions outdoors.

Security Because a wireless device emits radio signals that can cover a wide area, security becomes a major concern. It is possible for an intruder to be lurking outdoors with a laptop computer and a wireless NIC with the intent of intercepting the signals from a nearby wireless network. Because much of a business's network traffic may contain sensitive information, this is a real concern for many users.

However, some wireless technologies can provide added levels of security. A special coded number can be programmed into an authorized wireless device, which must then transmit this special number prior to gaining access to the network; otherwise, it is denied access. Network managers can also limit access to a wireless network by programming it with a list of approved wireless devices. Only those devices on the list will be allowed access. As a further protection, data transmitted between the access point and the wireless device is often encrypted in such a way that only the recipient can decode the message. If an unauthorized user were to intercept the radio signals being transmitted, he or she could not read the messages being sent.

Wireless networks are subject to jamming attacks that are difficult to locate and deal with without the proper troubleshooting tools. Rogue APs can be connected to a wired network by employees and can represent a significant security risk for companies. Fortunately, enterprise-class wireless equipment today provides many options for detecting and dealing with these types of threats.

Health Risks Wireless devices contain radio transmitters and receivers that emit radio frequency (RF) energy. Typically, these wireless devices emit low levels of RF energy while being used. Scientists know that high levels of RF can produce biological damage through heating effects (this is how a microwave oven is able to cook food). However, it is not known if lower levels of RF can cause adverse health effects. Although some research has been done to address these questions, no clear picture of the biological effects of this type of radiation has been found to date.

Most wireless devices also emit very low levels of RF energy when in stand-by mode. These levels are considered insignificant and do not appear to have health consequences.

In the United States, the Food and Drug Administration (FDA) and the Federal Communications Commission (FCC) set policies and procedures for some wireless devices, such as cellular telephones. However, only the World Health Organization (WHO) currently conducts and sponsors research on this topic. In May 2011, the WHO issued a warning that wireless devices can be "carcinogenic" but also included a statement that no clear adverse health effects had been directly linked to cancer or other biological problems in human beings. The announcement was more specifically directed at users of cellular handsets, which place the transmitter antenna very close to the head during a call. One of the ways to alleviate this danger is to always use a headset when talking on a cellular device.

The FCC and FDA, along with the Environmental Protection Agency (EPA), established RF exposure safety guidelines for wireless phones back in 1996. Before a wireless phone is available for sale to the public, it must be tested by the manufacturer and certified that it does not exceed specific limits. One of the limits is expressed as a Specific Absorption Rate (SAR). SAR relates to the measurement of the rate of absorption of RF energy by a wireless phone user. The FCC requires that the SAR of handheld wireless phones not exceed 1.6 watts per kilogram, averaged over 1 gram of tissue.

Science today does not yet permit us to draw a definitive conclusion about the safety of wireless mobile devices. Although there is no proof that using mobile wireless devices has adverse health effects, it is wise to be aware of the possibility and monitor ongoing scientific research.

Chapter Summary

- Wireless communications has become ubiquitous today and is quickly becoming the standard in the business world. Remote wireless Internet connections and entire wireless computer networks are making many network-based business activities faster and more convenient.

- There are many different types of wireless networks and devices. Home users can implement WLANs to connect different devices. Bluetooth and WiGig are being implemented on consumer devices, making it possible to connect many different types of home audio and video equipment over short distances. WLANs are also becoming the standard in business networks. Fixed broadband wireless is used to transmit data at various distances, and satellite transmissions can send data around the world. Digital cellular networks are used to transmit data at speeds over 100 Mbps.

- Wireless wide area networks enable companies of all sizes to interconnect their offices without the high cost charged by telephone carriers for their landline connections.

- RFID and NFC short-range wireless technologies have revolutionized counting inventory, item identification, and payment systems, using electronic tags that can store and transmit far more information than the traditional barcode systems. NFC enables two NFC-equipped devices to communicate with each other for a wider range of functions than what is provided by reading a tag.

- Digital convergence refers to the fact that data networks today carry digitized audio (voice and music), video, and graphics in addition to other types of data. Many of today's wireless communications technologies play an important part in enabling digital convergence, with smartphones, tablets, and computers being able to provide VoIP (voice) and video calls, as well as stream music, movies, and TV programs from the Internet over many types of wireless connections.

- Mobility—the ability to move around without being connected to the network by a cable—is the primary advantage of a WLAN. Other advantages include easier and less expensive installation, increased network reliability, and support for disaster recovery.

■ There are some challenges to a WLAN. Radio signal interference, security issues, and health risks may slow down the growth of these technologies for a while, but there are so many advantages that use of wireless data will very likely continue to grow and to be an integral part of our lives.

Key Terms

3G (third generation)   A digital cellular technology that can send data at up to 21 Mbps over the cellular network.

4G (fourth generation)   A digital cellular technology, often called LTE (Long Term Evolution), that can transmit and receive data at speeds over 20 Mbps when users are moving fast to well over 100 Mbps when users are moving slowly or are stationary.

802.16 (WiMAX)   A set of standards for fixed and mobile broadband wireless communications that allows computers to communicate at up to 75 Mbps and at distances of up to 35 miles (56 kilometers) in a point-to-point configuration. This set of standards also allows the use of both licensed and unlicensed frequencies.

Bluetooth   A wireless standard that enables devices to transmit data at an effective rate of 721.2 Kbps over short distances of up to 33 feet (10 meters). Bluetooth is popular for short-distance communications between wireless devices such as smartphones, laptops, speakers, headsets, printers, smartwatches, and keyboards.

cable modem   A technology used to transmit data as well as video signals over a television cable connection.

digital convergence   The power of digital devices such as desktop computers and wireless handhelds to combine voice, video, and data, as well as to be connected to business and home networks and to the Internet.

digital subscriber line (DSL)   A technology used to transmit data at high speeds over a telephone line.

fixed broadband wireless   A group of wireless technologies intended for communications between fixed points such as buildings or communication towers.

Institute of Electrical and Electronics Engineers (IEEE)   A nonprofit organization that creates standards related to electrical and electronics products and devices that are adopted by manufacturers worldwide. IEEE's core purpose is to foster technological innovation and excellence for the benefit of humanity.

link manager   Special software in Bluetooth devices that helps identify other Bluetooth devices, creates the links between them, and sends and receives data.

near field communication (NFC)   A technology similar and sometimes compatible with RFID that can store data that can be used to configure and activate a connection between two devices over Bluetooth or Wi-Fi. NFC tags are similar to RFID tags and can also store web addresses and may contain commands to be executed by a smartphone or tablet, such as opening a web browser and automatically entering an address.

optical fiber   A glass strand, about the thickness of a human hair, that carries data signals encoded in a laser beam.

piconet   A small network composed of two or more Bluetooth devices that are exchanging data with each other.

radio frequency identification (RFID)   A technology developed to replace barcodes that uses small tags placed on product packaging and boxes that can be remotely activated and read by sensors. The data about the product is then transferred directly to an information-processing system for inventory control, location tracking, and item counting.

radio module   Small radio transceiver built onto microprocessor chips and embedded into Bluetooth devices, which enable them to communicate.

repeater   A device commonly used in satellite communications that simply "repeats" the signal to another location.

RFID reader or **RFID interrogator**   A device that emits electromagnectic energy to power a typical RFID tag and can transmit to and read the data stored in the tag's memory.

RFID tag   Device embedded in or attached to an object that contains a chip and antenna. The chip is powered by the energy emitted by an RFID reader and can then transmit information contained in its memory back to the reader.

smartphone   A device that combines a cellular phone with the capabilities of a personal digital assistant (PDA). These devices provide the user with the ability to enter appointments in a calendar, write notes, send and receive email, play games, watch videos, and browse websites, among other functions.

smartwatch   Device that functions as a regular watch but also connects via Bluetooth to the owner's smartphone. Some of these devices can run applications that link directly to the same app on the smartphone, while others only display email messages, notifications, and calls from the smartphone. A few models are equipped with speakers and microphones that allow you to answer a call without having to use the smartphone and others give you the ability to respond to text messages using your voice, directly from the watch.

T1   An older wired technology used to transmit data over special telephone lines at 1.544 Mbps.

Ultra Wide Band (UWB)   A wireless communications technology that allows devices to transmit data at hundreds of megabits or even gigabits per second at short distances—up to 6 feet (2 meters) at the higher speeds and up to 150 feet (50 meters) at lower speeds.

USB   A common way of connecting peripherals such as flash drives, Wi-Fi NICs, printers, and other peripherals to a computer. Stands for Universal Serial Bus.

Voice over Internet Protocol (VoIP)   A technology that allows voice telephone calls to be carried over the same network used to carry computer data.

Wi-Fi   A certification label awarded to IEEE 802.11 WLAN-compatible wireless devices that pass all interoperability tests performed by an organization called the Wi-Fi Alliance. The acronym is often thought to stand for Wireless Fidelity, but this is a common misconception. The name was chosen by the alliance purely for marketing reasons and is not an acronym at all.

Wi-Fi hotspot   A public Wi-Fi network that is available at many stores, coffee shops, auto repair shops, fast-food outlets, etc., for use by its customers. Individuals can also use some smartphones to create a private Wi-Fi hotspot.

WiGig   A specification for connecting computers, communication, and entertainment devices over short ranges, using the 60 GHz band at multi-gigabit speeds, developed by an alliance of companies.

wireless access point (wireless AP or just **AP)**   A device that receives the signals and transmits signals back to wireless network interface cards (NICs), typically in a WLAN. APs connect wireless devices to a wired network such as the Internet.

wireless communications Generally refers to any type of communications that does not require the use of wires or cables. In this sense, smoke signals and police radio may be understood as forms of wireless communications, but for the purpose of this book, wireless communications is defined as the wireless transmission of digital data while connected to some type of network.

wireless local area network (WLAN) A local area network that is not connected by wires but instead uses wireless technology. Its range extends to approximately 330 feet (100 meters) and has a data rate of 600 Mbps and higher. Today's WLANs are based on IEEE 802.11a/b/g/n/ac/ad standards.

wireless metropolitan area network (WMAN) A wireless network that covers a large geographical area such as a city or suburb. The technology is usually based on the IEEE 802.16 (WiMAX) set of standards and can span an entire city, covering distances of up to 35 miles (56 kilometers) between transmitters and receivers or repeaters.

wireless network interface card (wireless NIC) A device that connects to a computer or other digital device to transmit and receive network data over radio waves. It includes an antenna for wireless communication between networked devices.

wireless personal area network (WPAN) A very small network that typically extends to 33 feet (10 meters) or less. Due to its limited range, WPAN technology is used mainly as a replacement for cables. *See also* piconet and Ultra Wide Band.

wireless residential gateway (often called a **wireless router)** Device used to set up a Wi-Fi network in a home or small office. These devices are used to connect a home or small office to the Internet and are often supplied by the service provider, integrated with a cable modem.

wireless wide area network (WWAN) A WAN that uses cellular phone technologies and encompasses any geographical region, including the entire globe.

ZigBee A specification based on IEEE 802.15.4 developed by the ZigBee Alliance, an organization that creates protocols and specifications for devices used for home automation that can wirelessly control lighting, as well as security and energy systems, in homes and industries.

Review Questions

1. Ultra Wide Band transmission technology is used primarily for ＿＿＿＿＿＿ .
   a. displaying webpages on a cellular phone
   b. connecting devices installed close together at very high speeds
   c. finding the location of a car within a city
   d. transmitting data at distances of up to 35 miles

2. Bluetooth devices communicate using small radio transceivers called ＿＿＿＿＿＿ that are built onto microprocessor chips.
   a. receivers
   b. transponders
   c. radio modules
   d. link managers

3. ZigBee devices transmit data at rates of up to _____.

   a. 250 kbps

   b. 1 Mbps

   c. 721.3 kbps

   d. 3 Mbps

4. IEEE 802.11n equipped devices can be as far as 375 feet (114 meters) apart and can send and receive data at rates over _____ Mbps, according to the IEEE standard.

   a. 75

   b. 600

   c. 100

   d. 54

5. Each Bluetooth device uses a _____, which is a special software that helps identify other Bluetooth devices.

   a. frame

   b. link manager

   c. repeater

   d. bridge

6. Bluetooth can send data through physical barriers, like walls. True or False?

7. Bluetooth devices can transmit at maximum data at rates 75 Mbps. True or False?

8. A wireless network interface card performs basically the same functions and looks similar to a traditional network interface (NIC) card. True or False?

9. An Earth station transmits to a satellite at one frequency, and the satellite regenerates and transmits the signal back to Earth on the same frequency. True or False?

10. Eliminating cable installation costs is an advantage of wireless technologies. True or False?

11. The automatic connection between various Bluetooth devices creates a network called a(n) _____.

    a. micronet

    b. small net

    c. piconet

    d. Intranet

12. 4G (fourth generation) cellular technology allows data connections at a maximum rate of over _____ in fast-moving vehicles.

    a. 2 Mbps

    b. 1 Gbps

    c. 20 Mbps

    d. 100 Mbps

13. An 802.11 wireless NIC, when configured to communicate with a wired network, sends its signals through invisible radio waves to _____ .

    a. another computer directly

    b. an access point

    c. a wireless server

    d. the Internet

14. _____ is a wireless technology that can be used for data communications and transmit as far as 35 miles.

    a. Wi-Fi

    b. Microwave

    c. WiGig

    d. WWAN

15. How can a ZigBee network be extended beyond its maximum range?

    a. By using network cables

    b. It can't, you would have to use Wi-Fi or another kind of wireless network.

    c. ZigBee devices can pass information through to other devices.

    d. By installing a ZigBee AP

16. Explain the role of an access point (AP) in a WLAN.

17. Describe the difference between WPANs, WLANs, WMANs, and WWANs with a single word.

18. What could you use a WLAN for, in a classroom setting?

19. Pick one of the types of wireless networks described in this chapter, and describe how it can reduce installation time.

20. Write a paragraph about how implementing a wireless network can be helpful in case of disaster recovery.

Hands-On Projects

Project 1-1

Understanding the terminology and being able to explain what something means to a person who does not work in the same field is an essential part of any support technician's job. Although many of the following terms will be discussed and reviewed in later chapters, you should become familiar with as many of them as possible. Research these terms and write a one-sentence description of each of them, in your own words.

Broadband	Unlicensed band (wireless communications)	Transceiver
Yagi antenna	Narrowband	Spread spectrum
Radio frequency	Forward error correction	Signal bandwidth
Carrier frequency	RF signal modulation	Baseband

Project 1-2

To be successful in today's job market, wireless technicians and engineers must be familiar with the industry and have a broad knowledge of the various products available. For example, you may have heard about the Verizon Palm Pre smartphone, but who actually makes this phone? If you needed a full set of specifications for this device, you would have to contact Hewlett-Packard because Verizon does not actually manufacture it and may not provide you with all the data that you need. Using the web, research one or two manufacturers (not distributors or resellers) of the products listed below, then provide links to information about the products.

Wireless bridge	Bluetooth access point	RFID reader
NFC-enabled tablet	Wireless controller	Independent vs. dependent access point
Wireless repeater	Active RFID tag	Real-time location services (RTLS)
Wireless ISP	Bluetooth Class 1 USB adapter	NFC tags
Web-managed AP	LTE transceiver	IEEE 802.11ad wireless router

Project 1-3

Following the news about the wireless industry is a very good way to learn who uses a particular technology and for what purpose. Use local news services or the Internet to find a school, hospital, manufacturing plant, warehouse, or other business in your area that is switching to wireless technology. If possible, try to interview some of the people involved to determine why they are making the change. Ask what benefits and drawbacks they considered. Write a one-page paper describing what you find out.

Project 1-4

Because a wireless device transmits radio signals over a broad area, security becomes a major concern. What are some of the security concerns with using a WLAN? What security options are available? Write a one-page paper that addresses these concerns. Use the Internet and information from hardware and security vendors as additional resources.

Project 1-5

Using the Internet, find the latest information about health concerns using wireless technologies. What studies have been completed or are currently under way? What issues are of concern? What are the official positions of the government departments on these issues? Write a one-page paper about your findings.

Real-World Exercises

Tenbit Wireless Inc. (TWI) is a company consisting of 50 wireless networking specialists who assist organizations and businesses with network planning, design, implementation, and problem solving. You have recently been hired by TWI to work with one of its new clients, Vincent Medical Center (VMC), a large healthcare facility, concerning their wireless needs.

Each day, doctors and nurses throughout VMC's facility attend to patients, update medical records, issue prescriptions, and order medical exams. VMC has deployed a sophisticated suite of medical software that stores all patient records, exam results, and diagnoses. The system is also fully integrated with VMC's pharmacy and can process purchase orders, payments, and receipts as well as inventory and shipments, and it meets the tightest patient information protection regulations established by the federal government.

Exercise 1-1

VMC is interested in learning about the possibilities of upgrading its infrastructure and deploying a wireless network to allow doctors, nurses, and all staff members to access information from anywhere within the medical facility (two buildings). VMC does not want to spend money installing additional network cabling connections to every patient room. VMC has asked you to make a presentation to its administrator regarding the use of a WLAN. Create a presentation to deliver to the staff about WLANs. Be sure to cover the following points:

- Greater mobility for doctors and nurses
- Ease and cost of installation
- Easier network modifications
- Increased network reliability
- Radio signal interference
- Security

Exercise 1-2

VMC would like to know about potential interference that medical equipment such as X-ray machines and CT and MRI scanners might cause on the WLAN, or vice versa. Prepare a report to present to the hospital administrators addressing their concerns.

Exercise 1-3

After your presentation, the physicians and nurses seem very interested in the potential of the WLAN. However, VMC also has an outdated telephone system that provides mobile cordless handsets but is no longer supported by the manufacturer. Without the ability to use voice communications from anywhere in the facility, the staff cannot see how a wireless network alone will solve their dilemma. Create a presentation that expands on your first one and proposes a solution based on the existing WLAN.

Exercise 1-4

Although some doctors have laptop computers already equipped with wireless NICs, VMC is also interested in providing other staff members with portable data communication equipment, but at a lower cost than laptops. The devices should be able to transmit prescriptions directly to the central system. The pharmacy would then deliver medications to patients right away. VMC would also like to be able to check on the status of these pharmacy orders. VMC administrators have asked your opinion regarding using smartphones on the WLAN or tablet computers, and they have told you that their software can handle these requirements through a web server. Prepare to present your recommendations to VMC's management team.

Challenge Case Project

CASE PROJECTS

A syndicated magazine is writing an article about Bluetooth technology and has asked Tenbit Wireless Inc. for information. Form a team of three or four consultants and research Bluetooth technology. Focus on the current specifications and on the future of Bluetooth. Provide information regarding its problems and concerns by some vendors. Also provide estimates regarding how you envision Bluetooth or any other proposed technology will be used in home, office, and personal applications.

chapter 2

Wireless Data Transmission

After reading this chapter and completing the exercises, you will be able to:

- Discuss the two types of wireless transmission
- Explain the properties of a wave, such as amplitude, wavelength, frequency, and phase
- Outline the basic concepts and techniques related to the transmission of data by radio waves
- Describe spread spectrum transmissions

Consider the cell phone or smartphone that may now be in your pocket or sitting on your desk. If you were to take that phone apart, you would find an array of pieces: chips, a microphone, a speaker, resistors, capacitors, and other parts. Yet much more than just the phone hardware is needed to complete a call. Some of the other elements involved are the cellular towers, the equipment that manages your call as you move from one cell to another, and all the equipment at the telephone company's central office that directs your call to the correct recipient. Moreover, if you're calling someone overseas, additional equipment, such as satellites or underwater cables, may be used to complete the international connection.

Trying to make sense of a modern communications system is truly mind-boggling because of the sheer number of components that are involved. How can we begin to understand how it all works?

One approach is the bottom-up method, which looks first at the individual elements or components that make up a system, then ties them all together to show how the system works. This chapter uses the bottom-up approach to set the foundation for our exploration of wireless communications and networks. You will apply the concepts covered in this chapter to the technologies that will be discussed in later chapters. If you are studying or working in the IT field, you already know how data is represented inside a computer or digital device. In this chapter, you will learn how the various types of wireless signals are used to transmit data. Finally, we'll delve a little deeper into how data is transmitted using radio waves.

To keep things simple and short, we will use the **American Standard Code for Information Interchange** (or **ASCII** code), which uses only 8 bits to represent all the letters of the alphabet, all the numerals, and several symbols. You can easily find ASCII tables on the web showing the hexadecimal value for all the characters and symbols.

Recall that all numbers—such as street-address numbers or any other numbers that are not intended to be used by the computer in calculations—are stored as text (i.e., as character data, without numerical value). In this case, the number is stored in a computer's memory in binary, using ASCII code. For example, the decimal value 47 is normally stored as its binary equivalent (00101111) in the computer memory. When using ASCII code, a decimal number 4 is stored as hexadecimal 34 (0x34), which uses 1 byte (00110100 in binary); and the number 7 is stored in another byte in the computer memory using the ASCII code 0x37 (00110111 in binary).

 A limitation of ASCII is that there are not enough unique codes for all the symbols used by international languages. When 1 bit out of every byte is used for error control (parity), the ASCII code can only represent 128 different characters. Another coding scheme, called **Unicode**, is the standard that is used today. Unicode can represent 65,535 different characters because it uses 16 bits, or 2 bytes, instead of 8 bits, or a single byte, to represent each character. This means that Unicode covers all of the different languages and scripts, such as Arabic, Japanese, and Chinese characters.

Wireless Signals

Wired communications use either copper wires or fiber-optic cables to send and receive data. Wireless transmissions, of course, do not use these or any other visible media. Instead, data signals travel on electromagnetic waves. All forms of electromagnetic energy—gamma rays, radio waves, even light—travel through space in the form of waves. The light from a flashlight or the heat from a fire also moves through empty space as waves. These waves, known as **electromagnetic (EM) waves**, don't require any special medium (such as air) or any type of conductor (such as a copper wire or optical fiber). Instead, wireless signals travel freely through empty spaces at the speed of light, or about 186,000 miles (300,000 kilometers) per second.

Practically everything in the universe either emits or absorbs electromagnetic radiation. Figure 2-1 illustrates the electromagnetic spectrum and compares each of the properties of electromagnetic radiation—such as the length of an electromagnetic wave—with the sizes of some common objects and items. The middle portion of the figure shows the commonly used names for these waves, and the bottom portion shows the range of frequencies—that is, how many waves occur in 1 second—along with where these waves usually originate. For example, in the visible light emitted by a light bulb, the number of waves that occur in 1 second is higher than 10^{13}, and each wave is about the size of a bacteria—that is, 3.281×10^{-6} feet (0.000001 meters). In this chapter, you will learn about the properties of electromagnetic waves and the significance they have in wireless data communications. There are two basic types of waves by which wireless data is sent and received: infrared light and radio waves.

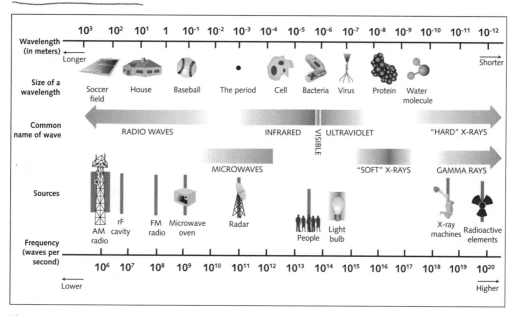

Figure 2-1 Electromagnetic spectrum

Many people, when asked what type of medium is used to send and receive wireless transmissions, answer "airwaves." If this were the case, radio signals would not propagate in space, where there is no air. Wireless transmissions use electromagnetic (EM) waves as the medium, not air or empty space.

Infrared Light

For centuries, flashes of light have been used to transmit information. Bonfires set on top of hills were once used to relay messages. Ocean vessels sent signals from ship to ship or from ship to shore using light. In 1880, Alexander Graham Bell demonstrated an invention called the photophone, which used light waves to transmit voice information. Transmitting modern computer or network data using light follows the same basic principle.

Because computers and data communications equipment use binary code, it is easy to transmit information with light. Just as binary code uses only two digits (0 and 1), light has only two properties (off and on). Sending a 1 in binary code could result in a light quickly flashing on; sending a 0 could result in the light remaining off. For example, the letter *A* (ASCII 0x41 or 01000001) could be transmitted by light as off-on-off-off-off-off-off-on. This concept is illustrated in Figure 2-2.

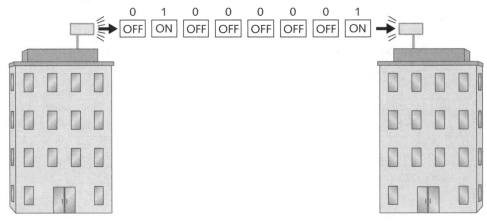

Figure 2-2   Transmitting a message using visible light

What type of light should be used to transmit these signals? Transmitting data using visible light flashes, such as a strobe light, would be very unreliable because other sources of light could be mistaken for the transmission signal or very bright light could wash out the light flashes. In addition, some types of light can be invisible to the human eye and can be blocked by various kinds of obstacles—fog, heavy rain, walls, etc.—and are therefore not a reliable medium for data transmissions.

Visible light is only one type of light. All the different types of light that travel from the Sun to the Earth make up the **light spectrum,** and visible light is just a small part of that entire spectrum. Some of the other forms of energy on both sides of the visible light portion of the spectrum, such as ultraviolet rays, are invisible to the human eye. **Infrared light,** some of which is also invisible, has many of the characteristics that visible light has because it is adjacent to visible light on the light spectrum. Yet, it is a much better medium for data transmission because it is less susceptible to interference from other sources of light, except for infrared light itself.

 Each wavelength within the spectrum of visible light represents a particular color. Differing wavelengths of light waves bend at different angles when passed through a prism, which in turn produces different colors. The colors that visible light produces are red (R), orange (O), yellow (Y), green (G), blue (B), indigo (I), and violet (V). Visible light is sometimes referred to as ROYGBIV.

Infrared wireless systems require that each device have two components: an **emitter**, which transmits a signal, and a **detector**, which receives the signal. (These two components are almost always combined into one device.) An emitter is usually a laser diode or a light-emitting diode (LED). Infrared wireless systems send data by the intensity of the light wave instead of whether the light signal is on or off. To transmit a 1, the emitter increases the intensity of the electrical current and, consequently, the intensity of the infrared light, which indicates a pulse to the receiver. The detector senses the higher-intensity pulse of light and produces a proportional electrical current (see Figure 2-3).

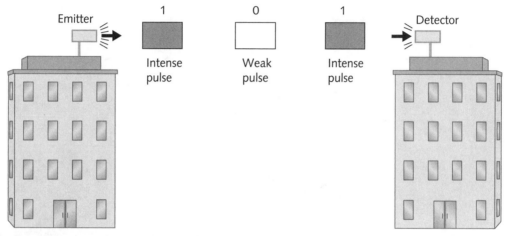

Figure 2-3   Intense and weak light pulses

Infrared wireless transmission can be either directed or diffused. A **directed transmission** requires that the emitter and detector be directly aimed at one another and not blocked by a solid object. This is called the **line of sight** principle and is shown in Figure 2-4. The emitter sends a narrowly focused or thin beam of infrared light. The detector has a small receiving or viewing area. A television remote control, for example, uses directed transmission, and this is the reason that most of us point the remotes at TV sets or other remote-controlled devices.

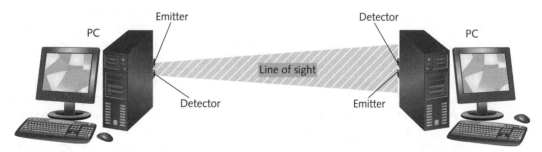

Figure 2-4   Directed infrared transmission

Although TV remote controls generally use directed transmission, with a fresh set of batteries you should be able to point the remote at a white or light colored wall directly across from the TV set and use it to change channels, increase the volume, etc.—as long as nothing else is blocking the path of the invisible infrared light.

A **diffused transmission** relies on reflected light. With diffused transmissions, the emitters have a wide-focused beam instead of a narrow beam. For example, the emitter might be pointed at the ceiling of a room and use it as a reflection point. When the emitter transmits an infrared signal, the signal bounces off the ceiling and fills the room with the signal. The detectors are pointed at the same reflection point as the emitter and can detect the reflected signal, as shown in Figure 2-5.

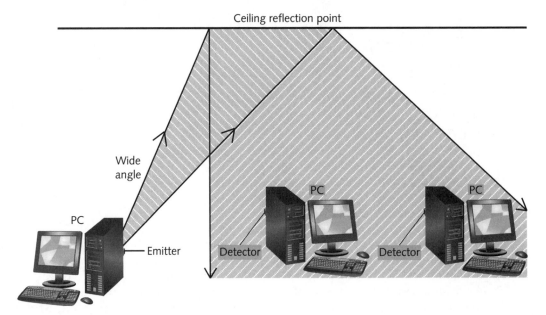

Figure 2-5   Diffused infrared transmission

Infrared wireless systems have several advantages. Infrared light neither interferes with other types of communications signals (such as radio signals) nor is it affected by other signals, except light. In addition, because infrared light does not penetrate walls, the signals are confined to the inside of a room that is surrounded by walls. This makes it impossible for someone elsewhere to listen in on the transmitted signal.

However, there are several serious limitations to infrared wireless systems. The first limitation involves the lack of mobility. Directed infrared wireless systems use a line-of-sight principle, which makes it challenging for mobile users because the alignment between the emitter and the detector would have to be continually adjusted. The second limitation is the range of coverage. Directed infrared systems, which require line of sight, cannot be placed in an environment where there is the possibility that anything could get in the way of the infrared beam (such as someone standing in front of your remote control while you are trying to change TV channels). This means that devices using infrared transmissions must be placed close enough to one another to eliminate the possibility of something moving between them. Due to the angle of deflection, diffused infrared can cover a range of only about 50 feet (15 meters), and because diffused infrared requires a reflection point, it can only be used indoors. These restrictions limit the range of coverage.

Another significant limitation of an infrared system is the speed of transmission. Diffused infrared can send data at maximum speeds of only 4 Mbps. This is because the wide angle of the beam loses energy as it reflects and spreads around the room (this is called attenuation). The loss of energy results in a weakening of the signal. The weak signal cannot be transmitted over long distances, nor does it have sufficient energy to maintain a high transmission speed, resulting in a lower data rate.

Infrared also shares the limitations of visible light and heat. Light waves, for example, cannot penetrate through most materials like wood or concrete, and heat rays are absorbed by most objects, including human skin (we feel infrared waves as heat). Solid, opaque objects, and even dust and humidity (water molecules in the atmosphere) can limit the distance that light and infrared waves can travel (see Figure 2-6).

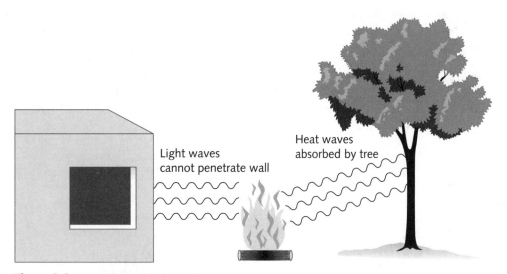

Heat waves
absorbed by tree

Light waves
cannot penetrate wall

Figure 2-6   Limitations of light and heat waves

Because of these limitations, infrared wireless systems are generally used in specialized applications, such as data transfers between laptop computers, digital cameras, handheld data collection devices, and other similar mobile devices. In the past, laptop computers were almost always equipped with infrared interfaces, which often made it easy to connect to a printer without using cables; sadly, this is no longer true. (Wireless printer connections are now implemented primarily via Wi-Fi or Bluetooth, both radio wave technologies.)

NOTE   A new system of transmitting data with light is Li-Fi. Created by Prof. Harald Haas at the University in Edinburgh, it has achieved data transmission speeds of 100 Gbps in laboratory experiments. You will look at Li-Fi again in Chapter 12. In the meantime, you can find out more about it by visiting *http://purelifi.com*.

Some specialized wireless local area networks are based on the infrared method of transmitting data signals. These are used in situations where radio signals would interfere with other equipment, such as in hospital operating rooms, or when security is a concern, such as in some government and military installations.

Is there a wave in the electromagnetic spectrum that does not have the distance and line-of-sight limitations of light or infrared? The answer is yes: radio waves.

Radio Waves

The second means of transmitting a wireless signal is by using **radio waves** (sometimes called **radiotelephony**). Radio waves provide the most common and effective means of wireless communications today.

To get an idea of how radio waves behave and begin to understand many of their properties, imagine the surface of a smooth pond of water. If you press down on the water with the palm of your hand, or throw a rock in the middle of the pond, you will cause a disturbance that will result in a series of continuously expanding circles. As the water moves up and down at the point where your hand pushed it down or the rock hit the surface of the water, more circles will appear, until the water stabilizes and the waves stop. As the waves expand away from the point where the water is moving up and down, the energy of the waves is dispersed into growing rings of waves, and the waves become smaller, lower than the waves at the center of the disturbance, where the rock or your hand hit the water (see Figure 2-7). This loss of energy and its result are also important concepts that you will learn more about later in this chapter.

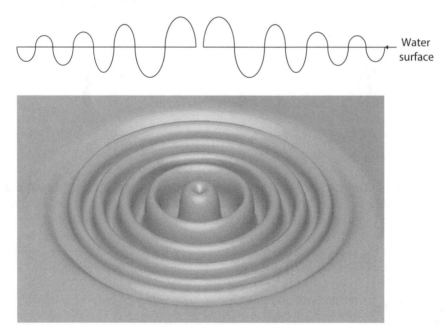

Figure 2-7   Waves created by rock thrown in water

The waves created in a pond have a shape that is similar to that of electromagnetic waves. Although when you throw a rock in a pond you can only really see the top, or high peaks of the waves created, in reality the waves extend below the surface of the water as well. At the top of Figure 2-7, you see a graphic representing what the waves in the pond would look like, if you could see them from the side. Recall that radio signals travel through empty space or air in electromagnetic waves. Infrared light, visible light from a flashlight, and heat from a fire also move through empty space or through the air in the atmosphere as waves.

With radio waves, an electric current passes through a wire, creating both magnetic and electric fields in the space around the wire. These fields radiate or move away from the wire and produce electromagnetic waves. Radio waves, like light and heat waves, are electromagnetic waves that occur in a particular range of frequencies. They move outward, away from the wire, much like the waves you see when you throw a rock in a pond.

Radio waves, however, are free from some of the limitations that affect light and heat (see Figure 2-8). Unlike heat waves, radio waves can travel great distances. Radio waves can also penetrate most solid objects (with the exception of metallic ones), whereas light waves cannot penetrate opaque or solid objects. We "see" visible light waves when they illuminate something, and we can feel heat waves, but radio waves are invisible. You cannot see, feel, touch, or smell them.

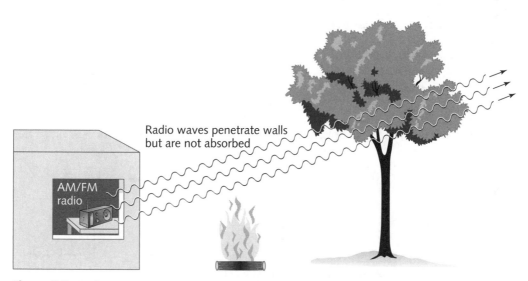

Figure 2-8   Radio waves can penetrate most solid objects and travel great distances

How Data Is Transmitted Using Radio Waves

Radio waves can be used to transmit data over long distances without the need for wires. The method by which radio waves transport data involves several concepts that will help you to better understand the technologies described in later chapters, how interference can affect transmissions, about speed of transmission and reliability issues, and how it may be possible to troubleshoot and resolve some of these problems. Understanding how radio waves transmit data will also give you a basis for learning about more advanced wireless data transmission technologies. We start by discussing the ways that analog and digital data can be transmitted over radio waves.

Analog and Digital

Waves are continuous, meaning that their up and down movement keeps happening so long as there is enough energy in the wave. An **analog signal** is one in which the waves vary continuously—in other words, the waves have no breaks in them. Figure 2-9 illustrates an analog wave. Audio, video, voice, and even light are all examples of analog signals. An audio signal that contains a tone or a song is continuously flowing and doesn't start and stop until the tone is turned off or the song is over. Sound can also vary in pitch and intensity.

Figure 2-9   Analog wave (continuous signal)

Now, suppose that instead of throwing a rock in a pond, you were to press a momentary switch on a flashlight to turn it on and off, as if you were transmitting a message in Morse code. Ignoring for a moment that light is a wave, the resulting on-off pattern of light is similar to a digital signal. A **digital signal** consists of discrete or separate pulses, as opposed to an analog signal, which is continuous. A digital signal has numerous starts and stops, on and off—like Morse code, for example, with its series of dots and dashes. Figure 2-10 illustrates a digital signal.

Figure 2-10   Digital signal (discrete or separate pulses)

Computers operate using digital signals. If analog data, such as a video image or an audio sound, needs to be stored on the computer, it must be converted into a digital format before it can be stored and processed or interpreted by a computer.

There are various techniques used to convert the different types of analog data to digital data. For CD-quality stereophonic music (two channels), the analog signal is measured (sampled) at the rate of 44,100 times per second; each sample is then stored in a digital format, using a minimum of 16 bits per sample. Using a number of other techniques, computers also compress digitized signals to minimize the total amount of storage space or the amount of data that needs to be transmitted.

To transmit a digital signal over a telephone line or TV cable, which are analog media and were not designed to carry a purely digital signal, a device known as a **modem (MOdulator/DEModulator)** is used. A modem takes the distinct pulses of electricity that make up digital signals from a computer and encodes them onto a continuous analog signal for transmission. The process of encoding the digital signals (bits) onto an analog wave is called **modulation**. The modem at the other end of the connection then reverses the process by receiving an analog signal, demodulating it, which means extracting the bits from it, to convert them back into a digital signal.

Frequency and Wavelength

The way in which a radio transmission circuit produces analog waves results in a different number of radio waves happening each second. This is a property of radio waves called **frequency**, that is, the number of times a complete wave cycle occurs each second. Each complete wave **cycle** is composed of one top (positive) peak and one bottom (negative) peak, as shown in Figure 2-11.

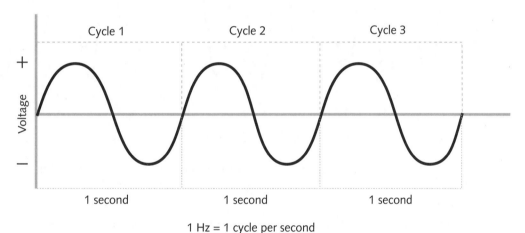

Figure 2-11   Analog wave; frequency = 1 Hz

Although frequency is a measure of the number of complete wave cycles that occur in one second, the shorter form **hertz (Hz)** is used when referring to the frequency of a wave, instead of cycles per second. A radio wave that has 710,000 Hz means that its frequency is 710,000 cycles per second. Because of the high number of cycles in typical radio waves, metric prefixes are always used when referring to their frequency. A **kilohertz (KHz)** is 1,000 hertz, a **megahertz (MHz)** is 1,000,000 (1 million) hertz, and a **gigahertz (GHz)** is 1,000,000,000 (1 billion) hertz. The wave measured as 710,000 Hz is referred to as 710 KHz.

Depending on how many wave cycles happen in 1 second (the frequency), the positive and negative peaks of the waves will be closer together or farther apart. This illustrates another property of waves, called the **wavelength,** or the length of a wave. The wavelength is the distance between any point in one wave cycle and the same point in the next wave cycle. The **amplitude** is the height of the wave from the starting point of the wave cycle to the maximum height of one of the peaks, either positive or negative. Figure 2-12 shows examples of two waves with different frequencies but the same amplitude.

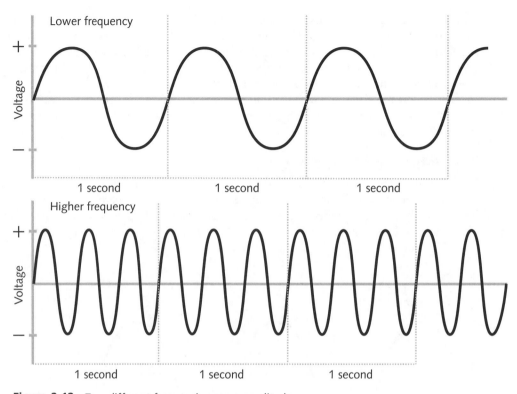

Figure 2-12   Two different frequencies; same amplitude

The top wave in Figure 2-12 has one cycle per second and the bottom one has three cycles per second. Note how the peaks of the top wave are farther apart than the ones in the bottom wave.

It is important to also notice that both the lower frequency waves and the higher frequency ones alternate to the same maximum and minimum voltage (amplitude), and that a change in voltage does not create a change in the frequency of a wave.

 The wavelength is inversely proportional to the frequency, which means that when the frequency is high, the wavelength is short and the peaks are closer together, and when the frequency is low, the wavelength is long and the peaks are farther apart.

 Frequency applies to music as well, since sound is an analog wave of air disturbances, in the form of air pressure. The frequency of the musical note A_4, for example, is 440 Hz. This means that when the note A_4 is played, 440 air pressure waves impact your eardrum each second.

To transmit information, radio transmitters use what is known as a **carrier wave**. When you want to listen to a radio station, you tune the receiver to the frequency of the carrier wave. The carrier wave has a fixed frequency, and the data to be transmitted is modulated onto it

before the signal is transmitted. In Chapter 3, you will learn more about transmitters and receivers. Before the information is modulated onto the carrier, it is simply a **continuous wave (CW)** of constant amplitude (measured in volts) and frequency. The CW is also commonly called an **oscillating signal** or **sine wave**. A CW carries no useful information by itself. Technically speaking, only after data, such as music, voice, or digital signals, is modulated onto a wave can we correctly refer to it as a carrier. However, when discussing waves used in radio transmission, it is common to refer to them as a carrier waves, even though they may not have any information modulated onto them.

 In electrical terminology, a continuously varying sine wave produces what is known as an alternating current (AC) because it flows between negative (–) and positive (+). AC is the type of current that runs to the electrical outlets in a house, and in North America it has a frequency of 60 cycles per second. Direct current (DC) is found in batteries. With DC, the current flows only in one direction, from the negative terminal (–) to the positive (+), and its voltage is static. The lack of up and down movement in DC also means that the power in a battery, for example, cannot be transmitted through empty space or a vacuum and because of this, DC cannot carry any information.

As you may know, radio waves are usually transmitted and received using an **antenna**. An antenna is a length of copper wire, or other electrically conductive material, with one end free and the other end connected to a receiver or transmitter. When transmitting, the radio waves created by the electronic circuit of the transmitter are fed to this antenna wire. This sets up an electrical pressure (**voltage**) along the wire, which causes a small electrical current to flow into the antenna. Because the current is alternating, it flows back and forth in the antenna at the same frequency as the radio waves. When the electricity moves back and forth in the antenna, it creates both a magnetic field and an electrical field around the antenna, perpendicular to each other, as illustrated in Figure 2-13. The continuous (analog) electrical pressure, the signal coming out of the transmitter, generates more waves, which move away (propagate) from the antenna the same way that water waves move away from the point of impact when you throw a rock in a pond. The result is an electromagnetic (EM) wave.

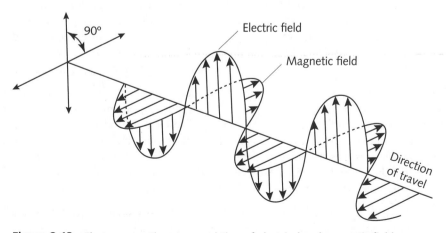

Figure 2-13 Electromagnetic wave consisting of electrical and magnetic fields

Antennas are also used to "pick-up" transmitted radio signals. An extremely small amount of electricity moves back and forth in the receiving antenna in response to the radio signal (EM wave) reaching it. This results in a very small amount of current flowing from the antenna into the receiver, as shown in Figure 2-14. In Chapter 3, you will learn what needs to be done to this small current so that the receiver can demodulate it and retrieve the data that was encoded onto the wave when it was transmitted.

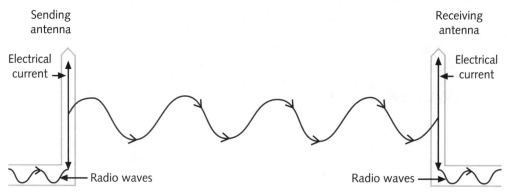

Figure 2-14   Radio antennas transmitting and receiving

Transmission Speed

Several different terms are used when referring to the transmission speed of radio waves. The electromagnetic waves themselves always travel at the speed of light, which is 186,000 miles (300,000 kilometers) per second. When digital information is transmitted using radio waves, the speed of transmission is usually shown in **bits per second (bps)**, since the primary concern is how efficiently the data can be moved from one place to another.

Another term used in measuring the speed of radio transmission is baud rate. Recall that radio transmissions send out a carrier signal and that this signal can be changed or modulated with some kind of information. A **baud** is a change in that signal, and every time the signal changes, as you will learn later in this chapter, it defines the boundary of a signal unit. **Baud rate**, then, refers to the number of signal units (changes) per second that are required to represent the bits transmitted. The fewer signal units required per second the easier it will be to demodulate it and retrieve the information stored in the wave. However, this usually also means that fewer bits can be transmitted every second.

Sometimes the terms *bps* and *baud rate* are used interchangeably, although they are not synonymous. This confusion originated with early computer modems. The first modems, for example, had speeds of 300, 600, and 1,200 baud. These early modems used a simple modulation technique and were capable of transmitting one signal unit per bit transmitted; therefore, their speed in bps was the same as the baud rate, or 300, 600, and 1,200 bps. For example, to transmit the letter U (0x55 ASCII or 01010101), it would take eight signal changes, one for each bit. Thus, the number of bits transmitted per signal unit (baud) was 1.

However, with later modems, it became possible to have a change in signal (a baud) represent more than 1 bit. A signal can be changed in several different ways, as described later in this textbook. In Table 2-1, each different change represents a combination of two bits.

Signal Change (Baud)	Bit Combination Represented
Signal W	00
Signal X	01
Signal Y	10
Signal Z	11

Table 2-1 **Bit representation of four signal changes**

The letters in Table 2-1 are simply used to differentiate between four types of signal changes. As an example, the most advanced telephone line modems transmit at a maximum rate of 4,800 baud (4,800 changes per second), which is the maximum number of signal changes that a typical phone line can support. However, because each change represents more than 1 bit, along with compression of the data, these modems can transmit data at speeds of up to 33,600 bps and receive data at up to 56,200 bps (56 Kbps modems).

56 Kbps capable modems are a little different from 33.6 Kbps modems in that one end of the connection must be a digital connection. To achieve 56 Kbps download speed, the signal conversion from analog to digital or from digital to analog must only happen at one end of the phone line. Because of this limitation, these modems achieve a downstream speed of 56 Kbps. The maximum speed from the modem side, or upstream, is 33.6 Kbps.

A signal change—that is, the change that is made to the signal that represents 2 bits—is known as a **dibit**. When a signal change can represent 3 bits, it is called a **tribit**. If 16 different signal changes are used, then 4 bits per signal unit can be represented (known as a **quadbit**). These characteristics are summarized in Table 2-2.

Name	Number of Signal Units Needed	Number of Bits Encoded per Signal Unit
Standard	1	1
Dibit	4	2
Tribit	8	3
Quadbit	16	4

Table 2-2 **Signal changes (baud) vs. number of bits represented**

Another term used when referring to transmission speed is **bandwidth**. Although this term is used to refer to the maximum data transmission capacity in digital systems, this is accurate only when referring to purely digital systems. Strictly speaking, in analog systems, bandwidth is defined as the range of frequencies that can be transmitted by a particular system or medium. In simple terms, bandwidth is the difference between the higher frequency and the lower frequency. Consider that the human voice, both male and female, falls between the range of 300 and 3,400 Hz. The difference between the two frequencies (3,400 Hz minus 300 Hz) is

3,100 Hz, which happens to be the bandwidth of human voice that is transmitted in a traditional telephone system, which is analog.

Digital Subscriber Line (DSL) modems usually transmit at speeds ranging from a few hundred Kbps to 25 Mbps and higher on a telephone line, at a distance of up to 2.5 miles (4 kilometers). The usable bandwidth of the pair of copper wires in a modern phone line is about 1 MHz. DSL takes advantage of the higher frequencies that can be transmitted on a phone line but that are not used for voice (above 4,000 Hz); it divides these into a large number of separate frequencies and transmits data bits at a few bps over several of them at the same time, resulting in the higher data rates described earlier. Full coverage of DSL technology is beyond the scope of this book, but later chapters cover technologies that work in a very similar fashion.

Analog Modulation

Recall that the carrier signal sent in analog radio transmissions is simply a continuous electrical signal. It carries no information and is more correctly referred to as a CW. Only after information is added to it by modulation should it be called a carrier. **Analog modulation** is the representation of analog information by an analog signal. There are three basic types of modulation that can be applied to an analog signal to enable it to carry information: the height of the signal, the frequency of the signal, and the relative starting point, or **phase**, of the signal. Let's look at each type of modulation separately.

The height, frequency, and relative starting point of a signal (phase) are sometimes called the "three degrees of freedom."

Amplitude Modulation (AM) The height of a wave, known as the amplitude, can be measured in volts (electrical pressure). This is illustrated in Figure 2-15 with a typical sine wave. In **amplitude modulation (AM)**, the height of the wave is changed in accordance with the height of another analog signal, called the modulating signal. In the case of an AM radio station, the modulating signal is the voice of the announcer or the music, which are also analog signals. The carrier wave's frequency and phase remain constant.

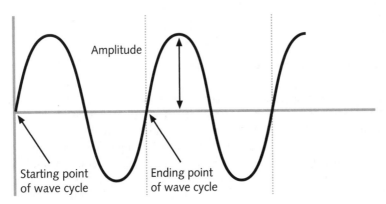

Figure 2-15 Amplitude of a signal

Amplitude modulation is used by AM broadcast radio stations. Because pure AM is very susceptible to interference from outside sources, such as lightning, it is not generally used by itself for data transmissions. Figure 2-16 shows a modulating wave, a carrier wave, and the resulting waveform after the modulation process, on the bottom. Note that the shape of the top of the modulated signal is the same as that of the modulating wave. At the bottom, the shape is also the same but is inverted (upside down) forming a kind of "envelope" or channel. In addition, note that there is no change in the frequency of the carrier wave.

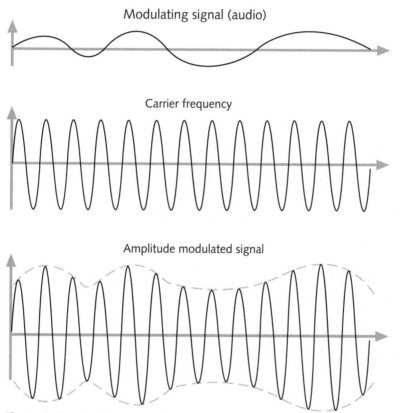

Modulating signal (audio)

Carrier frequency

Amplitude modulated signal

Figure 2-16   Amplitude modulation

Frequency Modulation (FM)

In frequency modulation (FM), the number of waves that occur during 1 second undergoes change based on the amplitude of the modulating signal, while the amplitude and the phase of the carrier remain constant. Figure 2-17 illustrates an FM signal and a simple modulating sine wave (top graphic). The bottom portion of the figure shows the result of modulating the FM carrier in frequency. Note how the frequency of the modulated wave changes proportionally, based on the change in amplitude of the input signal, which effectively allows the receiver to reproduce the modulating signal with the correct amplitude (or the volume) of the sound. The rate of change of the modulated signal (the frequency) follows the rate of change of the input, or modulating signal, which, in turn, allows the receiver to reproduce the frequency (pitch or tone) at the output. The last characteristic of the wave that also needs to be encoded in the modulated wave is the polarity (positive or negative) of the input signal. This is represented by the change in the frequency of the carrier. As you can see in the figure, when the polarity of the modulating signal is positive, the frequency of the modulated wave is high. Conversely, when the polarity of the modulating signal is low, the frequency of the modulated wave is low.

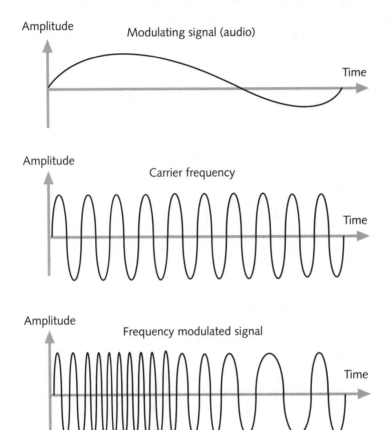

Figure 2-17   Frequency modulation

Like amplitude modulation, frequency modulation is often used by broadcast radio stations. However, FM is not as susceptible to interference from outside sources and is most commonly used to broadcast high fidelity (Hi-Fi) music. In addition, an FM carrier has a wider bandwidth, which allows it to carry stereophonic signals, with two separate sound channels.

In most countries, FM radio stations broadcast between 88 and 108 MHz, whereas AM stations transmit between 535 and 1,700 KHz.

Phase Modulation (PM) In contrast to AM, which changes the amplitude of a wave, and FM, which changes the frequency of a wave, **phase modulation (PM)** changes the starting point of the wave cycle, relative to or with reference to the starting point of the previous wave cycle, while the amplitude and frequency of the carrier remain constant. Phase modulation is not generally used to modulate analog input signals.

A signal composed of sine waves has a phase associated with it. This phase is measured in degrees, and one complete wave cycle spans 360 degrees. A phase change is always measured with reference to the wave cycle that happened immediately before. PM systems always use the previous wave cycle as the reference signal. Figure 2-18 shows an example of four different phase shifts with respect to a reference signal shown at the top of the figure, to illustrate changes in phase.

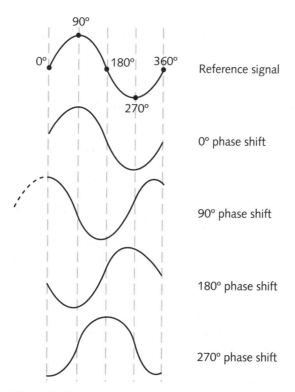

Figure 2-18   Visual representation of phase changes

Although radio broadcasts use either amplitude modulation (AM) or frequency modulation (FM), television broadcasts actually use AM, FM, and phase modulation (PM). Analog television transmissions use amplitude modulation, the sound uses frequency modulation, and the color information uses phase modulation.

Digital Modulation

How can digital data be transmitted by an analog carrier signal when the medium used for transmission cannot be used with digital signals? The simple answer is that it can be done by modulating the analog signal or changing it to represent a 1 bit or a 0 bit.

Modern wireless systems use **digital modulation**, which is the method of encoding a digital signal onto an analog wave for transmission over a medium that does not support digital signals, such as the atmosphere or the vacuum of space. In an analog system, the carrier signal is continuous, and amplitude, frequency, and phase changes also occur continuously because the input or modulating signal is still analog and therefore continuous. However, in a digital system that uses binary signals, the changes are distinct, which results in one of two states: a 1 or a 0, a constant positive or a constant negative voltage, on or off. For a computer to be able to understand these digital signals, each bit must have a fixed duration to represent a 1 or a 0 (more on digital signals later). Otherwise, the computer would not be able to determine when one bit ends and another one begins.

There are four primary advantages of digital modulation over analog modulation:

- It makes better use of the bandwidth available.
- It requires less power to transmit.
- It performs better when the signal experiences interference from other signals.
- Its error-correcting techniques are more compatible with other digital systems.

With digital modulation, as with analog modulation, there are three basic changes that can be made to the signal to enable it to carry information: the height, the frequency, and the relative starting point (phase) of the signal. However, with the never-ending demand for faster transmission speeds, more bits have to be crammed into the same number of wave cycles. Wireless communication uses many different types of modulation. For the most sophisticated modulations, it is practically impossible to show a graphic example of what the signals look like, because of how complex the signal looks. This chapter covers a few basic methods of digital modulation; these methods serve as the basis for more sophisticated modulation techniques.

Binary Signals Recall that with an analog signal the carrier wave alternates between the positive and negative voltage in a continuous cycle—that is, it doesn't stop. A binary signal can alternate between positive and zero volts or between a positive and a negative voltage. Data transmissions are typically sent in bursts of bits, meaning that some bits are transmitted, then the transmission stops, then more bits are transmitted. The best way to visualize this is that digital information sometimes has long strings of 0s and 1s and when there are no bits to be transmitted, nothing is transmitted at all. In analog systems, even when a radio station is not transmitting any sound, the carrier wave continues to be transmitted; in this case, your radio receiver simply does not detect any modulation of the carrier and therefore does not extract the original signal. Consequently, the receiver does not reproduce any sound even though the continuous carrier signal is still being transmitted and received.

Three basic types of binary signaling methods are used to represent digital data. The **return-to-zero (RZ)** technique calls for the signal to rise (the voltage to increase), for example, to represent a 1 bit. In this case, a 0 bit is represented by the absence of voltage, or 0 volts. This is illustrated in Figure 2-19. Notice that the voltage is reduced to 0 before the end of the period for transmitting a 1 bit. The signal shape does not quite "fill" the bit period; this transition of the signal in the middle of a bit period is used to synchronize the transmitter and receiver.

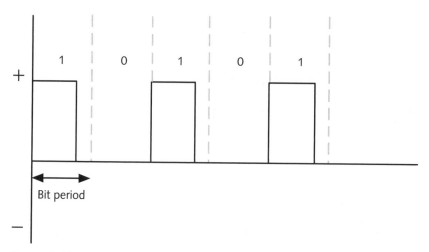

Figure 2-19   Return-to-zero

The second method is known as the **non-return-to-zero (NRZ)** technique. With non-return-to-zero, the voltage of the signal does not change for the entire length of the bit period. When the next bit to be transmitted has the same binary value as the previous bit, the signal does not change, remaining high for a 1 and low (0 volts or no voltage) for a 0. This effectively reduces the number of signal transitions (baud) required to transmit the message. As with RZ, there is no voltage when transmitting a 0 bit (see Figure 2-20) in this particular example.

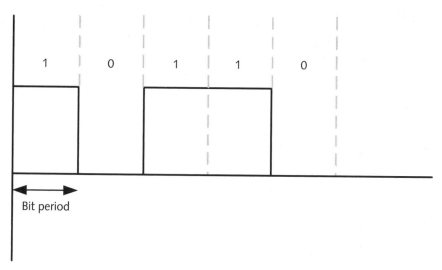

Figure 2-20   Non-return-to-zero

The final method, **polar non-return-to-zero (polar NRZ)**, uses a positive voltage to represent a 1 bit and changes the voltage to a negative value to represent a 0 bit. This technique is more commonly referred to as **non-return-to-zero-level (NRZ-L)** because the signal never returns to the 0 volts level. NRZ-L is illustrated in Figure 2-21.

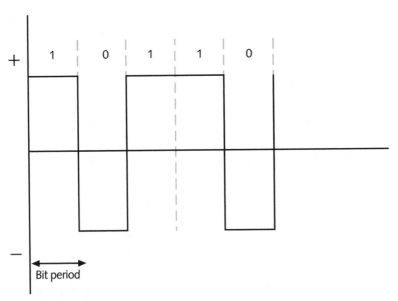

Figure 2-21   Polar non-return-to-zero

 The difference between NRZ and polar NRZ is that polar uses two voltage levels, positive and negative.

A variation of NRZ-L is **non-return-to-zero, invert-on-ones** (**NRZ-I**). NRZ-I is used to reduce the baud rate required to transmit a digital signal. In NRZ-I, a change in voltage level represents a 1 bit, whereas no change in voltage level indicates that the next bit is a 0. NRZ-I is illustrated in Figure 2-22.

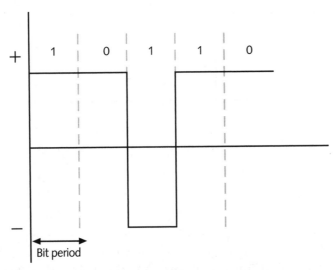

Figure 2-22   Non-return-to-zero, invert on ones

Why are there so many binary signaling methods? Here are two important reasons:

- Transmitters and receivers have a tendency to get out of synchronization with each other. If the transmitter sends a long string of 1s or a long string of 0s, the lack of transitions makes it difficult to keep both devices in sync. The transitions act like a clock pulse that helps the two radios stay synchronized.

- Digital electronic circuits tend to average the level of a signal that exhibits a lot of transitions. The result is that the more transitions the signal has, the greater the tendency of the circuit to average the amplitude of the signal, lowering it and making it harder for a receiver to detect the voltage change and understand it as a 0 or a 1. Using bipolar signals helps but does not eliminate the problem completely.

While trying to minimize the number of transitions, we must also be concerned with having enough of them to ensure good synchronization between the transmitter and the receiver. The methods just described are the most basic ones that are employed when transmitting at lower speeds. Several more sophisticated and complex methods of transmitting digital signals over wires and cables exist, but they are beyond the scope of this book. You will certainly learn about them in later, more advanced courses and books.

In digital modulation, there are three types of changes that can be made to the carrier to enable it to carry information: the height of the signal (amplitude shift keying), the frequency of the signal (frequency shift keying), and the relative starting point of the signal (phase shift keying).

Amplitude Shift Keying (ASK) Amplitude shift keying (ASK) is a binary modulation technique similar to amplitude modulation in that the height of the carrier signal can be changed to represent a 1 bit or a 0 bit. When a 1 bit and a 0 bit are transmitted, as with amplitude modulation, ASK employs NRZ encoding. The presence of a carrier signal represents a 1 bit (positive voltage), whereas the absence of a carrier signal represents a 0 bit (zero voltage). Figure 2-23 illustrates the letter A (ASCII 0x41 or 01000001) being transmitted using ASK.

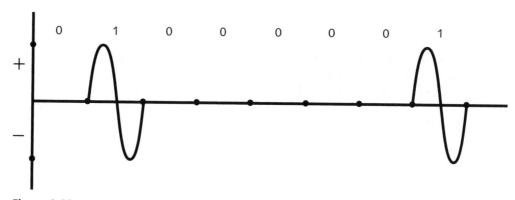

Figure 2-23 Amplitude shift keying (ASK)

The signals for transmission using digital binary modulation are shown in Figure 2-23 as sine waves because wireless transmissions use a medium (electromagnetic waves) that can only support analog signals. Recall that the direct transmission of purely digital signals (discrete pulses) can only be done using a medium that conducts electricity, such as copper wiring. Transmitting in ASK as shown in Figure 2-23 is not common, because the presence of an interference signal when there is no carrier being transmitted could be misinterpreted by the receiver as a bit with a value of 1. ASK systems typically use two amplitude levels, so there will always be a carrier wave present, making it easier for the receiver to differentiate between the two bit values. The absence of a carrier needs to be understood by the receiver as no data being transmitted at all, instead of a string of 0 bits. You will learn more about this in a later chapter that discusses RFID and NFC.

Frequency Shift Keying (FSK) Similar to frequency modulation, **frequency shift keying (FSK)** is a binary modulation technique that changes the frequency of the carrier signal to represent different bit values. Because it is sending a binary signal, the carrier signal does start and stop when the data transmission stops. As an example, when using FSK, more wave cycles are needed to represent a 1 bit and, respectively, fewer wave cycles represent a 0 bit. Figure 2-24 illustrates the letter *A* (ASCII 0x41 or 01000001) being transmitted using FSK. In this example, the number of wave cycles used to represent a 1 bit is double that of the number of wave cycles used to represent a 0 bit.

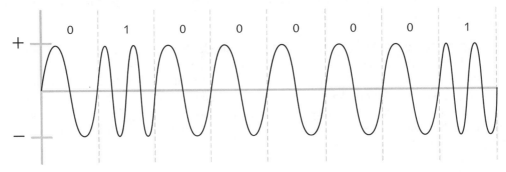

Figure 2-24 Frequency shift keying (FSK)

Phase Shift Keying (PSK) **Phase shift keying (PSK)** is a binary modulation technique, similar to phase modulation, in which the transmitter varies the starting point of the wave. The difference between PSK and phase modulation is that the PSK transmission starts and stops, because the signal being encoded onto it is binary. Figure 2-25 illustrates the letter *A* (ASCII 0x41 or 01000001) being transmitted using PSK.

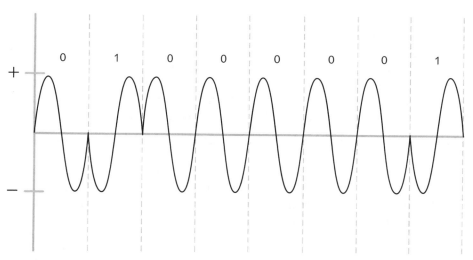

Figure 2-25 Phase shift keying (PSK)

Notice that whenever a bit being transmitted changes from 1 to 0 (or 0 to 1), the starting point (i.e., the direction of the wave) changes. For example, after the first 0 bit is represented by a "normal" carrier wave cycle, the next bit is a 1 bit. However, instead of this being indicated by another normal carrier wave cycle in which the signal goes into the positive range (goes up on the sine wave), it starts by going into the negative range. The change in starting point (going down instead of up) represents a change in the bit being transmitted (0 to 1).

In the preceding example, the change in the starting point of the wave means that the wave will start moving in the opposite direction—in this case, 180 degrees from the original direction. Note that phase modulation can change the starting point at various points (angles), as shown in Figure 2-26.

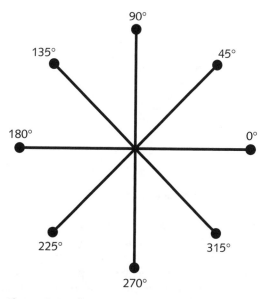

Figure 2-26 Phase modulation angles

In this case, there are eight possible starting points for a signal (0 degrees, 45 degrees, 90 degrees, 135 degrees, 180 degrees, 225 degrees, 270 degrees, and 315 degrees), with each dot in the figure representing a different starting point. You will recall that to transmit a tribit (3 bits per signal change or baud), eight different signals are needed. Using phase modulation with 45-degree angle changes results in eight different signal changes. In wireless communications today, phase modulation is combined with amplitude modulation, which is easier for receivers to detect than very small angles of phase change and this can provide 16 or more different signal changes.

In Figure 2-27, each dot represents a different signal change, for a total of 16 different combinations that can be used to transmit quadbits. This technique of combining amplitude and phase modulation is called **quadrature amplitude modulation (QAM)**. Due to the potential complexity of the resulting signal, most graphical representations of QAM only show the starting point of each wave with a dot. This representation is called a **constellation diagram**.

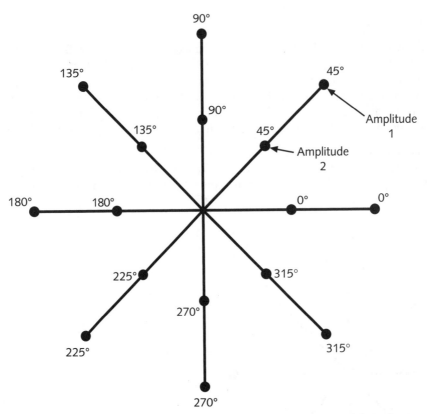

Figure 2-27   Constellation diagram (QAM-quadrature amplitude modulation)

In the presence of background electromagnetic noise (interference), receivers can detect a phase change much more reliably than a frequency or amplitude change. Noise (interference) usually occurs as a spike or sudden change in the amplitude of the signal and can also occasionally be detected as a change to a higher frequency at a particular point in the wave, although the latter happens less frequently. Because the phase of a signal is always referenced to the phase of the last wave cycle that was correctly detected, it is much less likely that noise will occur at the same time in a wave and at an amplitude level that would make the receiver detect it as a phase change; that's because noise is random. These benefits make PSK-based systems more attractive for high-speed digital wireless communications.

Figure 2-28 shows an approximate representation of the resulting waveform of this modulation technique for sending a series of 10 bits. It would be practically impossible to visualize this signal with any kind of electronic instrument, such as an oscilloscope. The graphic in Figure 2-28 is only an approximation of what this type of signal would look like.

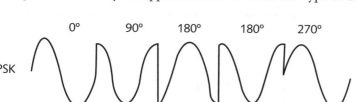

Figure 2-28 Transmitting dibits using PSK and four angles of phase change

Spread Spectrum

Radio signal transmissions are, by nature, **narrow-band transmissions**. This means that each signal transmits on one radio frequency or on a very narrow range of frequencies. An FM broadcast radio station, for example, would require you to "tune the receiver to 90.3 MHz" because this is the frequency at which it transmits. The next-lower frequency that listeners would be able to tune to would be 90.1 MHz; and 90.5 MHz would be the station with the next-higher frequency. This ensures that the station at 90.3 MHz can broadcast roughly between 90.2 and 90.4 MHz without interfering with other stations. The actual bandwidth used by FM stations is less than the difference between 90.2 and 90.4 MHz, allowing for some unused "frequency space" between the highest frequency used by the next-lower station on the FM band, the station you are tuned to, and the next station operating at a higher frequency.

Narrow-band transmissions are vulnerable to outside interference from another signal. Another signal that is transmitted at or near the broadcast frequency—90.3, in this case—can easily render the radio signal inoperable or make it difficult to detect and decode the information contained in the signal.

Broadcast radio stations work effectively with narrow-band transmissions because each station is allowed to transmit on only one frequency in a specific area. Radio stations broadcast using high-powered transmitters and use frequencies that are licensed by the Federal Communications Commission (FCC) in the United States. In contrast, Wi-Fi devices, for example, use the same frequency band but transmit at very low power levels. This means that the signals have a short-distance useful range, helping to ensure that minimum interference occurs.

An alternative to narrow-band transmission is **spread spectrum transmission**. Spread spectrum is a technique that takes a narrow-band signal and spreads it over a wider range of frequencies, as shown in Figure 2-29. Spread spectrum transmissions are more resistant to outside interference because any noise is likely to affect only a small portion of the signal instead of the entire signal. As an analogy, although an accident in one lane of an eight-lane highway slows down traffic and is very inconvenient, there are still seven other lanes that traffic can use. Likewise, spread spectrum is more "resistant" to interference and consequently spread spectrum transmission experiences fewer errors due to interference. Two common methods used in spread spectrum transmissions are frequency hopping and direct sequence.

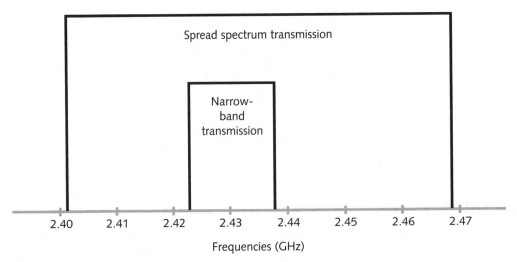

Figure 2-29   Spread spectrum vs. narrow-band transmission

Frequency Hopping Spread Spectrum (FHSS)

Instead of transmitting on just one frequency, **frequency hopping spread spectrum (FHSS)** uses a range of frequencies and changes the frequency of the carrier several times during the transmission. With FHSS, a short burst of data is transmitted in one frequency, and then another short burst is transmitted at another frequency, and so on until the transmission is completed.

Hedy Lamarr, a well-known film actress during the 1940s, and George Antheil, who had experience synchronizing the sounds of music scores with motion pictures, conceived the idea of frequency hopping spread spectrum during the early part of World War II. Their goal was to keep the Germans from jamming the equipment that guided U.S. torpedoes against German warships. Lamarr and Antheil received a U.S. patent in 1942 for their idea.

Figure 2-30 shows how an FHSS transmission starts by sending a burst of data at the 2.44 GHz frequency for 1 millisecond. Then the transmission switches to the 2.41 GHz frequency and transmits for the next millisecond. During the third millisecond, the transmission takes place at the 2.42 GHz frequency. This continual switching of frequencies takes place until the entire transmission is complete. The sequence of changing frequencies is called the **hopping code**. In the example shown in Figure 2-30, the hopping code is 2.44–2.41–2.42–2.40–2.43. The receiving station must also know and follow the same hopping code in order to correctly receive the transmission. The hopping codes are predefined and are usually part of the standard that defines how the radio circuit will be designed and implemented. Hopping codes can change so that multiple radios can each use a different sequence of frequencies within the same area and never interfere with one another, but the transmitter and receiver have to agree beforehand on which sequence to use.

Here is an analogy that may help you understand how FHSS works. Imagine that you and a friend both speak the same five languages and you want to have a conversation that would be difficult for other people around you to understand, since they do not speak the same languages, except possibly one of them. You agree before starting the conversation that you will use a particular sequence of languages and will speak in each one of them for a few words at a time. However difficult this may be to do, it would certainly accomplish your goal of not allowing anyone else around to understand the entire conversation.

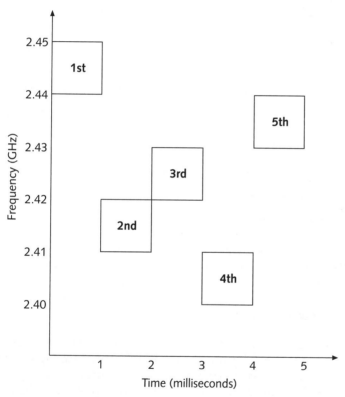

Figure 2-30   Frequency hopping spread spectrum (FHSS)

If interference is encountered while transmitting with FHSS on a particular frequency, only a small part of the message is lost. Figure 2-31 shows an example in which the second transmission has been affected by interference. Each block of data transmitted in FHSS is only about 400 bytes long. Typical FHSS systems can detect errors at the lower protocol layers and request retransmission before passing the data to higher protocol layers. Transmitter and receiver swap roles with each change of frequency, meaning that the transmitter becomes a receiver and vice-versa. When an error is detected by the receiver, it informs the transmitter during the next "slot" when it transmits back to the original transmitter. The original transmitter will retransmit the same data that was received in error when they switch roles again, using the next frequency, thus hopefully avoiding the interference from causing errors again.

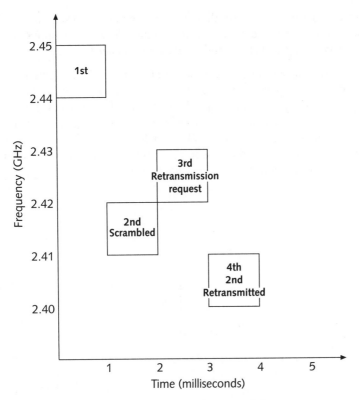

Figure 2-31   FHSS error detection and retransmission

 Some technologies make use of **forward error correction (FEC)**, a technique that sends redundant data to minimize the need for retransmission of the messages. Error handling and error detection and correction at the lower protocol layers are discussed in greater detail in later chapters.

Frequency hopping can reduce the impact of interference from other radio signals. An interfering signal will affect the FHSS signal only when both are transmitting at the same frequency and at the same time. Because FHSS transmits short bursts of data and switches frequency, the extent of any interference will be very small, the error can be detected, and the same portion of the message can be retransmitted quickly. FHSS signals also cause minimal interference with other signals. To an unintended receiver, FHSS transmissions appear to be of a very short duration (similar to noise), and unless the receiver knows the exact hopping sequence of frequencies, it is also extremely difficult to eavesdrop on the message.

A variety of devices use FHSS. Several of these devices are consumer-oriented products, because FHSS devices are relatively inexpensive to manufacture. Cordless phones, including multi-handset units, typically use FHSS. Bluetooth, which is covered in Chapter 5, also uses FHSS.

Direct Sequence Spread Spectrum (DSSS)

Another type of spread spectrum technology is **direct sequence spread spectrum** (DSSS). DSSS uses an expanded redundant code to transmit each data bit and then a modulation technique such as **quadrature phase shift keying** (QPSK). This means that a DSSS signal is effectively modulated twice. The first step before transmission is shown in Figure 2-32. At the top of the figure are two original data bits to be transmitted: a 0 and a 1.

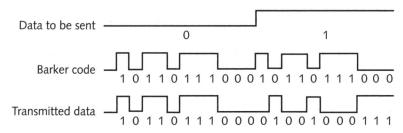

Figure 2-32   Encoding before modulation in a DSSS transmission

Instead of simply encoding these two bits over a carrier wave for transmission, the value of each data bit is first added to each individual 1 and 0 in a sequence of binary digits called a Barker code. A **Barker code** (or **chipping code**) is a particular sequence of 1s and 0s that has properties that make it ideal for modulating radio waves as well as for being detected correctly by the receiver. These 1s and 0s are called "chips" instead of bits to avoid confusing them with the actual data bits. The chipping code is sometimes called a **pseudo-random code** because it is usually derived through a number of mathematical calculations as well as through practical experimentation.

The term *Barker code* is correctly used only when referring to 802.11 transmissions at 1 and 2 Mbps. When referring to most other spreading codes used in DSSS-based systems—such as CDMA cellular phones—the terms *pseudo-random code, PN code, spreading code,* and *chipping code* may be used interchangeably.

The result of the addition is the actual set of 1s and 0s (the chips) that will be modulated over a carrier wave and transmitted (as seen in the bottom line of Figure 2-32). Let's take another look at how this sequence of chips is created. If a 1 bit is to be transmitted, then a 1 is added to each bit of the chipping code:

Bit to be transmitted: 1	1	1	1	1	1	1	1	1	1	1	1
Add Barker code:	1	0	1	1	0	1	1	1	0	0	0
Resulting sequence of chips transmitted:	0	1	0	0	1	0	0	0	1	1	1

If a 0 data bit is to be transmitted, then a 0 is added to each bit of the chipping code:

Bit to be transmitted: 0	0	0	0	0	0	0	0	0	0	0	0
Add Barker code:	1	0	1	1	0	1	1	1	0	0	0
Resulting sequence of chips transmitted:	1	0	1	1	0	1	1	1	0	0	0

The adding of the chipping code and the specific value to be added are arrived at by the Boolean operation of "exclusive or" (XOR) on a bit-by-bit basis, which is equivalent to a modulo 2 addition. In modulo 2 addition, there is no carryover, which means that 1 + 1 = 0 and 1 is not carried over to the next digit to the left. Other than that, a modulo 2 addition works exactly like a normal sum of two digits. See "Boolean Operations, XOR (Exclusive Or)" at *www.cplusplus.com/doc/papers/boolean.html*.

Instead of transmitting a single 1 or 0, a DSSS system transmits these combinations of chips. The 11 chips are transmitted at a rate 11 times faster than the data rate; in other words, the data rate does not change. However, the result of transmitting at a higher rate is the spreading of the signal over a much wider bandwidth than that of the frequency channel being used. In the case of Wi-Fi, to continue with the example given earlier, the signal is spread 11 MHz to each side of the center frequency of the channel and ends up occupying a total bandwidth of 22 MHz. Figure 2-33 illustrates the results.

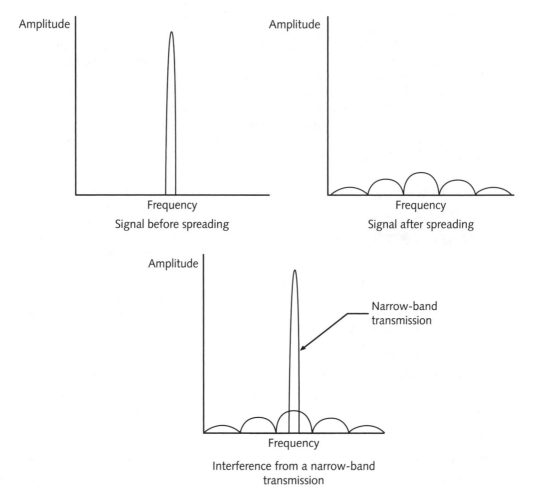

Figure 2-33   Result spreading has on frequency bandwidth and narrow-band interference effect on spread signal

This spread signal has three important characteristics:

- The frequency of the signal's digital component (or chipping rate) is much higher than that of the original data.
- A plot of the signal's frequency spectrum looks similar to random noise to narrow-band receivers.
- All the information contained in the original signal (a 0 bit or a 1 bit) is still there.

The most important aspect of this, however, is not the spreading of the signal but the fact that the power level (amplitude), *at any given frequency,* has dropped significantly as a result of spreading by using a chipping code at a higher rate than the data. In similar fashion to FHSS, a DSSS signal appears to an unintended narrow-band receiver to be low-powered noise, which is one major advantage of this method of transmission.

At the intended receiver, the signal is first demodulated and then de-spread. One of the techniques the receiver uses to detect which bit was transmitted is to count the number of 0 chips. If the pattern of chips received contains six 0s, the value of the data bit is 1. Conversely, if the pattern contains six 1s, the value of the data bit is 0.

Another major advantage of using DSSS with a chipping code is that in conventional narrow-band transmissions, any interference, even if it caused the loss of only 1 bit, would require the entire message to be resent, which takes time. In DSSS, if there is any noise or other type of narrow-band interference that may cause some of the chips to change value, the receiver can employ statistical calculations—mathematical algorithms that are used to recover the original data bit, thus avoiding the need for retransmission.

Devices that use DSSS are typically higher-end products because they are more expensive to manufacture than FHSS systems, but they also have many advantages over FHSS, as previously described. Wi-Fi WLANs use DSSS along with products that interconnect networks located in several buildings that comprise a campus setting, such as a school, a large corporation, a manufacturing plant, or a convention center.

FHSS and DSSS are not the only transmission techniques used for spread spectrum transmission. There are other techniques that are even more resistant to interference and to different kinds of phenomena that can cause data loss or reduce the performance of this type of wireless transmission. Some of the techniques are based on variations of DSSS; others are completely different. Later chapters of this book discuss some of the more sophisticated techniques as well as the types of problems that can affect wireless transmissions.

Chapter Summary

- One of the character coding schemes, which uses the numbers from 0 to 127, is called the ASCII. A character that will be stored in or transmitted by the computer is represented by its ASCII equivalent, then that number is stored as a hexadecimal value in binary.
- Whereas traditional wired communications use copper wires or fiber-optic cables to send and receive data, wireless transmissions do not use a visible medium. Instead, they travel on electromagnetic waves. There are two basic types of waves by which wireless signals are sent and received: infrared light and radio waves.

- Infrared light, which is next to visible light on the light spectrum, has many of the same characteristics as visible light. Infrared wireless transmission can be either directed or diffused. A directed transmission sends a narrowly focused beam of infrared light from the emitter to the detector. A diffused transmission relies on reflected light.

- The second means of transmitting a wireless signal is by using radio transmission. Radio waves provide the most common and effective means of wireless communications today. Radio waves have fewer limitations than light waves. Light does not go through solid objects, whereas radio waves are able to penetrate most objects.

- Radio transmissions use a carrier signal, which is a continuous wave (CW) of constant amplitude (voltage) and frequency. This signal is essentially an up-and-down wave called an oscillating signal or sine wave. The carrier signal sent by analog radio transmissions is simply a continuous electrical signal that carries no information.

- The carrier signal can undergo three types of modulation (i.e., change) to enable it to carry information: the height (amplitude) of the signal, the frequency of the signal, and the relative starting point. Amplitude modulation (AM) changes the signal height. Frequency modulation (FM) changes the number of wave cycles that occur in one second. Phase modulation (PM) changes the starting point of the cycle.

- In digital modulation, there are also three types of changes that can be made to the carrier to enable it to carry information: the height (amplitude) of the signal, the frequency of the signal, and the relative starting point. Amplitude shift keying (ASK) changes the height of the carrier to represent a 1 bit or a 0 bit. A carrier is transmitted for a 1 bit, and no signal is transmitted for a 0 bit. Frequency shift keying (FSK) is a modulation technique that changes the frequency of the carrier signal. Phase shift keying (PSK) is a modulation technique similar to phase modulation. The difference is that the PSK signal starts and stops because it is a binary signal.

- Radio station signals are by nature a narrow-band type of transmission, which means that they transmit on one radio frequency or a narrow range of frequencies. An alternative to narrow-band transmission is spread spectrum transmission. Spread spectrum is a technique that takes a narrow signal and spreads it over a broader portion of the radio frequency band.

- Spreading the signal over a wide range of frequencies and reducing the amplitude has the advantage of making the signal look like noise to an unintended narrow-band receiver, reducing the effects of interference.

- A common spread spectrum method is frequency hopping spread spectrum (FHSS). Instead of sending on just one frequency, frequency hopping uses a range of frequencies and changes frequencies during the transmission. Another spread spectrum method is direct sequence spread spectrum (DSSS). DSSS uses an expanded redundant code to transmit each data bit.

Key Terms

American Standard Code for Information Interchange (ASCII) An arbitrary coding scheme that uses the numbers from 0 to 127 to represent alphanumeric characters and symbols.

amplitude The height of a carrier wave.

amplitude modulation (AM)   A technique that changes the height of a carrier wave in response to a change in the height of the input signal.

amplitude shift keying (ASK)   A digital modulation technique whereby a 1 bit is represented by the existence of a carrier signal, whereas a 0 bit is represented by the absence of a carrier signal.

analog modulation   A method of encoding an analog signal onto a carrier wave.

analog signal   A signal in which the intensity (amplitude or voltage) varies continuously and smoothly over a period of time.

antenna   A copper wire, rod, or similar device used to send and receive radio signals that has one end up in the air and the other end connected to the ground through a receiver.

bandwidth   The range of frequencies that can be transmitted.

Barker code (or chipping code)   A bit pattern used in a DSSS transmission. The term *chipping code* is used because a single radio bit is commonly referred to as a chip.

baud   A change in a carrier signal.

baud rate   The number of times that a carrier signal changes per second.

binary phase shift keying (BPSK)   A simple digital modulation technique that uses four phase changes to represent 2 bits per signal change.

bits per second (bps)   The number of bits that can be transmitted per second. digital data.

carrier wave   An analog wave having a frequency that a receiver is tuned to. Although the term is commonly used to refer to any wave at a particular frequency that is used to transmit a wireless signal, technically speaking, a wave is only a carrier if some kind of data is encoded into it. Until data is encoded onto the wave, it is more correct to refer to it as a continuous wave (CW).

constellation diagram   A graphical representation that makes it easier to visualize signals using complex modulation techniques such as QAM. It is generally used in laboratory and field diagnostic instruments and analyzers to aid in design and troubleshooting of wireless communications devices.

continuous wave (CW)   An analog or sine wave that is modulated to eventually carry information, becoming a carrier wave.

cycle   An oscillating sine wave that completes one full series of movements.

detector   A diode that receives a light-based transmission signal.

dibit   A signal unit that represents 2 bits.

diffused transmission   A light-based transmission that relies on reflected light.

digital modulation   A method of encoding a digital signal onto an analog carrier wave for transmission over media that does not support direct digital signal transmission.

digital signal   Data that is discrete or separate.

direct sequence spread spectrum (DSSS)   A spread spectrum technique that uses an expanded, redundant code to transmit each data bit.

directed transmission   A light-based transmission that requires the emitter and detector to be directly aimed at one another.

electromagnetic (EM) wave   A signal composed of electrical and magnetic forces that in radio transmission usually propagates from an antenna and can be modulated to carry information.

emitter   A laser diode or a light-emitting diode that transmits a light-based signal.

forward error correction (FEC)   A technique that is used to correct bit errors in transmissions by sending extra redundant bits that are used to calculate which bit was lost or changed during transmission, so the receiving equipment can correct the error. This saves time in the case of single-bit errors because no retransmission is required.

frequency   A measurement of radio waves that is determined by how frequently a cycle occurs.

frequency hopping spread spectrum (FHSS)   A spread spectrum technique that uses a range of frequencies and changes frequencies during the transmission.

frequency modulation (FM)   A technique that changes the number of wave cycles in response to a change in the amplitude of the input signal.

frequency shift keying (FSK)   A digital modulation technique that changes the frequency of the carrier signal in response to a change in the binary input signal.

gigahertz (GHz)   1,000,000,000 (1 billion) hertz.

hertz (Hz)   The number of cycles per second.

hopping code   The sequence of changing frequencies used in FHSS.

infrared light   Light that is next to visible light on the light spectrum and that has many of the same characteristics as visible light.

kilohertz (KHz)   1,000 hertz.

light spectrum   All the different types of light that travel from the Sun to the Earth.

line of sight   The direct alignment as required in a directed transmission.

megahertz (MHz)   1,000,000 (1 million) hertz.

modem (MOdulator/DEModulator)   A device used to convert digital signals into an analog format, and vice versa.

modulation   The process of changing a carrier signal.

narrow-band transmission   Transmission that uses one radio frequency or a very narrow portion of the frequency spectrum.

non-return-to-zero (NRZ)   A binary signaling technique that increases the voltage to represent a 1 bit but provides no voltage for a 0 bit.

non-return-to-zero, invert-on-ones (NRZ-I)   A binary signaling technique that changes the voltage level only when the bit to be represented is a 1; a variation of NRZ-L.

non-return-to-zero-level (NRZ-L)   See polar non-return-to-zero.

oscillating signal   A wave that illustrates the change in a carrier signal.

phase   The relative starting point of a wave, in degrees, beginning at 0 degrees.

phase modulation (PM)   A technique that changes the starting point of a wave cycle in response to a change in the amplitude of the input signal. This technique is not used in analog modulation.

phase shift keying (PSK)   A digital modulation technique that changes the starting point of a wave cycle in response to a change in the binary input signal.

polar non-return-to-zero (polar NRZ)   A binary signaling technique that increases the voltage to represent a 1 bit but drops to negative voltage to represent a 0 bit.

pseudo-random code   A code that is usually derived through a number of mathematical calculations as well as practical experimentation.

quadbit   A signal unit that represents 4 bits.

quadrature amplitude modulation (QAM)   A combination of phase modulation with amplitude modulation to produce 16 different signals.

quadrature phase shift keying (QPSK)   A digital modulation technique that combines quadrature amplitude modulation with phase shift keying.

radio wave (sometimes called **radiotelephony)**   An electromagnetic wave created when an electric current passes through a wire and creates a magnetic field in the space around the wire.

return-to-zero (RZ)   A binary signaling technique that increases the voltage to represent a 1 bit, but the voltage is reduced to 0 before the end of the period for transmitting the 1 bit, and there is no voltage for a 0 bit.

sine wave   A wave that illustrates the change in a carrier signal.

spread spectrum transmission   A technique that takes a narrow signal and spreads it over a broader portion of the radio frequency band.

tribit   A signal unit that represents 3 bits.

Unicode   An international encoding standard that is capable of supporting numeric character codes to represent all the different languages and scripts in the world, such as Arabic, Hebrew, multiple Chinese and Japanese scripts, Sanskrit, etc.

voltage   Electrical pressure.

wavelength   The length of a wave as measured between two positive or negative peaks or between the starting point of one wave and the starting point of the next wave.

Review Questions

1. Which range of the electromagnetic spectrum is less susceptible to interference from sources of visible light?

   a. Ultraviolet

   b. Gamma light

   c. Infrared

   d. Yellow light

2. The distance between one positive peak and the next positive peak of a wave is called _____.

   a. frequency

   b. wavelength

   c. elasticity

   d. intensity

3. Which type of transmission is used when human voice is modulated directly onto a carrier wave?

   a. Analog

   b. Digital

   c. Diffused

   d. Directed

4. Why do computers and data transmission equipment use binary?

    a.   They are electrical devices, and electricity has only two states.

    b.   Base 2 is too difficult to use.

    c.   Base 10 was developed before binary.

    d.   Binary is the next step beyond quadecimal.

5. Eight binary digits grouped together form which of the following?

    a.   Byte

    b.   Bit

    c.   Binary

    d.   2x quad

6. The American Standard Code for Information Interchange (ASCII) can represent up to 1,024 characters. True or False?

7. Letters of the alphabet and symbols are stored using the ASCII code, but not numbers used in calculations. True or False?

8. Infrared light, though it may be invisible, has many of the same characteristics of visible light. True or False?

9. Infrared wireless systems require that each device needs to have only one component: either an emitter that transmits a signal or a detector that receives the signal. True or False?

10. Infrared wireless systems send data by the intensity of the light wave instead of whether the light signal is on or off. True or False?

11. Infrared wireless transmission can be either directed or _____.

    a.   analog

    b.   digital

    c.   diffused

    d.   detected

12. Radiotelephony or radio travels in waves known as _____ waves.

    a.   electromagnetic

    b.   analog

    c.   magnetic

    d.   electrical

13. Unlike a digital signal, a(n) _____ signal is a continuous signal with no "breaks" in it.

    a.   magnetic

    b.   visible

    c.   light

    d.   analog

14. Changing a signal to encode data onto it is known as _____.

    a. baud

    b. demodulation

    c. modulation

    d. continuity

15. PSK is an example of _____.

    a. ASCII encoding

    b. unicoding

    c. phase modulation

    d. digital modulation

16. Explain how a radio antenna works when transmitting a signal.

17. Explain the difference between bps and baud rate.

18. Explain the difference between amplitude modulation, frequency modulation, and phase modulation.

19. What is quadrature amplitude modulation (QAM) and how does it work?

20. List and describe the three different types of binary signaling techniques.

Hands-On Projects

Project 2-1

In this project, you will write your name in both hexadecimal and binary.

1. Search the web for an ASCII chart, then look up the hexadecimal ASCII value for each of the letters of your last name. (Note that the ASCII table contains codes for both uppercase and lowercase letters.) Here is what the author's last name looks like in hexadecimal, with a dash placed between successive letters, to make it easier to read:

    O–l–e–n–e–w–a = 4F–6C–65–6E–65–77–61

2. Convert each hexadecimal value to binary. The easiest way to do this is to break the hexadecimal code for each character into two separate digits. In the case of an uppercase O, this would be 4 and F. Each digit represents 4 bits out of 1 byte (also called a nibble).

3. Convert each digit to its binary equivalent in the range 0000 (0x0) to 1111 (0xF). Put the two groups of 4 bits together into a byte. For the purposes of this project, the most significant bit, which is generally used for parity, will always be a 0.

4. Write your full last name in binary. Again, use a dash between each group of 8 bits to make it easier to read. Here is what the author's last name looks like:

    01001111–01101100–01100101–01101110–01100101–01110111–01100001

    You will use these results in the following projects.

Project 2-2

This project helps you develop an appreciation for the topic of modulation and what it takes to transmit data—analog or digital—over the wireless medium. As you know, this book introduces many different wireless technologies that use various modulation techniques. In this project, you perform amplitude modulation.

1. In Figure 2-34, an analog input signal is shown at the top of the grid. To draw a wave that is modulated in amplitude, begin by copying the input signal to the top two rows of the grid shown in Figure 2-34. The goal is to create an "envelope" to guide you and make it easier to draw the carrier wave, showing what it will look like after it is modulated. Use a dashed line to draw the input signal.

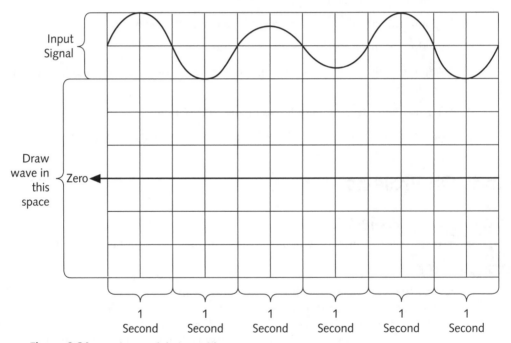

Figure 2-34   Analog modulation grid

2. Complete the envelope by drawing a mirror-image (vertically inverted) version of the input signal in the bottom two rows of the grid. Again, use a dashed line.

3. You are now ready to draw the modulated carrier. Considering a carrier with a frequency of 4 Hz, so that it will be easier to draw and visualize, draw a sine wave with four complete cycles for each second. The wave must fit inside and follow the contour of the envelope you created in the previous two steps. The frequency of the modulated carrier must remain constant at 4 Hz for each 1-second interval on the grid. The high and low peaks of the modulated carrier must reach all the way to the upper and lower guides you just drew, the envelope.

4. Check your results with your instructor, or see Figure 2-16 to make sure you got it right.

Project 2-3

As you have learned, digital modulation makes it possible to transmit a digital signal using an analog medium such as an electromagnetic wave. In this project, you draw a waveform to show how a digital signal can be encoded onto a carrier using 1 bit per phase change (PSK).

1. In Figure 2-35, a grid and an analog reference wave are shown without an input signal. Input the binary ASCII code for the first letter of your last name in the spaces provided at the top of the grid.

2. The modulated carrier wave should have the same amplitude as the original carrier. Begin at the 0 level indicated on the left side of the grid and draw a 4 Hz carrier to represent the first bit, a 0.

3. At the end of the first second, continue drawing the carrier but change the phase if the second most significant bit is a 1. If not, continue drawing the carrier at the same phase.

4. Keep drawing the 4 Hz carrier wave, changing phase as required to show a change from a bit with a value of 1 or 0.

5. After you have drawn the carrier wave for all 8 bits of the ASCII code, compare your results with Figure 2-35 to make sure it looks correct.

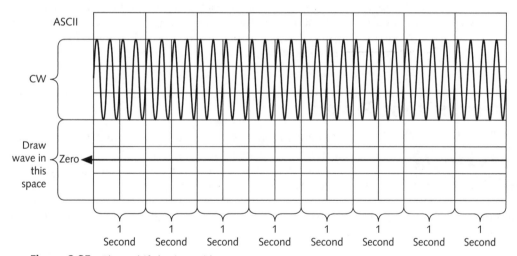

Figure 2-35 Phase shift keying grid

Real-World Exercises

The Baypoint Group (TBG), a company of 50 consultants who assist organizations and businesses with issues involving network planning and design, has hired you as a consultant. One of their oldest clients, Woodruff Medical Group, needs your help with the following tasks.

Exercise 2-1

Woodruff Medical has been approached by a vendor who is trying to sell it an infrared WLAN for its office. Because the equipment is proprietary, the cost is quite high, and this is one of their main concerns. Although none of the networking equipment will be placed around sensitive medical equipment, the office manager prefers infrared because he believes that other types of wireless networking equipment could interfere with the medical equipment in another hospital campus building that is located about 125 meters away.

Exercise 2-2

Prepare a PowerPoint presentation outlining how infrared and radio wireless transmissions work. This will be presented to the office manager, who is not technically inclined, and the LAN manager, who has a strong technology background. Be sure to list the advantages and disadvantages of both. The presentation should contain at least 10 slides. You will only have 20 minutes to explain both technologies.

Exercise 2-3

After listening to your presentation, the office manager has several questions. One of the questions involves wireless transmission speeds. The office manager wants to know how the transmission speed compares between infrared and RF WLANs. For this, he wants a written report instead of a presentation. Write a one-page summary regarding different transmission speeds and the advantages and challenges of each technology. He also remembers the time when he used a telephone modem to access the Internet and is very curious about the difference between bits-per-second and baud rate, so be sure to write a brief explanation for him.

Challenge Case Project

CASE PROJECTS

A local community college has contacted The Baypoint Group for information about modulation for a networking class, and TBG has passed this request on to you. Form a team of two or three consultants and research AM, FM, PM, ASK, FSK, and PSK. Specifically, pay attention to how they are used, as well as their strengths and weaknesses. Provide your conclusions regarding which of these methods, or combination of methods, is now the dominant player in wireless data transmission and why you think this is the case.

chapter 3

Radio Frequency Communications

After reading this chapter and completing the exercises, you will be able to:

- List the basic components of a radio system
- Describe the factors that affect the design of a radio system
- Discuss why standards are beneficial and list the major telecommunications standards organizations
- Explain the radio frequency spectrum

As you already learned, radio frequency (RF) communications is the most common type of wireless communications. It comprises all types of radio communications that use radio frequency waves, from radio broadcasting to wireless computer networks. In this book, we focus primarily on wireless data communications.

Unlike light-based communications, which is also wireless and is briefly discussed in this chapter, RF communications can cover long distances and is not always blocked by objects in the path of the signal, as light-based communications can be. RF is also a mature communications technology, the first radio transmission having been sent well over 100 years ago.

RF communications can be very complex, but this chapter attempts to demystify the subject to provide a very generic and simplified introduction to how RF transmitters and receivers work. First, we explore the basic components of RF communications. Then, we look at the issues regarding the design and performance of an RF system. Next, we explore the national and international organizations that create, regulate, and promote standards, which are so important, especially in the RF data communications field. These standards help ensure that we can travel all over the planet and are able to maintain wireless data communications virtually anywhere. Finally, we examine some of the issues around RF spectrum allocation.

Components of a Radio System

Several basic hardware components are common to all radio systems, even though the functions of the radio systems themselves may vary. These components include filters, mixers, amplifiers, and antennas. The first three are covered in this chapter. The fourth component, antennas, is important enough to warrant a chapter of its own (Chapter 4), especially given the accelerated growth of the wireless data communications field.

Filters

A **filter** does exactly what its name indicates: it filters RF signals to get rid of all the ones that are not wanted. The world around us is filled with RF signals that cover virtually every frequency in the electromagnetic spectrum (refer back to Figure 2-1). Most of these signals are generated by transmission equipment, such as cellular phones, communications satellites, and radio and television station transmitters; some reach us from outer space. After radio receivers have picked up these RF waves that are "flying" around us, a filter sifts out the frequencies that we do not want to receive. Think of a home-based water filter that removes particles and other impurities, or an automotive oil filter that prevents large contaminants from reaching the engine while allowing the oil itself to pass through. An RF filter either passes or rejects a signal based on the signal's frequency or range of frequencies. The block diagram symbol for a filter is shown in Figure 3-1.

Figure 3-1   Filter symbol

The block diagram symbols shown here are universal and are commonly used to illustrate radio frequency as well as microwave components.

There are three basic types of RF filters: low-pass, bandpass, and high-pass. With a **low-pass filter**, a maximum frequency limit or threshold is set and all signals below that value are allowed to pass through, as shown in Figure 3-2.

Maximum threshold: 900 MHz

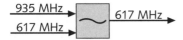

Figure 3-2   Low-pass filter

A **high-pass filter** has a minimum frequency threshold. All signals above this minimum threshold are allowed to pass through, whereas those below the minimum threshold are blocked. A high-pass filter is shown in Figure 3-3.

Minimum threshold: 2.4 GHz

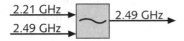

Figure 3-3   High-pass filter

A **bandpass filter**, instead of having either a minimum or maximum frequency threshold, has a range called a **passband**, which includes both a minimum and a maximum threshold. Only those RF signals that fall within the passband are allowed through the bandpass filter. This is shown in Figure 3-4.

Passband: 300 Hz to 3,400 Hz

Figure 3-4   Bandpass filter

Some of the figures depicting filters show multiple inputs, but a filter typically has only a single input.

Filters are also found in transmitters, where they are used to eliminate unwanted **harmonics**. This is because the process of modulating a signal generates additional oscillations that fall outside of the range of frequencies that are going to be transmitted, called harmonics. The way a filter functions in a transmitter is shown in Figure 3-5, which is a partial block diagram. The input is the information that needs to be sent; it can take the form of audio, video, or data. The transmitter takes the input data and modulates the signal (using either analog or digital modulation) by changing the amplitude, frequency, or phase of the sine wave, or in some cases, a combination of these modulation methods (see Chapter 2 if you need to refresh your memory about RF signal modulation). The output from the modulation process is known as the **intermediate frequency (IF)** signal; in the example shown in Figure 3-5, this output includes the frequencies between 8 and 112 MHz. The IF signal is then filtered through a bandpass filter to remove any undesired high-frequency or low-frequency signals and produce an output with a frequency range of between 10 and 100 MHz, which is the signal to be transmitted. This is also done to prevent frequencies that fall outside the transmission range from interfering with other transmitters operating in an adjacent frequency range.

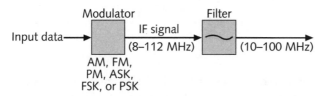

Figure 3-5   Filter function in a radio transmitter

Mixers

The purpose of a **mixer** is to combine two frequencies, the input signal and the transmission carrier frequency, and create a single output. The mixer symbol is shown in Figure 3-6. The single output of a mixer is in the range of the highest sum and the lowest difference of the two frequencies. In Figure 3-7, the input signal—the information to be transmitted—is between 300 and 3,400 Hz, and the carrier frequency is 20 KHz (20,000 Hz).

Figure 3-6   Mixer symbol

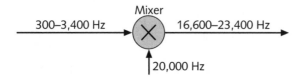

Figure 3-7   Mixer output

The mixer adds the input frequencies to the mixed-in frequency to produce the sums:

$$
\begin{array}{cc}
20{,}000 \text{ Hz} & 20{,}000 \text{ Hz} \\
+\ 300 \text{ Hz} & 3{,}400 \text{ Hz} \\
\hline
20{,}300 \text{ Hz} & 23{,}400 \text{ Hz}
\end{array}
$$

In this example, 23,400 Hz is the highest sum. The mixer also determines the lowest difference between the input frequencies and the mixed-in frequency, for example:

$$
\begin{array}{cc}
20{,}000 \text{ Hz} & 20{,}000 \text{ Hz} \\
-300 \text{ Hz} & -3{,}400 \text{ Hz} \\
\hline
19{,}700 \text{ Hz} & 16{,}600 \text{ Hz}
\end{array}
$$

In this example, the lowest difference frequency would be 16,600 Hz. Therefore, the output from the mixer would be a signal with a frequency range between 16,600 and 23,400 Hz. The sum and the difference are known as the **sidebands** of the frequency carrier because they fall above and below the center frequency of the carrier signal.

One way to think about sidebands is by considering AM radio signals. AM broadcast radio is confined to a frequency range of 535 to 1,605 KHz. In an AM broadcast radio signal, the sidebands are typically 7.5 KHz wide, so a radio station on the AM dial uses a total of about 15 KHz of bandwidth to transmit a single audio channel or voice. An example of sidebands is shown in Figure 3-8. In addition, there is always an unused range of frequencies below and above the sidebands, which are used to further prevent interference between two adjacent radio stations. These unused frequency spaces are called **guard bands**.

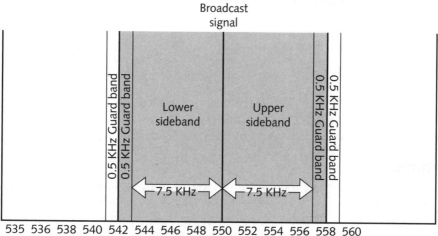

Figure 3-8   AM radio sidebands and guard bands

Mixers are used to convert an input frequency to a specific desired output frequency. For example, let's say that you wish to transmit data using an 800 MHz carrier. Figure 3-9 illustrates how a mixer functions in a radio transmitter. The transmitter takes the input data and modulates the signal to produce an IF signal. In this example, the output from the modulator is a range of frequencies from 8 to 112 MHz, which also includes some undesirable harmonic frequencies. This signal is then put through a bandpass filter to produce the desired IF signal range of 10 to 100 MHz. This IF signal then becomes the input to the mixer along with the desired carrier frequency of 800 MHz. The output of the mixer is a signal with a frequency range between 698 and 903 MHz, which is finally run through another bandpass filter to remove any frequencies outside the transmission range—in other words, those that fall outside the intended sideband limits.

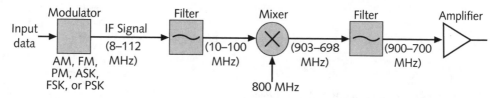

Figure 3-9   Mixer function in the final stage of radio transmitter circuit

Amplifiers

An **amplifier** increases the amplitude, or strength of an RF signal. Figure 3-10 shows the symbol for an amplifier. The amplifier is one of the first stages in a radio receiver circuit and one of the last stages in a transmitter (shown in Figure 3-9). Its function is to boost the power of the signal received from the last filter stage before it is transmitted. Amplifiers are critical components in a radio system because RF signals tend to lose intensity (amplitude) when they move through filters and mixers as well as when they travel through empty space in the form of electromagnetic waves. Filters and mixers are passive devices, meaning that they do not add power to a signal; instead, they take power away from the signal. Likewise, when an electromagnetic wave carrying a modulated signal leaves the antenna and travels from the transmitter to the receiver antenna, a large portion of its power is lost or attenuated (reduced in amplitude) when it is absorbed by water particles in the air, walls, trees, and so on.

Figure 3-10 Amplifier symbol

The amplifier is called an active device, because unlike filters and mixers, it must be supplied with electricity. Amplifiers use this electricity to increase the input signal's intensity or strength and then output an exact copy of the input signal at a higher amplitude.

Antennas

Finally, for an RF signal to be transmitted or received using electromagnetic waves, the transmitter and receiver must have an antenna, the symbol for which is shown in Figure 3-11. Table 3-1 shows the list of radio system components along with their functions and block diagram symbols. Antennas will be discussed in greater detail in Chapter 4.

Figure 3-11 Antenna symbol

Component Name	Function	Block Diagram Symbol
Filter	Accept or block RF signal	
Mixer	Combine two radio frequency inputs to create a single output	
Amplifier	Boost signal strength	
Antenna	Send or receive an electromagnetic wave	

Table 3-1 Radio system components and their symbols

Design of a Radio System

Filters, mixers, amplifiers, and antennas are necessary components of all radio systems, but designers also need to consider how the systems will be used. In radio signal broadcasting, this may be as straightforward as determining the size and location of the antenna as well as a signal that will be strong enough to cover a very large area. However, in a radio system that incorporates two-way communications—for example, cellular phones connected via a wireless network—there are other considerations, including multiple user access, transmission direction, switching, and signal strength.

Multiple Access

Because the number of frequencies available for radio transmission is limited, conserving the use of frequencies is important. One way to do this is by sharing a particular frequency among multiple users, which reduces the number of frequencies needed. In Figure 3-12, a group of people is using walkie-talkies, with everyone using the same frequency channel. If the three people on the left transmit at the same time, the three on the right will not be able to understand the messages, because the transmitters will interfere with each other and the people on the right will only hear noise. The only way for all the users to share a channel is if they take turns transmitting.

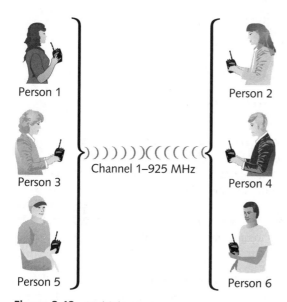

Person 1
Person 3
Channel 1–925 MHz
Person 5
Person 2
Person 4
Person 6

Figure 3-12   Multiple access

Another example of multiple access is when employees of a company send multiple envelopes or packages from one office to another office. All the envelopes and packages are shipped at the same time and share space in the same courier truck on the same trip (multiple access). When the courier truck arrives at the destination, the envelopes and packages are sorted and delivered to their respective recipients.

Several methods allow multiple access. The most significant, in terms of wireless communications, are Frequency Division Multiple Access (FDMA), Time Division Multiple Access (TDMA), and Code Division Multiple Access (CDMA).

Frequency Division Multiple Access (FDMA) Frequency Division Multiple Access (FDMA) divides the bandwidth of a frequency channel (a range of frequencies) into several smaller frequency bands (narrower ranges of frequencies, or channels). For example, a transmission channel with 50 KHz of bandwidth can be divided into 100 channels, each with a bandwidth of 500 Hz. Each channel can then be dedicated to one specific user. This concept is illustrated in Figure 3-13. FDMA is most often used with analog transmissions.

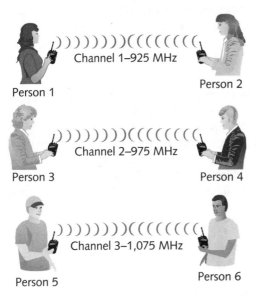

Channel 1–925 MHz
Person 1   Person 2

Channel 2–975 MHz
Person 3   Person 4

Channel 3–1,075 MHz
Person 5   Person 6

Figure 3-13   Frequency Division Multiple Access (FDMA)

Another example of FDMA is analog cable television, although most cable TV today is digital. In analog cable TV, all channels were transmitted using FDMA over coaxial cable. Each analog television channel uses about 6 MHz of the 500 MHz bandwidth of the cable. All of the TV channel signals, each in its own frequency, are transmitted simultaneously on the same cable. At the TV receiver end, a user would select (or tune) the TV set to a particular channel in order to view the programming (the TV tuner was essentially an adjustable bandpass filter).

Think back to the example in Figure 3-12. If each of the three people on the left uses a different portion of the same frequency band by selecting a different channel on the walkie-talkie and if each of the three people on the right select the same channel as the person they want to speak with, the people on the left can transmit simultaneously and each of the people on the right will receive the different transmissions intended for them.

One of the drawbacks of FDMA is that when signals are sent at frequencies that are grouped closely together, occasionally signals from one frequency may encroach on its neighbor's channel frequency. This phenomenon, known as **crosstalk**, causes interference on the other frequency channel and, in extreme cases, crosstalk can even cause image problems or you can hear sounds from a different frequency channel. Crosstalk was very common in old analog radios using FDMA, such as the early cellular phones. The digital technology used today has practically eliminated this type of problem.

Time Division Multiple Access (TDMA) To overcome the problem of crosstalk, **Time Division Multiple Access (TDMA)** was developed. Whereas FDMA divides the bandwidth into several frequencies, TDMA divides the transmission time into several slots. Each user is assigned the entire frequency channel for a fraction of time on a fixed, rotating basis. Because the duration of each time slot is short, the delays that occur while others are using the frequency are seldom noticeable. Figure 3-14 illustrates TDMA for six users. TDMA is most often used with digital transmissions.

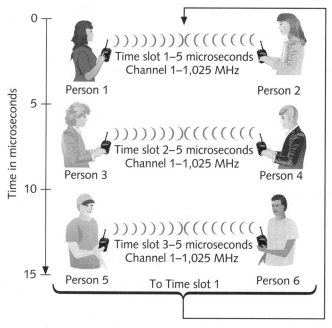

Figure 3-14 Time Division Multiple Access (TDMA)

In traditional TDMA, if a user has no data to transmit during his or her assigned time slot with TDMA, the frequency remains idle—in other words, no one else uses that frequency. In more modern systems, the unused time slots can be assigned to users that are currently communicating.

Cellular phones based on GSM technology, which until recently was the most common cellular technology used outside of North America, transmit and receive voice using the TDMA method and use FDMA to exchange control information with the tower base stations.

TDMA has two significant advantages over FDMA. First, it uses the bandwidth more efficiently. Studies indicate that when using a 25-MHz bandwidth, TDMA can achieve over 20 times the capacity of FDMA, meaning it can handle a much larger number of transmitters sharing the same frequency band. Second, TDMA allows data and voice transmissions to be mixed using the same frequency. However, one of the disadvantages of TDMA is that when all channels are being used simultaneously by different users, the quality of the voice calls can degrade very quickly, which can be very annoying.

Code Division Multiple Access (CDMA) Code Division Multiple Access (CDMA) is another transmission method used in cellular telephone communications. Rather than separate RF frequencies or channels, CDMA uses direct sequence spread spectrum (DSSS) technology with a unique digital spreading code (called a **PN code**) to differentiate the multiple transmissions in the same frequency range. Before transmission occurs, the high-rate PN code is combined with the data to be sent; this step spreads the signal over a wide frequency band, lowers the amplitude of the signal, and is more resistant to interference.

What is different between the CDMA and the DSSS techniques discussed in Chapter 2 is that to implement multiple access, the transmission to each user begins on a different chip. Recall that, in DSSS, the 1s and 0s of the spreading code are referred to as "chips" to avoid confusing them with the data bits; this imprints a unique address on the data. Each "address" is then used only by one of the receivers sharing a frequency. Figure 3-15 illustrates the concept of the spreading code.

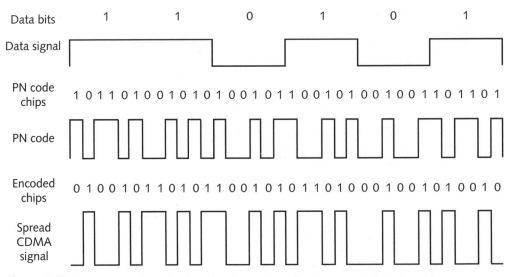

Figure 3-15   CDMA spreading of a data signal by a PN code

The unique-address concept works this way:

Channel 1:   1 0 0 1 1 0 1

Channel 2:   0 0 1 1 0 1 1

Channel 3:   0 1 1 0 1 1 0

and so on, until the sequence of chips wraps around.

Note that each of these codes starts on a different chip of the same sequence of 1s and 0s. In the above example, the code for channel 2 begins on the second chip of channel 1. The code for channel 3 begins on the second chip of channel 2, and so on, until there are no more unique codes available and the sequence of chips wraps around. The longer the code is, the larger the number of different PN codes, and consequently the larger the number of users who will be able to share a channel. In the previous unique-address example, there are seven chips per code, which allows for a maximum of seven unique PN codes.

The number of chips in the code determines the amount of spreading or bandwidth that the transmitted signal will occupy. Because the amount of spreading is limited by the bandwidth allocated to the system, the length of the spreading code also determines the number of unique code sequences and, consequently, the number of users that can share that frequency band.

In CDMA technology, the spreading code is called a pseudo-random code (PN code), because the code appears to be a random sequence of 1s and 0s, but it actually repeats itself over and over.

The spreading process is reversed at the receiver, and the code is de-spread to extract the original data bit transmitted. Because all receivers are on the same frequency, they all receive the same transmission. The PN code is designed so that when a receiver picks up a signal that was spread with the PN code that's being used by another receiver and then attempts to recover the original data, the decoded signal still looks like a high-frequency signal instead of data, so it is ignored. Figure 3-16 illustrates the decoding of the data in CDMA, and Figure 3-17 shows an example of what happens when a receiver attempts to de-spread another receiver's signal and recover the data bits. Note that the bits of the decoded data signal in Figure 3-17 are not long enough to match the minimum size of a data bit as shown in Figure 3-16.

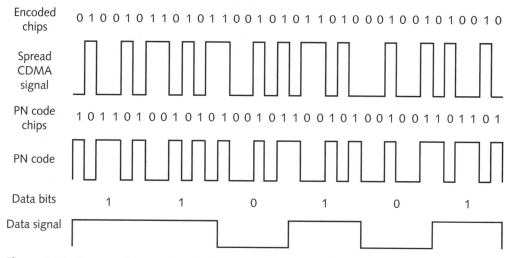

Figure 3-16 De-spreading a CDMA signal to recover data bits

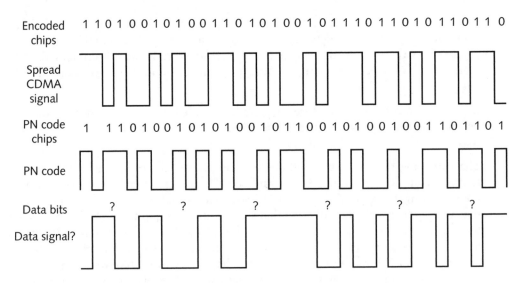

Figure 3-17 Attempting to de-spread another receiver's CDMA signal with wrong PN code

To understand CDMA, imagine a room with 20 people in it who are having 10 simultaneous one-on-one conversations. Now suppose that all the pairs of people are talking at the same time but in different languages. Ignoring the issue of the noise level in the room, because none of the listeners understands any language other than that of the individual with whom they are speaking, the other nine conversations don't bother them.

There are several advantages to CDMA:

- It can carry up to three times the amount of data as TDMA.
- Transmissions are much harder to eavesdrop on, because the would-be eavesdropper would have to know how many chips and the exact sequence of chips used to encode the original digital signal.
- A would-be eavesdropper must also know the exact chip in which a particular transmission starts and, in the case of cellular telephony, the PN code changes if the user is moving, when his cellular phone connects to a different tower, thus making eavesdropping extremely difficult.

CDMA-based cellular technology is extremely complex. Because this book is not specifically focused on CDMA technology, the preceding description is included merely to provide an overview of this multiple access method.

Transmission Direction

In most wireless communications systems, data must flow in both directions, and the flow must be controlled so that the sending and receiving devices know when data will arrive or when it needs to be transmitted. There are three types of data flow: simplex, half-duplex, and full-duplex.

Simplex transmission occurs in only one direction, from device 1 to device 2, as shown in Figure 3-18. A broadcast TV station is an example of simplex transmission: The signal goes from the TV transmitter to the viewer's TV, but the viewer has no way of communicating with the station using the same TV signal. Except for broadcast radio and television, simplex is rarely used in wireless data communications today. That's because the receiver is unable to give the sender any feedback regarding the transmission, such as whether it was received correctly or if it needs to be resent. Such reliability is essential for the successful and correct exchange of data.

Figure 3-18   Simplex transmission

Half-duplex transmission occurs in both directions, but only one way at a time, as shown in Figure 3-19. This type of communication is typically used in consumer devices such as citizens band (CB) radios or walkie-talkies, emergency services, and aircraft radio. In order for User A to transmit a message to User B, he must hold down the "talk" button while speaking. While the button is being pressed, User B can only listen and not talk. User A must release the "talk" button before User B can press his "talk" button. Both parties can send and receive information, but only one at a time.

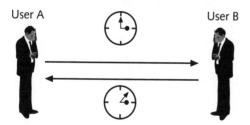

Figure 3-19   Half-duplex transmission

Full-duplex transmission occurs in both directions simultaneously, as shown in Figure 3-20. A telephone system is a type of full-duplex transmission. Both parties in a telephone call can speak at the same time, and they are able to hear each other throughout the call. Modern wireless communications systems, such as cellular and satellite telephones, also use full-duplex transmission.

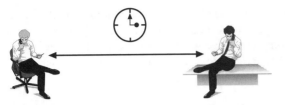

Figure 3-20   Full-duplex transmission

 Both cellular and satellite full-duplex communications require the use of two separate channels, regardless of whether they use FDMA, TDMA, or CDMA.

If the same antenna is used for wireless transmission and reception, a filter can be used to handle full-duplex transmissions. RF communications equipment that works in full-duplex mode using FDMA sends and receives on different frequencies. A transmission picked up by the antenna on the receiving frequency passes through a filter and is sent to the receiver, while the transmission signal on the sending frequency is passed on to the same antenna, but on a different frequency. The frequency channels are selected so as to cause minimal signal interference with each other. An example is shown in Figure 3-21, but not using "real" frequency channels.

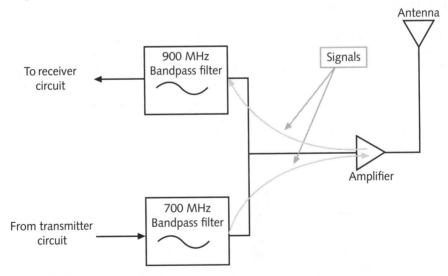

Figure 3-21   Using a single antenna in full-duplex RF communications

Switching

The concept of **switching** is essential to all types of telecommunications, wireless as well as wired. Switching involves moving the signal from one wire or frequency to another. Consider for a moment the landline telephone in your home. You can use that one telephone to call a friend across the street, a classmate in another town, a store in a distant state, or anyone else who also has a phone number anywhere in the world. How can one single telephone be used to call any other telephone in the world? This is accomplished through a switch at the telephone company's central office. The signal from your phone goes out your telephone's wire all the way to a telephone company's switching office and is then switched or moved to the wire of the telephone that belongs to your friend across the street, as shown in Figure 3-22.

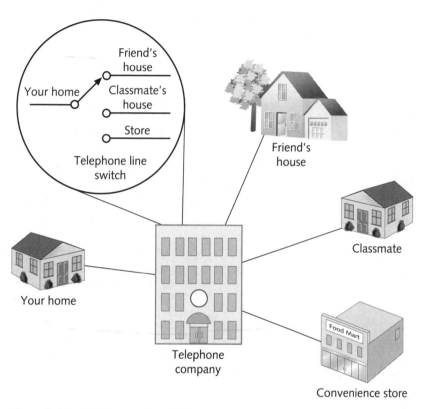

Figure 3-22   Telephone call switching

 The first telephone switches were not automatic. Human operators connected (switched) each two lines manually. Today, the telephone system is known as the Public Switched Telephone Network (PSTN), and the collection of equipment used in this network, including the home telephone sets, is commonly referred to in the data communications field as the Plain Old Telephone Service (POTS).

To better understand why switches are necessary, imagine a telephone network in which each telephone must be wired to every other telephone without using switches. If this network had 500 telephones, each telephone would require 499 cables to connect to all the others, and a total of 124,750 cables would be needed to connect all the telephones to one another. If you draw a simple network of five telephones on a piece of paper, you'll notice that you need 10 cables to interconnect all of them. This type of connection is called a "mesh network."

You can quickly calculate how many cables would be required to interconnect several telephones or computers in a mesh network by using the formula n(n-1)/2, where n is the total number of devices you want to connect. Of course, this is not a very practical solution. To connect all the telephone sets in a city with 100,000 telephones would require that each set be connected to an enormously large number of wires.

The type of switching used by telephone systems today is known as **circuit switching**. When a telephone call is placed, a direct physical connection is made, through the switch, between the caller and the recipient of the call. While the telephone call is taking place, the connection is "dedicated" and remains open only to these two users. Ignoring, for the moment, some of the advanced features available in today's telephone networks, such as call waiting and conference calling, no other calls can be made from or received by the two connected phones while this conversation is taking place, and anyone who calls that phone will receive a busy signal. This direct connection lasts until the end of the call, at which time the switch drops the connection and makes the two telephone lines available once more to receive or make calls.

Circuit switching is ideal for voice communications. However, it is not efficient at transmitting data, because data transmission occurs in "bursts," with periods in between, when nothing is transmitted. These periods with nothing being transmitted result in wasted connection time in a circuit switched network, since the connection is dedicated to the two devices and another connection cannot be made. As an example, imagine that you called a friend and neither of you said anything for long periods of time. No one else would be able to use the phones until you both hung-up the call.

Instead of using circuit switching, data networks use **packet switching**. Packet switching requires that the data transmission be broken into small units called **packets**. Each packet is then sent independently through the network to reach a specific destination device, based on an address contained in the packet, as shown in Figure 3-23.

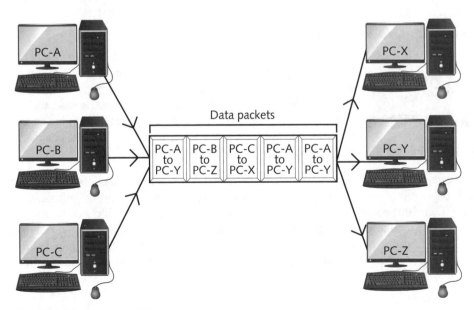

Figure 3-23 Packet switching

Packet switching has a couple of important advantages for data transmissions. One advantage is that it allows better utilization of the network, that is, the connections are not tied up by any two devices. In Figure 3-23, if PC-A does not have any data to send, PC-B and PC-C can use the available bandwidth on the network to send more data. Any PC can send data to any other PC at any time. Each packet will be sent on the medium (cable), when the medium is available (is not being used by another PC). Packets can be sent from any PC to any destination PC. Circuit switching ties up the communications line until the transmission is complete, whereas packet switching allows multiple computers to share the same line or frequency, if this is a wireless transmission. Another advantage of packet switching has to do with error correction. If a transmission error occurs, it usually affects only one packet. Only those packets affected by errors must be resent, not the entire message.

Circuit switching is currently used for both wired telephone systems and most wireless cellular telephone networks. Modern cellular technologies, currently being deployed in many parts of the world, use packet switching even for voice calls.

Signal Strength

In a radio system, a signal's strength must be sufficient for it to reach the receiver(s) with enough amplitude for the signal to be picked up by the antenna and amplified so that the information can be correctly extracted from it. Managing signal strength is much more complicated in a wireless system than in a wired network. Because the signal is not confined to wires, many types of electromagnetic interference can wreak havoc with the transmission. In addition, many types of objects, both stationary and moving, can negatively impact the signal. Some examples of electromagnetic interference include high-voltage power lines, various types of radiation emitted by the sun, other transmissions using the same frequency, and lightning (see Figure 3-24).

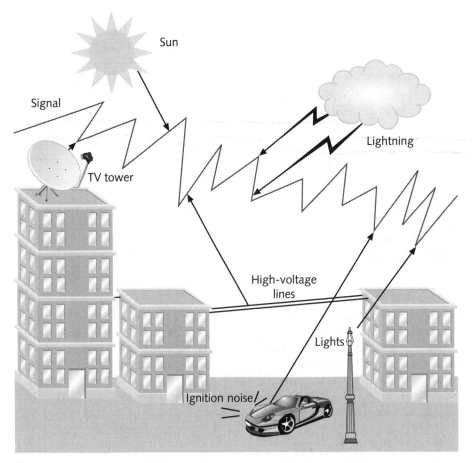

Figure 3-24   Sources of EMI (or noise) that can cause interference in RF transmissions

Electromagnetic interference (EMI) is also called **noise.** Consider a room with 20 people in it who are having 10 one-on-one conversations. If everyone talks freely, there is a great deal of "racket" or background noise, which interferes with all conversations. With radio waves, background electromagnetic "noise" of various types can negatively affect a signal and reduce the receiver's ability to reliably receive the transmission.

A measurement called **signal-to-noise ratio (SNR)** compares the signal strength with the background noise (see Figure 3-25). When signal strength falls close to or below the level of noise (low SNR), interference can take place. However, when the strength of the signal is well above the noise, interference can be easily filtered out. Consider again the example of the room with 20 people having 10 conversations. Someone who moves closer to her partner so she can be heard above the background noise is trying to increase the SNR, so the other person can better and correctly understand what she is saying.

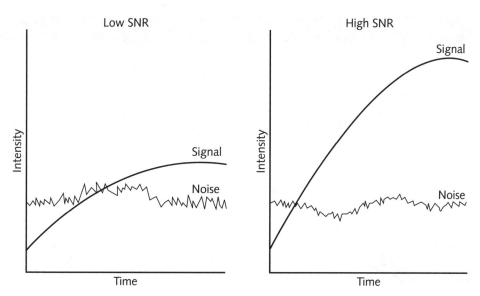

Figure 3-25 Signal-to-noise ratio

There are various ways to reduce the interference caused by noise, thereby creating an acceptable SNR. You can use more powerful amplifiers to boost the signal strength, you can better filter the signal on the receiving end, or you can use transmission techniques such as frequency hopping or direct sequence spread spectrum.

 With a highly complex and expensive device, such as an extremely sensitive radio telescope receiver, the temperature of the circuits is lowered to –459 degrees Fahrenheit to maximize the performance and minimize the noise and loss of signal strength caused by the circuits themselves. Recall that filters and mixers are passive devices that tend to reduce the amplitude or strength of the signal. Cooling these circuits down to –459 degrees Fahrenheit virtually eliminates the losses of signal strength and dramatically reduces the noise. However, it is not practical to do this in a handheld transmitting device.

Loss of signal strength, or **attenuation** is caused by various factors, but objects in the path of the signal, including man-made objects such as walls, are what cause the most attenuation. Table 3-2 shows examples of different building materials and their effect on radio transmissions. Amplifying a signal both before it is transmitted (to increase the power level) and after it is received helps to minimize the effects of attenuation.

Type of Material	Use in a Building	Impact on Radio Waves
Wood	Office partition	Low
Plaster	Inner walls	Low
Glass	Windows	Low
Bricks	Outer walls	Medium
Concrete	Floors and outer walls	High
Metal	Elevator shafts and cars	Very high

Table 3-2   **Materials and their effects on radio waves**

At certain frequencies, attenuation can also be caused by heavy rain or snow. Consequently, attenuation decreases as the altitude increases because of the decrease in air and water vapor density at higher altitudes.

As a radio signal is transmitted, the electromagnetic waves spread out like the waves in a pond, and lose strength. Some of these waves may also reflect off surfaces and continue toward the receiver. This results in the same signal reaching a receiver's antenna at different times. Since it takes longer for reflected waves to reach a receiver (see Figure 3-26), the waves that arrive at different times can interfere with each other.

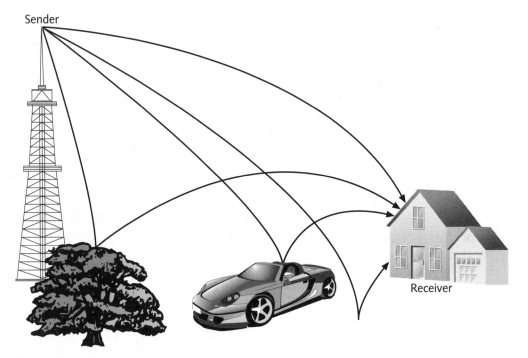

Figure 3-26   Multipath interference or distortion

This phenomenon, known as **multipath distortion,** can happen indoors as well outdoors, and can negatively affect the strength of signal, preventing a receiver from picking up a signal strong enough for reliable reception (see Figure 3-27).

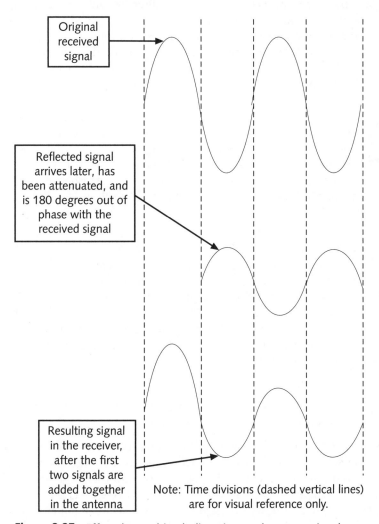

Figure 3-27   Effect that multipath distortion can have on a signal

Multipath distortion gets its name from the fact that some of the waves get reflected, travel different paths between the transmitter and the receiver, and arrive at the receiver antenna at different times and out of phase with a signal that travels a more direct path. The resulting signal at the input of the receiver gets distorted because the peaks of the waves of both signals—one positive and one negative, for example—get added to each other. The result can be a reduction or an increase in the amplitude of the signal at the receiver's antenna, both of which can cause problems. Multipath distortion is a very complex topic, and a full discussion of it is beyond the scope of this book. Newer wireless standards—such as 802.11n and 802.11ac—actually take advantage of multiple signals arriving at the receiver at different times to improve reception.

There are various ways to minimize multipath distortion, including using a directional antenna, using multiple receiver radios and antennas, or changing the height of the transmitter antenna to provide a stronger signal with a clear line of sight to the receiver's antenna. **Directional antennas** radiate the electromagnetic waves in one direction only and can help reduce or eliminate the effect of multipath distortion if there is a clear line of sight between the receiver and transmitter antennas. Other methods include using a more powerful amplifier in front of the receiver circuit to help increase the SNR or transmitting the same signal on separate frequencies. Multipath distortion is particularly problematic in cities with large buildings and structures where the receiver is in constant motion, such as in cellular telephony.

Multipath distortion affects FM reception as well, particularly in the downtown districts of metropolitan areas. FM stations are usually free from noise; however, while moving through the downtown area of a large city you may have noticed occasional static-like noise while listening to an FM station. This noise is caused by the signal reflecting off large buildings and reaching the receiver out of phase, sometimes canceling the signal for very brief moments.

Multipath distortion in RF communications works very similarly to the way an echo affects sound. A good way to simulate multipath distortion is to use an audio editor such as Audacity (on a computer running Windows) or GarageBand (on an Apple Macintosh running OS X) to record a sentence like "This is what happens when multipath affects a wireless transmission," then add an echo effect to the recording. Experiment with different degrees of echo. When you play the recording with a lot of echo, try to pick out only the individual words in the middle of the sentence.

Understanding Standards

As you continue to learn about the various wireless communications technologies discussed in upcoming chapters, you will find many references to standards and regulations that play a part in how they work and how they are used. In place almost from the beginning of the telecommunications industry, standards have also had an important role in its growth. A knowledge of which standards apply and how they apply to the wireless communications systems you work with will enhance your ability to read and understand industry news, technical articles, and system specifications as well as help you design and deploy multivendor systems that offer excellent compatibility and scalability.

The Need for Standards

Some IT people believe that the standards set for computer technologies stifle growth in this fast-paced field today and that waiting for standards to catch up with their needs slows everything down. Nevertheless, standards ultimately benefit both manufacturers and consumers. The very nature of the telecommunications industry, in which pieces of equipment from one manufacturer interact with equipment from other manufacturers, requires that standards exist for the design, implementation, testing, and operation of the equipment. For example, using your laptop computer on virtually any network worldwide would be next to impossible without standards.

The world's first telecommunications standard was published by the International Telegraph Union (ITU) in 1885. The standard originated from a desire by the governments of many countries to have a compatible telegraph operation. It took 20 years for the first telegraph standard to be created and published.

Advantages and Disadvantages of Standards

There are pros and cons to developing and applying standards in the telecommunications industry. The advantages have to do with interoperability and corporate competition, whereas the disadvantages are primarily political in nature.

Advantages of Standards

One advantage of telecommunications standards is the guarantee that devices from one vendor will interoperate with those from other vendors. Devices that are not based on standards may not be able to connect and communicate with similar devices from other vendors. Standards ensure that a transmitter purchased from Vendor A can be seamlessly integrated into a communications network that contains a receiver from Vendor B.

A second advantage of standards is that they create competition. Standards are open to everyone; any vendor who wants to enter a marketplace can do so by manufacturing their equipment to comply with standards. Thus, standards can result in competition between vendors; and competition has several benefits. It results in lower costs for consumers and better-developed products. A vendor who has created a proprietary device gains no benefit from reducing prices because there is no competition. Instead, with a captive market, the vendor may raise prices at will. However, vendors making products based on the same standards may reduce their prices in order to compete in the marketplace. The competition usually results in lower costs to consumers.

Competition also results in lower costs for manufacturers. Because standards have already been established, manufacturers do not have to invest large amounts of capital in research and development. Instead, they can use the standards as a blueprint for their manufacturing. This reduces start-up costs as well as the amount of time needed to bring a product to the market. Also, because standards increase the market for products that follow those standards, manufacturers tend to employ mass production techniques and gain economies of scale in manufacturing and engineering. As a result, production costs may be lower, and these savings are usually passed on to the consumers.

A third advantage of standards is that they help consumers protect their investments in equipment. It is not uncommon for a manufacturer of a proprietary device to phase out a product line. Businesses that purchased that line are left with two choices. They can continue to support this now-obsolete legacy system, although the costs will dramatically escalate as replacement parts (and support specialists) become more difficult to locate. Or, they can get rid of the equipment and buy an up-to-date system. Both choices are usually very expensive.

Standards can help create a migration path. The organization that creates the initial standards continues to incorporate new technologies by regularly revising its standards. Generally, these revisions are backward-compatible, which reduces the risk of obsolete "orphan" systems that are incompatible with newer technologies.

 One example of a standard that has helped consumers is IEEE 802.11 that is used in Wi-Fi. Even if your equipment is compatible with IEEE 802.11n, it can usually be configured to support older Wi-Fi equipment that is only compatible with IEEE 802.11b or earlier.

Disadvantages of Standards   International standards can be perceived as a threat to the economies of some countries because their domestic markets become subjected to overseas competition. Manufacturers in countries where labor costs are lower may be able to produce a device more cheaply. Standards allow those manufacturers to produce and sell their products abroad, often threatening a domestic manufacturer's market share.

Another disadvantage of standards is that although they are intended to create unity, they can have the opposite effect. Periodically, a country will create a standard and offer it to other countries as a global standard. However, for political reasons having nothing to do with technology, other countries may reject the standard and attempt to create their own. Television broadcasting standards provide an example of this. Countries around the world have created various standards as a way of protecting their internal markets as well as their cultural heritages. With the advent of the Internet and global commerce, this type of protectionism appears to be on the way out, but multiple TV standards continue to be in effect, forcing many manufacturers to design and produce television sets and video recorders that support multiple standards. The consumer ultimately has to pay the cost of maintaining these more complex devices.

Most experts agree that the advantages of standards far outweigh the disadvantages and that standards are vital, particularly for the telecommunications industry.

Types of Standards

There are two major types of standards in the telecommunications industry: de facto standards and de jure standards. A third type, consortia standards, is increasingly influencing how standards are set.

De Facto Standards   De facto standards are not official standards. They are simply common practices that the industry follows for various reasons—because they're easy to use, perhaps, or because they've traditionally been used or they're what the majority of users have adopted. For the most part, de facto standards are established by their success in the marketplace. For example, most industry experts would agree that Microsoft Windows today is still the de facto standard for personal-computer operating systems. No organization proclaimed Windows the standard; its widespread use created what amounts to a standard.

 The term *de facto* comes from Latin and means "from the fact." As it applies to computer and communications technologies, those technologies that are adopted by the market voluntarily become known as de facto standards.

De Jure Standards

De Jure Standards De jure standards, also called **official standards**, are those that are controlled by an organization or body that has been entrusted with that task. Each standards group has its own rules regarding membership. You will read about some of these groups in the next section.

The process for creating standards can be very involved. Generally, the organization develops subcommittees responsible for specific technologies. Each subcommittee is composed of different working groups, which are teams of industry experts given the task of creating the initial draft of a standard's documentation. The draft is then published to the members, both individuals and companies, and requests for comments (RFCs) are solicited. These members are developers, potential users, and other people with an interest in the field. The original committee reviews the comments and revises the draft. This final draft is then reviewed by the entire organization and is usually put to a vote before the final standards are officially published and made available to the public.

De facto standards sometimes become de jure standards by being approved by a committee. The TCP/IP network communications protocol that is so widely used today is an example of a de facto standard that later became an official standard, when the Internet Engineering Task Force (IETF) became an official standards body.

Consortia One of the major complaints against de jure standards is the amount of time it takes for a standard to be completed. For example, the initial standard for wireless LANs took 7 years to complete. In the telecommunications and IT industries, this represents an extremely long period of time before products can be brought to the marketplace; in some cases, manufacturers release products long before the standards are approved, as was the case with the latest high-speed WLAN standard.

Responding to this criticism, consortia are often used today to create standards. **Consortia** are industry-sponsored organizations with the goal of promoting a specific technology. Unlike with de jure standards bodies, membership in consortia is not open to everyone. Instead, specific high-profile companies create and serve on consortia. The goal of consortia is to develop a standard that promotes their specific technology in a shorter period of time than what official standards organizations take.

One of the most well-known consortia is the World Wide Web Consortium (W3C at *www .w3.org*), which is composed of industry giants such as Microsoft, Google, IBM, and hundreds of other companies. The W3C is responsible for creating the standards that are widely used on the Internet today, including hypertext markup language (HTML), cascading style sheets (CSS), and the Document Object Model (DOM).

Telecommunications Standards Organizations

In the telecommunications field, standards organizations exist at the national, multinational, and international levels. The following sections discuss each of these levels.

National Standards Organizations In the United States, there are several standards organizations, each of which plays a role in setting telecommunications standards. The **American National Standards Institute (ANSI)** functions largely as a clearinghouse for all kinds of standards development in the United States. Most ANSI standards are developed by one of its over 270 affiliated organizations, which include diverse groups such as the Water Quality Association and the Telecommunications Industry Association, as well as the group that originally created the ASCII code for use in computers and data communications. ANSI represents the interests of over 125,000 companies and 3.5 million professionals worldwide.

One of the ANSI-affiliated organizations is the **Telecommunications Industries Association (TIA)**. It is made up of industry vendors from telecommunications, electronic components, consumer electronics, and electronic information. Working with vendors, the TIA publishes Recommended Standards (RS) for the industry to follow. For example, the TIA developed and published a standard that defines how a computer's serial port, connector pin-outs, and electrical signaling should function. This standard is generally known as TIA RS-232. More information on the TIA can be found at *www.tiaonline.org*.

The TIA represents more than 600 companies that manufacture or supply the products and services used in global communications. The function of the TIA is to advocate policies to legislative bodies and to establish standards in five areas: user-premises equipment, network equipment, wireless communications, fiber optics, and satellite communications.

Two other organizations play roles in establishing national standards for telecommunications technology. The **Internet Engineering Task Force (IETF)** is a large, open (to anyone interested in joining) community of network designers, operators, vendors, and researchers concerned with the evolution of the Internet's architecture and the smooth operation of the Internet. Although it is a U.S. organization, it accepts members from any country in the world and focuses on the upper layers of telecommunications protocols; it is the organization that designs and develops practically all of the protocols used on the Internet. The IETF existed informally for many years, and it was not an official standards body until 1986, when it was formalized by the **Internet Architecture Board (IAB)**.

The IAB is responsible for defining the overall architecture of the Internet; it also serves as the technology advisory group for the **Internet Society (ISOC)**, a professional-membership organization of Internet experts that comments on policies and practices and oversees a number of other boards and task forces dealing with network policy issues. You can find out more about the IETF and its parent organizations at *www.ietf.org*.

The **Institute of Electrical and Electronics Engineers (IEEE)**, like the IETF, establishes standards for telecommunications. However, it also establishes a wide range of other IT standards. The IEEE's most well-known standards include IEEE 802.3, which covers local area network Ethernet compatible equipment, and IEEE 802.11, which covers the lower protocol layers of wireless LANs.

You can learn more about the IEEE at *www.ieee.org*. You can also obtain a no-cost copy of the IEEE 802 standards that relate to networking and wireless networking, provided that these have been published for longer than 6 months, at the following website: *standards.ieee.org/getieee802/portfolio.html*.

Multinational Standards Organizations Multinational standards organizations span more than one country; many of them are based in Europe. For example, the **European Telecommunications Standards Institute (ETSI)** develops telecommunications standards for use throughout Europe. Its membership consists primarily of European companies and European government agencies, but they also interface with organizations in other countries, including the United States. You can learn more about ETSI at *www.etsi.org*.

International Standards Organizations Because telecommunications technology is truly global, there are also global organizations that set industry standards. The best known is the **International Telecommunication Union (ITU)**, an agency of the United Nations that is responsible for telecommunications. The ITU is composed of over 200 governments and private companies that coordinate global telecommunications networks and services. Unlike other organizations that set standards, the ITU is actually a treaty organization. The regulations set by the ITU are legally binding on the nations that have signed the treaty.

Two of the ITU's subsidiary organizations prepare recommendations on telecommunications standards. The ITU-T focuses on telecommunications networks, and the ITU-R focuses on RF-based communications, including the radio frequencies that should be used and the radio systems that support them. Although these recommendations are not mandatory and are not binding on the countries that have signed other treaties, almost all of the countries elect to follow the ITU recommendations, and these essentially function as worldwide standards. You can learn more about the ITU at *www.itu.int*.

ITU-T replaced a standards body known as the CCITT, whose origins date back to work on standards for telegraphs in the 1860s.

The **International Organization for Standardization (ISO)** is based in Geneva, Switzerland. (Note that it uses the acronym "ISO" instead of "IOS." That's because "iso" means "equal" in Greek, and the organization wanted to use the same acronym worldwide, regardless of language.) Started in 1947, the ISO promotes international cooperation and standards in the areas of science, technology, and economics. Today, groups from over 190 countries belong to the ISO. You can learn more about it at *www.iso.org*.

Several of the groups that belong to the ISO are actually national standards bodies. For example, the TIA interfaces with the ISO.

It might seem like there are too many standards organizations, but all these organizations, including the ones in the United States, cooperate with one another, seldom stepping over one another's authority or geographical jurisdiction. You will read more about this cooperation in the upcoming chapters.

Regulatory Agencies

Although setting standards is important for telecommunications, enforcing telecommunications regulations is equally important. In a sense, the nature of national and international commerce enforces some standards. A company that refuses to abide by standards for cellular telephone transmissions will find that nobody buys its products. Telecommunications regulations, however, must be enforced by an outside regulatory agency, whose role is to ensure that all participants adhere to the prescribed standards. These regulations typically involve defining who can use a specific frequency when broadcasting a signal. Almost all countries have a national organization that functions as the regulatory agency to determine and enforce telecommunications policies. Some small countries without a regulatory agency simply adopt the regulations used by another country.

In the United States, the **Federal Communications Commission (FCC)** serves as the primary regulatory agency for telecommunications. The FCC is an independent government agency that is directly responsible to Congress. It was established by the Communications Act of 1934 and is charged with regulating interstate and international communications by radio, television, wire, satellite, and cable. The FCC's jurisdiction covers the 50 states, the District of Columbia, and U.S. territories.

In order to preserve its independence, the FCC is directed by five commissioners who are appointed by the President of the United States and confirmed by the Senate for 5-year terms. Only three commissioners may be members of the same political party, and none of them can have a financial interest in any FCC-related business.

The FCC's responsibilities are very broad. In addition to developing and implementing regulatory programs, it processes applications for licenses to use a particular frequency or band and similar filings, analyzes complaints, conducts investigations, and takes part in congressional hearings. The FCC also represents the United States in negotiations with foreign nations about telecommunications issues.

The FCC plays an important role in wireless communications. It regulates radio and television broadcast stations as well as cable and satellite stations. It also oversees the licensing, compliance, implementation, and other aspects of cellular telephones, pagers, and two-way radios. The FCC regulates the use of radio frequencies to fulfill the communications needs of businesses, local and state governments, public safety service providers, military, aircraft and ship operators, as well as individuals.

The RF spectrum is a limited resource, meaning that only a certain range of frequencies can be used for radio transmissions. Because of this limitation, frequencies are almost always licensed by regulatory agencies in the different countries around the world. In the United States, the regulatory agency is the FCC, which has the power to allocate portions of the spectrum. Broadcasters are required to transmit only in the frequency or frequencies for which they obtained a license. Commercial companies such as radio and television stations must pay fees (which are sometimes quite large) for the right to use a frequency; naturally, they do not want anyone else to be allowed to transmit on the same frequency within their coverage area. The FCC and other countries' agencies continually monitor transmissions to ensure that no one is using a frequency without a license or is transmitting with more power than their license allows.

Radio Frequency Spectrum

The **radio frequency spectrum** is the entire range of all radio frequencies that exist, from 10 KHz to over 30 GHz. The spectrum is divided into 450 different sections, or **bands**. Table 3-3 lists some of the major bands, their corresponding frequencies, and some typical uses.

Band (Acronym)	Frequency	Common Uses
Very low frequency (VLF)	10 KHz to 30 KHz	Maritime ship-to-shore
Low frequency (LF)	30 KHz to 300 KHz	Radio location such as LORAN (Long Range Navigation) Time signals for clock synchronization (WWVB)
Medium frequency (MF)	300 KHz to 3 MHz	AM radio
High frequency (HF)	3 MHz to 30 MHz	Short wave radio, CB radio
Very high frequency (VHF)	30 MHz to 144 MHz 144 MHz to 174 MHz 174 MHz to 328.6 MHz	TV channels 2–6, FM radio Taxi radios TV channels 7–13
Ultra high frequency (UHF)	328.6 MHz to 806 MHz 806 MHz to 960 MHz 960 MHz to 2.3 GHz 2.3 GHz to 2.9 GHz	Public safety: fire, police, etc. Cellular telephones Air traffic control radar WLANs (802.11b/g/n)
Super high frequency (SHF)	2.9 GHz to 30 GHz	WLANs (802.11a/n)
Extremely high frequency (EHF)	30 GHz and above	Radio astronomy

Table 3-3   **Radio frequency bands**

NOTE Frequency bands are defined by each country's regulatory agencies, such as the FCC in the United States, and each range is allocated for a specific radio communications purpose. Search for "frequency allocation chart" in Google (images) to view samples of the charts for different countries.

Radio frequencies of other common devices include:

- Garage door openers, alarm systems: 40 MHz
- Baby monitors: 49 MHz
- Radio-controlled airplanes: 72 MHz
- Radio-controlled cars: 75 MHz
- Wildlife tracking collars: 215–220 MHz
- Global positioning system (GPS): 1.227 and 1.575 GHz

The United States is obligated to comply with the international spectrum allocations established by the ITU. However, the United States' use of its domestic spectrum may differ from the international allocations as long as those uses do not conflict with international regulations or agreements.

NOTE Until 1993, the ITU held conferences at 20-year intervals to review the international spectrum allocations. Since then, ITU conferences are convened every 2 to 3 years.

The U.S. Commerce Department's National Telecommunications and Information Administration (NTIA) serves as the principal advisor to the President on domestic and international communications and information issues. It also represents the views of the executive branch before Congress, the Federal Communications Commission, foreign governments, and international organizations.

Although a license from the FCC is required to send and receive on a specific frequency, there is a notable exception. This is known as the **license exempt spectrum,** or **unregulated bands.** Unregulated bands are, in effect, the parts of the radio frequency spectrum that are available to any users nationwide without charge and without a license. Devices that use these bands can be either fixed or mobile. The FCC designated the unregulated bands to promote the development of a broad range of new devices and stimulate the growth of new industries.

The FCC does impose power limits on devices using the unregulated bands, which in effect reduces their range and helps prevent interference.

Table 3-4 outlines a subset of the unregulated bands used by many of the technologies discussed in this book. The ITU-R has published recommendations for many additional unregulated bands; but as you learned earlier, not every country's domestic market follows all of the ITU-R's recommendations. One unregulated band is the **Industrial, Scientific and Medical (ISM) band,** which was approved by the FCC in 1985. Today, devices such as WLANs that transmit at speeds of 1 Mbps and above use this band. Another unlicensed band used in Wi-Fi is the **Unlicensed National Information Infrastructure (U-NII),** approved in 1996. The U-NII band is intended for devices that provide short-range, high-speed wireless digital communications. U-NII compatible devices are also widely used in Wi-Fi WLANs today.

Unlicensed Band	Frequency	Total Bandwidth	Common Uses
Industrial, Scientific and Medical (ISM)	902–928 MHz (Americas only) 2.4–2.4835 GHz 5.725–5.875 GHz	259.5 MHz	Cordless phones, WLANs, wireless public branch exchanges
Unlicensed Personal Communications Systems	1910–1930 MHz	20 MHz	WLANs, wireless public branch exchanges
Unlicensed National Information Infrastructure (U-NII)	5.15–5.25 GHz 5.15–5.25 (Low) 5.25–5.35 GHz (Mid) 5.47–5.725 (Worldwide) 5.725–5.825 GHz (Upper)	555 MHz	WLANs, wireless public branch exchanges, campus applications, long outdoor links
Millimeter Wave	59–64 GHz	5 GHz	In-home networking applications

Table 3-4   Unregulated bands

A recent development that has had an impact on the crowded radio frequency spectrum involves transmitting radio signals directly to a device without the use of special directional antennas. When radio signals leave the sender's antenna, they spread or radiate out (the word *radio* comes from the term *radiated energy*) and can be picked up by multiple recipients. A new technique known as **adaptive array processing** replaces a traditional antenna with an array of antenna elements. These elements deliver RF signals with increased strength to one specific user or device, instead of sending signals out in a broad pattern. This allows more transmissions to take place in a given range of frequencies, in a particular location.

Chapter Summary

- Several hardware components are essential for communicating using radio frequencies (RF): filters, mixers, amplifiers, and antennas. A version of each of these components is found on all radio systems.

- A filter is used to either accept or block a radio frequency signal. With a low-pass filter, a maximum frequency threshold is set. All signals that are below that maximum threshold are allowed to pass through. Instead of having a maximum frequency threshold, as with a low-pass filter, a high-pass filter has a minimum frequency threshold. All signals that are above the minimum threshold are allowed to pass through, whereas those below the minimum threshold are turned away. A bandpass filter has a passband, which is both a minimum and maximum threshold, thus allowing all frequencies that fall in between both, to pass.

- The purpose of a mixer is to combine two inputs to create a single output. The single output is the highest sum and the lowest difference of the frequencies.

- An amplifier increases a signal's intensity or strength, whereas an antenna converts an RF signal from the transmitter into an electromagnetic wave, which carries the information through the air or empty space.

- Although filters, mixers, amplifiers, and antennas are all necessary components for a radio system, there are other design considerations that must be taken into account when creating a radio system. Because there are only a limited number of frequencies available, conserving the use of frequencies is important. One way to conserve is by sharing a frequency among several individual users.

- Frequency Division Multiple Access (FDMA) divides the bandwidth of the frequency into several narrower frequencies. Time Division Multiple Access (TDMA) divides the bandwidth into several time slots. Each user is assigned the entire frequency band for his transmission but only for a small fraction of time on a fixed, rotating basis. Code Division Multiple Access (CDMA) uses spread spectrum technology and unique digital spreading codes called PN codes, rather than separate RF frequencies or channels, to differentiate between the different transmissions.

- The direction in which data travels on a wireless network is important. There are three types of data flow. Simplex transmission occurs in only one direction. Half-duplex transmission sends data in both directions, but only one way at a time. Full-duplex transmission enables data to flow in both directions simultaneously.

- Switching involves moving the signal from one wire or frequency to another. Telephone systems use a type of switching known as circuit switching. When a telephone call is made, a dedicated and direct physical connection is made between the caller and the recipient of the call through the switch. Instead of using circuit switching, data networks use packet switching. Packet switching requires that the data transmission be broken into smaller units called packets, and each packet is then sent independently through the network to reach the destination.

- Managing a signal's strength is much more complicated in a wireless system than in a wired system. Electromagnetic interference (EMI), sometimes called noise, comes from a variety of man-made and natural sources. The signal-to-noise ratio (SNR) refers to the measure of signal strength relative to the background noise. A loss of signal strength is known as attenuation. Attenuation can be caused by a variety of factors (such as objects) that can decrease the signal's strength as the RF waves pass through. As a radio signal is transmitted, the electromagnetic waves spread out. Some of these waves may reflect off surfaces and slow down. This results in the same signal being received not only from several different directions but at different times. This is known as multipath distortion.

- Telecommunications standards have been in place almost since the beginning of the industry and have played an important role in the rapid growth of the field. There are several advantages of having standards, including interoperability, lower costs, and a migration path. De facto standards are not standards per se, just common practices that the industry follows. Official standards (also called de jure standards) are those that are controlled by an organization or body that has been entrusted with that task. Consortia are often used today to create standards. Consortia are industry-sponsored organizations that have the goal of promoting a specific technology.

- Some standards organizations span more than one country. And because telecommunications is a truly global phenomenon, there are also multinational as well as international organizations that set standards. In the United States, the Federal Communications Commission (FCC) serves as the primary regulatory agency for telecommunications. The FCC is an independent government agency that answers directly to Congress.

- The radio frequency spectrum is the entire range of all radio frequencies that exist. This range extends from 10 KHz to over 30 GHz and is divided into 450 different bands. Although a license from the FCC is normally required to send and receive on a specific frequency, unregulated bands are available for use without a license in the United States and most other countries. Two unregulated bands are the Industrial, Scientific and Medical (ISM) band and the Unlicensed National Information Infrastructure (U-NII).

- A recent development that has had an impact on the crowded radio frequency spectrum is adaptive array processing. Systems that use adaptive array processing replace a traditional antenna with an array of antenna elements. Use of this technique can deliver RF signals with increased strength to one specific user or device, instead of sending signals out in a broad pattern.

Key Terms

adaptive array processing   A radio transmission technique that replaces a traditional antenna with an array of antenna elements.

American National Standards Institute (ANSI)   A clearinghouse for standards development in the United States.

amplifier   A component that increases a signal's intensity.

attenuation   A loss of signal strength.

band   A range of radio frequencies. Frequency bands are defined by each country's regulatory agencies, such as the FCC in the United States, and each range is allocated for a specific radio communications purpose.

bandpass filter   A filter that passes all signals that are between the maximum and minimum threshold, that is, within the passband.

circuit switching   A switching technique in which a dedicated and direct physical connection is made between two transmitting devices—for example, between two telephones during a call.

Code Division Multiple Access (CDMA)   A technique that uses spread spectrum technology and unique digital codes to send and receive radio transmissions.

consortia   Industry-sponsored organizations that have the goal of promoting a specific technology.

crosstalk   Signals from close frequencies that may interfere with other signals.

de facto standard   A common practice that the industry follows for various reasons.

de jure standard   A standard that is controlled by an organization or body.

directional antenna   An antenna that radiates the electromagnetic waves in one direction only. As a result, it can help reduce or eliminate the effect of multipath distortion if there is a clear line of sight between the two antennas.

electromagnetic interference (EMI)   Interference with a radio signal; also called noise.

European Telecommunications Standards Institute (ETSI)   A standards body that develops telecommunications standards for use throughout Europe.

Federal Communications Commission (FCC)   The primary U.S. regulatory agency for telecommunications.

filter   A component that is used to either accept or block a radio frequency signal.

Frequency Division Multiple Access (FDMA)   A radio transmission technique that divides the bandwidth of the frequency into several smaller frequency bands.

full-duplex transmission   Transmissions in which data flows in either direction simultaneously.

guard band   Frequency space in which no signal is transmitted. Intended to prevent interference between two transmitters using adjacent channels.

half-duplex transmission   Transmission that occurs in both directions but only one way at a time.

high-pass filter   A filter that passes all signals that are above a maximum threshold.

harmonics   Stray oscillations that result from the process of modulating a wave and that fall outside the range of frequencies used for transmission. Harmonics also occur when a signal goes through a mixer and must be filtered out at several points before the signal is finally fed to the antenna for transmission.

Industrial, Scientific and Medical (ISM) band   An unregulated radio frequency band approved by the FCC in 1985.

Institute of Electrical and Electronics Engineers (IEEE)   A standards body that establishes standards for telecommunications.

intermediate frequency (IF)   The output signal that results from the modulation process.

International Organization for Standardization (ISO)   An organization to promote international cooperation and standards in the areas of science, technology, and economics.

International Telecommunication Union (ITU)   An agency of the United Nations that sets international telecommunications standards and coordinates global telecommunications networks and services.

Internet Architecture Board (IAB)   The organization responsible for defining the overall architecture of the Internet, providing guidance and broad direction to the IETF. The IAB also serves as the technology advisory group to the Internet Society and oversees a number of critical activities in support of the Internet.

Internet Engineering Task Force (IETF)   A standards body that focuses on the upper levels of telecommunications protocols and Internet technologies.

Internet Society (ISOC)   A professional-membership organization of Internet experts that comments on policies and practices and oversees a number of other boards and task forces dealing with network policy issues.

license exempt spectrum   Unregulated radio frequency bands that are available in the United States to any users without a license.

low-pass filter   A filter that passes all signals that are below a maximum threshold.

mixer   A component that combines two inputs to create a single output.

multipath distortion   What occurs when the same signal reflects and arrives at the receiver's antenna from several different directions and at different times.

noise   *See* electromagnetic interference (EMI).

official standards   *See* de jure standards.

packet   A smaller segment of the transmitted signal.

packet switching   Data transmission that is broken into smaller units.

passband   A minimum and maximum threshold that spells out which range of frequencies will pass through a filter.

PN code   Pseudo random code; a code that appears to be a random sequence of 1s and 0s but actually repeats itself. Used in CDMA cellular telephone technology.

radio frequency (RF) communications   All types of radio communications that use radio frequency waves.

radio frequency spectrum   The entire range of all radio frequencies that exist.

sidebands   The range of frequencies, above and below the carrier frequency of the transmitted signal, in which a signal is transmitted.

signal-to-noise ratio (SNR)   The measure of signal strength relative to the background noise.

simplex transmission   Transmission that occurs in only one direction.

switching   Moving a signal from one wire or frequency to another.

Telecommunications Industries Association (TIA)   A group of more than 600 companies that manufacture or supply the products and services used in global communications.

Time Division Multiple Access (TDMA)   A transmission technique that divides the bandwidth into several time slots.

Unlicensed National Information Infrastructure (U-NII)   An unregulated band approved by the FCC in 1996 to provide for short-range, high-speed wireless digital communications.

unregulated bands   *See* license exempt spectrum.

Review Questions

1. Each of the following is a type of RF filter except _____.

   a. low-pass

   b. high-pass

   c. passband

   d. bandpass

2. A(n) _____ combines two inputs to create a single output.

   a. mixer

   b. codex

   c. filter

   d. amplifier

3. A(n) _____ actively increases a signal's intensity or strength.

   a. transmitter

   b. demodulator

   c. amplifier

   d. antenna

4. The result of using a PN code is that _____.

   a. it adds a unique address to the signal

   b. it spreads the signal over a wider range of frequencies

   c. it mixes the signal with the IF

   d. it decodes the signal

5. _____ is a method of transmission in which the information is broken up into smaller units.

   a. Error correction

   b. Circuit switching

   c. Electromagnetic interference

   d. Packet switching

6. A passband has both a minimum and maximum threshold. True or False?

7. The resulting output from the modulation process is known as the middle frequency (MF) signal. True or False?

8. When mixing two signals, the highest sum and the smallest difference between the carrier frequency and the range of frequencies at the other input define two limits known as the sidebands. True or False?

9. TDMA can carry three times the amount of data that CDMA can. True or False?

10. Without circuit switching, 1,225 cables would be required to interconnect 50 telephones. True or False?

11. When using the same antenna for full-duplex communications, the same frequency can be used for transmitting and receiving simultaneously. True or False?

12. _____ divides the bandwidth of the frequency into several narrower frequencies. Each user then transmits using its own narrower frequency channel.

   a. TDMA

   b. OFDM

   c. FDMA

   d. CDMA

13. When signals are sent at frequencies that are closely grouped together, an errant signal may encroach on a close frequency, causing _____.

   a. frequency conflict

   b. crosstalk

   c. time conflict

   d. channel mixing

14. Which of the following divides the bandwidth of the frequency channel into several time slots?

   a. FDMA

   b. OFDM

   c. CDMA

   d. TDMA

15. A(n) _____ transmission uses spread spectrum technology and unique spreading codes for each user.

   a. CDMA

   b. FDMA

   c. TDMA

   d. OFDM

16. List and describe the three types of data flow. Simplex is transmission in one direction only. Half-duplex is transmission in both directions, but only one at a time. Full-duplex is simultaneous transmission in both directions at the same time.

17. List the three general types of standards.

18. What is switching in communications? What type of switching is used with telephone transmissions, and what type is used for data transmissions?

19. Explain multipath distortion and how it can be minimized.

20. What does the Federal Communications Commission do regarding the licensing of radio frequencies?

Hands-On Projects

Project 3-1

In Figure 3-28, fill in the dashed lines on the right with the resulting output frequency ranges from the various filters. Begin by converting the input frequencies to a common unit: KHz, MHz, or GHz. Then, show the results in the unit of your preference. (Recall that filters usually have only a single input but are shown here, for reasons of clarity, with two inputs.)

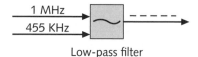

Maximum threshold = 600 KHz

1 MHz
455 KHz

Low-pass filter

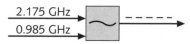

Minimum threshold = 1,800 MHz

2.175 GHz
0.985 GHz

High-pass filter

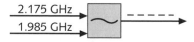

Passband = 1,800–1,900 MHz

2.175 GHz
1.985 GHz

Bandpass filter

Figure 3-28 Filters (1)

Project 3-2

In Figure 3-29, fill in the dashed lines at the right with the resulting output frequencies or ranges. Begin by converting the input frequencies to a common unit: KHz, MHz, or GHz. Then, show the results in the unit of your preference.

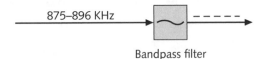

Maximum threshold = 2.312 GHz

2.49–2.89 GHz

Low-pass filter

Minimum threshold = 800 MHz

0.725–0.985 GHz

High-pass filter

Passband = 0.852–0.986 MHz

875–896 KHz

Bandpass filter

Figure 3-29 Filters (2)

Project 3-3

In Figure 3-30, fill in the dashed lines at the right with the resulting output frequency ranges. Begin by converting the frequencies to a common unit: KHz, MHz, or GHz. Then, show the results in the unit of your preference.

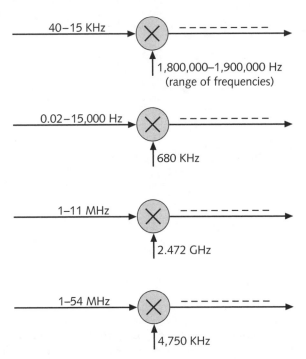

40–15 KHz

1,800,000–1,900,000 Hz
(range of frequencies)

0.02–15,000 Hz

680 KHz

1–11 MHz

2.472 GHz

1–54 MHz

4,750 KHz

Figure 3-30 Mixers

Project 3-4

Both natural and man-made objects located in a radio signal's path can cause attenuation—that is, a loss of signal strength. For this project, you will need a laptop computer equipped with a wireless LAN interface that is connected to an AP or wireless residential gateway. You will download, install, and configure Acrylic Wi-Fi Home to monitor the signal strength of the network that your computer is connected to.

1. In a web browser, enter the address **www.acrylicwifi.com/en**.

2. Click **Products,** then click **Acrylic Wi-Fi Home**.

3. Click the **Free Download** button. Save the file in the location of your preference, then locate the file and double-click it to install the application on your computer.

4. Once the program has finished installing, start the application and maximize the window. Acrylic Wi-Fi displays a list of all the wireless networks your computer has detected in the area around your current location, similar to Figure 3-31.

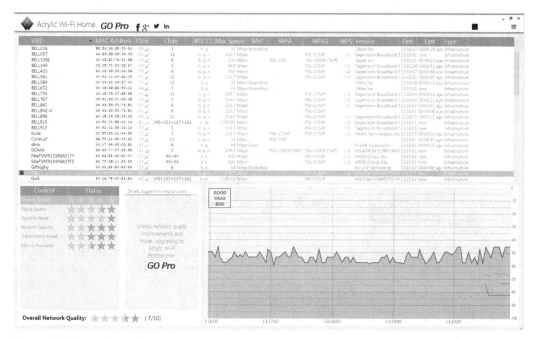

Figure 3-31 Acrylic Wi-Fi Home

Source: Screenshot from www.acrylicwifi.com/en

5. Right-click to the left of the WLAN network names, then click **Selection** and click **None** to deselect all WLANs. In the next project, you will monitor only the wireless network to which your computer is connected.

6. If you don't know it yet, ask your instructor to provide you with the SSID of your wireless network. Locate it in the SSID column in the Acrylic Wi-Fi window and click the

left mouse button in the blank space to the left of the network name. A colored square will appear next to the network name.

7. Leave the application open for the next project.

You will use Acrylic Wi-Fi Home in the following project as well as in other chapters of this book.

As an alternative to Acrylic Wi-Fi, if you have an Android smartphone, there are many similar free Wi-Fi utilities available from the Google Play store.

Project 3-5

In this project, you use Acrylic Wi-Fi Home to monitor the signal strength of your AP.

1. The graph at the bottom of the Acrylic Wi-Fi window (see Figure 3-31) displays the strength of the signal that your computer is receiving from the access points (APs) or Wireless Residential Gateways. The line will appear near the top of the graph if the signal strength is high and near the bottom of the graph if the signal strength is low.

Don't worry about the meaning of the numbers on either side of the Acrylic Wi-Fi time graph window for now. You will learn what they mean and how to use them in later chapters.

2. Monitor the strength of the signal while roaming away from the access point with the computer. Try to determine how far you can move from the access point before the signal is too weak for the connection to work reliably. To do this, you will need to attempt to open a webpage or download a file.

You can estimate the distance between you and the AP by any method available to you, such as counting tiles on the floor and multiplying by the size of the tiles or measuring your stride and counting the number of paces between the laptop computer and the AP.

3. As you move away from the AP, record all the obstacles between the computer and the AP, such as walls, doors, windows, and partitions. While monitoring the signal strength, record which items appear to have the greatest impact on the strength of the signal.

4. Record the distance at which the connection to the AP drops or becomes too slow or unreliable, such as when you can no longer access webpages or when a file download appears to stop for a minute or longer.

5. Monitor the strength of the signal while standing between 50 feet (15 meters) and 100 feet (30 meters) from the AP and covering the antenna of the network interface card with the following items:

   - Your hand (for a short period of time)
   - A piece of aluminum foil
   - A sheet of paper
   - A sheet of plastic (like a shopping bag)
   - A purse or briefcase with some metallic objects inside

If the NIC is built into the laptop computer, try using both hands to cover the back of the screen or the bottom of the computer until you see a definite reduction in the strength of the signal.

Project 3-6

Research the websites of the organizations listed in the left column of the table below and list some of the other standards that they publish that are not related to RF communications. Using Row 1 as a guide, identify other types of standards published by the same organization.

ISO—International Organization for Standardization *www.iso.org*	Screw threads, freight containers, computer protocols
IEEE—Institute of Electrical and Electronics Engineers *www.ieee.org*	
ITU—International Telecommunication Union *www.itu.int*	
ANSI—American National Standards Institute *www.ansi.org*	
ETSI—European Telecommunications Standards Institute *www.etsi.org*	

Real-World Exercises

The Baypoint Group (TBG), a company of 50 consultants who work with organizations and businesses on issues involving network planning and design, has again requested your services as a consultant. This time, the Good Samaritan Center, which assists needy citizens in the area, needs to modernize its office facilities. As part of its community outreach program, TBG has asked you to donate your time to help the Good Samaritan Center.

The Good Samaritan Center wants to install a wireless network in its offices. One local vendor has been trying to sell the center a proprietary system based on 5-year-old technology that does not follow any current standards. The price given for the product and its installation is low and is therefore attractive to the center. However, managers at the center have asked TBG for advice.

Exercise 3-1

Use PowerPoint or a similar presentation tool to create a slide presentation that outlines the different types of standards, the advantages and disadvantages of standards, and why they are needed. Include examples of products that did not follow standards and have vanished from the marketplace. Because the Good Samaritan Center is on the verge of buying the product, TBG has asked you to be very persuasive in your presentation. You are told that presenting the facts is not enough at this point; you must convince them why they should purchase a product that follows standards before you leave the room.

Exercise 3-2

Your presentation casts a doubt on the vendor's proprietary product, but the Good Samaritan Center is still not completely convinced it should go with a standard product. TBG has just learned that the vendor's proprietary product uses a licensed frequency that will require the center to secure and pay for a license from the FCC. TBG has asked you to prepare another presentation regarding the advantages and disadvantages of unregulated frequency bands. Because an engineer who sits on the Board of the Good Samaritan Center will be there, this slide presentation should be detailed and technical in its scope. Avoid focusing on the disadvantages of the vendor's proposal. Be prepared to answer questions related to potential interference by other wireless network users in nearby offices and what measures can be taken either to avoid such interference altogether or to deal with any problems that may arise.

Challenge Case Project

CASE PROJECTS

A local engineering user's group has contacted The Baypoint Group requesting a speaker to discuss multiple access technologies (FDMA, TDMA, and CDMA). Form a team of two or three consultants and research these technologies in detail. Specifically, pay attention to how they are used, and address their strengths and weaknesses. Provide an opinion about which technology will become the dominant player in the future of wireless.

chapter 4

How Antennas Work

After reading this chapter and completing the exercises, you will be able to:

- Define decibels, gain, and loss
- Explain the purpose of an antenna
- List different antenna types, shapes, sizes, and applications
- Explain RF signal strength and direction
- Describe how antennas work

So far, we have looked at the properties of radio frequency signals, most of the components that are required to generate these signals, and how to modulate RF signals with some kind of meaningful information to be transmitted, whether analog (like music or voice) or digital data (which is what this book is about). The last component required for transmission of these signals is an antenna, and this is such a vast topic that it deserves its own chapter.

Antennas mystify even some RF engineers and technicians, for they are responsible for the marvelous "magic" of RF communications. The purpose of an antenna is to convert electricity into electromagnetic (EM) waves, which then radiate or move away from the antenna at the transmitter end. At the receiver end, antennas "pick up" the EM radiation, which induces a tiny amount of electrical current into the antenna. It is this minute amount of electrical current, carrying the information, that is then amplified and demodulated by the receiver.

The field of wireless communications is growing at a very fast pace, with new standards and technologies being introduced seemingly every week. Wireless service providers, retailers, and in fact all kinds of businesses are beginning to deploy wireless networks everywhere—at airports, hotels, train stations, restaurants, cafes, shopping malls, and even in public parks or entire city blocks. The use of cellular telephones has exploded in ways that few people could imagine. Employees in all types of industries are being equipped with smartphones and tablet computers, so they can stay in touch through voice and email at all times from anywhere in the world, and also so they can access applications and corporate data. Wireless networks and wireless Internet hotspots are becoming commonplace in locations catering to businesspeople and the general public alike. No matter which type of RF communications, none of it could happen without antennas.

Antennas play a key role in the successful deployment of any kind of wireless connection. Proper design, planning, and installation of antennas is required to ensure good signal coverage, to permit user mobility, minimize or eliminate interference, and in some cases to enhance security. Cellular service providers spend a great deal of time and effort planning and analyzing utilization and traffic patterns in order to maximize the number of customers that can use the system in a given area and allow for continuous connectivity for both data and voice. In the rush to get wireless networks installed today, many are being deployed with little thought about where the signals originate or how far they reach.

This chapter takes you on an introductory technical tour of antennas—their types, sizes, and applications as well as some of the implementation issues. First, you learn about power gain and loss, then about the physical aspects of antennas. Mostly, this chapter discusses antennas used in a limited range of wireless communications technologies. However, the basic concepts cross over to other RF communications technologies, and the information provided here can be easily extended to other types of antenna systems.

Gain and Loss

Understanding RF signal transmission involves knowing:

- The strength or the power with which the transmitter is sending the signal
- The amount of reduction in signal strength caused by cables, connectors, and other components

- The transmission medium (electromagnetic waves)
- The minimum strength of the signal required by the receiver to be able to properly recover the data sent by the transmitter

These requirements mean that we need to know how much power the signal loses or gains at various points. For example, an analysis of the signal would determine the power level that was fed into the antenna and how much signal strength was lost in transit from the transmitter to the receiver, due to obstacles and other impediments.

Consider a wireless cable/DSL router for home networking, which typically sends out a signal with approximately 32 milliwatts (0.032 watts) of power. The router is on the lower level of the house, and by the time the signal reaches the wireless NIC in a laptop computer in the second-floor bedroom, it may only have a strength of about 0.000000001 (10^{-9}) watts, or 1 nanowatt. With received signals being sometimes several million times smaller than the signals that were transmitted, performing calculations with many digits to the right of the decimal point is challenging. It is easy to make a mistake reading, writing, or typing these long numbers, even with a calculator. Fortunately, engineers have had the same kind of difficulty with very large or very small numbers, which is why Bell Labs, in the 1920s, came up with a system to simplify these calculations.

Recall from the previous chapter that an amplifier boosts the power of a signal; when this happens, the effect is called a **gain**. Conversely, cables and connectors offer a resistance to the flow of electricity and therefore tend to decrease the power of a signal. Humidity, dust, and obstacles like walls and human bodies also cause the signal to lose strength. This effect is called a **loss**. Knowing how much gain or loss occurs in an RF system composed of radio transmitters, receivers, cables, connectors, and antennas is necessary to assist RF engineers and technicians in selecting the appropriate components and properly installing them for reliable signal transmission and reception.

It is also important to understand that a signal's power does not usually change in linear fashion. Instead, it changes *logarithmically*. Figure 4-1 shows a graph of two values: one that changes in linear fashion and one that changes in logarithmic fashion.

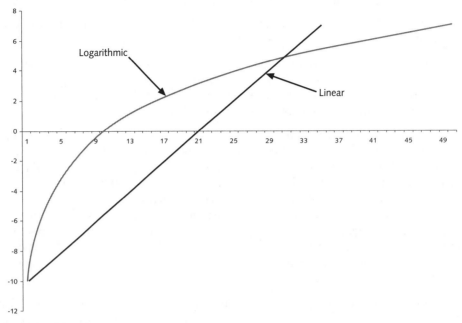

Figure 4-1   Linear vs. logarithmic values

Gain and loss are relative concepts, which means that you need to know the power level of the signal at two different points, such as at the transmitting antenna and at the receiving antenna. Relative concepts are best quantified with relative measurements, such as percentages. To calculate the signal loss, using percentages, for our sample wireless cable/DSL router used in a home network, you would still have to deal with numbers that are difficult to read, write, or type. Let's take a look at a much easier way to work with gain and loss, without using long numbers.

Decibel

Decibel (dB) is a ratio between two signal levels—a relative measurement (i.e., one in which a value is dependent on another value) that makes it much simpler to express and calculate power gain or loss. Here is how it's done.

The decibel is named in honor of Alexander Graham Bell, the inventor of the telephone. That is why the "B" in "dB" is written as a capital letter.

To calculate gain, all you need to remember, in practically all cases, is that:

- A gain of 3 dB (+3 dB) means the signal is two times bigger (twice the power).
- A gain of 10 dB (+10 dB) means the signal is 10 times bigger (10 times the power).

Loss is the opposite of gain, hence:

- A loss of 3 dB (−3 dB) means the signal is two times smaller (half the power).
- A loss of 10 dB (−10 dB) means the signal is 10 times smaller (1/10th the power).

To say "a loss of minus 3 dB" (−3 dB) is incorrect. The correct form is to say "a loss of 3 dB."

These rules are known as the *tens and threes of RF mathematics*. As you will see in the examples that follow, you can easily and quickly calculate the gain or loss with a reasonable amount of accuracy, without using a calculator, just by following these simple rules.

Using dB to represent gains and losses means that the only types of calculations required are simple additions and subtractions. There is no need for multiplication, division, or any kind of complex calculation to convert the values to the same unit in order to get a meaningful result. For example, if a transmitter is connected to a cable that has a loss of 4 dB and each connector—one on the transmitter end of the cable and one on the antenna end of the cable—has a loss of 1 dB, you can simply add the losses together like this: (−4 dB) + (−1 dB) + (−1 dB) = −6 dB, for a total loss of 6 dB.

Although dB is a relative measurement, at some point we have to make a "connection" or reference between dB and a linear, absolute measurement. One example of this is **dBm** (decibel-milliwatt), which is a relative way to indicate an absolute power level in the linear watt scale:

1 mW = 0 dBm

You can add or subtract any value represented in dB (dBm, etc.) using the "tens and threes" rule; you can also convert a dBm value directly to milliwatts of power. Let's look at some examples:

- +3 dB (3 dB of gain) will double the power: 10 mW + 3 dB = approximately 20 mW
- −3 dB (3 dB of loss) will halve the power: 10 mW − 3 dB = approximately 5 mW
- +10 dB will increase the power 10 times: 10 mW + 10 dB = approximately 100 mW
- −10 dB will decrease the power 10 times: 10 mW − 10 dB = approximately 1 mW

Converting to mW does not change the relative measurement characteristic of decibels. It simply means that you have a reference point for the values used in the calculations; you can still add or subtract any dB values as if they were all represented in the same units.

Therefore, if you want to know the absolute power level of a particular signal that is supplied by a transmitter and you know from the specifications for this particular unit that the strength of the output signal is +36 dBm, you can calculate the absolute power by breaking down this number like this:

36 dBm = 10 dBm + 10 dBm + 10 dBm + 3 dBm + 3 dBm

Because 0 dBm is equal to 1 mW, it follows that:

- Adding 10 dB makes the signal power 10 mW or 1 mW multiplied by 10.
- Adding another 10 dB multiplies the signal power by 10, making it 100 mW.
- Adding another 10 dB multiplies the signal power by 10 again, making it 1,000 mW or 1 W.

- Adding another 3 dB doubles the signal power, making it 2 W.
- Adding another 3 dB doubles the signal power again, making it 4 W.

In the rare instances in which using the "tens and threes" rule does not work, the formula for converting milliwatts (mW) to dBm is $P_{dBm} = 10\log P_{mW}$. Conversely, the formula for converting dBm to mW is: $P_{mW} = \log^{-1}(P_{dBm}/10) = 10$ dBm, where P_{mW} is power in milliwatts, and P_{dBm} is the equivalent figure in dB. These formulas are provided here for your reference only.

When assigning a dB factor to the gain of an antenna, the measurement must relate to some absolute value. The most perfect radiator of electromagnetic waves is an **isotropic radiator**, a theoretically perfect sphere that radiates energy equally in all directions. It is not possible to build a real isotropic radiator because it would need a power and a signal cable connected to it at some point on the surface of the sphere. The cable connection means that the sphere would no longer be perfect and would not be able to radiate with equal intensity in all directions.

An antenna does not transmit a signal where the cable is connected to it; however, the signal being fed into the antenna from the transmitter circuit does not change. That energy will still result in an electromagnetic wave, as well as a slight increase in the energy that did not propagate from the point where the cable is connected to the antenna. This is why antennas exhibit a gain (more on this later in this chapter).

As a reference point, an isotropic radiator has a theoretical gain of 0 dBm. Antenna gain is expressed using **dB isotropic (dBi)**, a relative measurement of the gain of an antenna as compared to the gain of an isotropic radiator.

The closest thing to an isotropic radiator is the sun. However, even the sun is not perfect because of a phenomenon called sunspots, which are dark areas on the surface of the star that change periodically and radiate energy levels different from the rest of the sun's surface.

For microwave and higher frequency antennas, antenna gain is usually expressed in **dB dipole (dBd)**. A **dipole** is the smallest, simplest, most practical type of antenna that can be made and exhibits the least amount of gain. A dipole has a fixed gain of 2.15 dB over that of an isotropic radiator. Therefore, if the gain of an antenna is 5 dBd, to convert to dBi, you simply add 2.15 to the 5 and get 7.15 dBi. Table 4-1 shows a summary of the decibel measurements used in RF communications.

Nomenclature	Description	Refers To
dBm	dB milliwatts	0 dB = 1 mW of power
dBd	dB dipole	The gain an antenna has over a dipole antenna at the same frequency
dBi	dB isotropic	The gain an antenna has over a theoretical isotropic (point source) radiator

Table 4-1   Decibel values and references

Antenna Characteristics

Now that you have an understanding of gain and loss, it is time to get acquainted with antenna types, sizes, and shapes.

 Antennas are reciprocal devices, which means that an antenna that works well for transmitting a signal on a particular range of frequencies is also effective at receiving signals in the same range of frequencies.

Antenna Types

Antennas used in wireless communications can be characterized as either passive or active. Each type of antenna can be constructed as either passive or active; however, most antennas are passive.

Passive Antennas Passive antennas are the most common type and are constructed of a piece of metal, wire, or similar conductive material. A passive antenna does not amplify the signal in any way; it can only radiate a signal with the same amount of energy that appears at the antenna connector minus any losses introduced by the antenna cable and connector. However, as you will learn, certain shapes of passive antennas radiate the RF energy supplied by the transmitter in one direction and consequently exhibit an effective gain that is similar to amplification of the signal and is called **directional gain**. Consider the two lamps in Figure 4-2. The light bulb on the left emits light energy all around it, except from the base, much like an omnidirectional antenna. Conversely, if you put a reflector around the light bulb, all of the light energy will be concentrated and emitted in one direction only, much like a directional antenna does.

Figure 4-2 Demonstrating directional gain by adding a reflector to make the light beam more directional

Active Antennas Active antennas are essentially passive antennas with built-in amplifiers. The amplifier is connected directly to the piece of metal that forms the antenna itself. Most active antennas have only one electrical connection. The RF signal and the power for the amplifier are supplied on the same conductor. This is intended to reduce the cost and make active antennas easier to install. Active antennas are not common, due to their much higher cost.

Antenna Sizes and Shapes

Antennas come in many sizes and shapes, depending on the following three characteristics:

- The frequency that the antenna is designed to transmit and receive
- The direction of the radiated electromagnetic wave
- The power with which the antenna must transmit or how sensitive it needs to be to receive very weak signals

The size of an antenna is inversely proportional to the frequency of the signal it is designed to transmit or receive. Lower frequency signals require larger antennas. Conversely, higher frequency signals require shorter antennas. For example, the antenna for an AM radio station transmitting at the frequency of 530 KHz (530,000 Hz) is 566 feet (172.5 meters) long, whereas that of a cellular telephone operating at a frequency of 900 MHz (900,000,000 Hz) is just over 13 inches (33.33 centimeters) long. Antenna shapes vary according to their specific applications.

Omnidirectional Antennas Omnidirectional antennas are used to transmit and receive signals from all directions with relatively equal intensity. Figure 4-3 shows two examples of omnidirectional antennas for use in IEEE 802.11 wireless networks. On the left is a magnetic mount antenna, with an integrated cable designed for use in WLAN applications. These antennas are useful for improving signal reception over antennas that are built inside laptop computers or permanently attached to a wireless NIC. Magnetic mount antennas can be used in office environments, where they can be easily attached to any metal surface, or they can be attached to the roof of a car or a truck for mobile applications. On the right of Figure 4-3 is a "blister"-type ceiling mount antenna. Blister antennas are typically used to hide the antenna or to make it blend with the decor.

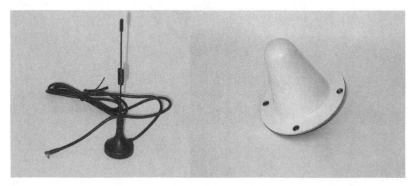

Figure 4-3   Magnetic mount and blister-type omnidirectional antennas

Longer omnidirectional antennas usually have higher gain but are more difficult to mount and hide. Later in this text, you will learn how the size of an antenna can affect its gain. Figure 4-4 shows an example of a high-gain antenna of this type.

Figure 4-4   High-gain omnidirectional antenna

Omnidirectional antennas exhibit passive gain because they emit a signal in two dimensions only, not in three dimensions, like an isotropic radiator. When viewed from the side, the RF waves from an omnidirectional antenna propagate from the sides or the length of the antenna, forming a doughnut-shaped pattern around it and are therefore somewhat focused.

Directional Antennas   The shape of an antenna also affects the intended direction of the radiated RF waves. A **directional antenna** is used to transmit a signal in one direction only. Although this may sound obvious, it represents an important difference between omnidirectional and directional antennas. Directional antennas, by focusing the RF waves mostly in one direction, concentrate the energy in one direction at the transmitter, or receive more energy, in the case of a receiver antenna, from one direction. This means that they exhibit more gain than an omnidirectional antenna.

Some types of directional antennas focus the RF energy more or less than others. A **yagi antenna** emits a wider, less-focused RF energy beam, whereas a **parabolic dish antenna** emits a narrow, more concentrated beam of RF energy. Yagi and dish antennas are both used for longer distance outdoor applications, and dish antennas are typically used for links of 16 miles (25 kilometers) or more. Dish antennas are used in point-to-point links, each aimed at one other dish antenna, but yagi antennas, in addition to being used in point-to-point links, are also sometimes used to enhance the signal quality and extend the distance of links to and from an omnidirectional antenna. One common application of a dish antenna is to receive satellite signals. Figure 4-5 shows two different models of yagi antennas. Note that it is not always easy to tell what type of antenna it is just by how it looks. Figure 4-6 shows a typical parabolic dish antenna. In a dish antenna, the parabolic surface of the dish is used to reflect the received signal onto the antenna element. At the transmitter end, the signal leaving the antenna element is reflected by the dish and leaves the antenna in one direction only.

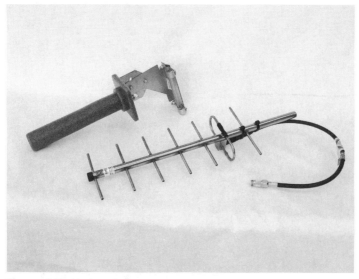

Figure 4-5 Yagi antennas

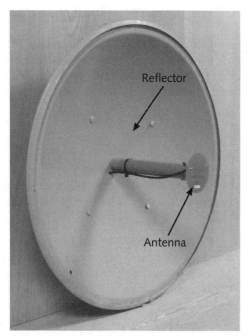

Figure 4-6 Parabolic dish antenna (protective weather dome removed)

Patch antennas emit an RF energy beam that is horizontally narrow but vertically wider, or taller, than that of a yagi antenna. Considered a semidirectional antenna, it is often used to send RF energy down a long, narrow corridor, although some varieties are designed for installation on the walls of buildings—for example, to send an RF signal in one direction away from the structure where they are mounted. Cellular telephony antennas are also designed to emit signals away from the tower or side of a building, where they are usually mounted. Figure 4-7 illustrates an example of antennas used in a cellular telephone tower, and Figure 4-8 shows a small patch antenna for use indoors.

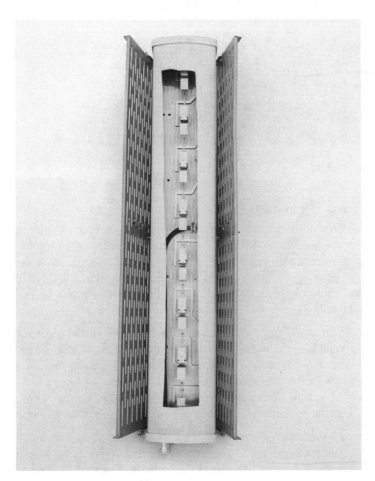

Figure 4-7 Cellular antenna with cutout to show internal construction

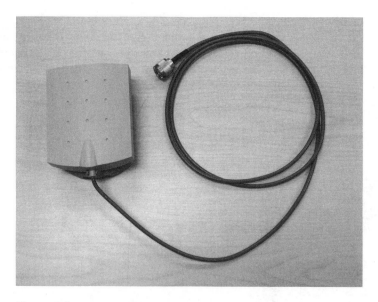

Figure 4-8 Indoor patch antenna

Signal Strength and Direction

The distance between the transmitter and receiver determines the strength of the signal you need to send, which in turn determines what size and shape of antenna you need for your application. Recall that most antennas are of the passive type and that transmitters can only produce finite amounts of RF energy. For most applications, active antennas can be extremely expensive, and frequency-licensing restrictions limit the amount of power with which signals may be transmitted.

What is the best solution? An omnidirectional antenna installed high and in a central location works well for sending a signal in all directions, but the strength of the signal is divided more or less equally in a 360-degree circle around the antenna. A directional antenna, on the other hand, sends most the energy in the direction the antenna is pointed; therefore, the RF wave travels farther than a signal sent from an omnidirectional antenna because the power is concentrated in one direction, an effect similar to the light bulb example shown in Figure 4-2.

Signals also lose energy as the electromagnetic wave travels away from the antenna. This behavior is primarily the result of free space loss. **Free space loss** happens because RF waves tend to spread away from the source of the signal (the antenna) similar to a circular wave created by throwing a stone in a pond. The farther the waves move away from the stone's impact point, the smaller they get because the amount of energy the wave originally had when the stone hit the water is distributed over an ever-growing and wider area. Eventually the wave fades to the point that you can no longer detect much movement on the surface of the water. If you place two floating objects on the water's surface—one near the point where the stone hits the water and another farther away—the one closer to the center point will move more than the one farther away because less of the wave's energy reaches the farther object. This energy loss means that a receiver gets less of the energy sent by the transmitter because the RF wave is spreading and its energy is dispersed over a wide area. However, if you experiment with dropping a stone into water in a confined space, such as a bathtub, the movement of the wave is contained by the sidewalls of the tub, and the waves will travel back and forth within the confines of the tub several times before they fade, the result is similar to multipath distortion, with waves getting affected by interacting with the reflected waves.

Free space loss can be calculated based on the strength of the signal coming out of the transmitter, the loss caused by cables and connectors, the gain of the antenna, and other objects in the path of the signal including, but not limited to, molecules of water (humidity) in the air. You can find many free space loss calculator tools on the Internet by using your favorite search engine to look for "free space loss calculator."

When discussing passive antennas, remember that antenna gain is directional gain (not power gain) due to focusing of the energy in one direction.

Radio stations transmit their signals in all directions to reach the largest number of listeners. Although they transmit with a lot of power, as you travel away from the city where the station's antenna is located, the signal gets weaker and weaker until your receiver can no longer detect it and all you may be able to hear are intermittent fragments of the transmission mixed with noise.

Some AM stations in the United States transmit with as much as 50,000 watts of power, and FM stations may send a signal with as much as 150,000 watts of power. Higher-frequency signals need more power to reach the same distance. In comparison, a typical enterprise-class WLAN AP transmits with only 100 milliwatts (0.1 watts) of power, and a typical home wireless gateway (router) transmits with only about 30 milliwatts of power.

How Antennas Work

Designing antennas and understanding how they perform the magic of sending RF signals out into air or space requires in-depth knowledge of physics, mathematics, and electronics. The details of the science behind how antennas work are beyond the scope of this book and are probably best left to higher-level courses in RF electronics. However, some general coverage of basic antenna functionality should help you develop a better appreciation of the science behind antennas. This section explains how antennas work as transmitters (radiators) and receivers of radio frequency signals.

Wavelength

The length of a single RF sine wave, known as the wavelength, is what determines the size of an antenna. An antenna transmits and receives a signal most efficiently at a specific frequency when it is as long as the full length of the wave; this is called a **full-wave antenna**. In most cases, this is not practical. For example, a full-wave antenna for an AM station might be about 1857 feet (over 566 meters) long, whereas a typical cellular telephone antenna would have to be just over 13 inches (33.33 centimeters) long. For practical reasons, antennas are more commonly designed to be as long as an exact fraction of the wavelength, and these are called **half-wave antennas, quarter-wave antennas**, and **eighth-wave antennas**. Though not as efficient as full-wave antennas, these smaller antennas work well enough to ensure reliable transmission and reception. The AM station antenna, for example, could be built as a quarter-wave antenna at about 464 feet (141 meters), which is still quite large, and the cellular antenna, using the same ratio, would only be about 3.25 inches (8.25 centimeters) long, which is about the size of one of today's smartphones.

When antennas with a higher gain are required, you can increase the size of the antenna to the next bigger fraction. A larger antenna exhibits a higher gain than a shorter antenna. Almost any metallic object or any object that conducts electricity can act as an antenna, but if you use an antenna that is much shorter than the wavelength of a particular frequency, it will not radiate any significant amount of RF. Alternatively, if the antenna is much longer than the wavelength, it will send out some RF energy, just not very efficiently, and this may affect the reliability of the transmitter circuits as well.

The wavelength of an RF signal is usually given in metric values. The formula for calculating the length of the wave, given that RF waves travel through air or space at the average speed of light (300,000 kilometers per second) is: *wavelength = speed of light/frequency*. Using a value in feet-per-second or inches-per-second for the speed of light will yield a result in feet or inches, respectively, for a particular wavelength. The average speed of light in miles-per-second is 186,000.

Antenna Performance

Antenna performance is a measure of how efficiently an antenna can radiate an RF signal. The design, installation, size, and type of antenna can affect its performance.

Radiation Patterns

In antenna design, certain items such as fasteners, brackets, and support structures can affect the way the antenna emits RF waves. During the testing phase of an antenna, engineers develop a graphic called an **antenna pattern** by measuring the signal radiating from the antenna. The antenna pattern indicates the direction, width, and shape of the RF signal beam coming from the antenna. An antenna pattern is usually drawn as if you were looking at it from the top. In the case of directional antennas, sometimes you will see an arrow indicating the direction in which the RF signal is being emitted. Figure 4-9 shows examples of antenna patterns.

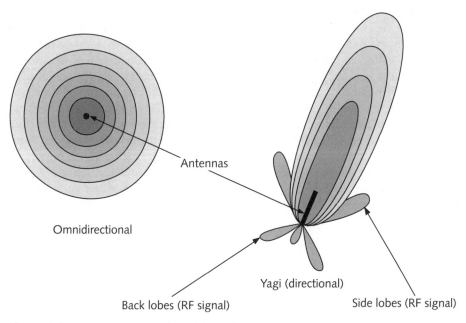

Figure 4-9   Antenna patterns viewed from above

Recall that antennas emit signals in two dimensions: horizontally and vertically. Antenna specifications almost always include the vertical beam angle that a particular antenna emits. Figure 4-10 illustrates the shape of RF waves emitted by an omnidirectional antenna, as viewed from the side.

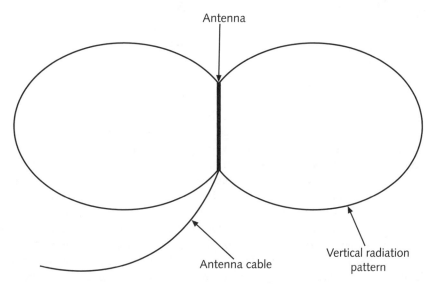

Figure 4-10   Vertical antenna pattern (side view of omnidirectional antenna pattern)

Antenna Polarization

When a signal leaves an antenna, the waves have a particular orientation; in other words, the oscillations are oriented either horizontally or vertically. The orientation of the wave leaving the antenna is called **antenna polarization**. If you hold a cellular phone straight up in your hand, the antenna is usually positioned vertically. The signal leaving the antenna in this case will be vertically polarized, meaning that the sine waves will travel up and down when leaving the antenna. If you are lying down when talking on the cellular phone, the signal leaving the antenna is horizontally polarized, which is to say that the sine waves travel from side to side on a horizontal plane. Cellular base station (tower) antennas are mounted vertically and send out signals that are also vertically polarized. Antenna polarization is important because the most efficient signal transmission and reception is experienced when the sending and receiving antennas are equally polarized—that is, they are both either vertically or horizontally polarized. Figure 4-11 illustrates this concept.

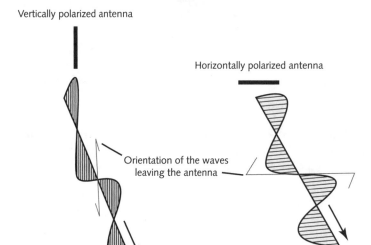

Figure 4-11 Antenna polarization

Most add-on USB wireless NICs used in laptop computers that stick out the side of the computers are horizontally polarized, provided that the laptop computer is on top of a desk or on your lap. The wireless residential gateways that the wireless NIC is transmitting to or receiving from usually have their antennas mounted in a vertical position, which means that the signal is not polarized the same direction as the signals emitted or received by the laptop computer. Conversely, the built-in wireless NICs in laptops usually have the antennas mounted on the back of the screen. Different polarization between devices can cause poor communication between them. The utility software supplied with wireless NICs can show the strength of the signal. If you experience poor reception, try placing the computer on its side (carefully, of course) while monitoring the strength of the signal. You will most likely see a small increase in signal strength due to the antennas having the same polarization. Figure 4-12 shows a laptop computer with an add-on wireless NIC (horizontally mounted antenna) and an AP with the antennas mounted vertically.

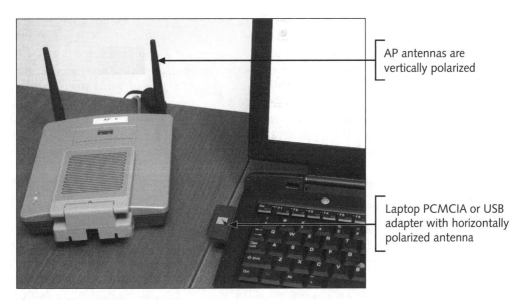

AP antennas are
vertically polarized

Laptop PCMCIA or USB
adapter with horizontally
polarized antenna

Figure 4-12 Mixed vertical and horizontal antenna polarizations

Antenna Dimensions

The design and construction of an antenna dictates whether it is one-dimensional or two-dimensional.

One-Dimensional Antennas One-dimensional antennas are basically a length of wire or metal. They can be built as a straight piece or bent in some shape, such as the old "rabbit ear" antennas that used to be placed on top of television sets.

A **monopole antenna** is basically a straight piece of wire or metal, usually a quarter of the wavelength, with no reflecting or ground element. As you learned earlier, dipole is the smallest, simplest, most practical type of antenna. Dipoles are commonly built as two monopoles mounted together at the base (the place where the cable(s) connect(s) to the antenna) and laid out in a straight line, with the two ends facing away from each other. Figure 4-13 shows an example of a dipole antenna.

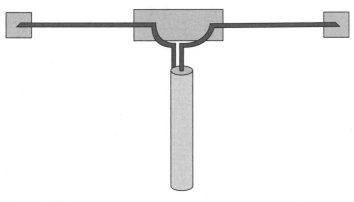

Figure 4-13 Common dipole antenna

A monopole antenna is less efficient than a dipole. Dipoles can be built larger because they are usually laid out horizontally. To work properly, monopole antennas are mounted in such a way that they are practically sticking out of the ground (or very close to it) or some other type of large structure that reflects the electromagnetic energy. Because the ground reflects the waves, it acts as a reflector, and this makes the monopole antenna behave like a dipole, rendering it more efficient. Alternatively, a monopole can be equipped with a large metal base called a **ground-plane** to simulate the signal-reflecting effect of the ground and increase its efficiency. The most common application of ground-planes is on boats that have fiberglass hulls. Fiberglass is nonconducting and does not reflect radio waves; therefore, antennas for nautical radios usually have either a horizontal metal plate near the base or, alternatively, four lengths of wire sticking out horizontally from the base, to act as the ground-plane.

Two-Dimensional Antennas Antennas organized in a two-dimensional pattern, with both height and width, are known as **two-dimensional antennas**. Examples include patch and satellite dish antennas. A satellite dish works like a signal collector, scooping up any signal that comes in a straight line with the center axis of the antenna. A patch antenna is usually a flat piece of metal, with different heights and widths, depending on the desired vertical and horizontal radiation angles. Another type of two-dimensional directional antenna is a **horn antenna**, such as the one shown in Figure 4-14, which resembles a large horn with the wide end bent to one side, in a parabolic curve. These antennas are common in telephone networks and are used to transmit high-power microwave signals between two very distant towers, usually over 18 miles (30 kilometers).

Figure 4-14 Telephone transmission tower showing two horn antennas

Smart Antennas

A newer development in antenna technology is the smart antenna. Used primarily in cellular telephony and WiMAX, **smart antennas** use the strength of the signal coming from a mobile device and "learn" where it is located, track it, and focus the RF energy in the device's direction to avoid wasting energy, which also prevents interference with other antennas. Instead of sending signals with wide beams, or spreading the energy over 360 degrees like omnidirectional antennas, smart antennas send narrow beams of energy toward the receiver. Figure 4-15 illustrates this concept. The illustration on the left shows a regular directional antenna. The one on the right shows a smart antenna tracking a mobile receiver.

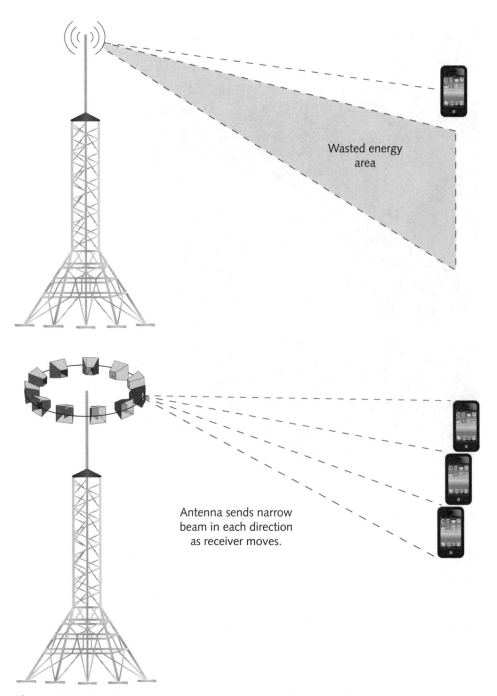

Figure 4-15 Directional antenna vs. smart antenna (switched-beam)

There are two classes of smart antennas:

- A switched beam antenna uses several narrow beam antennas pointing in different directions and turns each one on or off as the receiver moves across the path of the beams, as shown in Figure 4-15.

- An adaptive or phased array antenna is similar to a patch antenna but, instead of being just a single piece of metal, is divided into a matrix of radiating elements. A computer-based signal processor controls circuits in the antenna system, turning elements of the matrix on or off as well as adjusting the phase of the transmission signal supplied to each one as the mobile user moves across the front of the antenna. This has the effect of sending the energy beam in a particular direction and is sometimes called "beam forming." The signal processor is also able to determine the relative position of a mobile device by calculating its position based on the time difference of receiving the signal in different antennas as well as the strength of the signal.

Phased array antennas are used extensively in ultramodern radar systems. For example, you may have noticed that newer warships have far fewer rotating radar antennas than older ones. Phased array antennas are also used in aircraft nose radar systems. Because there are no moving parts to wear out or break, this also makes these antennas a lot more reliable and long lasting. This, in turn, helps to justify the higher cost of the smart electronics in these antennas. Figure 4-16 shows an example of a large land-based phased array radar antenna. Note the multiple antenna elements that make up the array.

Figure 4-16 Phased array antenna showing a matrix of transmission elements (multiple small, antenna elements)

Figure 4-17 shows a comparison between the mechanical movement parabolic dish antenna nose radar of an F4D warplane vs. the fixed phased array nose radar antenna on an F16.

Figure 4-17 F4D Phantom (left) vs. F16 (right) nose radar

Figure 4-18 shows how a transmitter varies the phase when transmitting the same signal from different elements in an array. This makes the signal arrive in phase at a particular physical location where the waves from different elements cross, which maximizes the signal's strength at the receiver.

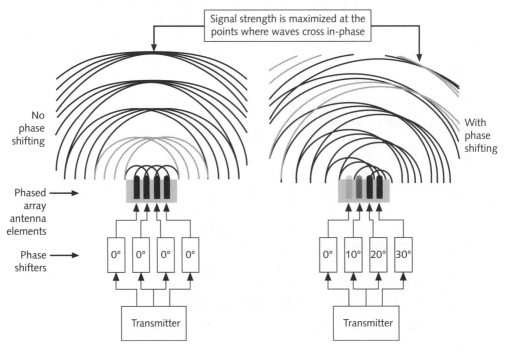

Figure 4-18 Phased array transmission

Phased array and switched beam smart antenna systems can be used for other applications as well, such as cellular telephony and even for radio stations in areas where interference from nearby radio transmitters operating in the same frequency range is very high. This can happen where large cities are relatively close to each other and the limited frequency spectrum in the area is very crowded. However, due to the very high cost of these smart antenna systems, they are not very common.

Antenna System Implementation

The proper installation of antennas requires knowledge of the user's requirements as well as an ability to deal with various challenges, including physical obstacles, municipal building codes, and other regulatory restrictions.

As mentioned at the beginning of this chapter, cellular providers spend a great deal of time and effort designing and testing their antenna networks in order to provide the best signal coverage and, hence, the best service to their customers. They also need to know what the user traffic patterns are in a given area, and they need to obtain the proper permissions for installation of antenna towers and atop buildings. In North America, obtaining permits from the government or from private land or building owners takes longer and is more expensive than in other countries around the world. As a result, cellular providers also need to be smarter and more thorough at both maximizing coverage and minimizing interference.

The purpose of a single RF antenna or a system consisting of multiple antennas is to allow a group of users to communicate reliably without wires. The system's performance and reliability are major concerns for the RF technician, and so is security. This is especially true today, when unlicensed frequencies are often accompanied by maximum signal power restrictions, a lack of support from regulatory agencies in case of conflict or interference, and easy access to a wide range of equipment and software by untrained and inexperienced users and hackers.

When implementing wireless communications—such as when setting up a WLAN—using the antennas supplied with the wireless devices limits you to placing the transmitters and receivers where you can achieve a good connection. If you need to go beyond the standard setup, however—if, for example, you purchase several different external antennas to ensure good signal reception in a difficult area or to create a long-distance outdoor link—there are a few additional things to consider.

You should not attempt to install towers or antennas outdoors without proper training and insurance. Instead, you should always hire a professional, insured installer for outdoor antennas, whether you are installing them in towers, on the sides of buildings, or on the roofs of houses or buildings.

Antenna Cables

Most antennas are connected to the transmitter or receiver using coaxial cable. This type of cable is built in layers of wires (conducting) and insulators (nonconducting). Figure 4-19 illustrates the construction of a coaxial cable.

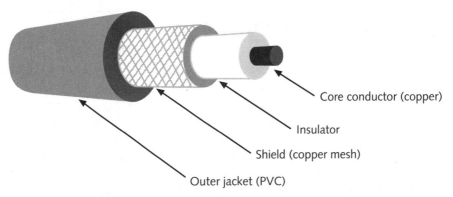

Figure 4-19 Coaxial cable construction

 Coaxial cable is also used for audio, cable television, and a variety of other applications. It is very important to always use the cable with the right specifications for the intended application in order to avoid problems that are difficult to troubleshoot.

Coaxial cables come in many sizes (thicknesses) and specifications. In an RF system, it is very important to use the correct type of cable, per the equipment and antenna manufacturer specifications. Among the specifications is the **impedance** of the cable, which is the opposition to the flow of alternating current in a circuit. Represented by the letter Z and measured in ohms, impedance is the combination of the circuit's resistance, inductance, and capacitance. The cable's impedance must match that of the transmitter circuit as well as that of the antenna. When you need to connect an external antenna and it is not possible to attach it directly to the transmitter output, you must consider the signal loss caused by the connectors and by the cable itself. Almost all conducting materials add a resistance to the flow of electricity on a wire. This is particularly important in antenna cables and more so in equipment that transmits at very low power—such as those used in IEEE 802.11 WLANs.

Cable loss is measured in relation to the length of the cable. The longer the cable, the more loss occurs. In RF antenna applications you should use special low-loss antenna cables to minimize signal loss. Table 4-2 lists LMR low-loss cables of varying thicknesses along with the losses that occur at 2.4 GHz for every 100 feet (30 meters) of cable.

Part Number	Diameter	Loss at 2.4 GHz (per 100 ft.)
LMR-100	1/10"	−38.9 dB
LMR-240	3/16"	−12.7 dB
LMR-400	3/8"	−6.6 dB
LMR-600	1/2"	−4.4 dB

Table 4-2 Low-loss LMR cables

To calculate the total cable loss, divide the loss per 100 feet by 100 and multiply by the required length of your cable. For example, if you needed to install the antenna about

10 feet (3 meters) away from the transmitter, LMR-100 cable will introduce a loss of 3.9 dB (39 dB/100 = 0.39 dB per foot × 10 = 3.9 dB), which means that significantly more than half of the energy produced at the transmitter output is lost, and that is before adding the connector losses! Using LMR-400, the loss introduced by the cable will be only about 0.7 dB.

To keep loss at a minimum, you may have to use a cable that is too thick for the connector type used in your transmitter, antenna, or both. The first consideration when deciding to change the manufacturer-provided or equipment-mounted antennas should be the locations of the transmitter and antenna(s). In addition, you should be aware that LMR cable is significantly more expensive than regular coaxial cable, easily costing over 10 times the price. LMR cable is also difficult to add connectors to and difficult to bend, often making its installation a challenge.

RF Propagation

The way that radio waves propagate, or move, between the transmitter and the receiver through the atmosphere of our planet depends on the frequency of the signal. RF waves are classified in three groups, as shown in Table 4-3. Ground waves follow the curvature of the Earth. Sky waves bounce between the ionosphere and the surface of the Earth. RF waves transmitted in frequencies between 30 MHz and 300 GHz require a line-of-sight path between the transmitter and the receiver antennas.

Group	Frequency Range
Ground waves	3 KHz to 2 MHz
Sky waves	2 to 30 MHz
Line-of-sight waves	30 MHz to 300 GHz

Table 4-3   RF wave propagation groups

Figure 4-20 illustrates how these different waves propagate through Earth's atmosphere and, consequently, how this affects the implementation of antenna systems.

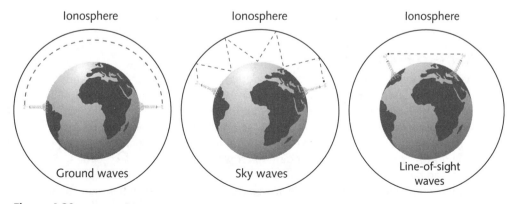

Figure 4-20   How radio waves propagate

Point-to-Multipoint Links

In most wireless communications applications, one transmitter communicates with several mobile clients. This is called a **point-to-multipoint wireless link**. If the receiver is installed in a fixed location, as in the case of a central building in a campus with wireless links to other buildings, it is possible to maximize the performance of an RF link by using an omnidirectional antenna at a central location and directional, higher-gain antennas at the remote locations. Figure 4-21 illustrates this type of application.

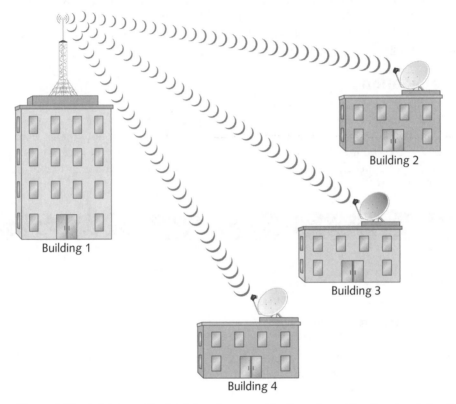

Figure 4-21   Point-to-multipoint links using a combination of omnidirectional and directional antennas

Point-to-Point Links

Two computer networks in different buildings can be connected by a **point-to-point** wireless link. In this case, directional antennas provide the most reliable method of transmitting RF waves. Their narrow beams and high gain ensure that most of the energy of the RF wave will be used between the two antennas. The cost is often much lower and the performance comparable to or higher than that of a digital telephone company line. Telephone companies make extensive use of point-to-point microwave links, instead of cables, for long-distance voice and data communications. Although repeater towers are required, the cost of maintaining a wireless link is usually much lower than the cost of installing and maintaining cables, which can be easily damaged and are harder to troubleshoot. Figure 4-22 shows an example of a point-to-point link.

Figure 4-22   Point-to-point link using directional antennas

Fresnel Zone

Although the transmission path for point-to-point links is usually represented by a straight line, recall that RF waves have a tendency to spread out. This means that the space between the two antennas would be more accurately represented by something similar to an ellipse (see Figure 4-23). This elliptical region is called the **Fresnel zone**, and its shape is an important consideration in wireless links. When planning a wireless link, at least 60 percent of the Fresnel zone must be kept clear of obstructions, which may affect the height of the antenna tower. If any obstruction, such as a tree or building, blocks more than 40 percent of the RF signal, it blocks the radio signals completely. The Fresnel zone is sometimes referred to as RF line of sight, and it is far more critical than visual line of sight, meaning that although a person standing next to an antenna may be able to see the other antenna, the transceivers at either end of a point-to-point wireless link may not be able to communicate.

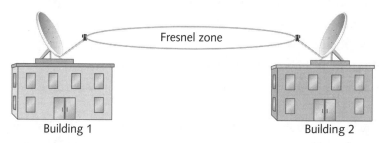

Figure 4-23   Fresnel zone

 The name "Fresnel" (pronounced Fray-nel) comes from the French physicist Augustin-Jean Fresnel, who studied the polarization of light waves.

Link Budgets

Once you have considered the cables, antenna types, link type, and Fresnel zone of your transmission, you still need to calculate whether you will have enough signal strength to meet the receiver's minimum requirements. This calculation is called a **link budget** and is used in every type of outdoor wireless link, whether across the road or between a satellite and an earth station.

The process involves all the variables that you have read about in this chapter. The calculations are not very complex, but there are many factors to consider. One of the simplest ways to calculate a link budget is to download a spreadsheet or tool that is available on the Internet at little or no cost. To calculate your link budget, you will need information from the equipment specifications, including the gain of the antennas, cable, and connector losses for the receiver and the transmitter, receiver sensitivity, and the free space loss figure.

Search the web for "Link Budget Calculator" and download one of the spreadsheets. If you do not have access to Microsoft Excel or a compatible spreadsheet application, you can also use one of the online link budget calculators.

Antenna Alignment

One of the challenges of implementing a point-to-point link is to position the antennas at the same height and point them toward one another to maximize the strength of the signal. Recall that you must ensure that a minimum of 60 percent of the Fresnel zone is not blocked by obstructions. The height at which the antenna will be mounted can be affected by trees, buildings, and the curvature of the Earth. Some transmitters and receivers are equipped with tools designed to assist the installers in aligning the two antennas. Others may require the rental or purchase of additional tools to ensure perfect alignment. Some basic tools are essential, such as:

- A compass to position the antenna in the correct direction
- A spotting scope or binoculars, if the other antenna site is within visible range
- A means of communication, such as a walkie-talkie or a cellular phone
- A light source such as a flashlight or laser pointer, if the distance is reasonably short
- A topological map that shows ground elevations in the area
- Some way of determining the height of the building or tower where the antenna is to be mounted

Technicians who often perform long-distance link installations and who need to align antennas with a great degree of accuracy to ensure maximum reliability (as is the case with dish antennas) are usually equipped with a spectrum analyzer, such as the one shown in Figure 4-24. This tool displays the signal amplitude and bandwidth used by the signal, showing a graphic of a signal in the frequency domain, instead of an oscilloscope which displays a signal in the time domain (real-time wave graph). Spectrum analyzers can also display interference happening in a particular frequency channel, offer multiple display options, and are expensive instruments, ranging in price from about $10,000 to over $100,000, depending on usable frequency range and other features.

Figure 4-24   Spectrum analyzer showing amplitude (vertical size of on-screen graph) and bandwidth used by signal (bottom of on-screen graph)

Antenna system implementation, including alignment and troubleshooting, demands hours of practical training. Although it is beyond the scope of this book, this overview is included here to give you a sense for the complex issues involved. Before moving on to other more practical aspects of wireless communications, we will discuss some of the other challenges that affect implementation, particularly of outdoor links.

Other Challenges of Outdoor Links

Recall that radio waves can reflect off, diffract, or be absorbed by various materials. Weather phenomena (such as heavy fog, rain, dust, or snowstorms), air disturbances (such as air masses rising quickly from the ground because of the sun heating up the surface in deserts and other very hot areas), and significant drops in temperature that occur in deep valleys during the course of a day—all can affect the performance and reliability of wireless links. Seasonal changes can also impact a wireless link. For example, say it was set up in the winter, when there were no leaves on the trees; when spring arrives, and the leaves grow, a tree can block more than 40 percent of the Fresnel zone, absorbing most of the RF waves.

When planning an outdoor link, you should always consider the possibility that the link performance will be seriously affected or the link will go down completely as a result of one or more of the environmental conditions described. Check the history of the region's weather. Contact the municipal planning, parks, and building permit departments to identify short- and long-term plans that may interfere with your intended link. And always take into account how the positioning of an antenna may be affected by vegetation growth.

The possibility of another company or person setting up a link in which the RF wave beam interferes with the one you set up is an additional concern. If you are using unlicensed frequencies, such as the ISM or U-NII bands, you cannot count on assistance from regulatory agencies or authorities. Of course, you should always be a good citizen and make sure you are not interfering with anyone else's signal before you set up an outdoor link.

Chapter Summary

- By the time an RF signal reaches the receiver, it can be a billion times smaller than when it left the transmitter. Cables, connectors, antennas, and the distance between the transmitter and receiver are all factors that affect how much energy a signal has when it is transmitted and when it is received. A gain occurs when a signal power is increased—for example, when most of the signal's energy is focused in one direction or when it is put through an amplifier before being routed to the antenna. A loss occurs when the energy of a signal is decreased.

- The decibel (dB) is a relative measurement used by engineers and technicians to simplify the calculations of gain and loss as well as to indicate the strength of a signal. A gain of 3 dB doubles the signal's power. A loss of 3 dB halves the signal's power. A gain of 10 dB increases the signal strength 10 times, and a loss of 10 dB decreases the signal strength 10 times. Gains and losses expressed in dB can simply be added or subtracted together.

- An isotropic radiator is a theoretically perfect sphere that radiates power equally in all directions. The two most basic types of antennas are the theoretical isotropic radiator, which is only used as a reference (given that it is not possible to build a working one), and the dipole.

- The most common type of antenna is a passive antenna, which is basically a piece of wire or metal that can only radiate a signal with as much power as is provided by the transmitter. An active antenna has a built-in amplifier to boost the signal power and compensate for the losses caused by cables and connectors.

- The size of an antenna depends primarily on the frequency or range of frequencies that it is designed to transmit or receive, and this is directly proportional to the wavelength of the signal and inversely proportional to the frequency—that is, a longer antenna is required for lower frequencies, and a shorter antenna is used for higher frequencies. To keep antennas at a manageable size, most are built as half-wave (half the wavelength), quarter-wave (a quarter of the wavelength), or eighth-wave (an eighth of the wavelength).

- Omnidirectional antennas transmit and receive signals from all directions. Directional antennas focus the signal energy in one direction only, which has an effect (called directional gain) in passive antennas that is similar to the gain provided by an amplifier, only without adding any additional electrical power.

- Yagi, patch, and dish are different types of directional antennas.

- Free space loss is caused by the natural tendency of RF waves to spread out and is a measure of the amount of loss of signal strength between the transmitter antenna and the receiver antenna.

- Larger antennas have a higher gain; conversely, smaller antennas have lower gain.

- Antennas have a horizontal and a vertical radiation pattern. Antennas also emit a signal that is either vertically polarized or horizontally polarized. The most efficient communications link is when the transmitter and the receiver antennas have the same polarization.

- There are two basic types of one-dimensional antennas: monopole and dipole. The dipole antenna is more efficient than the monopole antenna. Monopoles that are not mounted at or near the ground can make use of an artificial ground-plane. Patch, phased array, and dish antennas are examples of two-dimensional antennas.

- Smart antennas, used mostly in cellular telephone applications, can track a mobile user and send a narrower, more efficient beam of RF energy directed at the user, which also prevents interference with other transmitter antennas. A switched beam antenna uses several narrow beam antennas pointing in different directions. An adaptive array (or phased array) antenna has a matrix of radiating elements and uses a signal processor to enable or disable elements in order to send a focused beam of RF energy in the direction of the mobile user.

- Special LMR antenna cables are used to reduce the signal loss between the transmitter and the antenna.

- RF waves propagate differently depending on the frequency of the signal. Ground waves follow the curvature of the Earth. Sky waves bounce between the ionosphere and the surface of the Earth. RF waves transmitted in frequencies between 30 MHz and 300 GHz require line-of-sight path between the transmitter and the receiver antennas.

- Directional antennas build point-to-point links that connect two buildings using a wireless link; they are also used by telephone carriers for long-distance microwave communication links. Point-to-multipoint links can also be set up using an omnidirectional antenna and multiple directional antennas.

- A Fresnel zone is an elliptical area between two directional antennas. When setting up a wireless link in this way, maintaining a reliable connection requires that no more than 40 percent of the Fresnel zone be blocked by obstructions.

- Directional antennas must be aligned with each other to maximize the strength of the signal between the two. Although some wireless equipment manufacturers include built-in tools to facilitate the alignment of antennas, technicians also use spectrum analyzers to ensure high reliability, accuracy, and for troubleshooting wireless links.

- RF waves can be blocked, partially or completely, by weather phenomena and conditions such as heavy rain, dust, or snowstorms. When designing a long-distance wireless link, you should always check with the local authorities to make sure no buildings or trees are planned for the area, because that could interfere with your connection.

Key Terms

active antenna   A passive antenna with an amplifier built-in.

antenna pattern   A graphic that shows how a signal radiates out of an antenna.

antenna polarization   An indication of the horizontal or vertical orientation of the sine waves leaving an antenna.

dB dipole (dBd)   The relative measurement of the gain of an antenna when compared to a dipole antenna at the same frequency.

dB isotropic (dBi)   The relative measurement of the gain of an antenna when compared to a theoretical isotropic radiator.

dBm A relative way to indicate an absolute power level in the linear watt scale.

decibel (dB) A ratio between two signal levels.

dipole An antenna that has a fixed amount of gain over that of an isotropic radiator.

directional antenna An antenna that focuses RF energy, sending the signal in one direction.

directional gain The effective gain that a directional antenna achieves by focusing RF energy in one direction.

eighth-wave antenna An antenna that is one-eighth of the wavelength of the signal it is designed to transmit or receive.

free space loss The signal loss that occurs as a result of the tendency of RF waves to spread, resulting in less energy at any given point, as the signal moves away from the transmitting antenna.

Fresnel zone An elliptical region spanning the distance between two directional antennas that must not be blocked more than 40 percent to prevent interference with the RF signal.

full-wave antenna An antenna that is as long as the length of the wave it is designed to transmit or receive.

gain A relative measure of increase in a signal's power level.

ground-plane A metal disc or two straight wires assembled at 90 degrees, used to provide a reflection point for monopole antennas that are not mounted on or near the surface of the ground.

half-wave antenna An antenna that is half as long as the wavelength of the signal it is designed to transmit or receive.

horn antenna A two-dimensional directional antenna typically used for microwave transmission; it resembles a large horn with the wide end bent to one side.

impedance The opposition to the flow of alternating current in a circuit. Represented by the letter Z and measured in ohms, impedance is the combination of a circuit's resistance, inductance, and capacitance.

isotropic radiator A theoretically perfect sphere that radiates power equally in all directions; it is impossible to construct one.

link budget The process of calculating the signal strength between the transmitter and receiver antennas to ensure that the link can meet the receiver's minimum signal strength requirements.

loss A relative measure of decrease in a signal's power level.

monopole antenna An antenna built of a straight piece of wire, usually a quarter of the wavelength with no ground point or reflecting element.

omnidirectional antenna An antenna that sends out the signal in a uniform pattern in all directions.

one-dimensional antenna A straight length of wire or metal connected to a transmitter at one end.

parabolic dish antenna A high-gain directional antenna that emits a narrow, focused beam of energy and is used for long-distance outdoor links.

passive antenna The most common type of antenna. Passive antennas can only radiate a signal with the same amount of energy that appears at the antenna connector.

patch antenna   A semidirectional antenna that emits a wide horizontal beam and an even wider vertical beam.

point-to-multipoint wireless link   A link in which one central site uses an omnidirectional antenna to transmit to multiple remote sites, which may use omnidirectional antennas or directional antennas to maximize the distance and the quality of the signal.

point-to-point   The most reliable link between two antenna sites using directional antennas to maximize the distance and the signal quality.

quarter-wave antenna   An antenna that is one-quarter of the wavelength of the signal it is designed to transmit or receive.

smart antenna   A new type of antenna that uses a signal processor and an array of narrow beam elements to track the user and send most of the RF energy in the direction of the mobile receiver in order to prevent interference and avoid wasting RF energy. There are two types of smart antennas, switched-beam and adaptive or phased array antenna.

two-dimensional antenna   An antenna, such as a dish or patch, that has both height and width. In omnidirectional antennas, the thickness of the pole or wire is not considered a second dimension.

yagi antenna   A directional antenna that emits a wide, less-focused beam and is used for medium-distance outdoor applications.

Review Questions

1. Antennas are _____ devices.

   a. powered

   b. connection

   c. amplification

   d. reciprocal

2. Decibel is a relative measurement that requires a(n) _____.

   a. distance

   b. antenna

   c. power level

   d. comparison

   e. gain

3. A gain of 6 dB means that the signal level or strength _____.

   a. increases very little

   b. doubles

   c. doubles twice

   d. does not increase at all

4. A transmitter generates a 15-dBm signal and is connected to an antenna using a cable that introduce 2 dB of loss. The cable has two connectors, one at each end, that introduce a loss of 2 dB each. What is the signal level at the input of the antenna in dBm and milliwatts?

   a.   9 dBm, 8 mW

   b.   10 dBm, 10 mW

   c.   21 dBm, 18 mW

   d.   6 dBm, 4 mW

5. The simplest and most practical type of antenna is a _____ antenna.

   a.   straight wire

   b.   dipole

   c.   yagi

   d.   monopole

   e.   passive

6. A(n) _____ antenna transmits a signal in all directions with relatively equal intensity.

   a.   multidirectional

   b.   phased array

   c.   directional

   d.   omnidirectional

   e.   smart

7. Between the transmitting antenna and the receiving antenna, a signal will always be subject to _____.

   a.   gain

   b.   amplification

   c.   free space loss

   d.   reflection

   e.   diffraction

8. For the best performance between transmitter and receiver, the two antennas should have the same _____.

   a.   format

   b.   angle

   c.   gain

   d.   polarization

9. In a direct, point-to-point link, the Fresnel zone should never be obstructed more than _____.

    a. 40 percent

    b. 60 percent

    c. 30 percent

    d. 50 percent

10. To work as efficiently as a dipole, a monopole antenna requires a(n) _____.

    a. LMR cable

    b. longer length

    c. ground plane

    d. amplifier

11. A lower frequency signal uses a _____ antenna, whereas a higher frequency signal uses a _____ antenna.

    a. shorter, longer

    b. longer, shorter

    c. higher, lower

    d. lower, higher

12. The gain of an antenna is the measure of how an antenna _____ the beam.

    a. focuses

    b. widens

    c. enlarges

    d. lowers

13. A directional antenna typically has a low gain. True or False?

14. Passive antennas can be designed in a way that effectively increases the strength of a signal in a particular direction. True or False?

15. The _____ of an antenna depends upon the frequency of the RF signal and the gain.

    a. length

    b. amplification

    c. width

    d. height

16. When planning an outdoors wireless link, you should always prepare a _____ to ensure that the signal that reaches the receiver meets the minimum signal strength requirements for a reliable connection.

    a. free space loss

    b. proposal

    c. link budget

    d. specification

17. List two types of directional antennas.

18. How do smart antennas function?

19. How do sky waves propagate?

20. What happens if someone sets up a pair of antennas that interfere with your point-to-point link between two buildings, using the same unlicensed frequency channel as you do?

Hands-On Projects

Project 4-1

Using the Internet and other sources, write a one-page paper on adaptive array or phased array antenna systems. Other than for cellular telephony and military radar, what applications is this type of antenna being used for? What are its advantages and disadvantages?

Project 4-2

Write a one-page paper that recommends the type of antenna and the gain that would be required to transmit a signal over a 16-mile outdoor link. The transmitter is capable of generating a signal with a maximum signal strength of +36 dBm at its output, and it will be installed indoors, whereas the antenna will be installed on the roof. The cable provided is 50 feet of LMR-400 at both ends, which is about 10 feet longer than what you need to connect between the antenna and the transmitter. The receiver has a sensitivity of −86 dBm. Use an online or spreadsheet-based Link Budget Calculator available on the web. Write down the antenna gain and type that you would use to setup this wireless link.

Project 4-3

Search the web for antenna manufacturer's websites, locate the specifications for at least two different types of antennas, such as blister, Yagi or parabolic dish, and high-gain omnidirectional. Then find and compare the diagrams showing the horizontal and vertical antenna patterns. Write down your findings and include the antenna pattern images and the typical application for the antennas you chose.

HANDS-ON PROJECTS

Project 4-4

Many people have Wi-Fi reception issues in large houses or in apartment buildings where there may be a lot of interference. You may be able to improve the signal quality significantly by building a simple parabolic reflector. Search the web for "home-made Wi-Fi (or wireless) signal booster" and you should be able to find printable templates as well as videos that will guide you on how to make reflectors for a wireless router that is equipped with external antennas or a portable reflector if you have an external USB Wi-Fi NIC. Which one you decide to build will depend on the materials and tools you have available, but the cost to build one is either very low or free. Test your setup with a laptop or other mobile device that can display the signal strength, and record the results. To test for signal strength, you can use Acrylic Wi-Fi Home that was also used in Project 3-4, in Chapter 3. Start the application, right-click to the left of the SSID column, click **Selection** in the pop-up context menu, and then click **Invert.** Point to the SSID (or the name of your Wi-Fi network) and left-click to the left of your Wi-Fi network name to show only the signal graph for your network on the bottom part of the screen. Write a brief report showing the strength of the signal you detected with and without the reflectors installed on the antennas of the router or access point. Make sure your PC is at least 20 feet (6 meters) away from the transmitting device while measuring. You should also test the speed of data transfer with and without the reflector and report on any changes.

Real-World Exercise

Exercise 4-1

The Baypoint Group (TBG), a company of 50 consultants who assist organizations and businesses with issues involving network planning and design, has again requested your services as a consultant.

Triangle Farms is a cooperative that grows vegetables and has two greenhouse locations within 6 miles of each other on the outskirts of Bennington, Vermont. It wants to install a wireless network in both locations but also wants to interconnect the two facilities. The local telephone company has proposed to install a dedicated digital line to link Triangle's two locations and has argued that wireless links are not reliable and that they will end up costing more than the $1,500 per month that the dedicated line will cost. Triangle has asked TBG for an opinion. TBG has asked you to become involved because you are the expert they always call upon to discuss and recommend antenna systems for wireless links.

TBG is providing the network design and implementation, along with all the wireless networking equipment required for the connection, except for the antennas linking the two sites. The location of the warehouses allows for line-of-sight access to each other, and the building codes do not allow tall buildings or towers in the area, as they are located near an airport.

Each Triangle location has an office with about 10 staff members. The office area is large and fairly open. Each of the greenhouses has two 500-foot corridors that require wireless access because staff members perform periodic checks on the plant beds. The staff members would like to be able to upload the updates and harvest predictions directly to the central server using the wireless network.

Create a PowerPoint presentation that outlines the different types of connections and antennas and the advantages and disadvantages of each. Include examples in the form of pictures and stories about similar successful wireless links. TBG has asked you to be very persuasive in your presentation, because Triangle is on the verge of signing the contract with the phone company. You are told that presenting the facts is not enough at this point; you must convince them why they should select a wireless link.

After your presentation, TBG asks you to prepare a presentation regarding the advantages and disadvantages of unregulated bands. Because an engineer who sits on Triangle's project team will be there, this PowerPoint presentation should be detailed and technical in its scope.

Challenge Case Project

CASE PROJECTS

A local manufacturing company with several plants located around the city has contacted The Baypoint Group requesting a speaker to discuss different types of antennas for medium- and long-distance links, such as dish, yagi, and horn antennas. Each of the manufacturing company's plants is located between 5 and 15 miles (8 to 32 kilometers) from each other. Form a team of two or three consultants and research these antennas in detail. Pay specific attention to how they are used as well as their strengths and weaknesses. Provide an opinion about which antenna type is the best for medium- and long-distance fixed wireless links.

chapter 5

Wireless Personal Area Networks

After reading this chapter and completing the exercises, you will be able to:

- Describe a wireless personal area network (WPAN)
- List the IEEE 802.15 WPAN standards and their applications
- Explain how Bluetooth and ZigBee RF WPANs work
- Describe some of the security features and threats in WPAN technologies

For many years, there were few options for connecting and synchronizing your smartphone with your laptop or desktop computer without carrying around a collection of cables that matched each of the devices used. Each new type of device usually required consumers to use a different type of cable. Controlling lights, security systems, heating, and cooling was limited to the existing wiring in the home, and could only be done from inside the house, even with some innovative systems that allowed control from a central location within the house.

One of the first wireless technologies that appeared on the market used infrared light (IR). Although infrared interfaces had been available for quite a long time in TV remotes, IR's original maximum speed of 115,200 bps limited the ability of a person to use it for transferring large amounts of data to or from wireless devices. The IR specification was later enhanced, and speeds of 4 Mbps and even up to 16 Mbps were reached—comparable to Fast Ethernet at the time. Despite being secure and extremely easy to use, however, IR required close-range, point-to-point connectivity, and the lack of mobility eventually forced manufacturers to abandon an interface technology that had dominated the world of portable devices for a few decades.

Since the late 1990s, many alternative technologies have appeared on the market, with the primary goal of eliminating cables and allowing data devices and peripherals to communicate without wires. This chapter discusses the now-popular Bluetooth, which is available on computers, keyboards, mouse devices, smartphones, portable speakers, and many other products. It also discusses some of the latest developments in short-range, personal area networking, especially those products that are designed to eliminate some of the wires necessary in homes and buildings for lighting, environmental controls, and home security.

What Is a Wireless Personal Area Network?

A **wireless personal area network (WPAN)** is a group of technologies used for short-range communications—from a few inches or centimeters to usually about a maximum of 33 feet (10 meters), but occasionally up to 100 feet (30 meters). Most of these technologies were designed to eliminate the need for the large number of wires and cables to interconnect devices such as computers, smartphones, and even room lights and security systems, and smoke and fire detectors. The WPAN technologies discussed in this chapter are typically designed to support applications in which high-speed data transmission is not required and are thus known as low-rate WPAN technologies. A large number of Bluetooth devices support a maximum data rate of only 723.5 Kbps, for example. This is sufficient to handle up to three simultaneous voice channels, but it is not enough to handle applications such as high-definition video.

Current Applications

Current and future applications for WPAN technology with low data rates include:

- Home control systems (smarthome)
- Connecting headsets to computers, smartphones, and other audio devices for voice communications or listening
- Portable device data exchange
- Industrial control systems

- Real-time location services—smart tags used to track the location of people and equipment around the home or office
- Security systems
- Interactive toys
- Keyboard and mouse connection to computers and portable devices

In addition to helping eliminate wires and cables, WPANs offer three other key advantages:

- Because they are designed to communicate at short ranges, they generally use very little power to transmit. Devices can be small and powered by batteries that usually last a long time.
- The short-range nature of transmissions, along with the fact that they seldom carry sensitive personal data, helps provide a small amount of security and privacy.
- Short-range transmissions also cause very little interference with other nearby RF systems.

Existing Standards

The IEEE 802.15 group of standards discussed in this chapter covers the standards for two wireless technologies: IEEE 802.15.1 for Bluetooth and 802.15.4 for ZigBee.

The IEEE 802.15.x standard covers all the different Working Groups for WPANs. The last digit in the standard (indicated by the "x" above) identifies a specific working group, such as "1" for Bluetooth, and "4" for ZigBee.

As with the majority of other wireless standards created by the IEEE, they apply to both the **physical layer (PHY)** of the OSI, which is responsible for converting the data bits into an electromagnetic signal and transmitting it on the medium, and the **Media Access Control (MAC)** sublayer of the **data link layer,** which is responsible for the hardware addressing and controlling medium access and transfer of data between nodes in the same network segment and also provides basic error detection. With a few exceptions, the **Logical Link Control (LLC)** sublayer of the data link layer, which is responsible for establishing and maintaining logical connectivity to the local network, and all layers above it are usually defined in the specifications for each technology.

Although the OSI model is most often associated with local area networks, it is actually used as a model for most types of network communications.

Relationship Between the OSI Model and IEEE Project 802

At about the same time the International Organization for Standardization (ISO) was creating the Open Systems Interconnection (OSI) model, the IEEE started working on Project 802, which is intended to ensure interoperability among data networking products at the two lower layers of the OSI. As you know, the seven-layer OSI is a theoretical model of how data communication networks function, whereas IEEE 802 sets actual standards for the implementation of hardware and software at the two lower layers. The IEEE used the OSI model as a framework for its Project 802 specifications, but with some important differences (see Figure 5-1).

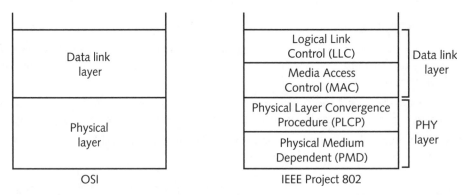

Figure 5-1 OSI model versus IEEE Project 802 layers

IEEE 802 divides the data link layer of the OSI model into two sublayers: the Logical Link Control (LLC) and the Media Access Control (MAC). The PHY layer in IEEE 802 is also divided into two sublayers: the **Physical Layer Convergence Procedure (PLCP)** and the **Physical Medium Dependent (PMD)** sublayers. The PLCP formats the data received from the MAC for transmission by adding a header and a trailer appropriate to the medium to be used, creating what is called a frame—the same way an envelope "frames" a letter. A **frame** is a string of data link layer bits that include the header and trailer required by the physical medium for transmission by the PMD. It is at the PMD that the precise method for transmitting and receiving data, such as frequency hopping spread spectrum (FHSS), for example, is implemented.

RF WPANs

The remainder of this chapter discusses RF WPANs, beginning with IEEE 802.15.1 and Bluetooth and continuing with IEEE 802.15.4 and ZigBee.

IEEE 802.15.1 and Bluetooth

Bluetooth is an industry specification that defines small-form-factor, low-cost, short-range wireless radio communications operating in the 2.4 GHz Industrial, Scientific, and Medical (ISM) band. In spite of how simple Bluetooth may be for users, it is a vast and complex technology. More than 14,000 companies, including hardware and software manufacturers, are members of the Bluetooth Special Interest Group (SIG). This introductory text covers some of the most important aspects and functionality of Bluetooth.

Because Bluetooth works in the same 2.4 GHz frequency band as Wi-Fi and other wireless technologies, the IEEE used a portion of the original Bluetooth specifications as the base material for creating the 802.15.1 standard. This standard was designed to ensure that

Bluetooth networks can operate reliably in the same area as other technologies using the 2.4 GHz band, with a minimum of interference. The IEEE 802.15.1 standard received final approval on March 2, 2002, and was then incorporated into version 1.2 of the Bluetooth specification. Previous versions of Bluetooth had significant issues when working in the vicinity of Wi-Fi networks.

You can find out more about Bluetooth technology and compatible products by visiting *www.bluetooth.com.*

Practically all smartphones sold today are Bluetooth compatible, which means you can use wireless headsets, synchronize the smartphone's phone book with a computer, download pictures from a camera-equipped phone, and connect to external speakers for playing and sharing music. You can also find printers, print servers, GPS devices, computer keyboards, computer mouse devices, tablets, medical equipment, gaming consoles, and even cooking stoves that connect with microwave ovens using Bluetooth. Current laptop models already include Bluetooth interfaces, and even if they don't, adding Bluetooth capability is as easy as plugging in a tiny, low-power USB adapter. Many other devices will likely incorporate Bluetooth in the future, as an alternative to cables.

Bluetooth Protocol Stack

To help you learn how Bluetooth works, let's begin with a tour of its protocol stack.

The functions of the lower layers of the Bluetooth protocol stack are implemented in the hardware, whereas the functions of the upper layers are implemented in software. These functions are discussed in the sections that follow. Figure 5-2 illustrates the Bluetooth protocol stack and compares it to the OSI and overall IEEE 802 protocol models.

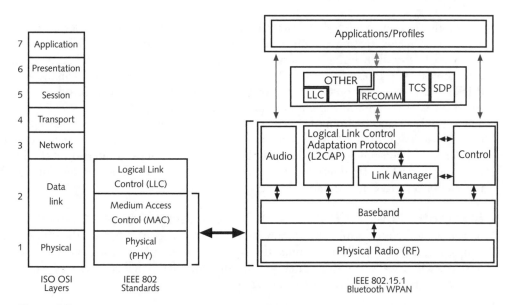

Figure 5-2 Bluetooth protocol stack compared with the OSI protocol model

Bluetooth RF Layer At the lowest level of the Bluetooth protocol stack is the RF layer. It defines how the basic radio hardware controls the transmissions. At this level, the data bits (0 and 1) are converted into radio signals and transmitted. As shown in Figure 5-2, this layer is equivalent to the OSI Physical layer.

Radio Module At the heart of the Bluetooth RF layer is a single radio transmitter/ receiver (transceiver) called a **Bluetooth radio module.** (See Figure 5-3 to get a sense of its size when compared to the tip of a pencil.) This device includes a tiny Bluetooth chip, which houses the radio module. Except for the antenna, which is part of the printed circuit board where the chip is mounted, this chip is the only hardware required for Bluetooth to work. Power is provided via a USB interface chip that is also included in the device shown in Figure 5-3. Bluetooth was designed so that the transceiver that performs all the MAC and PHY functions would fit into a single chip, be as generic or "mainstream" as possible, be low cost, require a minimum of off-chip supporting components, and consume a very small amount of power.

Figure 5-3 Bluetooth transceiver (transmitter/receiver)

Bluetooth can transmit at a data rate of up to 1 Mbps under Bluetooth specification versions 1.1 and 1.2. The actual maximum data rate is only approximately 721 Kbps because of the overhead bits used in frame headers. Version 2.1 adds two new modulation schemes that can increase data rates of 2.1 or 3 Mbps. The higher speeds are called **enhanced data rate (EDR).** Version 3.0 introduced four other enhancements designed to resolve issues related to power consumption in EDR that could cause momentary loss of headset connections, a connectionless data streaming feature, as well as an optional add-on radio that can achieve data transmission rates of up to a maximum of 24 Mbps, but at the cost of adding more hardware and consuming a considerably larger amount of power. Version 4.0 adds a low-energy transmission capability to extend battery life. All these versions of Bluetooth maintain full backward compatibility with versions 1.1 and 1.2.

Bluetooth Power Classes and Transmission Ranges Bluetooth has three
power classes that determine the communication range between devices; the classes are summarized in Table 5-1. Keep in mind that because Bluetooth is based on RF transmission, objects such as walls as well as interference from other RF signal sources (such as Wi-Fi networks) can reduce the range of transmission.

Name	Power Level	Typical Range
Power Class 1	100 mW	330 feet (100 meters)
Power Class 2	2.5 mW	33 feet (10 meters)
Power Class 3	1 mW	3 feet (1 meter)

Table 5-1   Bluetooth power classes

Modulation Techniques Versions 1.x of Bluetooth use a variation of frequency shift keying (FSK) that uses two different carrier signal frequencies (nothing is modulated onto the carriers). Bits transmitted at a higher frequency have a value of 1, and those sent at a lower frequency have a value of 0. The variation of FSK used by Bluetooth is known as **two-level Gaussian frequency shift keying (2-GFSK)**. This is illustrated in Figure 5-4.

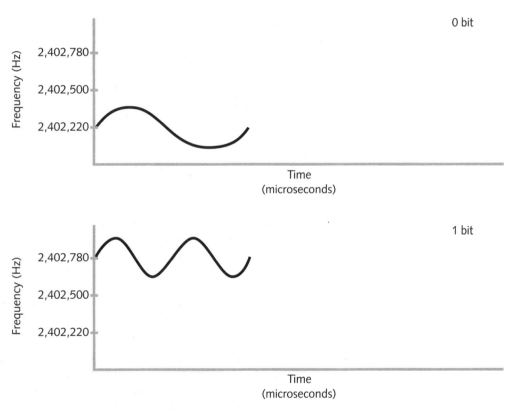

Figure 5-4   Two-level Gaussian frequency shift keying (GFSK)

The two new modulation schemes in Bluetooth version 2.x are **pi/4-DQPSK** (for 2 Mbps transmission) and **8-DPSK** (for 3 Mbps transmission). Figure 5-5 shows a pi/4-DQPSK waveform. As for 8-DPSK, it can only be used when the signal quality between two devices is robust—in other words, when there is very little or no interference. In fact, it may only be possible to achieve 3 Mbps in Bluetooth when there are no other transmissions of any kind nearby, especially in the same frequency range.

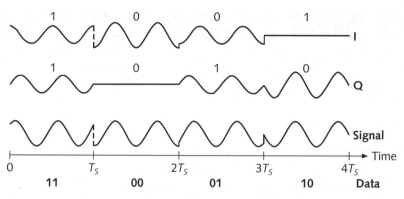

Figure 5-5 Pi/4-DQPSK I and Q waveforms and transmitted signal

The Bluetooth version 3.0 less power-hungry modes of operation allow batteries to last longer by detecting the signal quality and reducing the transmit power when possible. Version 3.0+HS (also referred to as version 3.1) added an **alternate MAC/PHY (AMP)**. AMP uses a separate radio module that transmits using a method that is similar to Wi-Fi (discussed in the next chapters). Once devices establish a normal Bluetooth connection, if both devices support AMP, then they can switch to the alternative radio module for faster data transfers. Due to the simpler Bluetooth protocol stack when compared to Wi-Fi, it may be possible to achieve data rates as high as 24 Mbps. In this case, all control communications continue to be handled by the RF layer that is compatible with Bluetooth version 1.x, which also ensures backward compatibility with previous versions of the specification.

Bluetooth version 4.0, ratified on June 30, 2010, introduced **Bluetooth Low Energy (BLE)**. BLE was based on Nokia's Wibree specification, which was developed in 2001, and BLE-capable devices are designed to transmit at a maximum rate of 270 Kbps (although typically 128 Kbps). This also has the effect of increasing the transmission range to approximately 50 feet (15 meters) while reducing power consumption from tens of milliamps to an average of just a few microamps. As a comparison with non-BLE devices, this could make a button-sized battery last up to one year before needing to be replaced. The technology is partially aimed at competing with near-field communications (NFC, discussed in Chapter 11) and can be implemented by simply enhancing existing Bluetooth radios, thus avoiding costly design and deployment of additional devices to support NFC. BLE can also compete with ZigBee (discussed later in this chapter).

Most current smartphones and tablet computers already support Bluetooth Smart Ready, the marketing brand for BLE. As early as March 2011, the Apple iPhone 4S and iPad 2 included support for BLE and were compatible with a number of devices—heart monitors, smartwatches that display emails and caller ID information, and several others. Bluetooth specification version 4.1 also allows devices such as a smartwatch to act as a data collection hub, gathering information off line from sensors such as a heart rate monitoring belt and other similar types of sensors. This means that the user does not need to have a smart device such as a phone turned on or even be near it while gathering data. The information will be transferred to the smartphone at a later time, when the user turns the phone on or is near the phone again.

Bluetooth Baseband Layer The Baseband layer lies on top of the RF layer in the Bluetooth stack. This layer manages physical connection channels and links, handles packets, and performs the functions required to locate and connect to other Bluetooth devices in the area.

Radio Frequency The part of the spectrum in which Bluetooth operates is the 2.4 GHz ISM band. Bluetooth divides the 2.4 GHz frequency into 79 frequencies, each 1 MHz wide, and uses the FHSS technique to transmit data. The specific sequence of frequencies used in FHSS—the hopping sequence—is called a **channel**. In other words, the frequency used for transmitting data could be said to hop (i.e., change rapidly) through the 79 different frequencies during transmission. The FHSS technique is shown in Figure 5-6. In just 1 second of a Bluetooth transmission, the frequency changes 1,600 times, or once every 625 microseconds.

Normally, the term *channel* would refer to a frequency range in RF. In FHSS, the term is also used to refer to a group of 79 frequencies that form the hopping sequence in a Bluetooth piconet.

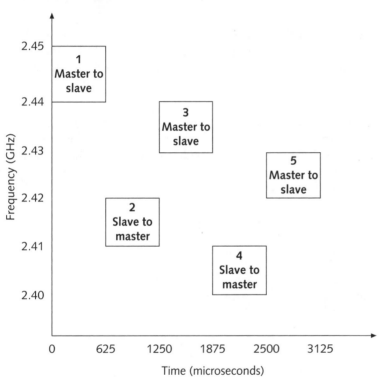

Figure 5-6 Bluetooth FHSS

The Bluetooth hopping sequence is significantly faster than that of most residential cordless telephones that also work in the 2.4 GHz band and that usually switch frequencies approximately 100 to 150 times per second. The interference to a Bluetooth transmission that is caused by cordless phones can result in data errors or significant breakups in the voice stream. This interference is caused by the wider frequency channels used by cordless phones.

Because they use the same frequency band as IEEE 802.11b/g/n WLANs, Bluetooth transmissions can interfere with 802.11 WLANs and vice versa. However, after the ratification of IEEE 802.15.1 and subsequent inclusion of this standard in Bluetooth version 1.2 specification, Bluetooth networks coexist with 802.11 WLANs with a minimum of interference and disruption. That is because version 1.2 added a feature called **adaptive frequency hopping (AFH)**, which greatly enhances compatibility with 802.11 WLANs operating in the 2.4 GHz band. Bluetooth accomplishes this by allowing the master device in a Bluetooth network to change the hopping sequence so that devices will not transmit in the RF channel occupied by 802.11 in the piconet area.

Coexistence with other wireless devices operating in unlicensed frequency bands is covered under the IEEE 802.15.2 standard. For more information, see *http://standards.ieee.org/getieee802/index.html.*

Bluetooth Network Topologies A Bluetooth device can scan the wireless medium, discovering and connecting to devices in its transmission range, which varies depending on the power class of device used. A Bluetooth network, called a **piconet,** can have up to one **master** and seven **slave** devices. The master device initiates the discovery of slave devices within RF range.

When two Bluetooth devices come within range of each other, they can automatically connect with one another. The master controls all communications in the piconet and slaves can only communicate with the master, never with each other. A Bluetooth network that contains one master and at least one slave, and that uses the same FHSS channel, forms a piconet. Examples of piconets are shown in Figure 5-7.

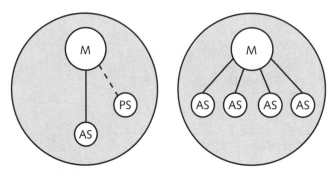

M = Master
AS = Active slave
PS = Parked slave

Figure 5-7 Two Bluetooth piconets

Each Bluetooth device is preconfigured with an address that is needed when participating or not participating in the piconet. The different addresses used in a Bluetooth piconet are described in Table 5-2.

Name	Description
Bluetooth device address	Unique 48-bit number (IEEE 802 hardware or MAC address), which is preconfigured in the hardware
Active member address	3-bit number valid only as long as device is an active slave in a pic
Parked member address	8-bit number valid only as long as device is a parked slave; a parked device does not retain the 3-bit active member address

Table 5-2 **Piconet radio module addresses**

All devices in a piconet must change frequencies at the same time and in the same sequence in order for communication to take place. The timing in the hopping sequence, called the phase, requires that each active slave be synchronized with the master's clock. The hopping sequence is unique for each piconet and is determined by the master's Bluetooth device address combined with the master's clock.

In a Bluetooth piconet, the master and slaves alternately transmit. The master transmits in odd-numbered time slots, and the slaves transmit in even-numbered time slots.

Bluetooth Connection Procedure Before two devices communicate using Bluetooth, the first thing that needs to happen is they need to be paired to each other. For security reasons, pairing requires user intervention to make the devices discoverable. Each Bluetooth device has its own way of accomplishing this task, and that is listed in the device's documentation. **Pairing** is a two-step process:

1. The first step is performed by the Bluetooth devices without user intervention. This is known as the **inquiry procedure**, and it enables a device to discover which other Bluetooth devices are in range and determine the addresses and clocks for those devices. When a Bluetooth device enters the range of other devices, it first attempts to find other Bluetooth devices in the area.

2. The second step is known as the **paging procedure**, and it is when an actual Bluetooth connection between two devices is established. During this step, a user must enter a pairing code in at least one of the devices. The pairing code is usually preset by the manufacturer for smaller devices such as headsets or speakers. To connect smartphones and computers, a random pairing code is usually generated by one of the devices and entered by the user on the other one. Once a Bluetooth device is paired with another it receives a 3-bit active member address and communication can begin. The master periodically sends out a page in an attempt to establish a connection with known or paired devices, so that when they are turned on and in range, they will reconnect automatically. The device that carries out a paging procedure and establishes a connection will automatically become the master of the connection.

Multiple piconets can be active in the same area. Because each piconet has a different master and hop sequence, the risk of collisions between two devices attempting to transmit at the same time on the same frequency is slim.

It is possible for a Bluetooth device to be a member of two or more overlapping piconets. This is called a **scatternet** (see Figure 5-8). To communicate in each piconet, the device must use the master device address and clock of that specific piconet; these are supplied by the master of each piconet.

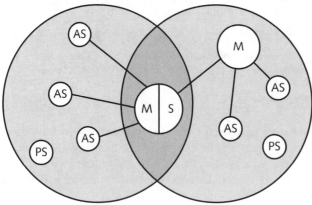

M = Master
AS = Active slave
PS = Parked slave

Figure 5-8 Bluetooth scatternet

A Bluetooth device can be a slave in several piconets, but it can be a master in only one piconet. A master and slave can switch roles in a piconet, but only devices, such as smartphones or computers, are usually capable of becoming a piconet master. Most headsets and similar smaller devices can only be paired to one master, although a few are capable of connecting to more than one.

Bluetooth Packets Because Bluetooth transmissions are limited to very small networks, they use a very simple packet structure. The basic packet format for Bluetooth transmissions is shown in Figure 5-9. Each packet consists of three parts:

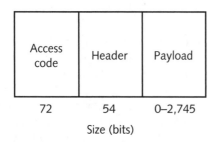

Figure 5-9 Bluetooth MAC frame (packet)

- *Access code (72 bits)*—Used for timing synchronization, paging, and inquiry
- *Header (54 bits)*—Used for packet acknowledgment, packet numbering, slave address, type of payload, and error checking
- *Payload (0–2,745 bits)*—Can contain data, voice, or both

Bluetooth Link Manager Layer

The Link Manager layer of the Bluetooth stack can be divided into two broad functions: managing the piconet and security.

Managing Links Between Bluetooth Devices Managing the piconet involves regulating the steps for attaching and detaching slaves from the master as well as overseeing the master-slave switch. To accomplish this, different types of links have to be established between Bluetooth devices. There are three basic types of physical links between devices:

- A **synchronous connection-oriented (SCO) link** is a bidirectional, symmetric point-to-point link, meaning that the data rate is the same between a master and a single slave in both directions, using 1, 2, or 3 reserved time slots. This link functions like a circuit-switched link by using reserved time slots at fixed intervals and is used to send user data only. A master and slave can each support up to three simultaneous SCO links. A SCO link carries mainly voice transmissions at a speed of 64 Kbps. This type of link is typically used for a full-duplex connection, such as when using a headset connected to a smartphone during a phone call. To reduce latency, packets are never retransmitted in a SCO link.

- An **extended synchronous connection-oriented link (eSCO) link** is similar to a SCO link. It is also bidirectional, but can be symmetric or asymmetric (different data rates for master to slave and slave to master), and is used for point-to-point, constant rate data, but with limited retransmissions in case errors should happen.

- An **asynchronous connectionless (ACL) link** is a reliable packet-switched link used for data transmissions. In case of errors data is retransmitted, but Bluetooth can use three different methods to reduce retransmissions (discussed later). A master can use ACL links to transmit data to a single slave (point-to-point) or to a group of slaves at the same time (point-to-multipoint). In the time slots not reserved for the SCO links, the master can establish an ACL and transfer data to any slave. A slave already engaged in an SCO link can also have an ACL link. ACL links are used to exchange control information or for user data.

There are also two other types of Bluetooth links that are used for sending unreliable, unidirectional (master to slaves), connectionless broadcast messages to all slaves in the piconet. These are discussed in the Bluetooth Power Usage section that follows.

Table 5-3 shows a summary of the basic types of link configurations in a piconet for both ACL and SCO links.

Configuration Options	Maximum Transmission Rate Upstream	Maximum Transmission Rate Downstream
Up to three simultaneous voice channels (SCO)	64 Kbps × up to three channels	64 Kbps × up to three channels
Symmetric data (SCO)	433.9 Kbps	433.9 Kbps
Asymmetric data (ACL)	721 Kbps	57.6 Kbps
Asymmetric data (ACL)	57.6 Kbps	721 Kbps

Table 5-3 Supported Bluetooth link configurations

If an error occurs on an ACL packet, that packet is retransmitted. A SCO packet is never retransmitted.

Error Correction Another management function of the Link Manager layer is error correction. There are three kinds of error-correction schemes used in the Bluetooth protocol:

- *1/3 rate Forward Error Correction (FEC)*—Repeats every bit three times for redundancy. The maximum data rate is effectively divided by 3, hence "1/3 rate."

- *2/3 rate Forward Error Correction (FEC)*—Adds extra bits that are examined by the receiving device to determine if an error took place in the transmission. The extra bits reduce the maximum data rate that can be achieved for a transmission but allows the receiver to detect multiple bit errors and correct single bit errors, avoiding the need to retransmit the data.

- *Automatic retransmission request (ARQ)*—If a Bluetooth packet is not using one of the above FEC schemes and is not acknowledged, the transmitting device will continuously retransmit a data-only or data-voice packet until an acknowledgment is received or until a timeout value is exceeded. Recall that this applies only to reliable ACL links. ARQ is not used in unreliable SCO links.

Bluetooth Power Usage Because most Bluetooth devices are designed to be mobile and because they consume power from what is often a very small battery, conserving power is essential. The power consumption of Bluetooth devices varies depending on their connection modes and the size and type of battery used. Voice transmissions through a headset use only 10 milliamps (mA). Data transmissions use only 6 mA and when not transmitting, Bluetooth uses only 0.3 mA, which means a battery charge can last from days to months if the device is left on but not used. The only way to know how long a battery will last is to consult the manual for a specific Bluetooth device.

Although amps and watts can sometimes be confusing, think of watts as a measure of the actual power used to push the radio signal out, and think of amps as a measure of the power that is needed to make that push.

Once connected to a piconet, a Bluetooth device can be in one of four power modes:

- *Active*—In **active mode**, the Bluetooth device actively participates on the channel and consumes an amount of power that corresponds to the type of data being transmitted. Over a period of time, this averages out to 2.5 mW in a Power Class 2 device.

- *Sniff*—In **sniff mode**, a slave device turns off its transmitter and only listens to the piconet master so that it uses less power. The interval is programmable and depends on the application. It is the least efficient of the power-saving modes.

- *Hold*—The master device can put slave devices into **hold mode**, in which only the slave's internal timer is running. Slave devices can also demand to be put into hold mode to conserve power. In this mode, devices are still active in the piconet and will turn their receivers on periodically to listen to the master.

- *Park*—In **park mode**, the most efficient of the power-saving modes, a device is still synchronized to the piconet but are not active in the piconet. These slaves occasionally listen to the traffic of their master in order to resynchronize and check for broadcast messages but cannot transmit unless the piconet has less than seven active slaves and they request permission from the master to rejoin. Power consumption in this mode is a mere 0.3 mA. There can be up to 255 parked slaves in a piconet.

A piconet master sometimes needs to send a broadcast message to parked slaves. This is the other type of logical link discussed previously, that can happen in a Bluetooth network, and it is used by the master to "unpark" a slave if there are packets waiting to be sent.

Other Bluetooth Protocol Layers and Their Functions

The Logical Link Control Adaptation Protocol (L2CAP; refer to Figure 5-2) is the layer responsible for segmenting and reassembling data packets, which are then sent through standard data protocols such as TCP/IP for transmission, multiplexing, and quality of service information. The Radio Frequency Communications (RFCOMM) protocol layer provides serial port emulation for Bluetooth data. This layer emulates a computer's serial port and packages the data so that it appears as if it were sent through the computer's standard serial port, which is another feature of Bluetooth.

Control information is also transmitted between devices, such as an instruction for a device to switch from master to slave. This control information comes through the **Link Manager** layer but then bypasses the L2CAP layer, which is only used when transmitting data streams.

Bluetooth Profiles
The ability of a Bluetooth device to perform certain types of functions is defined by a series of profiles that are located at the Application layer of the Bluetooth protocol stack. These are implemented in the software driver used with Bluetooth devices. Profiles define the interactions required between the Bluetooth protocol stack layers to accomplish a certain task, such as playing music and being able to control the music using buttons located in a headset or speaker. As an example, for a Bluetooth device to operate as a remote control—to control a slide show using Microsoft PowerPoint, for example—it must support the AVRCP (Audio/Video Remote Control) profile. A headset, on the other hand, would typically implement the Advanced Audio Distribution Profile (A2DP).

A comprehensive list of Bluetooth profiles currently adopted by the Bluetooth SIG can be found on the *bluetooth.com* website. Once you open the main page, use the search box to locate "Profiles." At the bottom of the page you should see a link to the most up-to-date list of Bluetooth profiles.

IEEE 802.15.4 and ZigBee

Another WPAN technology designed to replace cables and wires is ZigBee. Based on the IEEE 802.15.4 standard, ZigBee is primarily aimed at providing wireless connectivity between simple stationary devices or mobile devices—such as remote controls—that require very low data rates (between 20 and 250 Kbps), consume minimal amounts of power, and connect at distances from 33 feet (10 meters) to about 300 feet (100 meters). There are a couple of other specifications promoted by different organizations to perform similar smarthome monitoring and control functions like Insteon and ZWave, but ZigBee is the only truly global standard at this writing.

The **ZigBee Alliance**, formed in 2002, created a set of specifications for monitoring and controlling devices over a wireless link. At the time, there was no global, open standard that enabled manufacturers to build low-cost devices that could interoperate with those of other countries. The requirements for monitoring sensors and for control systems are different from those for other wireless computer networks. Although several manufacturers have implemented devices designed for control and monitoring functions using Wi-Fi and Bluetooth, these technologies were originally designed for the transmission of either large amounts of data, for cable replacement, or for voice and video. Unlike ZigBee, Bluetooth and IEEE 802.11 were also not originally designed to support mesh networking. The ZigBee specification is also far more open, and this helps reduce implementation costs.

The ZigBee specification uses the 802.15.4 standard for the PHY and MAC layers. ZigBee covers all of the layers above IEEE 802.15.4. You can access the ZigBee specifications at *www.zigbee.org*. The IEEE 802.15.4 standard is located at *http://standards.ieee.org/getieee802 /index.html.*

The ZigBee Alliance has expanded its specifications to include several industry-specific sets of interoperable standards, including ZigBee Health Care, ZigBee Home Automation, ZigBee Smart Energy, ZigBee Telecom Services, and the ZigBee Building Automation and ZigBee Retail Services specifications, among others.

IEEE 802.15.4 can operate in the 868 MHz range in Europe, 915 MHz in North America, and the 2.4 GHz range that is also part of the ISM band. Applications for ZigBee-compliant devices include:

- Lighting controls
- Automatic meter readers for natural gas, electricity, water, and similar systems
- Wireless smoke and carbon monoxide detectors
- Home security sensors for doors and windows
- Environmental controls for heating and air-conditioning systems
- Controls for window blinds, draperies, and shades
- Equipment for wireless patient monitoring, such as heart-rate and blood pressure monitors
- A universal remote control for televisions and set-top boxes, including home control functions—such as lighting and temperature
- Industrial and building automation controls for remote machine monitoring
- Location-based services; calculates distances and determine locations indoors, without using GPS
- And many others

The ZigBee specification is based on the relatively low-level performance requirements of sensors and control systems, such as light switches. ZigBee-compliant devices are designed to remain quiescent (without communicating) for long periods of time.

When a ZigBee device is connected to the network but is no longer needed, it can turn itself off, thereby consuming much less power. As a result, ZigBee battery-powered devices are capable of operating for several years before their batteries need to be replaced. Devices can wake up any time they need to communicate, follow the network access protocol, and then transmit on the specific network's channel, which is already known, from when the device first connected to the network. Once they have performed their functions, they can return to sleep mode by turning themselves off again. Their average duty cycle, the percentage of time they transmit or receive data, is between 0.1 percent and 2 percent of the time, which means that ZigBee-compliant devices use very little power. For example, if a ZigBee device wakes up every 60 seconds and turns on its radio for about 60 milliseconds while it communicates on the WPAN, its batteries can last for several years.

Although ZigBee transmissions are designed to be short in range, the specification includes full mesh networking. This means that ZigBee devices that are powered from an electrical outlet can route packets to other devices, which allows them to reach beyond their radio ranges. In fact, given that each network can simultaneously support 64,000 nodes, a ZigBee network can cover a large area, such as an entire house, conference center, office building, or manufacturing plant. This makes ZigBee technology ideal for sensors and control applications even in tall office buildings.

Mesh networking is supported, but not included, as part of the IEEE 802.15.4 standard. This means that other technologies that use IEEE 802.15.4 may or may not support mesh networking. However, mesh networking is an integral and important part of the ZigBee specification.

There are three basic classes of devices in a ZigBee network:

- *Full-function device (FFD)*—A full-function device can connect to other full-function devices and route control and data frames in addition to connecting to endpoint devices in a parent-child relationship. Full-function devices can maintain connections to multiple devices.

- *PAN coordinator*—The first full-function device that is turned on in an area usually becomes the PAN coordinator, and it starts and maintains the network. Coordinators are always plugged in to electricity and never turn themselves off, which allows the ZigBee network to remain available to all other devices. They can also be equipped with a backup battery.

- *Reduced-function device (RFD)*—This is an endpoint device—such as a light switch or a lamp—that can only connect to one full-function device on the network and can only join the network as a child device. Child devices do not connect to other child devices.

ZigBee Network Topologies
There are three basic topologies for ZigBee networks: star, tree, and mesh, as shown in Figure 5-10. Topologies are an important part of learning about ZigBee networks since many of its capabilities are dependent on the topology supported and implemented.

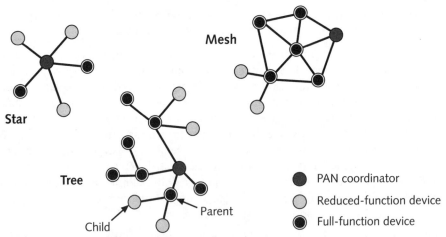

Figure 5-10 Topologies supported in ZigBee networks

In both tree and mesh topologies, alternate paths may be available for packets to reach an endpoint device. However, in tree and cluster tree networks, alternate paths may only be available to a child or to an FFD if another FFD is within its radio range. If a full-function routing device loses the connection to another full-function device, it will automatically use one of its alternate connections, if available, so that it can still route frames to other parts of the network. These are important considerations when installing a ZigBee network.

 The IEEE 802.15.4 standard defines only two topologies: star and peer-to-peer, given that a cluster tree network essentially consists of multiple star topology networks.

Figure 5-11 shows multiple paths for packets that are routed in a ZigBee mesh network. Note that the mesh network itself is made up of full-function devices connected in a peer-to-peer fashion, although each of these can have other RFD child devices connected to them. Provided that all full-function routing-capable devices are able to connect to one another, forming a mesh-like topology, packets can be routed along the network to other devices.

In a star or hub-and-spoke topology, a single device, the PAN coordinator, controls the network. All other devices are known as end-nodes, regardless of whether they are FFDs or not. Because all devices are connected to a coordinator, they only communicate directly with the coordinator, which will in turn transfer commands and data to all other devices.

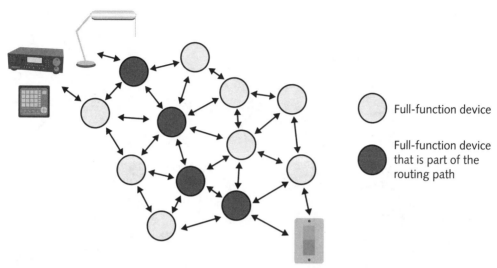

Figure 5-11 Routing of data packets in a ZigBee mesh network

Cluster tree topologies are made up of two or more tree topology networks that are inter-connected by FFDs. Cluster tree networks have a slight advantage over mesh networks. In a mesh network, performance is diminished because each FFD must maintain a routing table and make decisions on the best route to use when forwarding the packets. However, the reliability of a cluster tree network is not as high as that of a mesh network, because the failure of an interconnecting device can prevent an entire tree from communicating with other trees and other devices on the network, perhaps preventing a light switch from turning on a lamp located at the other end of the room or building. Figure 5-12 shows an example of a larger cluster tree network. Notice the connections between trees; also notice that each cluster tree uses a different channel to communicate between devices. Each ZigBee router (FFD) must be able to communicate on both channels in order to act as an interface between two trees of a cluster tree topology.

CH 1
CH 7
CH 13
CH 8
CH 4
CH 10
CH 15
Parent
Child

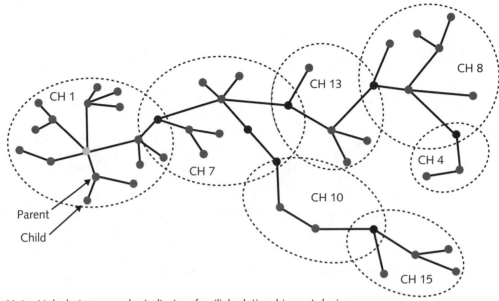

Note: Links between nodes indicate a familial relationship, not device or communications capability.

Figure 5-12 ZigBee cluster tree network

ZigBee Protocol Stack The ZigBee protocol stack is based on the OSI seven-layer model but defines only those layers that are relevant to achieving the specific functions required in the ZigBee specifications. Shown in Figure 5-13, the ZigBee protocol stack has the following characteristics:

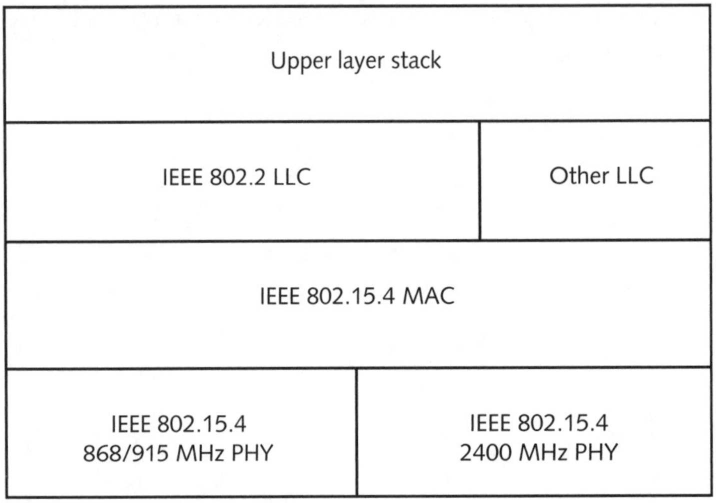

Upper layer stack
IEEE 802.2 LLC
Other LLC
IEEE 802.15.4 MAC
IEEE 802.15.4 868/915 MHz PHY
IEEE 802.15.4 2400 MHz PHY

Figure 5-13 ZigBee protocol stack

- It has two options for the PHY layer. Each one operates in a different frequency range. The lower-frequency PHY layer covers both the 868 MHz band used in Europe and the 915 MHz band used in North America and Australia. The higher-frequency PHY layer uses the 2.4 GHz ISM band; it is used worldwide.

- The MAC sublayer controls access to the radio channel. Its responsibilities include synchronization and providing error checking for the reliability of communications.

- The Logical Link Control (LLC) sublayer complies with the IEEE 802.2 LLC and is responsible for managing the data-link communication, link addressing, defining service access points, and frame sequencing. A second LLC sublayer is included in the specification to support alternative protocols and functionality.

The upper layers of the ZigBee protocol stack include specific procedures that devices use to join a network (called an **association**), leave a network (called a **disassociation**), apply security to frames, and perform routing. These layers are also responsible for device discovery, maintaining routing tables, and storing information about neighbor devices.

The PHY layer in a ZigBee device is responsible for turning the radio transceiver on and off, detecting the presence of an RF signal in the currently selected channel, analyzing and reporting link quality for received packets, assessing whether the channel is clear before initiating a transmission, selecting a frequency channel for operation, and transmitting and receiving data.

Altogether, there are 27 channels across the various frequency bands that can be used in IEEE 802.15.4. A single channel that is 600 KHz wide is available in the 868 MHz band; 10 channels that are 2 MHz wide are in the 915 MHz band; and 16 channels that are 5 MHz wide (although it only uses 2 MHz for transmission) in the 2.40 GHz band. Table 5-4 presents the frequency bands and data rates for 802.15.4 WPANs.

PHY Layer (MHz)	Frequency Range (MHz)	Chip Rate (kchips/second)	Modulation	Bit Rate (Kbps)
868/915	868–868.6	300	BPSK	20
	902–928	600	BPSK	40
2,450	2,400–2,483.5	2,000	O-QPSK	250

Table 5-4   **802.15.4 frequency bands and data rates**

You may recall from Chapter 2 that binary phase shift keying (BPSK) modulation uses two different starting points of an analog wave—typically at 0 degrees and 180 degrees—to encode a digital signal onto an analog wave. However, since DSSS transmission spreads the signal over the bandwidth of the channel, the carrier is modulated with a sequence of 15 chips, instead of the data bits themselves, in both the 868 and 915 MHz bands. To send a binary 1, the sequence 000010100110111 is transmitted at the chip rates indicated in Table 5-4; to send a binary 0, the sequence 111101011001000 is transmitted.

In the 2.4 GHz band, transmissions use 16 different 32-chip sequences called **symbols**. Each of the 16 different 32-chip sequences in this band transmits a different combination of 4 bits.

These 32-chip sequences are then modulated using a technique called **offset quadrature phase shift keying (O-QPSK)**, which uses two carrier waves, at different frequencies, that are exactly 90 degrees out of phase and therefore do not interfere with each other. It modulates some of the chips on one carrier and some on the other. Finally, the two signals are combined and transmitted. Figure 5-14 illustrates the modulation of each signal separately; one is called I-Phase, for "in-phase," and the other is called Q-Phase, for "quadrature signal." The resulting waveform, after combining the two carriers, is similar to QPSK, discussed in Chapter 2.

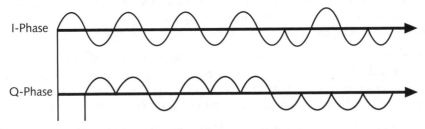

Figure 5-14 Offset quadrature phase shift keying (O-QPSK)

802.15.4 PHY Frame Format The PHY frame for IEEE 802.15.4, shown in Figure 5-15, has the following format:

4 octets	1 octet	7 bits	1 bit	Variable
Preamble	SFD	Frame length	Reserved	Payload

Figure 5-15 ZigBee PHY frame format

- *Preamble (32 binary 0s)*—Used for synchronization
- *SFD (8 bits)*—Start of Frame Delimiter; a fixed pattern of bits that indicates the end of the preamble and the start of the data
- *Frame length (8 bits)*—Seven bits that indicate the length of the payload, which can be from one to 127 octets; the additional bit is reserved and makes this field one octet long
- *Payload (variable)*—This field is either 5 octets long (containing an ACK) or 8 to 127 octets long. Frame lengths of 0 to 4, 6, or 7 octets are reserved in the standard

802.15.4 MAC Layer The MAC layer in 802.15.4 handles all access from the upper layers to the physical radio channel and is responsible for:

- Generating time synchronization frames if the device is a PAN coordinator
- Synchronizing the time synchronization frames for non-coordinator devices
- Device association and disassociation from the PAN

- Device security and support of security mechanisms implemented by the upper layers
- Managing channel access
- Giving priority for certain devices to transmit at specific times
- Maintaining a reliable link (error detection); 802.15.4 uses a 16-bit ITU cyclic redundancy check for validating the data

Most of the time, access to the wireless medium in a ZigBee network is contention-based, which means that all devices, before transmitting, listen to the medium to determine if the frequency channel is free. If the channel is busy, the devices will back off and not transmit for a random amount of time and then repeat the process of sensing if there are any transmissions, at which point they will wait for the channel to be clear before transmitting. This process is called **carrier sense multiple access with collision avoidance (CSMA/CA)**. Because a collision during a wireless transmission can only be detected if a packet is not understood by the intended receiver and acknowledgement is not sent back to the transmitting device, wireless transmissions can avoid, but not actually detect, collisions.

In Ethernet, collisions are detected by using a voltage sensor on the cable, but in wireless there is no way to know what the amplitude of the signal will be, at the receiver end, due to variations in attenuation that can be caused by distance-related loss or by obstacles in the path of the signal. In addition, wireless devices typically use a single radio, which means that they cannot receive and transmit simultaneously. Consequently, devices assume that there must have been a collision—or some other phenomenon that destroyed the frame—if they do not receive an ACK from the intended receiver.

ZigBee and IEEE 802.15.4 Communication Basics

When a ZigBee device needs to determine if a channel is clear, it can do it in one of two ways. The first way is by enabling the receiver to detect and estimate the amount of RF signal energy in the medium. In this case, the devices do not attempt to receive or decode any data—that is, they do not look for an IEEE 802.15.4 transmission; they only try to estimate the energy level in the wireless medium, which would indicate that another device is transmitting in the same frequency channel. (Note that in energy detection this could be any other type of device transmitting in the same frequency range—such as a laptop computer transmitting using Wi-Fi—and not necessarily another ZigBee device). This procedure is called **energy detection (ED)**.

The second way for a ZigBee device to decide if a channel is clear is to perform a carrier sense. In this case, the device looks for a specific 802.15.4 signal, and it attempts to decode the data transmission before deciding that the channel is busy. If the channel is not clear of transmissions, the device backs off—does not transmit—for a random amount of time. The process is repeated until the frequency channel is clear of other 802.15.4 transmissions.

Beacon-Enabled vs. Non-Beacon Communications

There are two types of network access used in IEEE 802.15.4: Beacon-enabled networks in which the frames contain contention-based periods for network access and may contain contention-free periods called **guaranteed time slots (GTSs)**, which are used for data transfer to specific devices. **Beacons** are a special type of frame transmitted by the coordinator only in star topology networks, or transmitted by routers to other devices, on request from a child device.

In contention-based communications, all devices that want to transmit in a particular frequency use CSMA/CA to determine if the channel is busy. In beacon-enabled networks, the PAN coordinator can transmit control information about which devices are allowed to transmit and when, and it will also inform devices about timing periods in which all devices can contend for access to the medium. Beacons can be transmitted at fixed intervals, during which devices will normally wake-up and turn on their receivers so they can find out if any messages are being held for them at the coordinator or a parent device.

In beacon-enabled networks, IEEE 802.15.4 can optionally use a **superframe** concept. The superframe is a mechanism for managing transmission time in the network. It consists of a continuously repeating set of time slots, bounded by beacon frames. The timing periods between two beacons will always include some contention access periods but may also contain GTSs for critical devices to transmit data between two beacons. If no devices need to transmit anything, the time slots are not used. A superframe always begins and ends with a beacon. A beacon signals the beginning of a superframe and contains information about the type and number of time slots contained in the time periods between beacons. The beacon is also the time synchronization frame for the network and is required for association when the network is using superframes. The ZigBee coordinator allocates GTSs but always leaves time slots available for use as contention access periods between two beacons. Figure 5-16 shows an example of an 802.15.4 superframe.

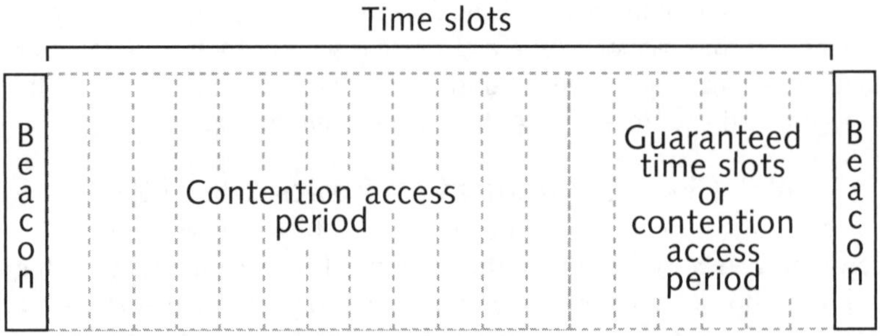

Figure 5-16   IEEE 802.15.4 superframe

Beacon frames are not required for device-to-device communications. In nonbeacon-enabled networks, the PAN coordinator will send beacons in response to beacon request frames from other devices. Beacons contain addressing and timing information required for new devices to associate with the network. The only exception to this is in ZigBee mesh networks, where beacons are not permitted and every device communicates in peer-to-peer fashion.

Network Association In 802.15.4, all the procedures for associating with and joining a network require only minimal configuration or interference by the user, the first time they connect. Installing a ZigBee network is limited to configuring the initial PAN address and then configuring which switch turns on a particular light or group of lights. Typically, the only field troubleshooting task in ZigBee networks is determining whether the RF signal from one device is within the range of another device so that they can communicate reliably or if interference may be causing problems with the PAN.

ZigBee devices are designed to automatically associate with and join or rejoin a PAN that has already been established by a coordinator, once they are powered on. The network topology is defined during initial installation, depending on the specific needs of the system being installed. When a ZigBee device is powered on for the first time, it will listen for traffic on the network and scan the medium in an attempt to identify which RF channel is being used. Then it will send a request to join the network.

ZigBee devices can query the coordinator or other FFDs to identify the number of devices that are connected to the network and their locations in a process called **device discovery**. Once the devices are associated with the PAN, they have the option of performing a **service discovery** to identify the capabilities of specific devices.

Coexistence with Other Standards Relatively wideband interference, such as that generated by IEEE 802.11 (Wi-Fi) networks in the 2.4 GHz band, appears like white noise to an IEEE 802.15.4 receiver because only a fraction of the 802.11 transmission falls within the 802.15.4 receiver bandwidth. This is because 802.15.4 transmissions only use 2 MHz of bandwidth, whereas 802.11 transmission use between 20 and 25 MHz, as you will learn in Chapter 6. Likewise, the impact of interference from Bluetooth (802.15.1) devices should be minimal due to the fact that Bluetooth changes the transmission frequency every 625 microseconds.

802.15.4 devices should only interfere with approximately three out of the 79 hops of a Bluetooth transmission, or approximately 4 percent. To an IEEE 802.11 receiver, the signal from an 802.15.4 transmitter looks like narrowband interference. The low duty cycles of 802.15.4 transmissions—the result of infrequent transmissions—further reduce the impact of interference.

Several companies manufacture ZigBee-compatible LED lights and control hubs for smarthomes and offices. Search the web for: GE Link®, Cree Connected®, TCP Connected®, Philips Hue®, and LIFX® for smart LED lights. You can also search for Wink, Smartthings® (Samsung), Revolv® (Nest/Google), and Almond+® (Securifi) to get more information on hubs used to control lighting and other devices. Be sure to also visit *wemo.com* a smarthome system by Belkin® that uses Wi-Fi instead of ZigBee, as a comparison.

Network Addressing The ZigBee specification defines four levels of addresses for identifying devices within a PAN: IEEE address, network (PAN) address, node address, and endpoint address. The IEEE address, also called an extended address, is a 64-bit static hardware address that is embedded in every radio transmitter. The PAN address is a unique 16-bit identifier for each PAN in an area. It is assigned by the PAN coordinator and is only used for a single network or cluster. The node address is a 16-bit address assigned by the PAN coordinator or parent device; this address comes from a group of addresses distributed by the coordinator and is unique for each radio on the network. The node address is used for the purpose of increasing the efficiency of ZigBee transmissions, given that the IEEE address is 64 bits long. The endpoint address uniquely identifies each endpoint device or service controlled by a single radio—a light bulb, for example.

To understand multiple levels of addressing, see Figure 5-17, in which two switches control three lights connected to a single ZigBee radio. Switch A, on the left, controls the bottom light. Switch B, on the right, controls the two top lights. The ZigBee module controlling the switches can be physically located far from the lamp. In this case, for either switch to send a command to the lamp, it needs the PAN address, the node address (to identify the radio module in the lamp), and the endpoint address (to identify the individual light bulbs). The process of creating a relationship between a light and a switch is called **binding**; this needs to be performed only when the WPAN is being set up, but can be reconfigured at any time.

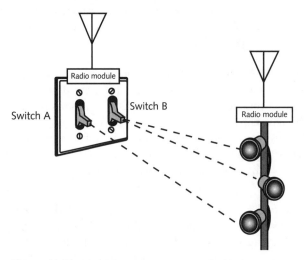

Figure 5-17   Multiple endpoints controlled by a single pair of radios in ZigBee

Note that not all addresses are used in every frame; which address is used depends on which two devices are communicating in the piconet. Although the example in the figure is extremely simple, imagine the same process applied to endpoint devices in a tall office building or a large factory. With ZigBee, if the office layout changes, it is possible to reconfigure all the light switches. As a comparison, in a traditional installation, this would require a significant amount of rewiring, which is often prohibitively expensive.

Power Management in ZigBee Networks Packet routing requires a lot of processing overhead and additional packet traffic, which diminishes the power-saving effect of ZigBee devices and also reduces the data throughput. In addition, ZigBee devices are designed to be very small—such as a light switch—and for this reason they are more likely to be equipped with low-speed, power-efficient CPUs. In a ZigBee PAN, only the devices that perform routing or are coordinators incur processing overhead and, consequently, consume more power. The 802.15.4 standard favors battery-powered devices but does not prevent devices from being connected to another power source, such as an electrical outlet. There is also no limitation on devices having additional data-processing power. Most FFDs, which are routing-capable ZigBee devices, typically connect to external power sources like an electrical outlet, although they can run on battery power as well. One example is an FFD that includes a temperature sensor and is configured to transmit every 30 seconds, such as those monitoring critical machinery.

The ZigBee specification includes a number of parameters that must be maintained by devices in case of localized or network-wide power failures or resets. These include the PAN ID, the network address, the address of every associated child device, and the channel in use. In addition, if there are alternate paths, FFDs must also maintain a routing table that lists all routing-capable neighbor devices, along with the length of the path or cost, to reach every other device in the PAN.

Other Technologies Using IEEE 802.15.4

There are two other technologies that take advantage of the IEEE 802.15.4 MAC and PHY: 6LoWPAN and WirelessHART.

6LoWPAN is a protocol that implements IPv6 on WPANs. It makes interfacing a WPAN to the Internet much simpler because it uses an adaptation layer between the MAC and Network layers of IPv6 to translate the IP information into a format that can be transmitted using the MAC frame format of 802.15.4-compliant hardware.

6LoWPAN supports mesh networking and is designed to be used in nodes that have limited memory space and processing capabilities and, like ZigBee, the Adaptation layer uses a compression algorithm to reduce the size of the 40-octet IPv6 header. It also uses fragmentation to allow the minimal-size IPv6 packets (1,280 octets) to be transmitted in a 802.15.4 payload, which has a maximum size of 127 octets. This makes it possible to access and manage a network node just like any other IP device.

WirelessHART is based on the Highway Addressable Remote Transducer (HART) protocol, designed for industrial-automation applications such as process control, equipment and process monitoring, and advanced diagnostics in wired networks. HART supports both a bus topology, in which several instruments are attached to the same cable, and a point-to-point connection that allows both digital and analog signals to be sent on the same cable. In 2007, the HART Communications Foundation (HCF) approved WirelessHART to protect process manufacturing companies' investment in the over 30 million HART devices installed while permitting their use over a wireless link.

WPAN Security

Although you might think that security shouldn't be a concern with WPANs, given that most of the transmissions are restricted to a short physical range, and no sensitive personal data are transferred, there is still the danger that hackers will try to break into devices or entire networks and access sensitive or critical controls, especially in industrial environments. Malicious hackers could break into WPANs to open smart door locks and gain access to homes and businesses. In this section, you will learn about the security models for each of the WPAN technologies discussed in this chapter.

Designing security for WPANs can be more difficult than for other networking technologies. A single solution is not likely to meet all the security requirements, for one thing. Users like to roam free while remaining connected, but they do not want anyone to eavesdrop on their telephone conversations, access their homes or offices, or interfere in any way with their systems. However, small battery-powered devices tend to have limited processing capabilities, and this makes it difficult to implement security measures like complex encryption, which tends to use a lot of processing cycles and consequently consumes a lot of battery power.

Banking and electronic funds transactions present even more difficulties for WPANs. To keep the transactions secure, both the user's identity and the transaction itself have to be verified. This is often done using public key infrastructure and a certificate authority. **Public key** infrastructure (PKI) uses a unique security code, or key, provided by an independent certificate authority. A **certificate authority** is a private company that verifies the authenticity of each user in order to discourage fraud. This kind of authentication will have to be in widespread use before financial institutions will adopt WPAN technology.

The data transmission must also be protected to prevent tampering; otherwise, hackers can intercept a packet, make changes to it, and then forward the changed packet, which by now may contain data that enables the hacker to access other network traffic. This is called a man-in-the-middle attack, and the process to prevent it uses both sequential packet freshness information and a message integrity check (or message integrity code). Both of these security mechanisms are discussed later in this chapter.

Security is an extensive and complex topic that is largely beyond the scope of this text. Nevertheless, you will find, on a chapter-by-chapter basis, a list of the security options that are available for each technology as well as a brief discussion of the security issues faced by each technology.

Security in Bluetooth WPANs

Bluetooth provides security through authentication or encryption. **Authentication** is based on identifying the device itself, not who is using the device. To accomplish that, Bluetooth uses a **challenge-response strategy** to determine whether the new device knows a secret key. If it does, it is allowed to join the piconet. Bluetooth data transmissions are "whitened," meaning that the data is scrambled according to a pattern determined by the clock and address of the master that is also used to synchronize all devices on the piconet. Although this is not a perfect security method, it does make Bluetooth data extremely difficult to capture (sniff) and decode in its entirety.

Encryption services are also available for Bluetooth networks, but because Bluetooth devices tend to be powered by very small batteries and have slower CPUs, encryption is seldom a good idea, except in government or military applications, where it often cannot be avoided.

Encryption is the process of scrambling the data using mathematical algorithms so that the transmission, if intercepted, still has to be decoded into the original data, which discourages many hackers. The Bluetooth specification supports three encryption modes:

- *Encryption Mode 1*—Nothing is encrypted
- *Encryption Mode 2*—Traffic from the master to one slave is encrypted, but traffic from the master to multiple slaves (broadcasts) is not encrypted
- *Encryption Mode 3*—All traffic is encrypted

The pairing key and the encryption key in Bluetooth are two very different things. The reason for separating them is to allow the use of a shorter encryption key without weakening its strength with a pairing key that may be extremely simple and common to different devices of the same type.

There are three levels of Bluetooth security:

- *Level 1: No security*—A Bluetooth device does not initiate any security steps.
- *Level 2: Service-level security*—Security is established at the higher levels of the protocol stack after a connection is made.

- *Level 3: Link-level security*—Security is established at the lower levels of the protocol stack before a connection is made.

Note that due to the difficulties in sniffing Bluetooth data, very few manufacturers implement security beyond the pairing key in Bluetooth. When transferring data other than voice or video, another option that Bluetooth users have is to encrypt the data before it is transmitted. However, you should consider that encryption usually increases the byte count significantly and therefore reduces the speed and efficiency of the piconet, in addition to needing far more processing and therefore consuming extra battery power.

A lot has and is being written about Bluetooth and RF WPAN security threats. Bluetooth threats have even been named Bluesnarfing, Bluebugging, and Bluejacking, along with a few others. However, keep in mind that once devices are paired and connected, unless they are again put into discoverable mode by the users, other devices cannot "see" them. If Bluetooth users are conscientious and do not approve pairings that they did not initiate themselves, it remains very difficult for would-be attackers to sniff data from Bluetooth wireless transmissions. In most cases the kind of data transmitted in a Bluetooth piconet or other RF WPANs, with few exceptions, does not demand a much more sophisticated degree of security than what is already available. While security attacks against Bluetooth piconets can potentially be very annoying, they are seldom dangerous to people or property.

To learn more about Bluesnarfing, Bluejacking, and other Bluetooth security threats, search the web for "Bluetooth security threats."

Security in ZigBee and IEEE 802.15.4 WPANs

ZigBee WPANs use a process called symmetric key for both authentication and encryption. A **symmetric key** is a sequence of numbers and letters, much like a password, that must be entered by the authorized user on all devices. No automatic key distribution or key rotation is included in the standard, although these options can be implemented at the higher protocol layers. The length of the key can be 4, 6, 8, 12, 14, or 16 octets, with longer keys providing more security than shorter ones.

In addition to symmetric key security, the IEEE 802.15.4 standard provides frame integrity, access control, and security services. Frame integrity is a technique that uses a **message integrity code (MIC)**, a sequence of bits based on a subset of the data itself, the length field, and the symmetric key. This code is used by the receiving device to verify that the data has not been tampered with during transmission from the sender to the receiver. In access control, a device maintains a list of other devices with which it is permitted to communicate. This list is called an **access control list (ACL)**. This technique allows ZigBee devices in a large building, for example, to communicate only with devices belonging to their own network and not with devices in other networks. **Sequential freshness** is a security service used by the receiving device that ensures that the same frames will not be transmitted more than once. The network maintains a sequential number that is continually incremented and tracked by the devices to verify that the arriving data is newer than the last data transmitted. This prevents a frame from being captured and replayed on the network by a hacker who does not have access to the encryption key.

There are three security modes in the 802.15.4 standard: unsecured mode, ACL mode (which uses access control), and secured mode (which uses full authentication and encryption). In secured mode, the MAC layer may optionally provide frame integrity and sequential freshness.

Whenever ZigBee devices and networks are used to control critical equipment in manufacturing, residential, or commercial buildings, security concerns must be addressed by a combination of the techniques discussed here, as well as encryption. In these cases, most critical ZigBee devices are not likely to be powered by batteries, except for backup purposes, and can make use of more powerful processors that are able to handle sophisticated encryption. Manufacturers of these types of control systems are aware of these concerns and their equipment is designed with security and safety in mind. End users should always be aware that security is not, and will likely never be, "set-and-forget." Instead, security is likely to always be a work-in-progress.

Chapter Summary

- Bluetooth is a wireless technology that uses short-range radio frequency (RF) transmissions, enabling users to connect to a wide range of devices without using cables. Bluetooth can also be used to create a small network.

- Bluetooth is supported by over 14,000 hardware and software vendors who make up the Bluetooth Special Interest Group (SIG). The IEEE used a portion of the Bluetooth specifications as the base material for its 802.15.1 standard. The standard is fully compatible with Bluetooth version 1.2 and higher.

- The Bluetooth protocol stack's functions can be divided into two parts based on how they are implemented: the lower levels and the upper levels. The lower-level functions are implemented in hardware, whereas the upper-level functions are implemented in software. At the lowest level of the Bluetooth protocol stack is the RF layer. It defines how the basic hardware that controls the radio transmissions functions. At the heart of Bluetooth is a single radio transmitter/receiver (transceiver) that performs all the necessary functions. Bluetooth can transmit at a speed of 1 Mbps and has three different power classes for transmitting.

- Up to version 1.2, Bluetooth uses two-level Gaussian frequency shift keying (2-GFSK) modulation and operates in the 2.4 GHz Industrial, Scientific, and Medical (ISM) band. Bluetooth uses the frequency hopping spread spectrum (FHSS) technique to send a transmission. Version 2 of Bluetooth added two modulation methods that help it achieve speeds of 2 Mbps and 3 Mbps. Version 3 added power-saving modes of operation, an alternative MAC, and PHY layers that use a second radio and Wi-Fi, all of which help it achieve transmission rates as high as 24 Mbps.

- When two Bluetooth devices come within range of each other, they automatically connect with one another. One device is the master and the other device is a slave. A Bluetooth network that contains one master and at least one slave using the same channel forms a piconet. A Bluetooth device can be a member of two or more piconets in the same area. A group of piconets in which connections exist between different piconets is called a scatternet.

- There are three kinds of error-correction schemes used in the Bluetooth protocol: 1/3 rate Forward Error Correction (FEC), 2/3 rate FEC, and the automatic retransmission request (ARQ).

- Devices in a piconet can be in active, hold, sniff, or park modes; device activity is lowered during the power-saving modes.

- ZigBee, created by the Zigbee Alliance, is a specification for low-rate WPANs. It offers a global standard for monitoring and controlling small, low-power, cost-effective, wirelessly networked products.

- ZigBee technology is geared toward devices such as lighting controls, wireless smoke and carbon monoxide detectors, thermostats and other environmental controls, medical sensors, remote controls, and industrial and building automation.

- The ZigBee specification includes full mesh networking to allow networks to encompass large buildings. Full-function devices can route frames across the network to remote devices. Reduced function devices are an endpoint device, such as a light switch or lamp.

- There are three ZigBee network topologies: star, tree, and mesh.

- The IEEE 802.15.4 standard defines three frequency bands: 868 MHz, 915 MHz, and the 2.4 GHz ISM band. The protocol stack has two PHY layers. One supports 868/915 MHz, and the other supports 2.4 GHz. There are 27 channels across the three bands. Modulation is BPSK for 868/915 MHz. For 2.4 GHz, it uses O-QPSK modulation with a fixed set of 16 chipping codes, each representing a 4-bit data pattern (also called a symbol).

- 802.15.4 is designed to coexist easily with other WPAN and WLAN technologies transmitting in the same frequency range. Access to the medium is contention based, but support for guaranteed time slots is also provided through the use of superframes.

- Security in Bluetooth supports only device authentication and limited encryption. Secure key distribution is not provided in the standard. ZigBee supports message integrity at the MAC layer and can also check for the freshness of the message to ensure that the same frame will not be transmitted more than once in a piconet.

Key Terms

1/3 rate Forward Error Correction (FEC)   An error correction scheme that repeats each bit three times for redundancy.

2/3 rate Forward Error Correction (FEC)   An error correction scheme that uses a mathematical formula to add extra error correction bits to the data sent.

6LoWPAN   The protocol that implements IPv6 on WPANs. Also the name of an IETF working group that defines how the Internet protocols—IPv6, in particular—are applied to the smallest devices so that they can participate in the "Internet of Things."

8-DPSK   A simple method of phase shift keying introduced in Bluetooth version 2 that uses eight degrees of phase to encode tribits. This method of modulation is very sensitive to co-channel and intersymbol interference.

access control list (ACL)   A list of addresses of other devices from which the device that maintains the list expects to receive frames.

active mode   A state in which the Bluetooth device actively participates on the channel.

adaptive frequency hopping (AFH)   A feature added by Bluetooth version 1.2 that further improves compatibility with 802.11b by allowing the master in a piconet to change the hopping sequence so that it will not use the frequency channel occupied by 802.11b in the piconet area.

alternate MAC/PHY (AMP)   A feature added in version 3 of the Bluetooth specification that makes it possible for Bluetooth radio manufacturers to add a second radio that uses 802.11 to transmit data at speeds of up to 24 Mbps. Compatible Bluetooth devices use FHSS to establish communications with each other and exchange commands and control information, while using the secondary radio for data transfers only.

association   A procedure for a device to join a network.

asynchronous connectionless (ACL) link   A packet-switched link that is used for data transmissions.

authentication   The process of verifying that the device asking to join the piconet should be allowed to join.

automatic retransmission request (ARQ)   An error-correction scheme that continuously retransmits until an acknowledgment is received or a timeout value is exceeded.

beacon   A frame that signals the beginning of a superframe and contains information about the type and number of time slots contained in the superframe.

binding   The process of establishing a relationship between endpoints in a ZigBee network.

Bluetooth Low Energy (BLE)   An amendment to the Bluetooth specification designed to save energy by sending transmissions at a maximum rate of 270 Kbps or lower.

Bluetooth radio module   A single radio transmitter/receiver (transceiver) that performs all the necessary transmission functions.

carrier sense multiple access with collision avoidance (CSMA/CA)   A device-access mechanism in which, before transmitting, a device must listen to the medium to determine if the channel is free.

certificate authority   An organization that supplies security keys and authenticates users.

challenge-response strategy   A process used to check if the other device knows a shared identical secret key.

channel   The frequency or range of frequencies used by a particular technology to transmit and receive data. In Bluetooth, a channel consists of all the frequencies in a hop sequence.

data link layer   The OSI layer responsible for the transfer of data between nodes in the same network segment; it also provides for error detection.

device discovery   The process of querying other devices on the network to identify their locations and how many of them there are.

disassociation   A procedure used by devices to leave (i.e., disconnect from) a network.

encryption   The process of encoding communications to ensure that the transmission, if intercepted, cannot be easily decoded, which discourages many hackers.

energy detection (ED)   One of two types of procedures used by IEEE 802.15.4 compatible devices to detect the presence of RF waves from another transmission in the medium.

enhanced data rate (EDR)   A feature of the Bluetooth version 2.0 specification that allows it to support data rates of 2 and 3 Mbps (by adding two modulations) while remaining fully backward compatible with Bluetooth versions 1.1 and 1.2.

extended synchronous connection-oriented link (eSCO)   A Bluetooth SCO link that can be either asymmetric or symmetric. eSCO links are used to send point-to-point constant-rate data with limited retransmissions in case of errors.

frame   A data link layer container that includes physical addresses in the header and a trailer required for transmission in the medium (wireless or wired), but does not include any synchronization bits.

full-function device (FFD)   A device used in 802.15.4 (ZigBee) networks that can connect to other full-function devices and has the capability of routing frames to other devices in a ZigBee network. It can also connect to endpoint or child devices. Full-function devices can maintain a connection to multiple devices and can become coordinators.

guaranteed time slot (GTS)   A reserved period for critical devices to transmit priority data.

hold mode   A state in which the Bluetooth device can put slave units into a mode in which only the slave's internal timer is running.

inquiry procedure   A process that enables a Bluetooth device to discover which other Bluetooth devices are in range and determine the addresses and clocks for the devices.

Link Manager   The Bluetooth layer responsible for establishing and maintaining connections on the piconet.

Logical Link Control (LLC)   One of the two sublayers of the IEEE Project 802 data link layer.

master   A device on a Bluetooth piconet that controls all the wireless traffic.

Media Access Control (MAC)   One of the two sublayers of the IEEE Project 802 data link layer.

message integrity code (MIC)   A code composed of a subset of the data, the length of the data, and the symmetric key; used by the receiving device to verify that the data has not been tampered with during transmission.

offset quadrature phase shift keying (O-QPSK)   A transmission technique in 802.15.4 that uses two carrier waves of the same frequency but with a phase difference of 90 degrees between them. This technique modulates even-numbered chips in the in-phase wave and odd-numbered chips in the other phase (Q-Phase), using quadrature amplitude modulation, before combining the waves for transmission.

paging procedure   A process that enables a device to make an actual connection to a piconet.

pairing   A two-step process for establishing a connection between a Bluetooth master and slave devices.

PAN coordinator   The 802.15.4 device that controls access to the piconet and optionally the timing as well.

park mode   A state in which the Bluetooth device is still synchronized to the piconet but does not participate in the traffic.

physical layer (PHY)   The OSI layer that is responsible for converting the data bits into an electromagnetic signal and transmitting it on the medium.

Physical Layer Convergence Procedure (PLCP)   The IEEE 802.15 sublayer that formats the data received from the MAC for transmission by adding a header and a trailer appropriate to the medium to be used, creating what is called a frame.

Physical Medium Dependent (PMD)   The IEEE 802.15 sublayer that is responsible for converting the bits into a modulated carrier wave and transmitting it on the medium.

piconet   A Bluetooth network that contains one master and at least one slave that use the same channel.

pi/4-DQPSK   A method of modulation introduced in Bluetooth version 2 that uses two different frequencies exactly 90 degrees apart and that therefore do not interfere with each other.

public key infrastructure (PKI)   A unique security code that can verify the authenticity of a user.

reduced-function device (RFD)   In ZigBee networks, a device (such as a light switch or lamp) that can only connect to one full-function device at a time and can only join the network as a child device.

scatternet   A group of piconets in which connections exist between different piconets.

sequential freshness   A security service available in 802.15.4 and used by the receiving device; it ensures that the same frames will not be transmitted more than once.

service discovery   The process of sending a query to other devices on the network to identify their capabilities.

slave   A device on a Bluetooth piconet that takes commands from the master.

sniff mode   A state in which the Bluetooth device listens to the piconet master at a reduced rate so that it uses less power.

superframe   A mechanism for managing transmissions in a piconet. The superframe is a continually repeating frame containing a beacon, contention access periods, channel time allocation periods, and management time allocation periods. Using the superframe is optional in 802.15.4 WPANs.

symbol   A data unit that can represent one or more bits.

symmetric key   A sequence of numbers and letters, much like a password, that must be entered by the authorized user on all devices.

synchronous connection-oriented (SCO) link   A symmetric point-to-point link between a master and a single slave in the piconet; it functions like a circuit-switched link by using reserved slots at regular intervals.

two-level Gaussian frequency shift keying (2-GFSK)   A binary signaling technique that uses two different frequencies to indicate whether a 1 or a 0 is being transmitted.

WirelessHART   A wireless sensor network protocol based on the highway addressable remote transducer protocol (HART), designed for interfacing manufacturing equipment and machines.

wireless personal area network (WPAN)   A group of technologies that are designed for short-range communications, from a few inches (centimeters) to about 33 feet (10 meters).

ZigBee Alliance   An association of manufacturers and interested organizations formed to promote the creation of a global standard for wireless devices used in monitoring and control applications.

Review Questions

1. A Bluetooth channel consists of _____.

    a. a specific frequency channel

    b. an IEEE 802.15.1 channel

    c. a hopping sequence including up to 79 frequencies

    d. a frequency range that the signal spreads across

2. Which of the following is not an example of a Bluetooth communication?

    a. Smartphone phone to headset

    b. Laptop computer to smartphone

    c. Hard drive to memory

    d. Laptop computer to GPS

3. Which of the following is not a feature of Bluetooth?

    a. Power-saving

    b. Master and slave changing roles

    c. Slave authenticates master

    d. Asymmetric transmission

4. What is the name of the organization that develops and promotes Bluetooth products and consists of over 14,000 hardware and software vendors?

    a. Bluetooth SIG

    b. IEEE 802.15.1 Task Group

    c. Bluetooth TIA

    d. Bluetooth Standards Organization

5. The lower layers of a Bluetooth WPAN protocol stack are implemented in the _____.

    a. software

    b. hardware

    c. IR

    d. data link layer

6. At the lowest level of the Bluetooth protocol stack is the _____ layer.

    a. RF

    b. L2CAP

    c. TCP/IP

    d. Link Manager

7. Which of the following is a feature of WPAN devices?

   a. They can transmit signals at a great distance.

   b. They are usually small and can operate on batteries.

   c. They transmit signals that do not penetrate walls.

   d. Their users cannot roam.

8. The _____ is when ZigBee devices have time reserved for priority transmissions.

   a. contention access period

   b. GTS

   c. beacon period

   d. time synchronization period

9. Which method of Bluetooth transmission uses two different frequencies to indicate whether the bit is a 1 or a 0?

   a. DSSS

   b. FHSS

   c. GFSK

   d. DPSK

10. The amount that the Bluetooth frequency varies, which is between 280 and 350 KHz, is called the _____.

    a. direct sequence

    b. modulation index

    c. hopping sequence

    d. i-phase

11. Bluetooth divides the 2.4 GHz frequency into 79 frequencies that are spaced how far apart?

    a. 5 MHz

    b. 22 MHz

    c. 11 MHz

    d. 1 MHz

12. A ZigBee coordinator cannot allocate guaranteed time slots for devices to transmit data. True or False?

13. Bluetooth has seven different power classes. True or False?

14. Objects (such as walls) and interference from other sources do not usually affect the range of Bluetooth transmissions. True or False?

15. Bluetooth devices are usually small and mobile, so conserving power is necessary. True or False?

16. What is the maximum data-transmission rate in ZigBee WPANs?

    a. 2 Mbps

    b. 721 Kbps

    c. 250 Kbps

    d. 40 Kbps

17. Which frequency band(s) can ZigBee networks utilize?

    a. ISM

    b. U-NII

    c. 3.1 GHz

    d. 60 GHz

    e. All of the above

18. Which of the following topologies are supported by ZigBee?

    a. Scatternet and SCO

    b. Tree, star, and mesh

    c. Inverted tree and ACL

    d. Piconet and master/slave

19. Which of the following topologies are supported by Bluetooth?

    a. Scatternet and piconet

    b. ACL and SCO

    c. WMAN and WLAN

    d. Star and cluster tree

20. What type of security is provided for in the ZigBee specification?

    a. Encryption

    b. MIC

    c. Short-range communications

    d. ACLs

    e. All of the above

Hands-On Projects

This Project assumes you are using Windows 7. Instructions for using Windows 10 are included in Appendix A.

Project 5-1

Different Bluetooth interfaces may have different software and procedures. For this project, you will need two computers equipped with Bluetooth interface adapters. The project instructions and illustrations below are based on a Dell laptop with Windows 7 that uses a built-in Dell 365 Bluetooth module. If you are not using a Dell laptop or are using an external Bluetooth adapter, you may need to adjust the specific steps to fit your hardware.

1. First, you need to make at least one of the computers discoverable. In Windows 7, if you don't see the Bluetooth icon in the system tray, click the up arrow at the bottom right-hand corner of the screen to show the hidden icons. Now, click the Bluetooth icon, then click **Open Settings**. You will see the arrows shown in Figure 5-18.

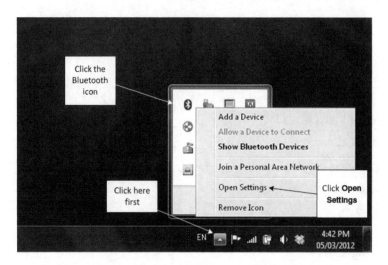

Figure 5-18   Opening Bluetooth settings from the Windows 7 system tray

2. In the Bluetooth Settings dialog box, click the **Options** tab and ensure that all the options in this dialog box are checked by clicking the boxes next to them. Your configuration dialog should look like what is shown in Figure 5-19. Click **OK** to set the configuration and close the page.

Figure 5-19 Configuring Bluetooth settings

3. Next, you need to pair the two computers. Once you have made the first one discoverable, click the up arrow in the system tray of the second computer and then click **Add a device**. Windows will now search for devices and display the ones that it discovers (see Figure 5-20).

Figure 5-20 Bluetooth devices discovered

4. Once an icon for the other computer appears in the Window, click it once to select it, then click **Next**. Remember that the two Bluetooth devices must be placed within a maximum of 33 feet (10 meters) of each other. Windows will now display a dialog page containing an automatically generated number. On the other computer, an information bubble will appear at the bottom right-hand side of the screen. Click the bubble to open a dialog box (see Figure 5-21) that asks you to verify that the pairing code is the same. Click **Next** to accept it. After Windows installs the necessary drivers, it will display a message indicating that the pairing was successful. If not, you may need to turn the Bluetooth device off and on again before attempting to pair.

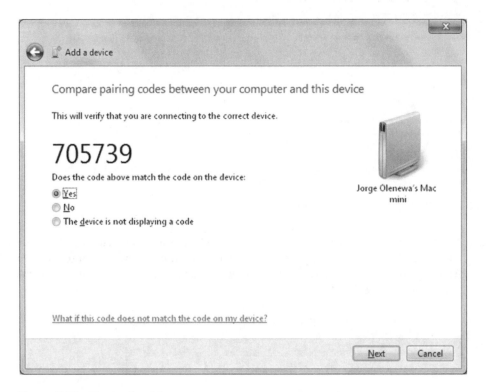

Figure 5-21 Bluetooth pairing

5. Open the Windows system tray on the second computer and click the Bluetooth icon. In the context menu, click **Show Bluetooth Devices**. You should see the other computer identified by name. Double-click it to open the dialog box shown in Figure 5-22.

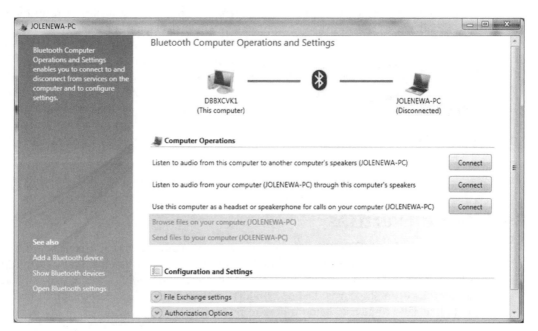

Figure 5-22 Bluetooth operations

6. Click **Send files to your computer** *<Name of the other Computer>* Windows will open a dialog page that allows you to select the files to send. Click the **Browse Files** button on this page and select a sample picture from the Windows Pictures folder. Click **Open** and then click **Next**.

7. Windows will open a dialog page that asks you to **Select the destination folder** and shows the other computer's name. Click **Send**. On the other computer, Windows will display a bubble confirming that the connection was successful and another bubble requesting authorization for the sending computer to copy a file over Bluetooth. Click the bubble to open the Bluetooth Image Push Service Access Authorization dialog page, and then ensure that **Allow access for the current request only** is checked. Then click **OK**.

8. Windows will now transfer the image using the image push profile mentioned in Step 7. Once the file has been transferred, the receiving computer will display another bubble for File Transfer notification. Click the bubble to open the containing folder and verify that the file was transferred correctly.

9. Experiment with Bluetooth by transferring other images and other types of files. Blue-tooth networking is somewhat complex and also sometimes clumsy. Devices must be able to support the right Bluetooth profiles; otherwise, you may not be able to transfer some types of files.

10. To verify which profiles are supported by your Bluetooth hardware and drivers, go to the **Show Bluetooth devices** page again, right-click the icon for the other computer or device with which you are trying to communicate, and click **Properties**. Click **Services** and check the list of Bluetooth services offered by the other device. If some of the

options are not checked and you had problems transferring a file, click all the services offered, click **OK**, and then attempt your file transfer again.

If you have an older laptop equipped with an infrared port (IrDA), you may wish to attempt a file transfer using this technology and compare the steps required with performing the same action on Bluetooth. In spite of its distance limitations and the requirement to have the computers' IrDA ports pointed at each other, the technology is much simpler to use and allows all types of data transfer between computers, usually at 4 Mbps.

Real-World Exercises

The Baypoint Group (TBG) has once again requested your services as a consultant. One of its clients, DeLuxe Builders, is interested in making sure that all their future construction projects include wireless control systems for lighting, heating and cooling, and energy management that are based on standards. DeLuxe Builders is aware that ZigBee is a global standard and would like TBG to advise them on how to proceed.

TBG will be in charge of evaluating the right type of technology and making recommendations to DeLuxe.

Exercise 5-1

Create a PowerPoint slide presentation that outlines how ZigBee technology works. Be sure to include information about the standards used, the advantages and disadvantages, and why ZigBee would be the best solution for DeLuxe.

Exercise 5-2

Your presentation convinced DeLuxe's management that using ZigBee would be a good solution. However, DeLuxe's management is concerned about the reliability of the system because it transmits using 2.4 GHz and this frequency band is also used by Wi-Fi and cordless phones. TBG has asked you to be involved in a demonstration to the client of both these technologies. Prepare a three-page paper discussing how ZigBee can coexist with other systems using the same frequency band and how ZigBee devices can also make use of other frequency bands.

Challenge Case Project

Microsoft has included full Bluetooth support in from Windows 7 on. Manufacturers of Bluetooth devices usually list the capabilities of their hardware but seldom tell you exactly which profiles are supported. If you have many Bluetooth devices or need specific information about your devices and you cannot locate this information on the Internet, sometimes it is useful to be able to obtain this type of information directly from your devices.

The following link at Softpedia (*www.softpedia.com/dyn-search.php?search_term=bluetooth*) has several utilities that can help you identify Bluetooth devices. Search the available utilities on the Softpedia site, and download and install one of the utilities (you may have to try more than one) on a computer equipped with a Bluetooth adapter. Most Bluetooth adapters should be supported, but some are limited to only certain manufacturer's adapters.

Now turn Bluetooth on in as many devices as you have available and use the utility to identify as many as you can. Remember that you may need to place the devices in discoverable mode. The utility should be able to identify cellular phones, headsets, etc. Some devices, such as the Apple iPhone, do not report their capabilities.

If you have a device that is already paired with another, such as a headset to a smartphone, do any of the utilities find the paired device? How might some of these utilities be useful to you in the field for identifying devices and capabilities or to troubleshoot? Write a short report answering these questions and outlining your approach for completing this project.

chapter 6

Introduction to Wi-Fi WLANs

After reading this chapter and completing the exercises, you will be able to:

- List the components of a WLAN
- Describe the modes of operation of a WLAN
- Discuss the first IEEE WLAN standards
- Describe coordinating communications in RF WLANs
- Explain the process of association and reassociation
- Outline the power management features of IEEE 802.11 networks
- Discuss 802.11 MAC frame formats

WLANs are probably the technology that has attracted the most attention since the introduction of personal computers to the consumer market. The explosive growth of wireless networks all over the world was initially driven by home and small-office sales, but after the ratification of the latest wireless networking standards—IEEE 802.11n in 2009 and 802.11ac in 2014—more companies are deploying wireless networks to allow staff and customers to connect their own devices and benefit from more flexible, mobile access. Globally, public Wi-Fi hotspot access continues to grow steadily, and the Wireless Broadband Alliance (*www.wballiance.com*) predicts that mobile phone carriers will continue to deploy Wi-Fi calling to offload some of the traffic from their networks. Total mobile data traffic is forecast to reach 30.6 **exabytes** (30.6×10^{18}) per month by 2020. This figure includes both smartphones and WLANs.

As a comparison, 5 exabytes (5×10^{18}) is estimated to be equal to all words ever spoken by human beings, so far. You can search the web for "global mobile data traffic" for additional statistics.

WLAN technology supports a very broad range of applications. Practically all laptop computers, tablets, and smartphones are equipped with Wi-Fi today. Popular coffee shops and restaurants, hotels, planes, trains and even some automobiles now offer Wi-Fi Internet access today.

This chapter begins by reviewing the basic concepts of how Wi-Fi WLANs work, focusing on low-speed WLANs (up to 11 Mbps). This background knowledge will help you better understand the higher-speed technologies, new standards, and compatibility issues covered in Chapter 7. Today, the widespread use of these wireless technologies means that working in this field requires a more in-depth understanding of how Wi-Fi works and how you can install and troubleshoot WLANs.

WLAN Components

The hardware needed to enable devices to connect to WLANs is surprisingly minimal. In addition to a mobile device and an Internet service provider, only wireless network interface cards (WNICs) and access points (APs) are needed for communications to take place.

Wireless Network Interface Card

The hardware that allows a computer to be connected to a wired network is called a network interface card (NIC) or a network adapter. A NIC is the device that connects the computer to the network so that it can send and receive data to other devices, either locally or via the Internet. A wired NIC has a port for a cable connection. The cable connects the NIC to the network, thus establishing the link between the computer and the network.

A wireless NIC (WNIC) performs the same functions as a wired NIC, with one major exception: There is no port for a wire connection to the network. In its place, there is an antenna to send and receive RF signals. Specifically, when WNICs transmit, they:

- Modulate the data onto RF carrier waves
- Determine when to send the packet
- Transmit the packet

Wireless NICs are available in many different formats. For desktop computers, WNICs are available as a card to be installed in an internal expansion slot or as an external wireless adapter that can be connected to a computer's USB port.

For laptop computers, WNICs are available as USB devices or **Mini PCI** cards. A Mini PCI is a small card that is functionally equivalent to a standard PCI expansion card for a desktop computer, but significantly smaller. The antenna is usually embedded in the part of the laptop that surrounds the screen. Today, the WNIC in laptops, smartphones, and other mobile devices consists of a set of chips mounted directly on the motherboard. These chips are the result of the development of components that consume a very small amount of power to allow handheld devices to operate longer on power supplied by relatively small batteries.

Access Points

As you learned in Chapter 1, an AP provides wireless LAN devices with a point of access into a wired network. APs consist of three major parts: (1) a radio transmitter/receiver to generate the signals that are used to send and receive wireless data, (2) an antenna to radiate these signals, and (3) an RJ-45 wired network interface port that is used to connect the AP to the wired network.

It is possible to use a PC as a wireless residential gateway or AP by using a WNIC, a standard NIC (which connects to the wired network), and special software that allows the PC to function as an AP. You can find free versions of this kind of software at: *www.microtik .com* as well as other websites.

The AP also acts as the wireless communications base station for the wireless network. With few exceptions, all the wireless devices that connect to the AP use the AP to transmit to other wireless devices that are connected to the same AP. The AP also acts as a bridge between the wireless and wired networks, as shown in Figure 6-1.

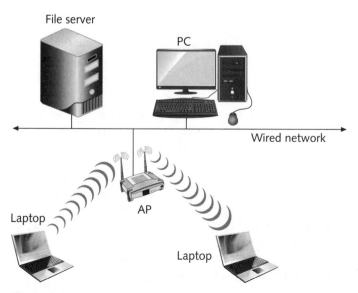

Figure 6-1 The AP as the point of access into a wired network

The range of an AP acting as the base station is a maximum of 375 feet (115 meters) in an unobstructed office environment, in which there is little interference. However, the data rate will drop as the signal strength, quality, or both begin to degrade due to distance or interference. The exact point at which the data rate begins to drop depends on the specific environment, the type and number of obstructions, and any sources of interference. The AP will automatically select the highest possible data rate for transmission, depending on the strength and quality of the transmissions it receives from mobile devices with which it is connected. This process is called **dynamic rate selection (DRS)**. Because the connection speed is so dependent on the environment, testing the signal before implementation of a WLAN is an extremely important part of the installation process. This preinstallation test is called a **wireless site survey**.

The largest number of devices that a single AP can be connected to varies, but is usually over 100. However, because the wireless medium is shared among all the connected devices, most vendors recommend one AP per maximum of 50 users if the network is lightly used—that is, for email, occasional web surfing, and occasional transferring of medium-sized files. On the other hand, if users are mainly working with large or time-sensitive data—such as digital pictures, video, or voice—the maximum number of users should be kept to between 20 and 25 per AP.

When the antennas are directly attached to the AP, the AP itself is usually mounted near the ceiling or in a similar area high off the ground to ensure the clearest possible path for the RF signal. However, electrical power outlets are generally not found in these locations and, due to building code restrictions, and installing these outlets near the ceiling can be very expensive. The IEEE has published two enhancements to the 802.3 Ethernet standard for wired networks —namely, 802.3af and 802.3at—that define how manufacturers may implement the distribution of **power over Ethernet (PoE)**. Instead of receiving power directly from an AC outlet, DC power is delivered to the AP through the same twisted pair Ethernet cables that connect the AP to the wired network. This makes the installation of APs much easier and more flexible.

WLAN Operating Modes

In an RF WLAN, data can be exchanged between devices in one of the two connection modes: ad hoc and infrastructure mode.

Ad Hoc Mode

Ad hoc mode is also known as **peer-to-peer mode**, although its formal name in the IEEE 802.11 standard is **Independent Basic Service Set (IBSS)**. In ad hoc mode, wireless devices communicate directly among themselves without using an AP, as shown in Figure 6-2. This mode is useful for a quick and easy setup of a wireless network anywhere that a network infrastructure, wired or wireless, does not already exist or is not permanently required. Examples of locations that use ad hoc mode WLANs include hotel meeting rooms or convention centers. The drawback is that the wireless devices can only communicate among themselves; there is usually no access to a wired network. Recent versions of PC, Mac, and Linux operating systems may support a feature called **Wi-Fi Direct**. This feature enables sharing of an Internet connection if one PC is connected to the wired network or to a cellular network through an embedded software-based AP into the operating system.

Laptop

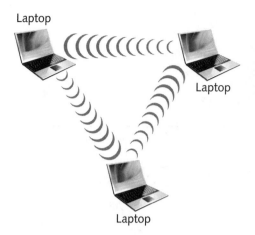

Laptop

Laptop

Figure 6-2 Ad hoc mode (IBSS)

Most smartphones also allow you to set up the phone as a wireless hotspot, which permits other devices to connect to it, so they can share a cellular connection to the Internet when not in range of a Wi-Fi network. Keep in mind that an IBSS can only effectively connect a maximum of 10 devices, depending on the processing capacity of the device that is sharing the Internet connection.

Infrastructure Mode

The second wireless network mode is **infrastructure mode**, also known as a **Basic Service Set (BSS)**. Infrastructure mode consists of at least one wireless device connected to a single AP. If the coverage area needs to be increased beyond the range of a single AP, or if you need to support more users, additional APs can be added to the network. When an infrastructure WLAN has more than one AP using the same **Service Set Identifier (SSID)**, it is called an **Extended Service Set (ESS)**. An ESS is simply two or more BSS wireless networks installed within the same area, providing users with uninterrupted mobile access to the network, as shown in Figure 6-3. The SSID is an alphanumeric character string that uniquely identifies each WLAN and is essentially the human-readable name of the network. In an ESS, each AP is tuned to a different frequency channel, but all APs are connected to the same wired LAN, creating a virtually seamless wireless connection. In an IEEE 802.11 WLAN, the MAC address of each AP is called the basic service set identifier or **BSSID**, and in the case of an ESS, where the alphanumeric SSID is the same for several different APs, Wi-Fi devices use the BSSID to identify which AP they are connected to.

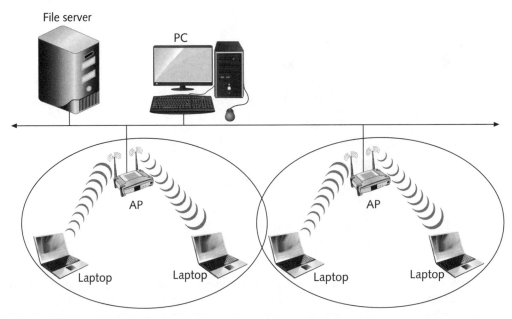

Figure 6-3 Extended Service Set (ESS)

When multiple APs are used, they create areas of coverage, much like the individual cells in a beehive. However, unlike in a beehive, these cells overlap to facilitate roaming. When a mobile user carrying a wireless device enters into the range of more than one AP, his wireless device chooses an AP with which to associate based on signal strength and quality. Once the AP accepts the connection from that device, the device changes to the radio frequency used by that particular AP.

Whenever a wireless device is not communicating on the WLAN, it monitors all the radio frequency channels on the network to determine if a different AP can provide a better-quality or stronger signal. If the device finds one (perhaps because the user has moved to another area of the building), it then associates with the new AP, changing to the radio frequency of the new AP. In an ESS, this transition is called a **handoff**. To the user, a handoff in an ESS is seamless, because the connection between the wireless device and the wired network is never interrupted. The device remains connected to the same WLAN.

A challenge of ESS WLANs is that all wireless devices and APs must be part of the same network segment for users to be able to roam freely between one AP and the other. Sometimes, it is difficult to manage one large network. Because of this, network managers usually subdivide large networks into units known as **subnets** that contain fewer computers. An ESS is almost always set up using a dedicated VLAN that spans all of the network switches in a building or campus. This way all APs can be part of the same network segment (IP addresses belonging to the same subnet) allowing users to roam freely around the building or campus while maintaining connectivity at all times.

First WLAN Standards

In this section, you will learn about the first IEEE standards for wireless LANs. All Wi-Fi WLANs are based on the original IEEE 802.11 standards, and even the latest standards still follow the same basic principles, albeit with a number of enhancements. These standards implement specific transmission technologies based on differences in the PHY and MAC layers.

IEEE 802.11

The original IEEE **802.11 standard,** ratified in 1997, defines a local area network that provides cable-free data access for devices that are either mobile or in a fixed location, at a rate of either 1 or 2 Mbps using either diffused infrared light or RF. In addition, when using RF technology, this standard defines the implementation of WLANs using FHSS or DSSS (discussed in Chapter 2).

The standard specifies that the features of a WLAN be transparent to the upper layers of the TCP/IP protocol stack or the OSI protocol model. That is, all differences between Ethernet LANs and WLANs are implemented in the PHY and MAC layers, so that no modifications are needed to any other OSI protocol layers, as shown in Figure 6-4. Because of this, any network operating system or LAN application will run on a WLAN without modifications.

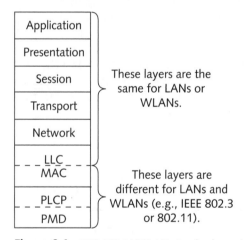

Figure 6-4   IEEE 802.11 WLAN standards are implemented in MAC sublayer and PHY layer

Because no IEEE 802.11 equipment has ever been introduced in the consumer market using either IR or FHSS, this book does not cover these technologies. Instead, this chapter focuses on the basics of 802.11 as it is available in the market today.

The slow maximum bandwidth of only 2 Mbps for the original 802.11 standard is not sufficient for most network applications. As a result, the IEEE revisited the 802.11 standard shortly after it was released to determine what changes could be made to increase the speed. In 1999, the 802.11b standard was published, increasing the speeds to a maximum of 11 Mbps in the 2.4 GHz ISM band. Even the IEEE 802.11n amendment to the standard is still backward compatible with the original maximum data rates from 1997 of 1 or 2 Mbps in the 2.4 GHz band, as well as with 802.11b. This backward compatibility makes it possible for older models of devices to connect to WLANs, which protects the user's investment in equipment.

IEEE 802.11a, 802.11ac, and 802.11ad are not mentioned in this chapter because they are not compatible with 2.4 GHz. They will be discussed in later chapters.

IEEE 802.11b

The IEEE **802.11b** amendment, ratified in 1999, was originally called Higher Speed Physical Layer Extension in the 2.4 GHz band by the IEEE. Today, it is generally referred to as High-Rate (HR). It added two higher speeds to the 1997 standard, 5.5 and 11 Mbps, and specified RF and direct sequence spread spectrum (DSSS) as the only way to encode and modulate bit streams for transmission. 802.11b also became known as **Wi-Fi** shortly after the establishment of the Wi-Fi Alliance.

Physical Layer Remember that the purpose of the PHY layer is to transmit and receive signals. The IEEE 802.11b PHY layer is also divided into two sublayers, as shown in Figure 6-4: the physical medium dependent (PMD) sublayer and the physical layer convergence procedure (PLCP) sublayer. The 802.11b standard made changes only to the PHY layer of the original 802.11 standard.

Physical Layer Convergence Procedure PLCP standards for 802.11b are based on direct sequence spread spectrum (DSSS). The PLCP must reformat the data received from the MAC layer (when transmitting) into a frame that the PMD sublayer can transmit. An example of an 802.11 PLCP frame is shown in Figure 6-5.

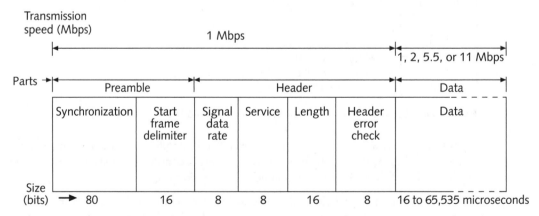

Figure 6-5   IEEE 802.11 PLCP frame

The PLCP frame is made up of three parts: the preamble, the header, and the data. The preamble allows the receiving device to prepare for the rest of the frame. The header provides information about the frame itself, and the data is the information to be transmitted. The fields of the PLCP frame are:

- *Synchronization*—Consists of alternating 0s and 1s to alert the receiver that a transmission is about to begin; the receiving device then synchronizes with the incoming signal.

- *Start frame delimiter*—Always the same bit pattern (1111001110100000); it defines the beginning of a frame.

- *Signal data rate*—Indicates how fast the data is being sent.

- *Service*—Most of the bits in this field are reserved for future use and must be set to 0. Bits 2, 3, and 7 are used in combination with the Length field for data rates higher than 5 Mbps.

- *Length*—Indicates how long, in microseconds, the data portion of the frame (the MAC frame) is. The value of the Data field ranges from 16 to 65,535 and it is measured in time slots, not bits or bytes. Approximately two pages of the 802.11b standard are devoted to calculating the length of the data. These details are beyond the scope of this book.

- *Header error check*—Contains a value that the receiving device can use to determine if the data was received correctly.

- *Data*—Can be up to 4,095 bytes (the maximum length of an IEEE 802.11 MAC frame).

The 802.11b PLCP frame preamble and header are always transmitted at 1 Mbps to allow slower devices to be able to "understand" the transmission, which is the key to avoiding frame collisions. The slow PLCP preamble and header transmission speed also means that a slower transmission, that uses a simpler modulation scheme, can be more easily "understood" by devices farther away. The disadvantage of using the lowest common denominator speed is that faster devices must still fall back to the 1 Mbps transmission rate for the preamble and header, and this affects the overall performance of the WLAN. However, the data portion of the frames can be transmitted at the faster rates, if supported by the devices.

Physical Medium Dependent Standards Once the PLCP has formatted the frame, it then passes the frame to the PMD sublayer of the PHY layer. Again, the job of the PMD is to translate the binary 1s and 0s of the frame into RF signals that can be transmitted via EM waves.

The 802.11b standard uses the Industrial, Scientific, and Medical (ISM) band (an unregulated band that you learned about in Chapter 3) for its transmissions. For use in 802.11 and 802.11b, the standard specifies 14 available frequencies, beginning at 2.412 GHz and incrementing by 0.005 GHz (or 5 MHz) of bandwidth per channel, except for channel 14. The frequencies for each channel are listed in Table 6-1.

Channel Number	Frequency (GHz)
1	2.412
2	2.417
3	2.422
4	2.427
5	2.432
6	2.437
7	2.442
8	2.447
9	2.452
10	2.457
11	2.462
12	2.467
13	2.472
14	2.484

Table 6-1 802.11 2.4 GHz ISM channels

NOTE The United States and Canada use channels 1–11; Europe permits channels 1–13, with the maximum power limited at 10 mW between 2,454 and 2,483 MHz; and Japan permits the use of all 14 channels but limits the use of channel 14 to 802.11b only.

Bear in mind that these frequencies and their associated limitations may change over time, as a result of the work of the ITU-T with the governments of various countries.

By employing dynamic rate selection, the PMD on an AP adjusts the transmission rate automatically from 1 to 2, 5.5, or 11 Mbps and down again depending on the latest signal strength and quality received from a device. For transmissions at 1 Mbps, two-level differential binary phase-shift keying (DBPSK) is specified as the modulation technique and encodes 1 bit per signal change (or symbol). For transmissions at 2 Mbps, differential quadrature phase-shift keying or DQPSK is specified and encodes 2 bits per symbol.

You may remember that DSSS uses an expanded redundant code, called the Barker code, to transmit each data bit. The Barker code is used when 802.11b is transmitting at 1 or 2 Mbps. However, to transmit at rates above 2 Mbps, **Complementary Code Keying (CCK)**, a table containing 64 8-bit code words, is used instead. As a set, these code words have unique, mathematically calculated properties that allow them to be correctly distinguished from one another by a receiver. The 5.5 Mbps rate uses four of these code words to encode 4 bits per signal unit, whereas the 11 Mbps rate uses all 64 code words to encode 8 bits per symbol.

Keep in mind that because all 802.11 transmissions use a single frequency channel, they are half-duplex, which means that the maximum throughput achievable in an 802.11b network is only between 5 and 6 Mbps.

Media Access Control Layer   The 802.11b Data Link layer consists of two sublayers: Logical Link Control (LLC) and Media Access Control (MAC). The 802.11b standard specifies no changes to the LLC sublayer (the LLC remains the same as for IEEE 802.3 wired networks); therefore, all the changes required for 802.11b WLANs to work are confined to the MAC sublayer.

Coordinating Communications in the Shared Wireless Medium

Because all devices in the same 802.11 WLAN must share the medium by transmitting on the same frequency channel, if two computers start sending messages at the same time, a **collision** results, the data becomes corrupted and cannot be correctly decoded by receivers. Figure 6-6 shows an example of a collision in a wired network. To prevent this, wireless network devices must use a variety of methods to access the frequency channel. One way to prevent network collisions, for example, is for each device to listen to the medium first, to make sure no other device is transmitting. In addition, after a device transmits a frame, it must wait to receive an acknowledgment from the receiving device. If it does not receive an **acknowledgment (ACK)**, it assumes there has been a collision. This process is called **distributed coordination function (DCF)**.

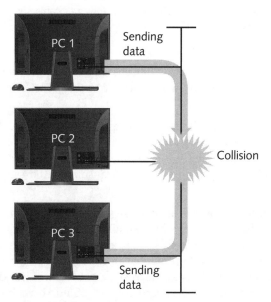

Figure 6-6   Frame collision in a wired network

CSMA/CA

In Chapter 5, you learned about a **channel access method** called carrier sense, multiple access with collision avoidance (CSMA/CA). In this chapter, we will explore CSMA/CA further to better understand how 802.11 networks work. This method of detecting collisions is based on the one used in IEEE 802.3 Ethernet. When Ethernet devices are connected using a shared medium, such as a coaxial cable, or when they operate in half-duplex mode using hubs and only two wires to communicate, they use a method to access the medium called carrier sense, multiple access with collision detection (CSMA/CD). CSMA/CD specifies that before a computer starts to send a message, it should listen on the cable to see if any other computer is transmitting. If it hears traffic, it should wait until that traffic is finished. If it hears no traffic, then the computer can send a packet. However, what if two computers simultaneously listen for traffic and hear nothing on the cable and both start to send at exactly the same time? A collision would result. CSMA/CD also specifies that each computer must continue to listen while sending its message. If it detects a collision, each computer stops sending data and broadcasts a jam signal over the network, which tells all other computers not to send any messages for a random period of time (the backoff interval) before attempting to resend.

CSMA/CD in Ethernet uses voltage sensors on the NIC. Whenever they detect a voltage higher than 5 volts, it means that more than one device is transmitting at the same time. This method of detecting a collision cannot be used in a wireless system. Collision detection is virtually impossible with wireless transmissions when the signals are transmitted and received in the same frequency. While a device is transmitting on a particular frequency, it cannot detect a collision. In addition, the amount of attenuation of an EM signal sent by another device is dependent on the environment in which it is being transmitted, as well as on reflected signals and other types of interference, and is therefore not predictable. Consequently, measuring the strength or voltage of an RF signal is not practical for detecting collisions in wireless systems.

 The maximum length of an Ethernet cable in wired networks is limited to about 300 feet (100 meters). Due to tight Ethernet cable specifications, this makes the signal attenuation in Ethernet networks predictable.

The entire family of 802.11 standards uses DCF or variations of it to avoid collisions. Whereas CSMA/CD is designed to handle collisions when they occur, CSMA/CA attempts to avoid collisions altogether.

When using a contention-based channel access method, the time at which the most collisions occur is immediately after a device completes its transmission. This is because all other devices wanting to transmit have been waiting for the medium to clear so they can send their messages. Once the medium is clear, they may all try to transmit at the same time, which results in collisions.

CSMA/CA in DCF handles the situation by making all devices wait a random amount of time (the backoff interval) after the medium is clear, which significantly reduces the occurrence of collisions. The amount of time that a device must wait after the medium is clear is measured in **time slots**. All devices must wait a random number of time slots as their backoff interval. Each time slot in a DSSS 802.11b WLAN is 20 microseconds. If a wireless device's backoff interval is three time slots, then it must wait 60 microseconds (20 microseconds times three time slots) before attempting to transmit, in an attempt to prevent collisions.

As a comparison, each time slot for an 802.3 Ethernet 10 Mbps transmission is 51.2 microseconds; for 100 Mbps Ethernet, it is 5.12 microseconds.

CSMA/CA also reduces collisions by using an explicit acknowledgment (ACK). An ACK frame is sent by the receiving device back to the sending device after each frame transmission to confirm that the frame arrived intact. If the sending device does not receive the ACK frame, either the original data packet sent was not received correctly or the ACK was not received correctly. In either case, the sending device assumes that a problem has occurred and retransmits the frame. Other devices are not allowed to transmit until after this process is completed. This explicit ACK mechanism can also handle interference and other radio-related problems, such as one device being able to hear the transmission from an AP but not being able to hear another device that may be too far away from it. Devices may be too far away from each other, but when connected, they should all be able to "hear" transmissions from the AP. Figure 6-7 shows a graphic example of the acknowledgment process.

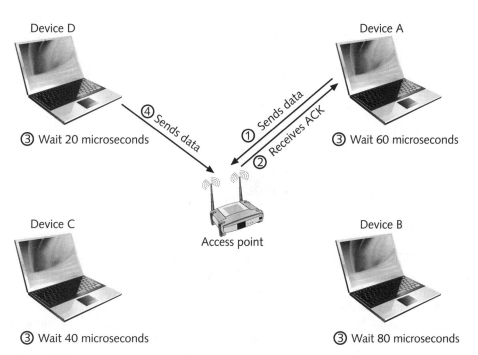

Figure 6-7 CSMA/CA and acknowledgment steps and process

CSMA/CA reduces potential collisions, but it does not eliminate them altogether. The 802.11b standard provides two additional methods for reducing potential collisions. The first is known as the **request-to-send/clear-to-send** (**RTS/CTS**) protocol (also called *virtual carrier sensing*). A graphic example of the RTS/CTS protocol is shown in Figure 6-8. The device wishing to transmit sends an RTS frame to the AP. This frame contains a "Duration" field that defines the length of time needed for both the transmission and the returning ACK frame. The AP then alerts all other wireless devices that device B needs to reserve the medium for a specific number of time slots by responding back to device B with a CTS frame. The CTS also tells all devices that the medium is now being reserved and that they should therefore suspend any transmissions. Once the device that sent the RTS to the AP receives the CTS frame, it can proceed with transmitting its message.

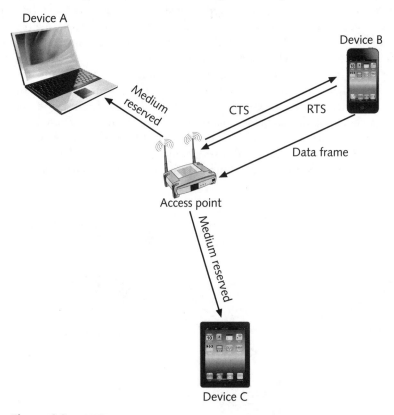

Figure 6-8   RTS/CTS

The RTS/CTS protocol imposes additional overhead, which reduces network performance, and is not used unless there are excessive collisions. The second method of reducing collisions is **fragmentation**. Fragmentation involves dividing the data to be transmitted from one large frame into several smaller ones. Sending many smaller frames instead of one large frame reduces the amount of time that the wireless medium is being used to transmit each frame, and because of this, it can also reduce the probability of collisions.

In fragmentation, if the length of a data frame to be transmitted exceeds a configurable value, the MAC layer will divide, or fragment, that frame into several smaller frames. Each fragmented frame is given a fragment number (the first fragmented frame is 0, the next frame is 1, and so on). After a frame is received and verified to be free of errors, the receiving device sends back an ACK and then is ready to receive the next fragment. After all the fragments are received at their destination, they are reassembled, based on their fragment numbers, back into the original frame by the MAC layer.

Fragmentation is an alternative to RTS/CTS; however, it does create additional overhead in two ways. First, more frames imply additional MAC and PLCP headers. Second, the receiving device must send a separate ACK for each smaller fragment received. Fragmentation does not always have to be used separately from RTS/CTS; in a busy WLAN, they may have to be combined to reduce collisions. The standard allows both methods to be used simultaneously.

Point Coordination Function

Another type of channel access method is **polling**. With this method, each device is sequentially "asked" by the AP if it has anything to transmit. After associating with the AP, devices cannot transmit unless they are polled. If the device has something to transmit, it will send a positive response to the AP. The AP then grants the device permission to transmit. If the device does not have anything to transmit, it will send a **null data frame** to the AP, and then the next device in sequence will be polled. It is a very orderly way of allowing each device to transmit a frame. Each device is given a turn, as shown in Figure 6-9. Polling effectively eliminates collisions because every device must wait until it receives permission from the AP before it can transmit.

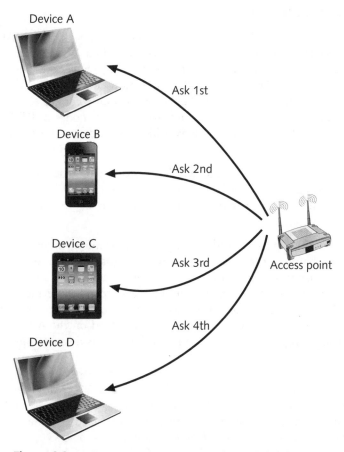

Figure 6-9   Polling in point coordination function (PCF)

This optional polling method is known as **point coordination function (PCF)**. With PCF, the AP serves as the polling device. When using PCF, the AP (the point coordinator) first listens for wireless traffic. This is because in order to allow other devices to associate with the AP and join the WLAN, PCF must still allow some time slots for contention access, in which case the WLAN uses DCF. If the AP hears no traffic on the wireless medium, it sends out a beacon frame to all devices. One field of this frame contains a value that indicates the number of time slots that will be used for PCF (polling), as well as the number of time slots that will be used for DCF (contention). Devices that are not yet associated with the AP but that receive the beacon will take advantage of the DCF period to contact the AP and join the WLAN.

Delays in transmission can result in a video that freezes on the screen or a voice conversation that has gaps of dead space. Data transmissions, on the other hand, are not time sensitive. DCF cannot distinguish between voice, video, and data frames. Although PCF was never actually implemented in any 802.11 APs or wireless residential gateways, a hybrid of this method and DCF is part of later amendments to the standard, so it is still important to understand the basics of how PCF works.

Association and Reassociation

Before a device can communicate in a WLAN, it must first join the network. The MAC layer of the 802.11 standard provides the functionality for a device to join a WLAN. The process for joining is known as **association**. In the case of an ESS, devices also have to connect to different APs when the user is roaming. This means that devices must connect to another AP in an ESS and must disconnect from the AP to which they were previously connected. The latter process is called **reassociation**. Remember that there are two different modes in RF WLANs: ad hoc and infrastructure. Regardless of which mode is being used, a device must first associate with the WLAN.

Association begins with a device scanning the wireless medium to discover an AP or ad hoc devices within RF range. The device that wants to join the WLAN must first listen or scan the medium for the information that it needs to begin the association process.

There are two types of scanning: passive and active. **Passive scanning** involves a device "listening" to each of the channels for a set period of time (usually 10 seconds). The device listens for beacon frames transmitted by APs or by other devices in an ad hoc network within a range. The information contained within the beacon frame includes how often beacon frames are sent, the supported transmission rates of the network, and the AP's SSID and BSSID. The transmission of the SSID can be disabled on the AP to attempt to hide the network from scanning devices. This hiding of the SSID is discussed in Chapter 8, under "WLAN Security."

SSIDs are case sensitive. For example, if you set the SSID on an AP as "AP1" and set the SSID on the device as "ap1," the device will not be able to associate with the AP using this configuration. The same is true for ad hoc networks. All devices must use the same SSID.

The second type of scan, **active scanning**, involves the device first sending out a special frame, called a **probe** frame, on each available channel. It then waits for an answer called the **probe response** frame, from the AP to which it sent the frame. Like the beacon frame, the probe response frame contains information the device needs to begin a dialog with the AP. According to the IEEE 802.11 standard, the probe response frame must always be sent back and must also include the SSID, regardless of whether the AP is configured to transmit it by default in the beacon or not. Devices do not normally perform active scans of the wireless medium, but every device is capable of sending probe frames. Some WLAN apps, such as those used for war driving, include this feature. **War driving** is the practice of discovering and recording information about WLANs in a neighborhood or around a city while driving or walking. In the early days of Wi-Fi, when WLANs were not so common, war drivers even used chalk on outside walls or sidewalks to mark the existence of WLANs at each location.

After devices receive the network information in the beacon, they can begin to negotiate a WLAN connection. To join the WLAN, the device will send an **associate request frame** to the AP that includes the device's own capabilities and supported transmission rates. The AP then returns an **associate response frame**, containing a status code and a device ID number that will be used as long as it remains connected to the same AP. At this point, the device becomes part of the WLAN and can begin communicating.

A device can be preconfigured to connect to a specific WLAN. In this case, the device is already configured with the SSID of the WLAN. Likewise, some APs can be configured to accept or reject a connection from certain devices, usually based on a device's MAC address. As it receives beacon frames from the different APs, the device compares its preconfigured profile's BSSIDs with the BSSID of the preferred AP. The device will not attempt to connect to APs until it finds a match, at which time it will send an associate request frame to that AP. If a device has not been preconfigured to connect with a specific AP, it will attempt to connect with the AP from which it has received the strongest radio signal. User intervention is required at the device to create a profile to connect to WLANs.

Devices can only be associated with one WLAN at a time. Reassociation happens when mobile devices roam beyond the coverage area of one AP in an ESS and are receiving a stronger signal from a different AP in the same ESS, in which case the device reassociates with the new AP. Reassociation can also occur when the signal from one AP weakens because of interference, but there is another AP using a different channel, within range.

When a device determines that the link to its current AP is poor, because it has been scanning the medium and maintaining information related to the various APs in an ESS, it will switch to the frequency of the AP with the strongest signal and send a **reassociate request frame**. If the new AP accepts the reassociation request, it will send a **reassociate response frame** to the device. The new AP will then send a **disassociate frame** to the previous AP that the device was connected to, via the wired network. This process is shown in Figure 6-10. The only time a device sends a disassociation frame to an AP is when it is made to disconnect from the WLAN by user intervention.

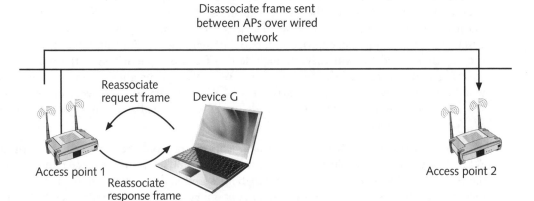

Disassociate frame sent between APs over wired network

Reassociate request frame   Device G

Access point 1

Reassociate response frame

Access point 2

Figure 6-10   Associating and disassociating in an ESS

In the 802.11 standard, multiple APs can only communicate with one another over the network cabling. In other words, they cannot communicate over a wireless connection. As you will learn in Chapter 8, there are two separate enhancements to the 802.11 standards that permit APs to communicate with each other over the wireless medium.

Power Management

Most devices in a WLAN are laptop computers, smartphones, or tablets, giving the users the freedom to roam without being tethered to the network by wires. When these devices are mobile (and consequently not connected to a power outlet), they depend on batteries as their primary power source. To conserve battery power, wireless NICs can go into **sleep mode**. When a device is participating in a WLAN, it must remain fully powered up to receive network transmissions. Missing transmissions because the NIC is in sleep mode may cause an application running on the device to drop a connection-oriented TCP session. The answer to the issue of a battery-powered device being able to shut down its radios to save energy is known as **power management**. In the 802.11 standard, power management allows the mobile device's NIC to turn off its radios as often as possible to conserve battery but still not miss out on data transmissions. Power management in 802.11 is transparent to all protocols and applications so that it does not interfere with normal network functions. Note that in 802.11 the power management function can only be used when devices connect in infrastructure mode.

A NIC going into sleep mode is not the same as when a laptop or other mobile device goes into sleep mode. As defined in 802.11, a NIC in sleep mode must remain powered up. When a laptop, for example, goes into hibernate or standby mode, the NIC also shuts down completely and the laptop is unable to maintain TCP sessions.

The key to power management is synchronization. Every device on a WLAN has its own local timer. At regular intervals, the AP sends out a beacon signal that contains a time stamp. Devices will turn on their radios during every beacon transmission to receive these frames from the AP and synchronize their local timers with that of the AP.

When a wireless device goes into sleep mode by turning off its wireless NIC radios, it first informs the AP of the change in its status. The AP keeps a record of those devices that are awake and those that are sleeping. When the AP receives frames from the network destined for devices that have the radios off, it will temporarily store the frames that are destined to the devices that are in sleep mode (this function is called **buffering**).

Since the AP has only a limited capacity to buffer frames, in the next beacon, it will add a **traffic indication map (TIM)** containing the IDs of the devices for which it has buffered frames. All devices that have been sleeping must awaken (by turning on their wireless radio) and go into an active listening mode during beacon transmissions. If a device learns that it has buffered frames waiting at the AP, it will send a request to the AP for those frames. If the TIM does not include the device ID of a particular device, signaling that it has no buffered frames, the device can return to sleep mode. This process is shown in Figure 6-11.

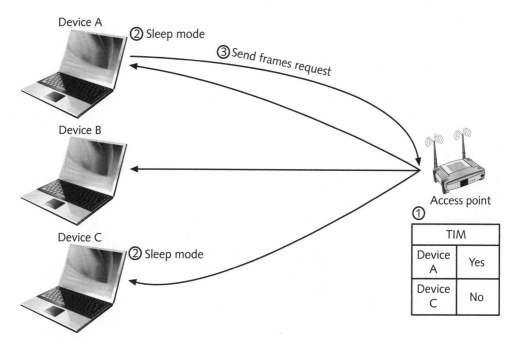

Figure 6-11   Power management in IEEE 802.11

 The typical sleep time for a battery powered device is usually set to about 100 milliseconds, which is the amount of time between beacon frames.

MAC Frame Formats

To understand many of the intricacies of how CSMA/CA works, how backward compatibility with legacy devices is handled by the latest amendments to the standard (covered in the next chapter), as well as some of the challenges of troubleshooting WLANs, it is important to understand the MAC frame formats. The 802.11b standard specifies three types of MAC frames. The first type of MAC frame is known as the **management frame**. These frames are used to set up the initial communications between a device and the AP. The association, reassociation request, the reassociation response frame, and the disassociation frames are all examples of management frames.

The format of a management frame is shown in Figure 6-12. The Frame control field indicates the current version number of the standard and whether encryption is being used. The Duration field contains the number of microseconds needed to transmit. This value will differ depending on whether the PCF or DCF modes are being used. The Sequence control field is the sequence number for the frame and, if necessary, the fragment number.

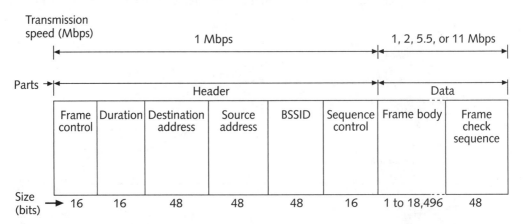

Figure 6-12 Structure of a management frame

Control frames are the second type of MAC frame. After association and authentication between the devices and the APs are established, the control frames provide assistance in delivering the frames that contain the data. RTS and ACK frames are examples of control frames. The format of a control frame is shown in Figure 6-13.

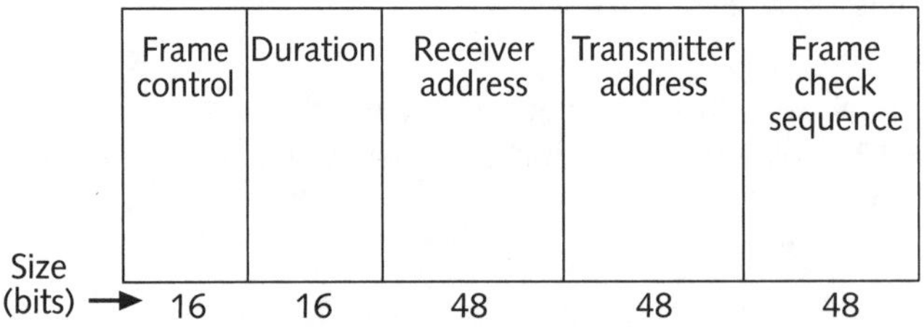

Frame control	Duration	Receiver address	Transmitter address	Frame check sequence
16	16	48	48	48

Size (bits) →

Figure 6-13 Control frame

Data frames are the third type of MAC frame. They carry the information to be transmitted to the destination device. The format of a data frame is shown in Figure 6-14. The fields Address 1 through Address 4 contain the destination MAC address, the source MAC address, and the transmitter MAC address and the receiver MAC address, depending on how the network is configured. The number of address fields varies depending on the type of MAC frame transmitted.

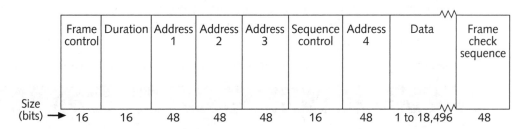

Frame control	Duration	Address 1	Address 2	Address 3	Sequence control	Address 4	Data	Frame check sequence
16	16	48	48	48	16	48	1 to 18,496	48

Size (bits) →

Figure 6-14 Data frame

A full discussion of the use of the address fields is beyond the scope of this book, but the reason for having four address fields, instead of the two used in Ethernet, has to do with the use of a wireless repeater, sometimes called a signal booster in consumer product ads. As you know, in a wired network, switches transfer frames at layer 2 and do not change the MAC address field. Conversely, routers must change the source and destination MAC addresses (but not the IP addresses) every time they forward a frame. Even though APs are not routers, they also use and change the source and destination MAC addresses whenever they forward frames in a WLAN. Note that only one repeater per AP is allowed by the 802.11 standard. For additional information regarding the content of the address fields, see the 802.11-1999 standard. You can find it at *http://standards.ieee.org/about/get*. Copies of the IEEE standards are usually available at no cost 6 months after the publication of a standard or amendment.

Interframe Spaces

To understand the message exchange process in a WLAN, you need to understand the collision avoidance mechanism in DCF that APs and wireless devices use to communicate. For CSMA/CA to work properly in DCF, the 802.11 standard defines a number of **interframe spaces (IFS)** or time gaps between frames in a WLAN. These are designed to handle the contention for the medium among several devices attempting to communicate.

To keep this explanation as simple as possible, we will only review the procedure and rules associated with using DCF. We will not look at the procedure or rules associated with RTS/CTS or PCF. For additional information, refer to the 802.11-1999 standard.

In 802.11, interframe spaces perform various critical functions:

- The **Short Interframe Space (SIFS)** is a time period used to allow all transmitted signals to arrive and be decoded at the receiving device, including multipath signals that take a longer trajectory and arrive later at the receiver. A SIFS occurs immediately after the transmission of each frame, regardless of type. No devices are allowed to transmit during the SIFS. If a frame has been transmitted to one specific device, and provided there were no errors, the receiving device will send an ACK immediately after the SIFS time.

- The **DCF Interframe Space (DIFS)** is a time period during which all devices must wait between transmissions of data frames. The DIFS occurs after the transmission of an ACK or right after the SIFS if the frame transmitted was a broadcast (no ACKs are transmitted in response to broadcast frames). A device waiting to transmit will listen to the medium during the DIFS. If it does not hear any transmissions during the DIFS, it will be allowed to transmit a frame, otherwise it will defer the transmission.

The times of these space intervals are measured in microseconds, as shown in Table 6-2.

DSSS Interframe Space	Duration in Microseconds
SIFS	10
DIFS	50

Table 6-2   Interframe space duration

The basic rules of communication in an 802.11 network are as follows (see Figure 6-15):

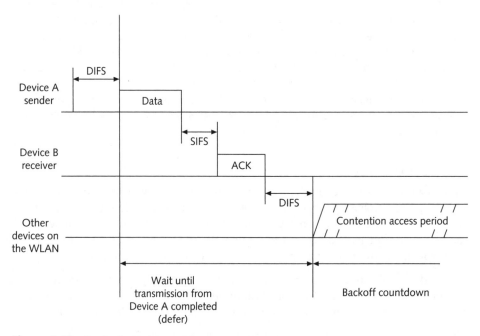

Figure 6-15   Single device transmitting

- A device that wants to transmit begins listening for an RF signal on the medium, which indicates the presence of frame traffic on the network, during the DIFS.

- If no RF signal is detected at the end of the DIFS and the device's backoff interval has counted down to 0, it can begin transmitting a frame.

- The size of a frame includes both the length of time necessary to send the data and the SIFS time, and every device that receives this information will not transmit for the duration or a frame transmission by another device, assuming it "heard" and understood its transmission. When the transmission is over, the sending device begins listening for an acknowledgment (ACK) from the receiving device.

- The receiving device must send the ACK immediately after the SIFS. After receiving an ACK, the transmitting device begins to wait for a random number of time slots, its backoff interval.

- If the transmitting device does not receive an ACK after the SIFS, it is allowed to maintain control of the medium and begin retransmitting the frame that was not acknowledged immediately after the DIFS time. It will try to do this a few times and then indicate an error to the upper protocol layers.

- If the frame was acknowledged correctly, the transmitting device listens to the medium and counts down while waiting its random backoff interval, except during the SIFS or DIFS or during a transmission by another device. Once the backoff interval ends, the device checks for traffic at the end of the next DIFS and the process repeats itself from the first point above.

In the case of two devices having frames to transmit, the process works as follows (see Figure 6-16):

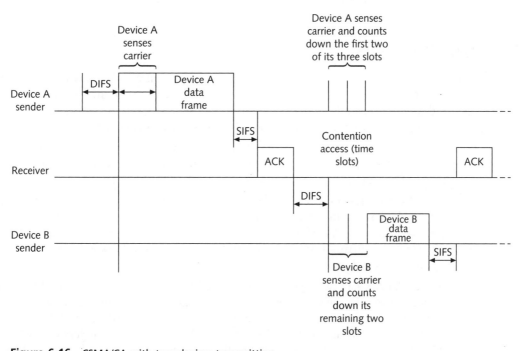

Figure 6-16 CSMA/CA with two devices transmitting

- Device A has a frame to transmit. Its backoff period counter is 0. It senses the carrier during the DIFS (the one on the left in Figure 6-16) and finds no traffic on the medium. At the end of the DIFS, it begins transmitting a frame.

- Device B had two time slots left to count down, but it can only do so during a contention access period.

- After Device A finishes the transmission of its data frame, it sets its random backoff counter to 3.

- The network enters a contention access period, and both Device A and Device B begin counting down their respective backoff time slots.

- After two time slots, Device B's backoff counter reaches 0 and it has something to transmit. Device B finds the medium free during the DIFS and transmits the frame immediately after.

- Like Device B before, Device A does nothing, except count down, after a DIFS and when the medium is free. Once Device B has received an ACK for its most recent transmission, the process described above starts over.

The process just described is what actually occurs in an IEEE 802.11 WLAN, and it is the essence of the DCF collision avoidance method. However, collisions may still happen. One of the most common causes is what is called the "hidden node" problem, when two (or more) devices are able to communicate with the AP but may be too far away or blocked by an obstacle and cannot "hear" each other. This is when RTS/CTS solves the problem. When an AP sends out a CTS frame, all devices are able to receive it. The CTS frame includes the amount of time required for a particular device to transmit its frame, so all other devices will refrain from transmitting until after they "hear" an ACK frame.

Chapter Summary

- The wireless technology that attracts the most attention today is wireless local area networks (WLANs). WLAN deployments continue to grow, and usage is increasing at a dramatic pace, all because WLANs allow users to access networks such as the Internet from a wider range of locations than was ever possible before.

- A wireless NIC performs the same functions as a wired NIC, except instead of a port for a cable connection to the network, the wireless NIC uses an antenna to send and receive RF signals. Wireless NICs are available in many different formats.

- An AP's main function is to interconnect the wired network and the WLAN. The AP acts as the base station for the wireless network and also serves as a bridge between the two networks. An AP consists of three major parts: an antenna, a radio transmitter/receiver, and an RJ-45 wired network interface that allows it to connect by cable to a standard wired network.

- An RF WLAN has two operating modes, ad hoc or infrastructure. In ad hoc (or peer-to-peer) mode, the wireless devices communicate directly with each other without using an AP. Ad hoc mode is known in the 802.11 standard as an IBSS. Infrastructure mode, also known as the Basic Service Set (BSS), consists of wireless devices and an AP. If more users need to be added to the WLAN or the range of coverage needs to be increased, more APs can be added using the same network name, or SSID. This creates an Extended Service Set (ESS), which consists of two or more BSSs.

■ The original IEEE WLAN standard was 802.11. The IEEE 802.11 standard defines a local area network that provides cable-free data access at a rate of up to 2 Mbps for devices that are either mobile or in a fixed location. The 802.11 standard also specifies that the features of a WLAN be transparent to the upper levels of the OSI protocol model. However, the slow bandwidth of only 2 Mbps for the 802.11 standard proved insufficient for most network applications. IEEE 802.11b was the first amendment to the original standard and it added two faster transmission speeds, 5.5 and 11 Mbps. The IEEE 802.11b amendment also removed both infrared and frequency hopping as technologies for implementing WLANs. (Later standards are covered in later chapters.)

■ The 802.11 standard uses a medium access method known as the distributed coordination function (DCF). DCF specifies that a modified procedure known as carrier sense, multiple access with collision avoidance (CSMA/CA) be used. CSMA/CA attempts to avoid collisions. The CSMA/CA process ensures that all devices wait until the medium is clear of all other transmissions in an attempt to reduce collisions. CSMA/CA also reduces collisions by using explicit packet acknowledgment (ACK). Although CSMA/CA reduces the potential for collisions, it does not eliminate them altogether. The 802.11 standard provides two other options that may be used to reduce collisions. The first is known as the request-to-send/clear-to-send (RTS/CTS) protocol. RTS/CTS reserves the medium for a single device to transmit. The second option to reduce collisions is fragmentation. Fragmentation involves dividing the data to be transmitted from one large frame into several smaller ones.

■ The MAC layer of the 802.11 standard provides the functionality for a device to join a WLAN. This functionality is known as association and reassociation. Association is the process of communicating with the other wireless devices in ad hoc WLANs or with the AP in order to become accepted as part of the network. To associate with a WLAN, the device first scans the wireless medium and listens for beacons from the APs. There are two types of scanning: passive scanning and active scanning. A device may drop the connection with one AP and reestablish the connection with another, which is known as reassociation.

■ Mobile WLAN devices often depend on batteries as their primary power source. To conserve battery power, they can go into sleep mode after a period of time. Power management, as defined by the 802.11 standard, allows the mobile device to be off as much as possible to conserve battery life but still not miss out on data transmissions by waking up and listening to beacons. The beacon may contain a Traffic Information Map (TIM) that indicates whether there is data waiting at the AP to be transmitted to the device. If so, the device will then remain awake and request the data from the AP.

■ The 802.11 standard specifies three different types of MAC frame formats. Management frames, the first type, are used to set up the initial communications between a device and the AP. Control frames, the second type, provide assistance in delivering the frames that contain the data. Data frames, the third type, carry user the information to be transmitted. The 802.11 standard also defines two different types of interframe spaces (IFS), or time gaps, which are standard spacing intervals between the transmissions of frames. Instead of being just dead space, these time gaps are used to allow enough time for a device to finish receiving transmissions, checking for errors, and sending an ACK. They form part of DCF to help prevent collisions.

- In 1999, IEEE approved the 802.11b standard. IEEE 802.11b added two higher speeds, 5.5 and 11 Mbps, to the original 802.11 standard. With the faster data rates, the 802.11b quickly became the standard for WLANs.

- The physical layer convergence procedure (PLCP) for 802.11b is exclusively based on RF and direct sequence spread spectrum (DSSS). The PLCP must reformat the data received from the MAC layer (when transmitting) into a frame that the PMD sublayer can transmit. The frame is made up of three parts, which are the preamble, the header, and the data. The 802.11b standard uses the 2.4 GHz Industrial, Scientific, and Medical (ISM) band for its transmissions and can transmit data at 11, 5.5, 2, or 1 Mbps.

Key Terms

802.11 standard An IEEE standard released in 1997 that defines wireless local area networks at a rate of either 1 or 2 Mbps. All WLAN features are confined to the PHY and MAC layers. This is the original IEEE standard for WLANs and the basis for later 802.11b, a, g, n, and ac/ad amendments.

802.11b An amendment to the IEEE 802.11 standard for WLANs that added two higher speeds, 5.5 and 11 Mbps, and is also known as Wi-Fi, a name given by the Wi-Fi Alliance to technology that has been certified for interoperability with equipment from different manufacturers.

acknowledgment (ACK) A procedure used to reduce collisions by requiring the receiving station to send an explicit packet back to the sending station, provided that the received transmission had no errors.

active scanning The process of sending frames to gather information.

ad hoc mode A WLAN mode in which wireless devices communicate directly among themselves without going through an AP.

associate request frame A frame sent by a device to an AP that contains the device's capabilities and supported rates.

associate response frame A frame returned to a device from the AP that contains a status code and device ID number.

association The process for a device to join a Basic Service Set (BSS) or Independent Basic Service Set (IBSS).

Basic Service Set (BSS) A WLAN mode that consists of at least one wireless device and one AP. *Also called* infrastructure mode.

BSSID In an infrastructure WLAN, the BSSID is the MAC address of the AP. In a peer-to-peer network, the BSSID is the MAC address of the first station to be turned on and configured to establish the ad hoc WLAN.

buffering The process that the AP uses to temporarily store frames for devices that are in sleep mode.

channel access methods The different ways of sharing resources in a network environment.

collision   The scrambling of data that occurs when two computers start sending messages at the same time in a shared medium.

Complementary Code Keying (CCK)   A table containing 64 8-bit code words used for transmitting at speeds above 2 Mbps. This table of codes is used instead of the process of adding a Barker code to the bit to be transmitted.

control frame   MAC frame that assists in delivering the frames that contain data.

data frame   MAC frame that carries the user information to be transmitted to a device.

disassociate frame   A frame sent by the new AP to the old AP in an ESS to terminate the old AP's association with a device. Disassociation frames are transmitted from one AP to another over the wired network only, not via the wireless medium.

distributed coordination function (DCF)   The default channel access method in IEEE 802.11 WLANs, designed to avoid collisions and grant all devices on the WLAN a reasonably equal chance to transmit on the selected channel.

DCF Interframe Space (DIFS)   The standard interval between the transmission of data frames.

dynamic rate selection (DRS)   A function of an AP that allows it to automatically select the highest transmission speed based on the strength and quality of the signal received from a device WNIC.

exabytes   One exabyte is equal to a one followed by 18 zeroes or 1 billion GB (1,000,000,000,000,000,000).

Extended Service Set (ESS)   A WLAN mode that consists of wireless devices and multiple APs using the same SSID, extending a WLAN seamlessly beyond the maximum range of an 802.11 transmission.

fragmentation   The division of data to be transmitted from one large frame into several smaller frames.

handoff   In an ESS, when a WLAN device reassociates with an AP on the network and disassociates with the one to which it was previously connected.

Independent Basic Service Set (IBSS)   A WLAN mode in which wireless devices communicate directly among themselves without using an AP. *Also called* ad hoc mode and peer-to-peer mode.

infrastructure mode   *See* Basic Service Set.

interframe spaces (IFS)   Time gaps used in CSMA/CA to allow devices to finish receiving a transmission and checking for errors before any other device is allowed to transmit.

management frame   MAC frame that is used, for example, to set up the initial communications between a device and the AP.

Mini PCI   A small card that is functionally equivalent to a standard PCI expansion card used for integrating communications peripherals onto a laptop computer but that is much smaller.

null data frame   The response that a device sends back to the AP to indicate that the device has no transmissions to make in PCF.

passive scanning   The process of listening to each available channel for a set period of time.

peer-to-peer mode   *See* ad hoc mode.

point coordination function (PCF)   The 802.11 optional polling function.

polling   A channel access method in which each computer is asked in sequence whether it wants to transmit.

power management   An 802.11 standard that allows the mobile device to be off as much as possible to conserve battery life but still not miss out on data transmissions.

power over Ethernet (PoE)   A technology that provides power over an Ethernet cable.

probe   A frame sent by a device when performing active scanning.

probe response   A frame sent by an AP when responding to a device's active scanning probe.

reassociate request frame   A frame sent from a device to a new AP asking whether it can associate with the AP.

reassociate response frame   A frame sent by an AP to a station indicating that it will accept its reassociation with that AP.

reassociation   The process of a device disconnecting from one AP and reestablishing a connection with another AP.

request-to-send/clear-to-send (RTS/CTS)   An 802.11 protocol option that allows a station to reserve the network for transmissions.

Service Set Identifier (SSID)   A unique network identifier assigned to an AP during configuration. In an Extended Service Set (ESS), all APs will be configured with the same SSID.

Short Interframe Space (SIFS)   A time period used to allow a receiving station to finish receiving all signals, decode them, and check for errors.

sleep mode   A power-conserving mode used by portable, battery-powered devices in a WLAN.

subnets   Subsets of a large network that use a different group of IP addresses belonging to the same domain IP address. Subnets are separated from other subnets by routers.

time slots   The measurement unit in a PLCP frame.

traffic indication map (TIM)   A list of the stations that have buffered frames waiting at the AP. The TIM is sent in the beacons by the AP.

war driving   The practice of discovering and recording information about WLANs in a neighborhood or around a city while driving or walking.

Wi-Fi   A trademark of the Wi-Fi Alliance, used to refer to 802.11b and later WLANs that pass the organization's interoperability tests.

Wi-Fi Direct   A feature defined by the Wi-Fi Alliance that enables a computer or other wireless device to act as an AP and share an Internet connection in an ad hoc WLAN.

wireless site survey   A test that is conducted before deployment of a WLAN to determine the best location for APs and antennas, in order to provide maximum coverage.

Review Questions

1. A wireless NIC performs the same functions as a wired NIC except that it _____ .

   a.   does not transmit the packet

   b.   uses an antenna instead of a wired connection

   c.   contains special memory

   d.   does not use parallel transmission

2. Some vendors have already integrated the components of a wireless NIC directly onto the laptop's _____ .

   a. motherboard

   b. floppy drive

   c. hard drive

   d. CD-ROM drive

3. Which of the following is not a function of an AP?

   a. Sends and receives RF signals

   b. Connects to the wired network

   c. Serves as a router

   d. Acts as a bridge between the wired and wireless networks

4. The range of an AP acting as the base station in a 2.4-GHz WLAN is approximately _____ .

   a. 573 feet (175 meters)

   b. 375 feet (114 meters)

   c. 750 feet (229 meters)

   d. 735 feet (224 meters)

5. The highest data transmission rate for an RF WLAN, as specified in the 1997 IEEE 802.11 standard, is about _____ Mbps.

   a. 22

   b. 1

   c. 2

   d. 54

6. The IEEE 802.11b standard that outlines the specifications for RF WLANs is based on _____ .

   a. FHSS

   b. DSSS

   c. infrared

   d. OFDM

7. Power over Ethernet delivers power to an AP through the same wires used for data in a standard unshielded twisted pair (UTP) Ethernet cable. True or False?

8. In ad hoc mode, the wireless devices communicate directly with the AP. True or False?

9. An Extended Service Set (ESS) consists of two or more BSSs. True or False?

10. On a regular basis, wireless devices will scan all the radio frequencies to determine if a different AP can provide better service. True or False?

11. Network managers like to subdivide large networks into smaller units known as subnets because this makes it easier to manage the entire network. True or False?

12. The IEEE _____ standard defines a local area network that provides cable-free data access at a rate of up to 2 Mbps for devices that are either mobile or in a fixed location.

    a. 802.3

    b. 802.21

    c. 802.11

    d. 802.3.1

13. Because all the IEEE WLAN features are isolated in the PHY and _____ layers, practically any LAN application will run on a WLAN without any modification.

    a. MAC

    b. network

    c. PLCP

    d. PMD

14. The Physical Layer Convergence Procedure (PLCP) for 802.11b are based only on _____ spread spectrum.

    a. frequency hopping

    b. QAM

    c. direct sequence

    d. BPSK

15. A PLCP frame is made up of three parts, which are the preamble, the header, and the _____ .

    a. error correction

    b. CRC

    c. SIFS

    d. data

16. The PLCP frame preamble is always transmitted at _____ Mbps in a network that supports backwards compatibility.

    a. 2

    b. 5.5

    c. 1

    d. 11

17. The method used in IEEE 802.11 to implement CSMA/CA is based on _____.

    a. DSSS

    b. DCF

    c. FHSS

    d. PCF

18. IEEE 802.11 operates in _____ mode, and each frame must be acknowledged.

    a. ACK

    b. FDMA

    c. half-duplex

    d. full-duplex

19. If the AP does not send the SSID of the WLAN in the beacon, devices can still obtain the SSID by _____.

    a. sending an associate request frame

    b. transmitting an SSID request frame

    c. sending a probe frame

    d. transmitting a special data frame

20. In PCF, the devices cannot transmit unless _____.

    a. the WLAN is operating in peer-to-peer mode

    b. the AP sends an ACK frame

    c. the AP sends data first

    d. the device is "polled" by the AP

Hands-On Projects

These Project assumes you are using Windows 7. Instructions for using Windows 10 are included in Appendix A.

Project 6-1

In this project, you will configure a wireless network connection in Microsoft Windows 7. As usual, there is more than one way to accomplish this task. Windows 7 provides a built-in tool called WLAN AutoConfig, which is designed to make it much simpler for the average computer user to connect to a wireless network. WLAN AutoConfig can be used to connect to WLANs in most homes, offices, hotspots, as well as hotels. The procedure presented in this project is generic and can be used regardless of the type or make of computer you have, provided that you are running the Windows 7 operating system. Setting up a connection to an Enterprise network, which typically uses a separate authentication server, is more complex and will not be covered in this exercise.

Manufacturers almost always provide WLAN utilities with their hardware, and in Windows you can choose to configure a WLAN with either the WLAN AutoConfig tool or the WLAN NIC manufacturer's utility. The manufacturer's utility often has additional features, but it can be more complex to use. For this project, you will be configuring an ad hoc WLAN. You will need two computers equipped with wireless NICs.

1. Log in to both computers as administrator or to an account with administrator privileges. Windows will not allow you to complete any of the following steps unless you are the system administrator or your account has administrator privileges.

2. Click the Windows **Start** button on the lower-left corner of the Windows taskbar, and then click **Control Panel** on the right-hand side of the Start menu.

3. In Control Panel, search for and click **Network and Sharing Center**.

4. When you set up an ad hoc network, your computer is not connected to a router or DHCP server that can provide you with an IP address. Because of this, you will need to configure a static IP address. You will also not have access to the Internet, only to shared files on the other computer(s) connected to the same ad hoc WLAN.

5. Once you have configured unique IP addresses on the WLAN NIC of each computer, return to the Network and Sharing Center window. Click **Manage wireless networks** on the menu in the left column of the window. If you have WLAN connections already configured and your NIC is enabled, you will see a list like the one shown in Figure 6-17.

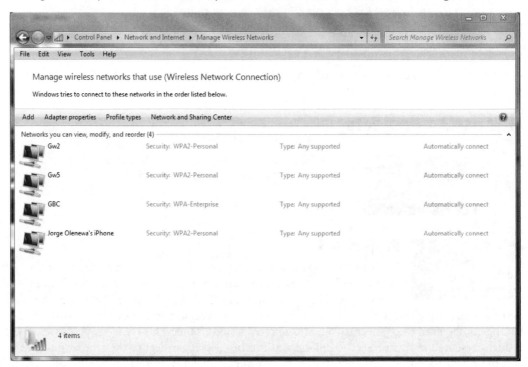

Figure 6-17 Managing wireless networks in Windows 7

6. Click **Add** in the toolbar above the network list area, then click **Create an ad hoc network** in the pop-up window.

7. Read the information on the "Setup a wireless ad hoc network" window that opens, then click **Next**. Type a unique name for this network, one that is not being used by any other students working on this project at the same time. Remember that the network name is the SSID of the network and is case sensitive.

8. Under Security type, click the drop-down box and select **No authentication (Open)**.

9. Click the check box next to **Save this network**, then click **Next**. Check the parameters of your network, then click the **Close** button. You should now see your network at the top of the list in the "Manage wireless networks" window. On the right-hand side of the ad hoc network entry you just created, you will see that the network is configured to "Manually connect." Perform the same steps on the other computer(s) you want to connect to your ad hoc WLAN.

10. If your ad hoc WLAN appeared at the top of the list in Step 9, once you finish configuring the second computer, they should connect automatically. To check this, click the Windows network icon located on the far right-hand side of your Windows taskbar. (If your taskbar is located at either side of your computer screen, the icon will appear at the bottom.) This is shown in Figure 6-18.

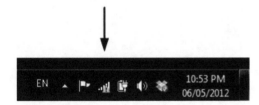

Figure 6-18 Windows network icon (indicated by arrow)

11. You will see a list of the networks available. Your ad hoc network name should be at the top of the list, and it should say "Connected." If it is not connected, click the ad hoc network entry and click the **Connect** button. The connected ad hoc network should look similar to the one highlighted by the ellipse in Figure 6-19, but with your own SSID.

Figure 6-19   Configuring Bluetooth settings

12. To test the connection to the other computer, click the Windows **Start** button on the left-hand side of the taskbar and type **cmd** in the "Search programs and files" text box to open a command window. At the command prompt, type **ping** and the IP address of the WLAN NIC of the other computer you are using for this project, then press **Enter**. You should receive three or four successful ping replies from the other computer, as shown in Figure 6-20. (Remember that your IP addresses must be unique and may be different than the one shown in the figure.)

```
C:\Users\jolenewa>ping 192.168.1.12

Pinging 192.168.1.12 with 32 bytes of data:
Reply from 192.168.1.12: bytes=32 time=1ms TTL=64
Reply from 192.168.1.12: bytes=32 time=1ms TTL=64
Reply from 192.168.1.12: bytes=32 time=1ms TTL=64
Reply from 192.168.1.12: bytes=32 time=3ms TTL=64

Ping statistics for 192.168.1.12:
    Packets: Sent = 4, Received = 4, Lost = 0 (0% loss),
Approximate round trip times in milli-seconds:
    Minimum = 1ms, Maximum = 3ms, Average = 1ms
```

Figure 6-20   Pinging another wireless device from the Windows 7 command line

13. Be sure to return the IP address settings to **Obtain an IP address automatically** and delete the ad hoc entry you just created from the "Manage wireless networks" window.

Project 6-2

In this project, you will manually configure a wireless residential gateway, which is more commonly known as a wireless router or broadband router, to create a WLAN. The device used in this project is a Linksys WRT54G, but you can use any model available to you and adapt the following instructions. The settings you will configure are very similar among different manufacturers' products, and even when different names are used for the parameters, they are usually easy to figure out. Remember that a wireless residential gateway includes an AP, a router, firewall, and a network switch, and in some cases it also includes a built-in DSL or cable modem.

1. Obtain a wireless residential gateway from your instructor, or you can use your own.

2. If the device has external antennas, make sure they are positioned vertically; and if they use a screw-in connector, make sure the antennas are finger-tight and do not fall to the horizontal position again. Never turn on a wireless device equipped with external antennas without first having them connected and tightened up. The absence of a proper load at the output of the transmitter can damage the circuit. In addition, despite the very low power levels of most WLAN devices, you are strongly advised to never touch the antennas when the device is turned on as this may represent a health risk.

3. Connect an RJ-45 Ethernet crossover patch cable to one of the switch ports in the back of the device. Note that one port is separated from the others and is usually marked "WAN." Do not connect anything to the WAN port. Plug the other end of the cable into an Ethernet port on your computer.

4. Plug in the power adapter and connect it to the back of your AP or broadband router.

5. Make sure the Ethernet adapter on your computer is configured to obtain an IP address automatically.

6. Open a web browser. In the address line, type **http://192.168.1.1** for a Linksys device. Other manufacturers' devices may use a different address. Consult the manual or download it from the Internet for the device you have.

7. At the login prompt, leave the user name blank and type **admin** in the password field. The Linksys setup page will appear. For this project, you will not use an Internet

connection. You can leave all the fields in the main Setup page in their default settings (see Figure 6-21).

Figure 6-21   Linksys WRT54G main setup page

Source: Linksys

8. Click the Wireless tab to display the wireless setup page.

If you are setting up more than one Linksys AP or wireless router in the same or an adjacent lab or classroom, make sure you select a different channel for each of the devices. Recall that to avoid interference, you can only use channels 1, 6, and 11.

9. Leave "Mode" as Mixed. Change the SSID to the same one you used in Project 6-1. Click **Save Settings**. A page should appear indicating that your settings are successful. Click **Continue** and you will be returned to the Wireless setup page (see Figure 6-22).

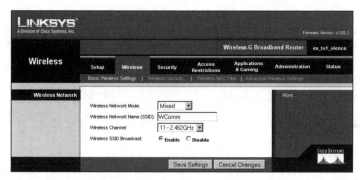

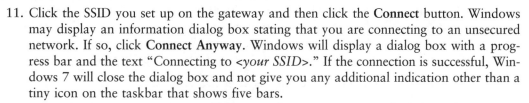

Figure 6-22   Wireless setup page on the Linksys WRT54G

Source: Linksys

10. On the computer, click the network icon on the right-hand side of the taskbar to view the wireless networks detected.

11. Click the SSID you set up on the gateway and then click the **Connect** button. Windows may display an information dialog box stating that you are connecting to an unsecured network. If so, click **Connect Anyway**. Windows will display a dialog box with a progress bar and the text "Connecting to *<your SSID>*." If the connection is successful, Windows 7 will close the dialog box and not give you any additional indication other than a tiny icon on the taskbar that shows five bars.

12. You can verify the connection using the same procedures described in Steps 11 and 12 of Project 6-1.

Real-World Exercises

Exercise 6-1

A hotspot is a public place—such as a train, bus station, coffee shop, or restaurant—that offers (usually) free Internet access to its customers. Using the Internet, search for hotspots by accessing the websites for various nationwide cellular phone companies, such as AT&T or Sprint. Alternatively, you can search the local media websites and local Internet service provider (ISP) sites. If you have access to a laptop computer, wireless-enabled smartphone, or tablet computer, and it is equipped with a WLAN interface, once you locate a hotspot, try to visit the site and get a connection to the Internet. If you do not have access to the Internet, but you can either telephone the provider or visit the hotspot location, interview the staff at the location and write a one-page report describing how the wireless access is provided. What steps did you have to go through to get a connection? For how long was the connection available? Was there a cost associated with accessing the Internet? How many people use the service daily? Were there any limitations? Who provides technical support for the site?

Exercise 6-2

Using the Internet, research wireless LAN applications. Compile a list of at least five WLAN applications that you had not thought about before, and write a one-paragraph description for each one. The paragraph should mention the challenges that you might face if you were asked to provide support for such an implementation. If possible, contact users of the new application and ask them about their particular experiences with the WLAN implementation. Add this information to your report.

Challenge Case Project

How do you measure a wireless network's performance? In this project, you will test your network and determine its speed of data transfer. Keep in mind, though, that most wireless networks communicate in half-duplex mode, so the data rate reported by the operating system does not reflect the maximum data rate the network is capable of.

There are many network performance-testing tools available on the web. One of the most popular is QCheck from *www.ixiacom.com*. You may be able to find others by opening your favorite browser and, using the search engine of your choice, typing in the question "How do you measure a wireless network's throughput?" Browse the results that appear, then download and install a free or trial version of one or more network-testing tools. Run as many of the following tests as possible, using Wi-Fi-enabled devices that are available to you, while copying a large file (over 10 MB) from one device to another:

- Create and test an ad hoc link between two devices.
- Test from a wired to a wireless device, and vice versa.
- Test with more than one pair of devices transmitting via the same AP.
- Run the tests in both directions.
- Try to test with both a clear channel and one that is already in use in the same area.

You can use Acrylic Wi-Fi Home from *www.acrylicwifi.com* to view available channels and signal strength.

Carefully record your results for each test, then write a one-page report detailing each of the results, the tools and devices you used, and your conclusions.

chapter 7

Enhancing WLAN Performance

After reading this chapter and completing the exercises, you will be able to:

- Explain how IEEE 802.11g enhances 802.11b networks
- Outline how IEEE 802.11a works and how it differs from 802.11 networks
- Discuss IEEE 802.11n and how it functions in both the 2.4 GHz and 5 GHz bands
- Describe the IEEE 802.11ac and 802.11ad amendments
- List other important current and future amendments to 802.11

Faster data rates and increased reliability have made 802.11 WLANs very competitive with wired networks, and corporations continue to deploy WLANs as a viable alternative to Ethernet. In terms of speed, WLANs have come a long way since the original IEEE 802.11 WLAN standard, established in 1997, offered speeds of only 1 and 2 Mbps. Today's WLANs can operate at data rates of 1 Gbps and higher.

At about the same time as the IEEE ratified 802.11b, they also released another specification for WLANs operating in the 5 GHz unlicensed national information infrastructure or U-NII band and could operate at up to 54 Mbps. These WLANs quickly became very attractive to users because the speed of transmission represented a significant increase over that of 802.11b systems. In addition, wider bandwidth available in U-NII meant that 802.11a offered an additional five channels, which gave it a clear advantage over the three usable channel limit of 802.11b, for ESS deployments.

IEEE 802.11g

The main drivers for the development of the IEEE 802.11g standard were the demand for higher Internet access speeds and the significantly higher throughput of wired networks. This amendment was published in June 2003. IEEE 802.11g operates in the same 2.4 GHz ISM frequency band as 802.11b, but supports data transmission rates of 6, 9, 12, 18, 24, 36, and 54 Mbps in addition to the 802.11b rates of 1, 2, 5.5, and 11 Mbps. This **802.11g** amendment is called **Extended Rate PHY (ERP)** in the standard.

 The IEEE 802.11b amendment is called High-Rate (HR).

802.11g PHY Layer

The PHY layer for 802.11g introduced a transmission technology called **orthogonal frequency division multiplexing (OFDM)** to the 802.11 standard. Instead of serializing the data and modulating bits onto a single carrier using DSSS or CCK as in 802.11 or 802.11b, respectively, OFDM divides 20 MHz of bandwidth in each of the three usable channels in the ISM band into 52 subcarriers and modulates the bits of data onto 48 of them, then transmits multiple bits and multiple copies of the same data at the same time at a slower data rate than 802.11 or 802.11b. The extra four carriers are used to monitor the strength and quality of the RF signal. The subcarriers are orthogonal to the adjacent subcarriers (on both sides), meaning that the bandwidth used by each of them overlaps as shown in Figure 7-1. When frequency channels overlap like this in the frequency domain, they do not interfere with each other.

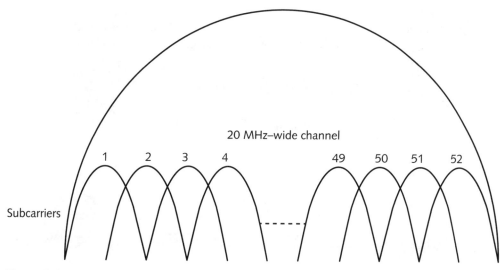

Figure 7-1   Subcarriers in a 20-MHz channel (OFDM)

   A full discussion of OFDM and why orthogonal frequencies do not interfere with each other is an advanced topic that is beyond the scope of this text.

In Chapter 3, you learned about multipath distortion, which occurs when the receiving device gets the same signal from several different directions at different times, due to signal reflections, diffraction, or scattering. Even though the receiving device may have already received the complete transmission, it must still wait until all reflections are received. If the receiver does not wait until all reflections are received, some of the signals that arrive later may spread into the next transmission because the reflected signals traveled a longer path and, as a result, have been delayed. This type of problem is called **intersymbol interference (ISI)**. Using more complex modulation schemes that increase data transmission speed through having more bits modulated onto each signal change—that is, making the transmission denser—tends to make multipath distortion worse and force the receiver to wait even longer before it gets the reflected signals. The required waiting time effectively puts a limit on the overall speed of the WLAN.

OFDM avoids problems caused by multipath distortion by sending the bits slowly enough that any delayed copies (multipath reflections) are late by a much smaller amount of time than those sent in 802.11b transmissions. This means that the network does not have to wait as long for the reflections to arrive at the receiver, thus the total throughput is actually increased. With OFDM, in other words, the total amount of data sent in parallel over a given unit of time is greater and the time spent waiting for reflections to arrive is less than with a single-carrier transmission. A comparison between the two systems is shown in Figure 7-2.

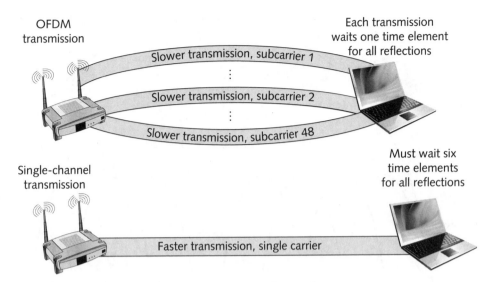

Figure 7-2 Comparison of OFDM and single-carrier transmission

Although the slower data transmission rate in OFDM may appear counterintuitive, the fact that multiple bits of data are being transmitted at the same time in parallel means that 802.11g is able to achieve nearly five times the data rate of 802.11b. These transmissions also use simpler modulation methods that are easier for the receivers to detect and decode.

Transmission Modes

The 802.11g amendment specifies two mandatory transmission modes along with two optional modes. The first mandatory transmission mode is the same one used by 802.11 and 802.11b; it supports data rates of 1, 2, 5.5, and 11 Mbps. The second mandatory transmission mode uses OFDM and supports 802.11g only.

Optional modes do not have to be implemented in a device, but will usually be tested for compatibility by the Wi-Fi Alliance, if they are implemented. The first optional transmission mode uses **PBCC (packet binary convolutional coding)** to transmit at either 22 or 33 Mbps. To transmit at 22 Mbps, PBCC is essentially a more complex version of CCK used in 802.11b that changes the modulation from QPSK to 8PSK and is optimized to increase the signal-to-noise ratio of the channel by 3 dB. To achieve the data rate of 33 Mbps using PBCC, the 802.11g standard specifies a change in the clock rate used to transmit the chips from 11 to 16.5 MHz. The preamble is transmitted with an 11-MHz clock (at 1 or 2 Mbps), and the change is accomplished in a 1-microsecond-long clock switch section of the PLCP frame, as shown in Figure 7-3.

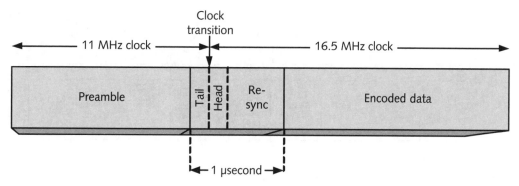

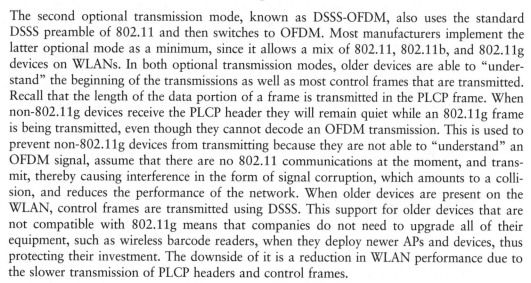

Figure 7-3 Clock switching during transition from 22 to 33 Mbps (PBCC)

The tail is 3 clock cycles at 11 Mchip/s, and the head is 3 clock cycles at 16.5 Msymbols/s (QPSK). The resync is 9 clock cycles at 16.5 Msymbols/s. The tail bits are 1 1 1, the head bits are 0 0 0, and the resync bits are 1 0 0 0 1 1 1 0 1. The modulation used for transmission at 22 or 33 Mbps is binary phase shift keying (BPSK), which you learned about in Chapter 2. PBCC was an effort by some chip manufacturers to increase the performance of 802.11b before the ratification of the 802.11g amendment.

The second optional transmission mode, known as DSSS-OFDM, also uses the standard DSSS preamble of 802.11 and then switches to OFDM. Most manufacturers implement the latter optional mode as a minimum, since it allows a mix of 802.11, 802.11b, and 802.11g devices on WLANs. In both optional transmission modes, older devices are able to "understand" the beginning of the transmissions as well as most control frames that are transmitted. Recall that the length of the data portion of a frame is transmitted in the PLCP frame. When non-802.11g devices receive the PLCP header they will remain quiet while an 802.11g frame is being transmitted, even though they cannot decode an OFDM transmission. This is used to prevent non-802.11g devices from transmitting because they are not able to "understand" an OFDM signal, assume that there are no 802.11 communications at the moment, and transmit, thereby causing interference in the form of signal corruption, which amounts to a collision, and reduces the performance of the network. When older devices are present on the WLAN, control frames are transmitted using DSSS. This support for older devices that are not compatible with 802.11g means that companies do not need to upgrade all of their equipment, such as wireless barcode readers, when they deploy newer APs and devices, thus protecting their investment. The downside of it is a reduction in WLAN performance due to the slower transmission of PLCP headers and control frames.

Another important change incorporated at the PHY layer of 802.11g to allow compatibility with legacy devices is related to signal timing. First, 802.11g specifies that any time a device is transmitting at a higher rate than 802.11b, a 6-microsecond quiet time (no transmission) is included at the end of every frame to allow additional processing time for all the reflected signals to arrive at the receiver and for the receiver to decode the data, but this also decreases the performance of the WLAN. This has the effect of increasing the Short Interframe Space (SIFS) duration from 10 to 16 microseconds. The PLCP frame format for 802.11g, used when supporting 802.11 and 802.11b devices, is shown in Figure 7-4. The PLCP frame format used in 802.11g is essentially the same as for 802.11b, with the exception of the added 6-microsecond quiet time at the end.

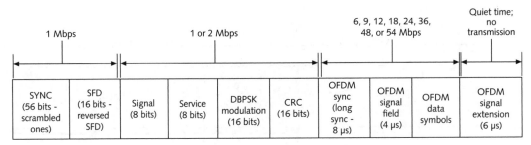

Figure 7-4   802.11g PLCP frame

802.11g MAC Layer

There is a significant performance penalty for 802.11g WLANs operating in mixed mode (with 802.11 or 802.11b legacy devices) because every PLCP header is transmitted at 1 Mbps. The 802.11g amendment includes a change to the MAC layer for compatible devices to slightly increase performance in this case by transmitting the entire PLCP frame using OFDM, while still preventing collisions. To accomplish this, some changes were incorporated in MAC layer. Devices wanting to transmit in 802.11g can ensure the medium is free, and then send a special control frame called CTS-to-Self using DSSS. A **CTS-to-Self** frame is transmitted with a destination MAC address of the same station that is transmitting the frame. Its purpose is to act as a **protection mechanism** notifying legacy devices (802.11 and 802.11b) to not attempt to "understand" or transmit during the entire frame exchange that follows. The issue is that legacy devices cannot decode OFDM frames, so while they may detect EM energy in the medium, they may attempt to transmit anyway and cause a collision due to corruption. After transmitting a CTS-to-Self, 802.11g devices can then complete the entire frame exchange using only OFDM.

To be fully compliant with the 802.11g amendment and 802.11a (discussed in the next topic), devices must be able to transmit at 6, 9, 12, 18, and 24 Mbps. Data rates of 36, 48, and 54 Mbps are not required for compliance with the IEEE standard.

Note that when the network is supporting only 802.11g devices, a setting that can be configured in APs and residential wireless routers, the standard allows each time slot to be reduced to 9 microseconds instead of 20 microseconds, which improves the performance of the 802.11g WLAN significantly.

IEEE 802.11a

The IEEE ratified and released 802.11b and 802.11a at roughly the same time in 1999. 802.11a products came to the market later because of technical issues and, at least initially, the high cost of implementation.

The **802.11a** standard maintains the same medium access control (MAC) layer frame formats as 802.11g WLANs, with practically all differences confined to the Physical layer. It achieves its increase in speed and flexibility over 802.11b through the use of OFDM and through a more efficient error-correction scheme than 802.11b. The major difference is that, unlike 802.11b and 802.11g, 802.11a works in the 5 GHz U-NII band only.

NOTE This book refers to the amendments to the standards by the lower-case letter appended to the end of the standard number (e.g., IEEE 802.11n). Every few years, the IEEE incorporates the content of several amendments into one document, publishes a new standard document and appends the year in which the work was completed (e.g., IEEE 802.11-2009, which includes the 802.11n amendment), but it is still important to know and be able to refer to each amendment, since some of them are optional in the published versions of the standard and are not implemented in every wireless NIC used in APs or devices.

U-NII Frequency Band

Recall that the 802.11b standard uses one part of the unlicensed Industrial, Scientific, and Medical (ISM) band for its transmissions and specifies 14 frequency channels that can be used. The U-NII band is intended for devices that provide short-range, high-speed wireless digital communications. Table 7-1 compares ISM and U-NII bands used in WLANs. Note that part of the ISM band overlaps with U-NII in a portion of the 5 GHz spectrum. In the ISM band these frequencies are not used for WLANs, but can cause interference. An example of this is 5 GHz cordless phones, some of which are still in use.

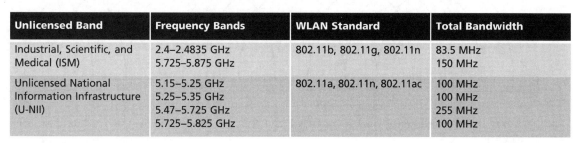

Unlicensed Band	Frequency Bands	WLAN Standard	Total Bandwidth
Industrial, Scientific, and Medical (ISM)	2.4–2.4835 GHz 5.725–5.875 GHz	802.11b, 802.11g, 802.11n	83.5 MHz 150 MHz
Unlicensed National Information Infrastructure (U-NII)	5.15–5.25 GHz 5.25–5.35 GHz 5.47–5.725 GHz 5.725–5.825 GHz	802.11a, 802.11n, 802.11ac	100 MHz 100 MHz 255 MHz 100 MHz

Table 7-1 ISM vs. U-NII

The U.S. Federal Communications Commission (FCC) has segmented the total 555 MHz of the U-NII spectrum into four bands. Each band has maximum power limits.

NOTE Usable frequencies, channels, and power limits in the U-NII band have changed significantly over the years, vary among different countries around the world, and may continue to change. The best way to stay up to date is to search the web for this information, looking for a link to your country's regulatory agency that provides this information. One example of this is that in 2008, the IEEE ratified the 802.11y amendment, which extended operation of 802.11a to the licensed 3.7 GHz band. This band offers increased power limits, which allows transmissions to achieve a maximum range of up to 16,400 feet (5,000 meters), but an FCC license is required to use it.

Although the U-NII band is segmented, the total bandwidth available for IEEE 802.11a WLANs using U-NII is almost seven times that which is available for 802.11b. The ISM band offers only 83.5 MHz of spectrum in the 2.4-GHz range, whereas the U-NII band offers 555 MHz.

Channel Allocation in 802.11a

The larger number of channels available is another reason for the better performance of 802.11a. Figure 7-5 shows a comparison of channel allocation with 802.11b/g and 802.11a.

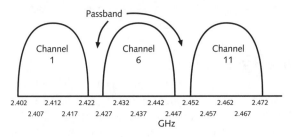

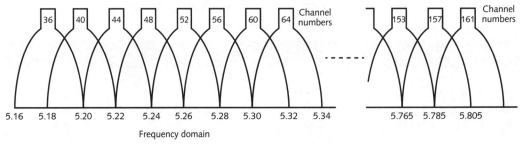

Figure 7-5   Comparison of usable channels in 2.4 GHz ISM band (802.11b/g) and 5 GHz U-NII band (802.11a)

In some countries, 802.11a has a total of 23 channels available. Each frequency channel is 20 MHz wide, and for 802.11a, as in 802.11g, each channel is divided into 52 subcarrier frequencies, with each subcarrier being 300 KHz. This is shown in Figure 7-6.

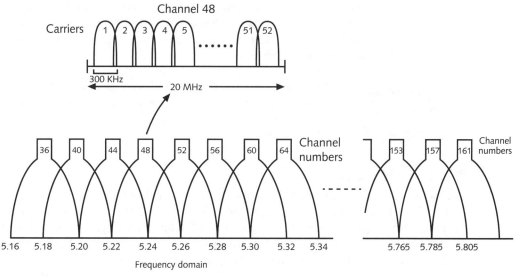

Figure 7-6 Dividing each U-NII channel into 52 subcarriers (802.11a)

 The channel numbers in the 5 GHz band are the result of a mathematical formula, whereas in the 2.4 GHz band, channel numbers 1 to 14 are arbitrarily assigned.

With only three channels available in the ISM band, it follows that a maximum of three APs can be installed within a radius of roughly 300 feet. Using 802.11g APs, for example, this would provide a maximum data throughput of only 162 Mbps (54 Mbps × 3) spread evenly across the three APs. Because there are more available channels than in the ISM band, additional APs can be installed in the same physical space, so more users can be supported simultaneously. A comparison of co-locating three APs in 802.11b versus co-locating, for example, eight APs in 802.11a is shown in Figure 7-7.

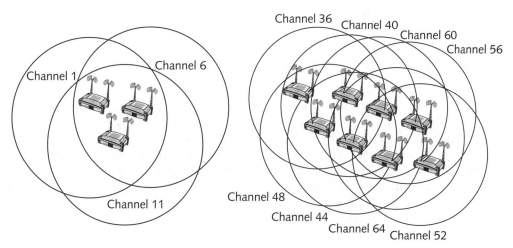

Figure 7-7 Co-locating APs in 802.11b/g vs. 802.11a (using only 8 of 23 channels)

This makes it easier to balance the user load per AP and increases WLAN performance as a result. Another advantage of having more channels available is that if a nearby WLAN is using the same channel as you are, you have more options and can set your AP to use a different channel to eliminate the interference.

OFDM is also the technology used for consumer-based digital subscriber line (DSL) service, which can provide Internet access over standard telephone lines at speeds ranging from 256 Kbps to over 100 Mbps in some areas.

802.11a PHY Layer

The modulation techniques used to encode the data vary depending on the speed. At 6 Mbps, binary phase shift keying (BPSK) is used (see Chapter 2). BPSK can encode 125 Kbps of data per each of the 48 subcarriers, resulting in a 6,000 Kbps (125 Kbps × 48), or a 6 Mbps data rate. (You may wish to review the waveform shown in Figure 2-28.) Note that this section describes only a few of the transmission rates and modulations used.

Whereas PSK has only two possible changes in the starting point of a wave, allowing 1 bit to be transmitted at a time, quadrature phase shift keying (QPSK) has four possible changes in the starting point of a wave, allowing it to transmit 2 bits per symbol (see Chapter 2), as shown in Figure 7-8. QPSK can double the amount of data encoded over PSK to 250 Kbps per subcarrier, which produces a 12 Mbps (250 Kbps × 48) data rate.

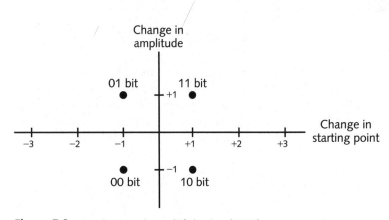

Figure 7-8 Quadrature phase shift keying (QPSK)

Transmitting at 24 Mbps uses 16-level quadrature amplitude modulation (16-QAM). 16-QAM has 16 different signals that can be sent, as shown in Figure 7-9. Each group of bits modulated into one signal change in a carrier is called a symbol. Whereas QPSK transmits 2 bits per symbol, 16-QAM can transmit 4 bits per symbol. For example, to transmit the bits 1110, QPSK would send two symbols, a 11 and then a 10 by changing the phase. 16-QAM would only send one symbol (1110). 16-QAM can encode 500 Kbps per subcarrier for a data rate of 24 Mbps.

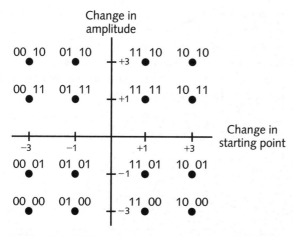

Figure 7-9 16-level quadrature amplitude modulation (16-QAM)

A data rate of 54 Mbps is achieved by using 64-level quadrature amplitude modulation (64-QAM), which can transmit at a rate of 1.125 Mbps over each of the 48 subcarriers (see Figure 7-10).

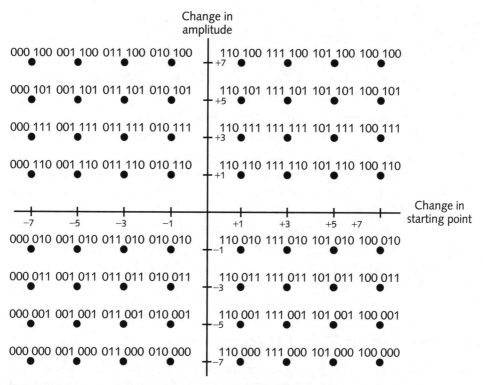

Figure 7-10 64-level quadrature amplitude modulation (64-QAM)

Hardware designers cannot increase the complexity of the modulation on the subcarriers beyond the maximum 54 Mbps rate because of the maximum amount of noise or the minimum signal-to-noise ratio (SNR) allowed, unless they use a more complex modulation. However, that would also make it harder for the receiver to decode the signal and the transmission would be less reliable. As you will see in the section on 802.11n, reliable transmissions at higher speeds requires a wider bandwidth and more subcarriers.

The IEEE made only minor changes to the PCLP frame format in 802.11a, as shown in Figure 7-11.

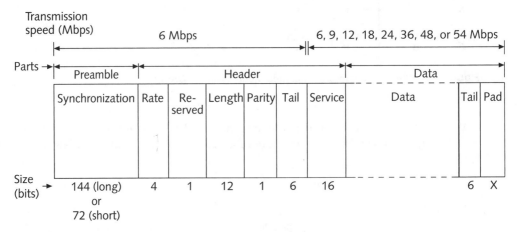

Figure 7-11 802.11a PLCP frame format

The differences between the PLCP frame for 802.11a, as compared to 802.11g, when it is transmitting in 802.11g-only mode, are outlined below.

- *Parity*—This single bit is used to check for errors in the previous fields.
- *Tail (Header portion of the frame)*—Indicates the end of the header. All six bits are set to 0.
- *Service*—The first seven bits are used to initialize part of the transmitter and receiver circuits and are set to 0; the remaining nine bits are reserved for future use and are also set to 0. The Service field is part of the header but is transmitted at the same rate as the Data field.
- *Tail (Data portion of the frame)*—Indicates the end of the Data field. All six bits are set to 0.
- *Pad*—The IEEE standard specifies that the number of bits in the Data field must be a multiple of 48, 96, 192, or 288. If necessary, the length of the Data field may need to be extended with padding bits to match this requirement.

Error Correction in 802.11a/g

IEEE 802.11g and 802.11a also handle errors differently than 802.11b. Because transmissions are sent over parallel subcarriers, interference from other signal sources is minimized. Instead of the interference impacting the entire data stream, it generally affects only one subcarrier. IEEE 802.11a/g uses a technique called forward error correction (FEC), which transmits extra bits per byte of data, in addition to multiple copies of the same data. The extra bits allow the receiver to recover (through sophisticated algorithms) bits that may be lost during the transmission. This can eliminate a lot of retransmissions when errors occur, which saves time and increases the total throughput of the WLAN. A full discussion of FEC is beyond the scope of this book, but it is widely employed in many modern digital communications systems.

The extra bits transmitted when using FEC means that transmission overhead is increased, but because of the higher data transmission rate, 802.11a/g can accommodate the FEC overhead with a negligible impact on WLAN performance.

IEEE 802.11n

As you have realized by now, work on dynamic standards such as those for WLANs has not stopped. User demand for faster and more reliable WLANs suggests that the IEEE will continue to enhance these technologies for the foreseeable future.

The IEEE began working on the **802.11n** amendment in 2004, shortly after the ratification of 802.11g in 2003. By then, it was clear that 54 Mbps was not enough for the 802.11 standard to compete effectively with wired networks. The work on 802.11n became the most widely discussed enhancement to this WLAN technology. A few consumer equipment manufacturers began introducing devices based on the first draft of the standard. Before we continue discussing this technology, it is important for you to understand that 802.11n is an extremely complex topic that could easily fill a book on its own, so this section provides an overview of the differences between 802.11n and the amendments discussed above, but it is not intended to offer complete coverage of 802.11n.

The excitement about this new technology reached a high point when the Wi-Fi Alliance began certifying equipment based on the second draft of the amendment in 2007, roughly 2 years before the members of the IEEE ratified the standard. The 802.11n amendment is called **high throughput (HT)**, and it was finally ratified and published by the IEEE near the end of 2009.

In Chapter 3, you learned about multipath interference and how it can degrade the quality of a signal to the point where the SNR is so low that the data can easily become corrupted and no longer understood by a receiver. HT utilizes a completely new approach to implementing the PHY layer. The 802.11n amendment uses multiple antennas along multiple radios in each device. This allows it to take advantage of multipath interference to actually increase the SNR, which results in an increase in the range and reliability of WLAN transmissions. Additional enhancements to the MAC layer, together with the changes to the PHY layer, help 802.11n achieve data rates that were not possible before.

Although the transmission techniques are somewhat different than those of previous versions of the standard, HT-capable devices are required to maintain backward compatibility with all previous amendments and published versions of 802.11. IEEE 802.11n was also a bit of a compromise, in that it works in both the 2.4 GHz ISM band as well as in the 5 GHz U-NII band. When operating in the U-NII band, it is also required to maintain backward compatibility with 802.11a.

MIMO and Beamforming

Multiple-input and multiple-output (MIMO) technology is based on using multiple radios, both transmitters and receivers, as well as multiple antennas. Until its introduction in 802.11n, most WLAN devices employed a single radio with two antennas and supported a technique called **antenna diversity**. With antenna diversity, the receiver senses which one of its two antennas is getting the strongest signal from the transmitter, and when it sends a response frame—an ACK, for example—it uses the antenna that received the strongest signal.

Instead of antenna diversity, 802.11n MIMO-capable devices use multiple radios, each with its own antenna, and they can employ a technique called **beamforming** to virtually direct a transmission back to the device from which they just received a frame, thus increasing the transmitted signal's range. Beamforming works very much in the same way that phase array antennas work, which you learned about in Chapter 4, by changing the phase of the signal transmitted by different radios to maximize the strength of the signal at the receiver end.

There are several videos available on YouTube that show how beamforming works. A good one from Cisco can be found at this link: *http://youtu.be/8rMtqRObvvU*.

Multiple radios can also increase the throughput. Instead of transmitting a frame via a single radio, 802.11n MIMO-capable devices break up a frame into multiple parts and transmit each part via a different radio. This is called **spatial multiplexing**. At the receiver end, the data is reassembled into a full PHY frame before being passed back to the MAC layer. Figure 7-12 shows a graphical example of this concept. Note how different part of the frames may travel different paths and be detected first by different receiver antennas, which is one of the ways that 802.11n uses to take advantage of multipath and increase the effective range of Wi-Fi signals.

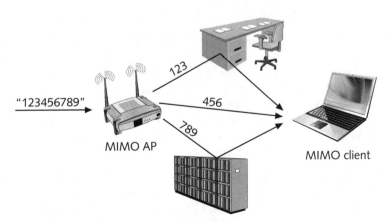

Figure 7-12   Spatial multiplexing with three spatial streams

The 802.11n amendment specifies radio configurations using multiple transmitters and receivers called **radio chains**, using up to four transmitters and four receivers, for a maximum transmission speed of 600 Mbps, or 150 Mbps per radio. No 802.11n equipment has yet been manufactured with four transmitters. Instead, equipment designers waited until the next amendment, discussed later in this chapter, to produce chipsets that support larger radio chains. To pass the Wi-Fi Alliance and be certified as 802.11n compatible, devices must support a minimum of two spatial streams, which is also the only way to achieve a data rate of 150 Mbps.

A 2 × 3 (two-by-three) device has two transmitters and three receivers, whereas a 3 × 3 device has three transmitters and three receivers, and so on. The number of transmitters must always be equal to or higher than the number of spatial streams supported. Consumer-class device specifications seldom list these capabilities in their specifications, on the box or in the user guide. Enterprise-class AP specifications often show how many spatial streams are supported by adding a colon and a digit to the end of the number of transmitters and receivers, such as 2 × 3:2, which means two transmitters and three receivers, and is capable of transmitting two spatial streams, for example.

Figure 7-13 shows examples of 2 × 3 and 3 × 3 MIMO APs. To take advantage of spatial multiplexing, the receiver needs to have the same number of radios as the transmitting device. If, for example, a device is only capable of receiving two streams, the transmitter will only send the maximum number of spatial streams that the receiving device can handle. The more radios a device has, the higher the cost as well as the higher the power consumption. Because of these two factors, practically no manufacturers have implemented devices beyond a 3 × 3 configuration in 802.11n.

2 × 3 MIMO AP

3 × 3 MIMO AP

Figure 7-13   802.11n MIMO APs

Consumer-class residential Wi-Fi routers are often listed as N900, suggesting that it can achieve 900 Mbps. This can be misleading. What it actually means is that this equipment is capable of operating in both the 2.4 and 5 GHz bands and is capable of transmitting at up to 450 Mbps in each band. However, keep in mind that no wireless device, other than the router itself, can transmit or receive in both bands at the same time. The N900 designation means that the device is MIMO-capable, has three transmitters and three receivers for each frequency band, and supports three spatial streams. An N300 device in comparison, has only two transmitters, but may have three receivers, would support up to two spatial streams, and 40 MHz of bandwidth.

Spatial multiplexing and beamforming can be combined to increase both the range and reliability of transmission. Both of these techniques rely on feedback information from the receiver, meaning that any two devices need to be able to somehow evaluate each other's capabilities and wireless medium information, such as signal quality. Information about spatial multiplexing capabilities is usually advertised by devices during association with the WLAN. Beamforming capability can be learned by the devices monitoring the pilot carriers or by an exchange of information using special wireless medium sounding frames. There are two different ways APs can establish a device's capability to support beamforming, which requires multiple radios. Most 802.11n devices either estimate the beamforming from the frames received from a device or infer the capabilities of the devices based on frames that are lost. The amendment also specifies an explicit way of determining a device's capabilities using special frames that devices reply to, and the reply is used by the transmitter to establish what method to use when transmitting data to the device. Explicit beamforming requires that both devices support this capability. Older 802.11a/g devices cannot participate in this type of frame exchange, so most APs determine a device's capabilities only via the implicit method.

Channel Configuration

One of the ways 802.11n is able to achieve higher data rates is by using more bandwidth in both the 2.4 and 5 GHz bands. IEEE 802.11a and 802.11g each consume 20 MHz of bandwidth to transmit using OFDM; 802.11b uses about 22 MHz of bandwidth.

HT radios can support both DSSS and OFDM in the ISM band, which means they can be configured to automatically use 22 or 20 MHz of bandwidth respectively, and support communications with 802.11b and 802.11g devices. However, the higher speeds of up to 300 or 600 Mbps can only be achieved if the radios are configured to utilize 40 MHz of bandwidth. In the ISM 2.4 GHz band, this means that HT will use either channels 1 and 6 or channels 6 and 11, and this can result in excessive interference in channel 6 if more than one AP is in use or if channel 6 is already being used nearby, whether in an office building, a public hotspot network—such as a coffee shop—or in a residential neighborhood.

The kind of interference that happens when two devices are using the same channel on a different BSS is called co-channel interference. Depending on how close the WLANs or the BSSs are, interference on channel 6 may prevent 802.11n devices from achieving their maximum data rates in the ISM band. The only viable solution in this case is to deploy equipment that works in the 5 GHz U-NII band.

When communicating with other HT devices, 802.11n radios divide the frequency space into 56 subcarriers for 20 MHz of bandwidth and use four of them as pilot subcarriers. When using 40-MHz-wide channels and communicating with other 802.11n devices that are also capable of using the wider bandwidth, the radios divide the frequency space into 114 subcarriers and use six of them as pilot subcarriers. In essence, HT combines two 802.11 channels in either the 2.4 or 5 GHz frequency band to allow it to carry more data. Figure 7-14 shows a graphical example of the channel bonding in 802.11n. Note how the channels overlap on channel 6 in the 2.4 GHz band when using 40-MHz-wide channels.

Keep in mind that the only way 802.11n can use 40 MHz channels in the 2.4 GHz band is when there are no other WLANs within range that are either not capable or are also using the wider bandwidth. The amount of interference on channel 6 will force all 802.11n-capable devices to use only 20 MHz and the maximum data rate will therefore be limited to about 150 Mbps.

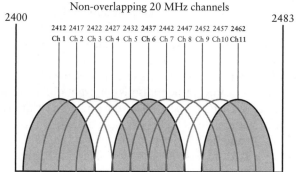

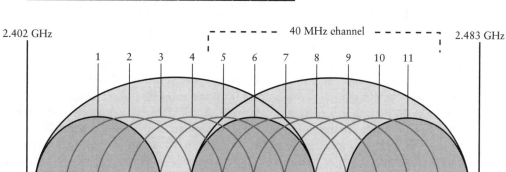

Figure 7-14   Channel bonding in 2.4 GHz 802.11n

Guard Interval As was discussed in the "IEEE 802.11a" section, to transmit digital signals, data is modulated onto a carrier in either single-bit streams or groups of bits called symbols. The more bits that are encoded in each symbol, the higher the data rate. In non-HT transmissions (compatible with 802.11a/g), because of multipath, a certain amount of delay is required at the end of every frame to allow all reflected signals to arrive at the receivers. This is called a **guard interval** (GI), and it prevents a new symbol from arriving at the receiver before the last multipath signal reaches the receiver's antenna, which can cause data corruption. As mentioned earlier, this kind of data corruption is called intersymbol interference (ISI). Although it normally takes a maximum of 200 nanoseconds for all the multipath signals to arrive at the receiver's antenna, the GI, in order to prevent data corruption, should always be two to four times larger than that. In 802.11a/g, the GI is set at 800 nanoseconds.

The 802.11n amendment specifies an 800-nanosecond GI for compatibility with 802.11a/g, but it optionally specifies a 400-nanosecond GI to reduce the symbol time and increase data rates by about 10 percent. When using the shorter GI, ISI can still occur, and the resulting data corruption means that frames would have to be retransmitted, which has the effect of reducing throughput.

Modulation and Coding Sets Because of the multiple factors involved in determining the data rate in 802.11n—the type of modulation, the number of spatial streams, the GI, the FEC coding, and so on—802.11n uses a combination of nine different factors to define the data rates. These combinations are referred to as **modulation and coding sets (MCSs)**. The 802.11-2012 version of the standard lists 77 different definitions that apply to both 20-MHz-wide and 40-MHz-wide channels, each specifying a different data rate. There are eight mandatory MCSs supporting data rates of up to 72.2 Mbps. All the other data rates, up to those for a 4×4 device supporting up to 600 Mbps, are optional. Some 802.11n MCSs support the use of unequal modulation in the same frame transmission from different radios and to the same destination device. Many of the MCSs specified in the amendment are seldom used and have never been implemented by manufacturers. One example of these is the unequal modulation MCSs. In comparison, 802.11a and 802.11g support only 6, 9, 12, 18, 24, 36, 48, and 54 Mbps, and the only mandatory rates, as discussed before, are 6, 9, 12, 18, and 24 Mbps.

HT PHY Layer The 802.11n HT PHY layer supports three different frame formats. The first frame format is used to transmit in non-HT mode when communicating with 802.11a/g devices. The second frame format is used in mixed environments, with both HT and non-HT (legacy 802.11a/g devices). This allows non-HT devices to decode the beginning of the preamble, which contains information about the duration of the frame, so that legacy devices will not attempt to communicate until the transmission ends, thereby avoiding collisions. The third frame format is used when the WLAN is exclusively supporting 802.11n devices. This mode of operation is called **greenfield** and is not compatible with non-HT devices. Though optional in 802.11n, it is the most efficient way to communicate with other HT devices if legacy support is not required. Greenfield mode is also not possible when there are legacy devices either present or within range of the WLAN, in an overlapping frequency channel.

HT MAC Sublayer The 802.11n MAC sublayer includes enhancements designed to address the increase in throughput and power management. Power management becomes really important in 802.11n because of the optional use of multiple radios. The more radios a device has, the faster it can communicate, but the more power it will consume, and this is particularly problematic for small handheld devices. The amendment addresses this issue by allowing devices to turn off all radios except one when they are not transmitting or receiving frames addressed to them.

Another enhancement deals with **frame aggregation**, a method of combining multiple MAC frames into one PHY frame to reduce frame transmission overhead, which contributes to increased WLAN throughput and reduced collisions.

There are two variations of frame aggregation. The first combines multiple MAC frames into one PHY frame, removing the individual headers. When using this method, all MAC frames must be of the same type, meaning that voice frames cannot be combined with video frames. The aggregated frames must also have a single destination—in other words, they must be unicast frames. As you know, in 802.11 the receiver must acknowledge each transmitted MAC frame, but in this case a single ACK is transmitted for the entire group of aggregated frames, which saves time and overhead, increasing throughput. The disadvantage of this method is that, should an error occur, the entire group of aggregated frames must be retransmitted.

The second method of frame aggregation combines individual MAC frames, including the headers, body, and trailers. Here again, the frames must all be unicast. In this case, the receiver sends an ACK for each individual MAC frame. However, if the receiving device is 802.11e compliant (discussed in the next section), then a block ACK frame is transmitted back to the sender acknowledging the multiple MAC frames transmitted. In case of an error, only the frames following the one in which an error was detected must be retransmitted.

Because of the higher power consumption of 802.11n devices with multiple radios, the standard defines two new power management methods. In **Spatial Multiplexing Power Save (SMPS)** mode, a MIMO device can shut down all but one of its radios. Beacons are transmitted on the primary channel only, when using 40 MHz of bandwidth. If the TIM in the beacon indicates that there is data waiting, the device turns on the other radios and informs the AP, which will then transmit the buffered data using MIMO and spatial multiplexing if the receiver is capable. In the second new power management method, called **Power Save Multi-Poll (PSMP)**, the devices also turn off all but one radio. When there is data to be transmitted to the device, the AP informs the devices by transmitting an RTS frame using DSSS. The destination device informs the AP when all of its radios are operating again, in preparation for receiving the data using HT.

The Wi-Fi Alliance website offers several resources on the topic of Wireless Multimedia (WMM) power management, especially for mobile devices. For more information, visit *wi-fi.org* and search for "WMM power save." Note that to download some of these resources you may need to register as a guest.

Reduced Interframe Space (RIFS) In greenfield mode, the 802.11n amendment allows for a **Reduced Interframe Space (RIFS)**—a shorter (2-microsecond) interframe space that can be used instead of a SIFS at the end of each transmitted frame, resulting in far less timing overhead and helping further increase the overall throughput of 802.11n. Remember that the SIFS interval in 802.11 is 10 microseconds long; in 802.11a/g, the SIFS is extended by 6 microseconds at the end of each frame to allow the receiver to process the OFDM signals.

HT Operation Modes To allow 802.11n WLANs to coexist with non-HT devices (both APs and clients) and to allow devices that can only support 20 MHz channels (maximum data rate of 150 Mbps) to participate in the WLAN, 802.11n can operate in one of four different modes, depending on the presence or absence of different types of devices. Here are brief descriptions of these four modes of operation:

- Mode 0, the greenfield mode, supports only HT-capable devices using either 20 or 40 MHz channels but not both in the same WLAN.

- Mode 1 is an HT mode, but if the AP detects stations that are not HT-capable and transmitting in a 20 MHz channel that interferes with either the primary or secondary channel in a 40 MHz channel, the AP will employ the CTS-to-Self protection mechanism to reduce or eliminate interference.

- Mode 2 supports either 20 or 40 MHz channels. If the AP detects a device that cannot communicate using a 40 MHz channel, it will employ protection mechanisms to allow 20-MHz-only devices to associate and communicate on the network.

- Mode 3, also called non-HT Mixed Mode, is used when one or more non-HT devices are associated with an HT AP. Mode 3 supports HT devices at 20 or 40 MHz and employs protection mechanisms to allow non-HT devices to participate in the BSS. Of all the modes, this is the one most commonly used and implemented by AP manufacturers, because many networks have to support non-HT devices.

When operating in mixed modes and 40 MHz of bandwidth, 802.11n transmits the headers in DSSS on the primary channel, to maintain backward compatibility with legacy devices as well as with other 802.11n devices using 20 MHz-wide channels. It also does this if a legacy device joins a WLAN operating in greenfield mode or if a legacy AP is detected within range.

IEEE 802.11ac

IEEE 802.11n introduced higher transmission speeds by using a wider 40 MHz channel, but the performance enhancement stretches the limit of the 83.5 MHz of bandwidth of the 2.4 GHz band, because it has only three usable channels for data transmission. One alternative to further increase the data rates would be to use more complex modulations and encode more bits per symbol, but that would also negatively affect the reliability and range. A better solution, introduced in the **802.11ac** amendment, was to limit transmissions to the 5 GHz band, which offers far more bandwidth and uses even wider channels with more subcarriers to transmit more data than 802.11n. The U-NII band is also less crowded, and there is no interference from Bluetooth, ZigBee, and other technologies.

The 802.11ac amendment increases data rates through the use of 80 and 160 MHz channels. In addition to using the same channel widths and subcarriers as 802.11n, 802.11ac includes 80 MHz channels divided into 242 subcarriers with 8 pilot subcarriers and 234 usable for data. A 160 MHz channel is divided into 484 subcarriers with 16 pilots and 468 usable. The amendment also specifies the use of 256-QAM modulation, although this requires an extra 5 dB of SNR to ensure reliable communications. However, it does away with the unequal modulation MCSs specified in 802.11n. With these channel configurations and 256-QAM modulation, 802.11ac can increase the data rates from 433 Mbps to roughly 6.9 Gbps, in addition to those data rates that can be achieved with 802.11n.

As of this writing, not all frequency ranges in the U-NII band are available in every country. The FCC in the United States has been working closely with international regulatory agencies to open up more of the band, but this process takes time. Note that 802.11ac continues to maintain backward compatibility with all previous standards in the 5 GHz band. However, because in some countries it may be difficult to bond eight channels for 160 MHz of bandwidth, the 802.11ac amendment does allow the use of two, nonadjacent 80 MHz channels, but in this case the data rates will be limited to the maximum achievable with the narrower channel.

 In 802.11ac, the theoretical maximum data rate for a single spatial stream, using 160 MHz of RF bandwidth is 780 Mbps. When using two, nonadjacent 80 MHz channels, the theoretical maximum data rate is 866.7 Mbps. Data rates of 6.9 Gbps can only be achieved when using eight spatial streams. You can check out all of the MCSs for 802.11ac by searching for "802.11ac MCS rates" on the Cisco support forums at: *https://supportforums.cisco.com.*

To achieve the higher speeds, 802.11ac, named **very high throughput (VHT)**, can use between two and eight radios to transmit a maximum of eight spatial streams per AP. If all eight radios are present in an AP but not all are being used to communicate with a single client device, the additional spatial streams can be used to communicate with multiple client devices simultaneously. This feature is called **multi-user MIMO (MU-MIMO)**, and it will be implemented in the second wave of the amendment. Figure 7-15 shows a graphical comparison between MU-MIMO and single-user MIMO.

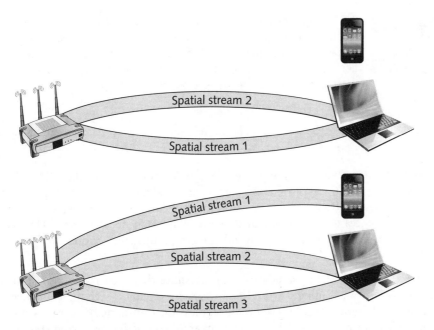

Figure 7-15 Single user MMO (top) vs. MU-MIMO (bottom)

IEEE 802.11ac simplifies the MCSs defined in 802.11n, most of which were never implemented, and trims the number down to only 10 MCSs. As more people purchase and install 802.11ac-capable devices, one of the drawbacks will no doubt be the increase in interference due to overcrowding and the use of wider channels.

IEEE 802.11ad

The IEEE **802.11ad** amendment was spawned by the Wireless Gigabit (WiGig) Alliance specification, which is discussed in the next chapter. The goal was to expand the 802.11 standard to work in the 60 GHz portion of the ISM band. Using the 60 GHz band comes at the cost of transmission range. At these high frequencies, even molecules of oxygen in the air absorb a large portion of the EM energy of the signal and this limits the range to an average of about 6 feet (2 meters). Although the maximum range is about 33 feet (10 meters), this can only be practically achieved in an environment with very few obstructions or other energy-absorbing items, such as human bodies.

One of the key advantages of the 60 GHz band is that it has approximately 2 GHz of spectrum available. This means that it can support very wide channels, carrying vast amounts of data such as, for example, multiple 4K ultra-high-definition television signal streams, without suffering from adjacent or co-channel interference. It can support data rates of 7+ Gbps per second.

At this writing, IEEE 802.11ad-compatible residential wireless routers are available from a few manufacturers and a few laptop computers support this amendment. The amendment specifies the ability of equipment to automatically switch to 802.11ac in the 5 GHz band when devices move out of range of the 60 GHz signal.

PLCP frame formats get progressively more complex as a new amendment is introduced. Coverage of advanced amendments quickly falls out of the scope of this introductory text. More information can be obtained by downloading a copy of the standard or amendments from *standards.ieee.org/about/get*.

IEEE 802.11e

The IEEE **802.11e** amendment was approved for publication in November 2005. It defines enhancements to the MAC layer of 802.11 to expand support for LAN applications that require Quality of Service (QoS), and it provides for improvements in the capabilities and efficiency of the protocol. When combined with enhancements to the PHY layer in 802.11a/b/g/n/ac, it promises to increase overall system performance and expand the application space for 802.11.

Unlike the 802.11a and 802.11g standards, which require that each frame be acknowledged before a transmission can continue, 802.11e allows the receiving device to acknowledge after receiving a burst of frames (i.e., after several frames are transmitted), which is also called delayed acknowledgement. Figure 7-16 shows a diagram comparing the two methods.

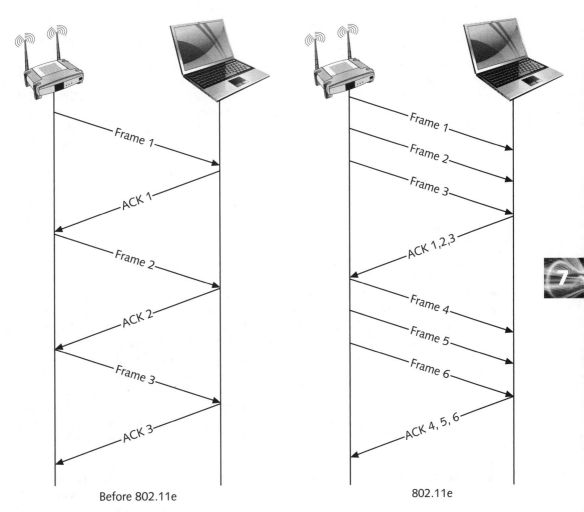

Before 802.11e

802.11e

Figure 7-16 802.11e frame acknowledgement

The 802.11e standard enables prioritization of data frames, which is essential to support voice streams over WLANs. In addition to delayed or burst acknowledgements, 802.11e implements two new coordination functions: **enhanced DCF (EDCF)** and **hybrid coordination function (HCF)**, discussed later in this chapter.

All APs that comply with the 802.11e amendment must implement both modes, although the network administrator has different levels of control over how these are configured. Both modes include a traffic class (TC) definition. Emails, for example, would be assigned a low priority, whereas voice communications would be assigned a higher-priority class. In EDCF, a station with higher-priority traffic class waits less time to transmit and therefore has a better chance of getting its traffic through, which is essential for Voice over IP (VoIP).

HCF is a combination of DCF and PCF. The interval between beacon frames is divided into a contention-free period and a contention period. During the contention-free period, the hybrid coordinator (the AP) controls access to the medium and, based on information about the traffic received from a client, allocates more time slots to the station with higher-priority traffic—such as VoIP frames. During the contention period, all stations work in EDCF mode.

This prioritization aspect is an important development for the 802.11 group of standards. The 802.11e standard enables voice, audio, and video to be transmitted reliably over WLANs by supporting traffic prioritization based on **QoS (quality-of-service)**. As you know, QoS is a network resource reservation mechanism that allows certain types of network traffic—voice and video, for example—to be transmitted with a higher priority than traffic that is not time sensitive, such as copying a data file. QoS also adds improved security features for both mobile and nomadic applications. A **nomadic user** is one who moves frequently from one location to another, but does not use the equipment while in motion.

IEEE 802.11r

The amount of time required by 802.11 devices to associate with one AP and disassociate from another in an ESS is in the order of hundreds of milliseconds. For 802.11 devices to be able to support mobile phones used for voice calls, the reassociation time cannot exceed 50 milliseconds; otherwise, the human ear will sense a break in the continuity of the voice stream. This will make users unhappy with the quality of the call, and they may stop using that phone service. To support **Voice over WLAN (VoWLAN)**, which enables organizations to implement and use VoIP in their ESSs, the 802.11 standard needs a way to provide quicker handoffs. As discussed previously, handoffs in a WLAN happen when a portable device connects with a new access point and disconnects from the previous one. Another issue is that the current 802.11 MAC protocol does not allow a device to find out if the necessary QoS resources, such as the required number of time slots and security features, are available on an AP before a telephone handset associates with it, which can affect the quality and reliability of a voice call.

The **802.11r** standard is designed to resolve these issues as well as security concerns regarding the handoff. It does so by refining the MAC protocol and providing a way for the mobile devices to communicate with multiple APs within range, on different channels, to establish all the necessary parameters, including security and available processing resources, before a handoff occurs. This amendment to the standard is designed to enhance the convergence of wireless mobile voice, data, and video.

IEEE 802.11s

Imagine that you need to deploy a WLAN over the entire downtown area of a medium-sized city and provide seamless connectivity to all city employees for events and functions. Though theoretically possible, connecting each of the APs to a wired network and configuring the system would be a monumentally expensive and complex undertaking because of the need for interconnecting all the different locations. Installing network cabling outdoors is not an option, so the only way to address this would be to lease communications lines from a local utility. Not only would this make the cost prohibitively high, but achieving high data rates might also be difficult, depending on the types of communications lines available.

The ideal solution would be to connect the wireless APs to each other over the wireless medium. However, as you recall from previous sections of this chapter, the original 802.11 standard did not provide a way for APs to communicate with each other over the wireless medium, much less forward wireless data frame traffic.

The **802.11s** amendment provides the solution. Figure 7-17 shows an example of a wireless mesh network. In this figure, AP 5 provides a single connection to the Internet to keep the landline connection costs low. The laptop associated with AP 3 and the smartphone connected to AP 7 would be able to access the wired network or the Internet because with 802.11s the APs can communicate with each other over the wireless medium and forward the frames to AP 5.

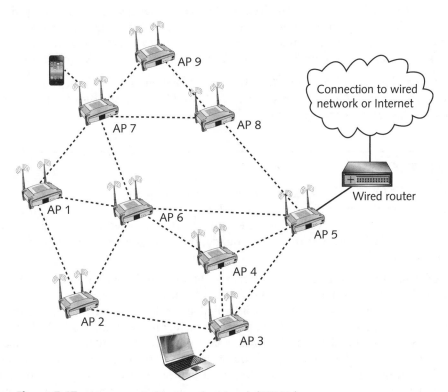

Figure 7-17   APs connected in a mesh network (802.11s)

Other Amendments and Amendments Currently Under Development

As you have likely gathered from your reading of this introductory text, work on new amendments to 802.11 is ongoing and shows no sign of slowing down in the near future. The amendments mentioned in this book are by no means the only ones implemented in the published versions of the 802.11 standard. For example, work has been completed on the 802.11ae amendment, which enables the prioritization of management frames to improve access for applications other than voice, and the 802.11af amendment, which uses the recently released analog over-the-air television frequency spectrum (Television White Spaces) to transmit at sub-1 GHz frequency, at lower data rates but at much greater distances.

Additional work is being done by the IEEE (802.11ah) to develop standards for wireless communications in other sub-1 GHz frequency bands (not TV White Space) to support Internet connectivity for low-duty-cycle devices including a wide variety of data collection devices and sensors that are part of the Internet of Things (IoT).

The IEEE is also working on the **802.11ax** amendment, an enhancement that will enable simultaneous communication with multiple devices (multiple access) within a single OFDM transmission. It differs from MU-MIMO in the sense that instead of using one or a group of radio chains to transmit to different devices, different subcarriers transmitted by the same radio chain will be assigned to different devices. This technology is already being tested and developed for cellular communications and is expected to reach data rates of over 10 Gbps. This work is expected to be completed in July 2018 and be ratified by March 2019.

Also under development is the IEEE **802.11ay** amendment, an improvement of 802.11ad that is expected to enable 60 GHz transmissions at 20 to 40 Gbps at distances of between 300 and 500 meters. This amendment is expected to be completed in 2017.

Chapter Summary

- IEEE 802.11g provided a significant improvement in performance over 802.11b and sparked the phenomenal expansion in WLANs, both at home and in the enterprise. This amendment preserved the features of 802.11b but increased the data transfer rates up to 54 Mbps. It also laid the foundation for future amendments with its use of OFDM and protection mechanisms.

- IEEE 802.11a networks use the Unlicensed National Information Infrastructure (U-NII) band. The total bandwidth available for IEEE 802.11a WLANs using U-NII is 555 MHz, almost seven times what is available for 802.11b networks using the ISM band. This amendment, published at approximately the same time as 802.11b, also has a maximum rated speed of 54 Mbps, but it had a slow start due to technical difficulties, as well as the initial cost of equipment. Like 802.11g, it achieves its increase in speed and flexibility over 802.11b through a higher frequency, more transmission channels, and a new multiplexing technique, along with greater reliability, despite its decreased range due to using higher frequencies. The availability of more channels allows the deployment of more APs per area, supporting a larger number of simultaneous users. IEEE 802.11a also uses OFDM and is less sensitive to multipath distortion of the signal because it divides each channel into multiple subcarriers and uses simpler modulation methods.

- IEEE 802.11n, in practice, increases the data rate in WLANs to 450 Mbps in each of the 2.4 and 5 GHz bands by bonding two channels and using 40 MHz of bandwidth as well as a larger number of OFDM subcarriers to transmit more bits simultaneously. This includes a number of necessary enhancements to the MAC and PHY layers and continues to maintain backward compatibility with 802.11a/b/g. This amendment uses multiple transmitters and multiple receivers (MIMO) to increase both the range and reliability of WLANs through the use of beamforming and can use spatial multiplexing to transmit multiple streams of data from each radio, further increasing performance.

- IEEE 802.11ac enhances WLAN performance even further, adding data rates from 433 Mbps up to 6.9 Gbps to the rates supported in 802.11n. It is limited to the 5 GHz band and bonds either four channels or eight channels to achieve bandwidths of 80 and 160 MHz, respectively. It also allows a 160 MHz channel to be split into two nonadjacent 80 MHz channels.

- The IEEE 802.11ad amendment works in the 60 GHz portion of the ISM band and supports data rates of 7+ Gbps. It allows multiple 4K television signal streams over short ranges of an average of 6 feet (2 meters) and can automatically switch to 802.11ac if devices move out of range.

- The 802.11e amendment adds QoS to the original 802.11 standard. In addition, it helps improve performance through burst acknowledgements and two new wireless medium coordination functions: enhanced DCF (EDCF) and hybrid coordination function (HCF). This amendment also supports QoS for prioritizing data frames, which is important to support voice communications in WLANs.

- The 802.11r amendment enables fast roaming and reduces the time required for a device to associate with a new AP from hundreds of milliseconds to less than 50 milliseconds. This permits WLANs to effectively support voice communications in ESS environments. It also allows a client device, prior to establishing a connection, to obtain information from multiple APs regarding bandwidth availability and security features.

- The 802.11s amendment enables APs to communicate and pass traffic from one to the other over a wireless connection, supporting cost-effective deployment of extensive mesh WLANs over a larger geographical area without the need to connect every AP to the wired network.

- The IEEE continues to work on further enhancements to the 802.11 standard. One of them is 802.11ax, which will allow independent communications with multiple devices within a single frame transmission. IEEE 802.11ay will improve 802.11ad with transmissions at 20 to 40 Gbps, at distances of between 300 to 500 meters.

Key Terms

802.11a   An IEEE 802.11 amendment developed in 1999, a standard for WLAN transmissions at speeds of up to 54 Mbps.

802.11ac   An IEEE 802.11 amendment that works exclusively in the 5 GHz band and can achieve data rates of up to 6.9 Gbps by supporting channel bandwidths of 80 and 160 MHz.

802.11ad   An IEEE 802.11 amendment that expands the standard to work in the 60 GHz portion of the ISM band and can reach speeds of up to 10 Gbps at distances of no more than 2 meters, due to signal attenuation that can be caused by molecules of oxygen in the air.

802.11ax   An IEEE 802.11 amendment currently under development that enhances MU-MIMO by allowing the AP to communicate with different devices by using different subcarriers within the same PHY frame.

802.11ay   An IEEE 802.11 amendment under development that will enable communications in the 60 GHz band to transmit between 20 to 40 Gbps at distances between 300 and 500 meters.

802.11e   An IEEE 802.11 amendment for WLAN applications that implements QoS for WLANs and provides for improvements in their capabilities and efficiency.

802.11g   An IEEE 802.11 amendment that allows for WLAN transmissions at speeds of up to 54 Mbps using the ISM band.

802.11n   An IEEE 802.11 amendment that increases the theoretical data rate up to 600 Mbps. Note than no 802.11n compatible equipment has ever been manufactured that achieves this rate. The maximum data rate achievable with 802.11n today is 450 Mbps.

802.11r   An IEEE 802.11 amendment aimed primarily at reducing the reassociation time in an ESS to less than 50 ms, to prevent breaks that reduce the quality of voice calls. It also enables mobile devices to communicate with APs within range, on different channels, ahead of reassociating with one of them, to determine whether they have enough processing resources to handle an ongoing voice call over the WLAN.

802.11s   An IEEE 802.11 amendment that enables APs to communicate with each other over the wireless medium. Prior to 802.11s, the standard only allowed APs to communicate with each other over the Ethernet medium and only for the purpose of disassociation of roaming mobile devices.

antenna diversity   A technique that uses two antennas to improve the range of 802.11 and transmits a signal through the antenna that received the strongest signal during the last transmission.

beamforming   A technique employed by 802.11n devices that uses multiple radios and antennas to virtually direct the transmission to the location of a device, similar to the way that phased array antennas work (*see* "Phased array antennas" in Chapter 4).

co-channel interference   Interference between two devices configured to use the same frequency channel.

CTS-to-Self   Short for "clear-to-send-to-self," a coordination method used by 802.11g devices that prevents 802.11 and 802.11b devices that do not "understand" OFDM from attempting to initiate a transmission while the 802.11g device is transmitting data.

enhanced DCF (EDCF)   An enhancement to the MAC protocol layer defined in 802.11e that enables prioritization of traffic, so that a station with higher priority frames, such as voice traffic, waits less time to transmit.

frame aggregation   In the 802.11n and 802.11ac amendments, MAC (layer 2) frames can be combined in a data frame to further increase throughput on the WLAN.

Extended Rate PHY (ERP)   The generic name given by the IEEE to refer to the 802.11g amendment.

greenfield   A mode of operation of 802.11n in which only HT-capable devices are supported, unless a legacy station joins the WLAN or a legacy AP is within range.

guard interval (GI)   An added 800-nanosecond delay at the end of each 802.11 that allows all reflected signals to arrive at the receiver's antennas before another symbol is transmitted.

high throughput (HT)   The generic name given to the 802.11n amendment.

hybrid coordination function (HCF)   An combination of DCF and PCF that enhances performance, with the AP assigning both contention and contention-free periods in the beacons. The AP can allocate more contention free periods to a device with higher-priority traffic.

intersymbol interference (ISI)   Interference caused when delayed multipath signals arrive at the receiver antenna while a later, different symbol taking a more direct path is already arriving at the antenna.

modulation and coding sets (MCSs)   A combination of modulation, guard interval, and FEC coding that defines the data rates in 802.11n/ac.

multiple-input and multiple-output (MIMO)   A technology that uses multiple antennas (usually three or four) and reflected signals (multipath reflections) to extend the range of the WLAN by attempting to correctly decode a frame from multiple copies of it received at different times.

multi-user MIMO (MU-MIMO)   A feature of 802.11ac that enables an AP with multiple radios to communicate with different devices simultaneously using different groups of radios and different spatial streams.

nomadic user   A user who moves frequently but does not use the equipment while in motion.

orthogonal frequency division multiplexing (OFDM)   A transmission technology that divides the available frequency bandwidth into multiple orthogonal subcarriers, then modulates bits onto different subcarriers and transmits multiple bits at the same time in each.

PBCC (packet binary convolutional coding)   An optional transmission mode of 802.11 that can send data at rates of 22 or 33 Mbps using either QPSK or 8PSK, respectively.

Power Save Multi-Poll (PSMP)   An alternate method of reducing power consumption defined in 802.11n that allows devices to switch off all but one radio.

protection mechanism   A protocol feature used to allow devices to participate in an 802.11 WLAN without interfering with transmissions and causing data corruption due to collisions because they are not able to "understand" the modulation and coding.

QoS (quality-of-service)   A resource reservation enhancement to the 802.11 MAC layer that enables prioritization of traffic and is most often used to support delivery of voice, video, and audio frames between WLAN devices.

radio chains   The name given in the 802.11 standard to devices that have multiple radios.

Reduced Interframe Space (RIFS)   A 2-microsecond interframe space that can be used in 802.11n networks working in greenfield mode to help reduce overhead and increase throughput.

spatial multiplexing   A transmission technique that uses multiple radios and multiple antennas to send different parts of the same message simultaneously, thus increasing the data rate.

Spatial Multiplexing Power Save (SMPS)   A power-saving mode defined in 802.11n in which devices can switch off all except one radio to reduce power consumption.

very high throughput (VHT) The generic name given to the 802.11ac amendment by the IEEE.

Voice over WLAN (VoWLAN) A term used to describe the transmission of telephone calls on WLANs.

Review Questions

1. Which technique is used in 802.11g APs to reduce the possibility of collisions when legacy 802.11b devices are within range?

   a. OFDM

   b. Changes to the PLCP frame format

   c. CTS-to-Self

   d. ACS

2. The maximum mandatory rate of an IEEE 802.11a WLAN, according to the standard, is _____ .

   a. 11 Mbps

   b. 24 Mbps

   c. 54 Mbps

   d. 108 Mbps

3. The most important change made to the MAC layer of 802.11a was _____ .

   a. to make the frames shorter

   b. to increase security

   c. to make the frames longer for efficiency

   d. none of the above

4. IEEE 802.11a achieves its increase in speed and flexibility over 802.11b by each of the following except _____ .

   a. higher frequency

   b. using less bandwidth

   c. more transmission channels

   d. a new multiplexing technique

5. The Unlicensed National Information Infrastructure (U-NII) band operates in the _____ frequency band.

   a. 2.4 GHz

   b. 33 GHz

   c. 5 GHz

   d. 16 KHz

6. The Federal Communications Commission (FCC) has segmented the 555 MHz of the original U-NII spectrum into four segments or bands. True or False?

7. All 5 GHz bands are available for use by WLANs worldwide. True or False?

8. Although such devices as 2.4 GHz cordless phones, microwave ovens, and Bluetooth devices may cause interference problems with 802.11b networks in the 2.4 GHz ISM band, they are not a problem with 802.11a. True or False?

9. Each frequency channel in an 802.11a WLAN is 20 MHz wide and is divided into _____ subcarriers that are modulated with data.

   a. 56

   b. 114

   c. 52

   d. 48

10. Although 802.11n can achieve data rates of 300 Mbps when using 40 MHz of bandwidth in the ISM band, one of the main challenges of deploying a WLAN in this frequency range is _____ .

   a. intersymbol interference

   b. co-channel interference on channel 6

   c. excessive multipath interference on channels 1 and 11

   d. interference from the U-NII band

11. How many pilot carriers are available to help evaluate the quality of the signal in 802.11n in the U-NII band when using 40 MHz of bandwidth by bonding two channels?

   a. 4

   b. 2

   c. 6

   d. 8

12. One of the reasons that 802.11n achieves a higher throughput is that it bonds two ISM or U-NII channels. Another important reason is that it _____ .

   a. eliminates multipath interference

   b. uses antenna diversity

   c. can transmit using multiple spatial streams

   d. can transmit in any two frequency channels simultaneously

13. When actively connected and using a WLAN while roaming in an ESS, the process of connecting to a new AP and disconnecting from another APs in one's path is called _____ .

    a. MIMO

    b. handoff

    c. switching

    d. nomadic

14. The 802.11e amendment made a change to the MAC layer to enable WLAN traffic to be prioritized. This is generally referred to as _____ .

    a. RSNA

    b. QoS

    c. VoWLAN

    d. WPA2

15. IEEE 802.11ac can use channels with a bandwidth of up to _____ in order to achieve data rates of up to 6.9 Gbps.

    a. 20 MHz

    b. 40 MHz

    c. 160 MHz

    d. 80 MHz

16. How many modulation and coding sets are defined in 802.11n?

    a. 10

    b. 27

    c. None, 802.11n does not define any MCSs

    d. 77

17. The acknowledgment mechanism in 802.11n and 802.11ac can enhance network performance because _____ .

    a. it transmits using more subcarriers

    b. the AP allows less time for receiving an ACK frame

    c. it uses frame aggregation

    d. multipath is eliminated

18. When communicating in greenfield mode in 802.11n, throughput can be increased slightly with the use of _____ .

    a. a reduced interframe space

    b. a shorter header for every frame

    c. a higher clock speed

    d. a more focused antenna

19. Because 802.11ac uses essentially the same transmission technology as 802.11n, which of the following is the main reason for its increased throughput?

    a. A more efficient protocol.

    b. The signal strength is higher.

    c. It does not suffer from interference at all.

    d. It can use wider frequency channels divided into more subcarriers.

20. Which of the following is a reason that 802.11a is more efficient than 802.11g when both operate at the same data rate?

    a. 802.11a does not have to support legacy devices.

    b. 802.11a devices can handle more data.

    c. 802.11a equipment is more sophisticated and expensive.

    d. 802.11a encoding is more efficient.

Hands-On Projects

Project 7-1

This Project assumes you are using Windows 7. Instructions for using Windows 10 are included in Appendix A.

This project covers the basic configuration of an 802.11n- or 802.11ac-compatible residential gateway (wireless router) or AP. You can do this project using any manufacturer's device. The brand of the equipment is not important, because in the real world you will likely be configuring a variety of different equipment makes and models. Although the configuration screens may be different than the ones shown in the figures, the point of the exercise is for you to understand which configuration items to modify and how these will affect the speed and performance of the wireless links.

The device used to create this exercise are a DLink DIR-825 simultaneous dual-band (2.4 and 5 GHz) wireless residential gateway and a Dell Latitude E4300 Notebook PC, but virtually any type of N300, N600, or N900 wireless residential gateway and PC compatible with 802.11n will work. The project covers only those settings that are relevant and assumes you already know (from Chapter 6) how to perform the basic configuration steps and connect a computer with a wireless NIC to the gateway.

1. Connect your computer to the gateway for configuration purposes. Whenever possible, you should use a wired connection to change settings on a gateway or access point.

Some of the settings, such as security, will cause your computer to disconnect until you reconfigure it to use the new settings.

2. Consult the documentation for your gateway on how to configure the wireless settings manually. Even if a configuration wizard is available, it often does not provide you with enough control over the parameter settings, so you will want to follow the procedures for manual configuration. Figure 7-18 shows an example of the settings you need to access to fully configure the 2.4 GHz wireless settings for 802.11n.

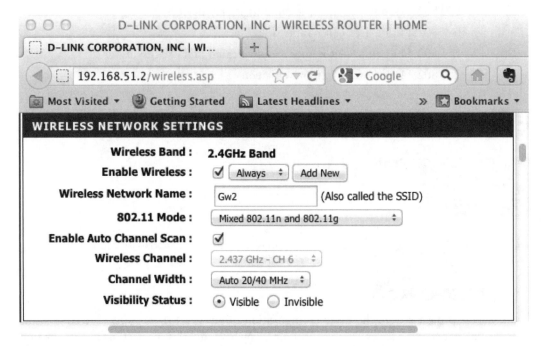

Figure 7-18 Configuring an 802.11n 2.4 GHz WLAN on a wireless residential gateway

Source: D-Link Systems

3. Configure a unique SSID for your WLAN. Consult your instructor in case there are other devices being used in the same room.

4. It is usually better, especially in 802.11n, to allow the gateway to automatically select the channel, but you can select the channel manually, if you prefer, keeping in mind that, with more than two gateways in the same room, there are really only two usable channels, 1 and 6, and that interference will affect the overall performance of your wireless link.

5. To achieve data rates of up to 300 Mbps, you need to configure the gateway to use Auto 20/40 MHz. Most gateways do not allow you to configure them for 40 MHz operation only. Make sure you turn off any devices in the room—cellular phones, and so on—that only support 802.11g and therefore can only use 20 MHz of bandwidth. Otherwise, you may find that the WLAN will perform slower and only

use 20 MHz of bandwidth, limiting your data rates to approximately 150 Mbps. This is because every time a broadcast frame is transmitted, the gateway needs to send it in a way that is compatible with non-802.11n devices if they are connected to the gateway.

6. You do not need to transfer any files to determine the maximum data rate (only to if you wish to determine the throughput) for the connection. Microsoft Windows provides this information in the Wireless Network Connection Status dialog box. To get to this dialog box in Windows 7, click the wireless network icon on the bottom-right-hand side of the taskbar and click **Open Network and Sharing Center**. On the right-hand side of the window, click **Wireless Network Connection**. Figure 7-19 shows the Wireless Network Connection Status dialog box.

Figure 7-19   Wireless Network Connection Status dialog box in Windows 7

7. You will see the data rate beside the label, Speed. If your data rate is showing anything less than 300 Mbps, you may need to modify the configuration of the NIC. To do this, click the Properties button at the bottom of the Wireless Network Connection Status dialog box (not the Wireless Properties button). This will open the Wireless Network Connection Properties dialog box.

8. Click the **Configure** button next to the name of your wireless NIC. Click the **Advanced** tab. Note that some NIC manufacturers do not provide you with the ability to configure advanced NIC parameters from this dialog box, in which case you may need to use the manufacturer's utility, which should have been installed when you set up your NIC. There

is no industry standard for configuring these parameters, so each manufacturer's adapters may use different parameter names. Figure 7-20 shows an example of the dialog box displayed for the Dell Wireless 1510 WLAN Mini-Card. Make a note of all the current settings for your card before changing any values, and then make sure that it is configured for 802.11n and for 20/40 MHz. Try changing some of the settings that appear to be related to bandwidth or standard support and observe the results as outlined in step 7 above.

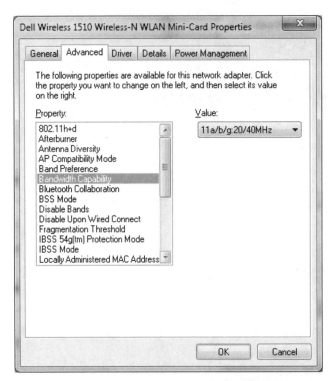

Figure 7-20 Wireless NIC configuration in Windows 7

9. Use Acrylic Wi-Fi Home, which you installed and learned about in Chapter 6, and check for interference from other networks using the same configuration you just completed. If your gateway device supports the 5 GHz band, perform the same configuration steps on the gateway, but configure the 5 GHz band instead. Check the interference with Acrylic Wi-Fi again and compare with the results you obtained for the 2.4 GHz band. What differences did you notice? How much bandwidth is being used in the 2.4 and in 5 GHz bands? Note that Acrylic Wi-Fi also shows the maximum data rate possible in your WLAN in the column labeled, Max Speed.

Project 7-2

Research the 802.11 standards and amendments since its introduction in 1997 until 802.11ad that affected the MAC and PHY layers. Start by reading this Wikipedia article, *https://en.wikipedia.org/wiki/IEEE_802.11*, which contains links to many articles and papers outlining what was done to achieve the ever-increasing WLAN data rates. Be sure to look at previous chapters in this book as required.

Create a table that lists what MAC and PHY layer enhancements were made to the standard from 802.11 to 802.11ad that helped increase the data rates to those achievable today in 802.11ac. Be sure to include bandwidth, MCSs and modulation types (BPSK, QAM, etc.), along with any changes introduced in the MAC layer.

Real-World Exercise

Exercise 7-1

The Baypoint Group (TBG) needs your help to prepare a presentation for Academic Computing Services Inc. (ACS), a nationwide organization that assists colleges and universities with technology issues. ACS would like to learn more about the differences and similarities between 802.11n and 802.11ac.

Prepare a Power Point presentation that outlines the features and functionality of both amendments to 802.11 and makes recommendations about which technology ACS should recommend to its customers in a variety of situations, such as when equipment is used for office applications and when wireless laptop computers are used by students. Your presentation should consist of a maximum of 15 slides.

Challenge Case Project

CASE PROJECTS

ACS found your presentation very useful but would like to know how interference from nearby WLANs can impact the performance of its WLAN. To prepare a report, you can use the same tools you used for the Chapter 6 Challenge Case Project. To use a better alternative and produce a more comprehensive report, visit *www.openmaniak.com/iperf* and review the tutorial on how to use Iperf tools to measure the bandwidth and quality of a network link. Then download and install Iperf from *sourceforge.net/projects/iperf* or from *https://github.com/esnet/iperf*.

Using the hardware and configuration you set up for Hands-On Project 7-1, measure the network's performance and record the results in both bands. Then write a one-page report outlining any differences in performance that you encounter. Be sure to calculate and provide a brief comparison of how long it would take to copy a 10 MB or larger file.

chapter 8

Expanding WLANs and WLAN Security

After reading this chapter and completing the exercises, you will be able to:

- Discuss how wireless bridges and repeaters can expand the functionality of WLANs
- Describe how wireless controllers can simplify management of WLANs
- Outline WLAN design considerations
- Discuss how Wi-Fi Direct can make it easier for end users to share resources, synchronize devices, and connect directly
- Describe developments in the use of WLANs in multimedia distribution
- List the security features and challenges of IEEE 802.11 networks, and how to manage them

Higher data rates and lower costs have made 802.11 WLANs very popular and competitive with wired networks. WLANs continue to be deployed, expanded, and enhanced at a very fast pace, especially in enterprises, as an alternative to wired Ethernet networks. This chapter wraps up everything you learned so far about Wi-Fi. It provides a review of the equipment, planning, and deployment of enterprise wireless networks, a task that is very different from installing a WLAN in a home or small office.

Since the early days, the design of enterprise WLAN equipment has changed significantly. The main reason behind this was to make it easier to plan, design, deploy, and manage large wireless networks in manufacturing plants, large offices, entire corporate campuses, educational institutions, hospitals, conference centers, and other large venues. Each of these environments demands careful planning and design to ensure user satisfaction, reliability, and security.

Wireless Bridges and Repeaters

Let's begin by looking at different types of equipment designed to address issues that are unique to enterprise-class environments.

Wireless Bridges

Wireless bridges can be used to interconnect wired or wireless networks between two campus buildings that are beyond the range of the Wi-Fi signal, especially when there are obstacles such as roads that need to be crossed, which can make using a wired connection either impractical or too expensive to install. Opening up a road to install fiber-optic cables can easily cost a few million dollars. Using existing wired technology deployed by telephone carriers or other kinds of providers often means paying high monthly fees. Instead, 802.11 bridges using directional antennas can be a good alternative. Multiple bridges and antennas can be combined in a single link to increase the throughput. For example, the combined data rate of three bridged connections at 300 Mbps each would be 900 Mbps. Even when you consider all of the transmission overhead in 802.11, the effective throughput of such a link might be enough to link two networks and support a significant number of users. Interference is usually not an issue because of the point-to-point nature of the connection; however, when deploying bridged links using unlicensed RF bands, it is up to the users to ensure that no other RF transmissions intersect the directional signal between the bridges. A bridge connection between two-wired LANs is illustrated in Figure 8-1.

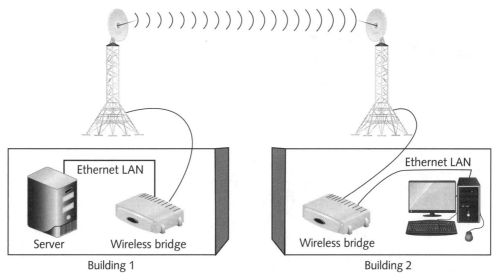

Figure 8-1   A bridged connection between two wired LANs

For long-distance links, in which the signal takes longer to arrive at the receiver, transmitting wireless bridges can extend the SIFS time, thereby allowing the receiver enough time to acknowledge a frame. (Recall that the ACK is always sent after the SIFS.) Extending the SIFS means that wireless bridges operate without fully conforming to the 802.11 standard, but it is an acceptable practice in a bridged, point-to-point configuration. Bridged connections can be up to 16 miles (25.7 kilometers), but the longer the distance, the slower the data rate. If you need to set up this type of connection, check your bridge specification carefully, and use the equipment vendor resources and expertise to test the connection before implementing and supporting users.

WLAN Range Extenders (Repeaters)

Wireless bridges as well as some APs and wireless routers can be configured as repeaters to extend the range of a WLAN. A bridge can often be configured to act as a repeater and connect to an AP. Devices that are out of the range of the access point can associate with the bridge, which will then forward the traffic between the devices and the AP. Some residential wireless routers and enterprise-class APs can also be configured as repeaters. Before purchasing an AP for this purpose, you should carefully check the user manual to make sure it meets your requirements. Figure 8-2 shows a WLAN with a repeater. The laptop in the figure is too far away to connect directly to the AP. Note that the 802.11 standard protocols allow only one repeater per AP. The same is true for home wireless routers. Note also that the repeater is not connected to the wired Ethernet network (see also the coverage of WIDS that follows). Because the laptop is out of range of the AP, it associates with the repeater instead. The laptop must follow all the DCF rules to transmit to the repeater, which must also acknowledge the frames. Then the repeater must go through the same process to forward the frames it receives from the laptop to the AP. The process is reversed when the AP transmits frames to the laptop.

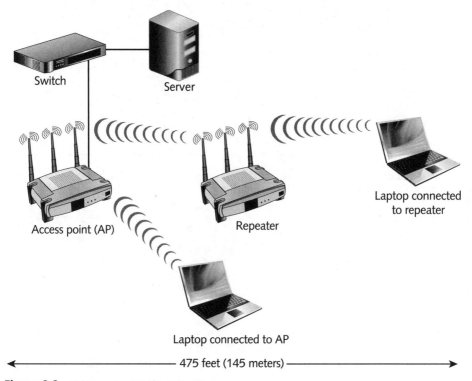

Figure 8-2   Using a repeater in a WLAN

Wireless repeaters are also available as stand-alone devices. In the consumer market, they are usually called Wi-Fi signal boosters or extenders.

Network designers should be aware of the extra delay introduced by a repeater in a WLAN. Certain kinds of business applications that connect to databases in client-server mode might not be able to tolerate the additional transmission delay, which could result in application issues. You also need to remember that this increased delay reduces the overall throughput of the link even further than if the laptop was communicating directly with the AP. This means that in a WLAN operating at a data rate of 300 Mbps, the maximum throughput will normally be about 150 Mbps or less. When you add a repeater to the WLAN, the throughput will be reduced by half again to about 75 Mbps due to the additional overhead.

Some APs and wireless routers (wireless residential gateways) can also be configured to extend the range of a WLAN. This feature is called **Wireless Distribution System (WDS)**, and it allows APs and wireless routers to communicate with each other without an Ethernet wired infrastructure. Devices can connect wirelessly to the WDS APs or routers that are not connected to the wired infrastructure, or they can use Ethernet cables as well. The WDS APs or routers act as repeaters or bridges, but also allow wired connections to client devices.

Search the web for the user manual for a late-model residential wireless router such as the ASUS RT-AC68U. Download the PDF of the manual, open it, and search for WDS to get an overview of how to configure a WLAN with WDS.

Wireless Controllers

When a large number of APs need to be deployed throughout a building or campus, managing the WLAN by managing each individual device becomes a challenge. Configuration settings can be distributed and administered remotely, but problems such as wireless connectivity and hardware failures usually demand that a technician be sent to the location—an expensive way to provide support.

In addition, APs often need to be deployed in branch offices, which increases support delays and cost when no technicians are stationed on-site. The more features an AP has, the more complex it can be to configure and manage. Signal coverage of APs is also difficult to monitor in remote locations.

An alternative way to simplify the management of a wireless network is to use a wireless controller. **Wireless controllers** include most of the functionality of an AP and include switch ports that can be used to connect to less complex APs. With a few exceptions, wireless controllers do not usually have any Wi-Fi radios. In the case of remote office locations, the controllers connect to the remote APs via a logical OSI Layer 2 or Layer 3 network connection. The simplified APs, usually called **lightweight APs** (**LWAPs**), consist of PHY-layer devices (radios) with some MAC-layer functionality. The wireless controller handles the interface and communications with the wired LAN and most of the MAC-layer functionality.

Using a wireless controller and LWAPs, the management of a WLAN can be effectively centralized. The administrator configures the WLAN on the wireless controller, including the parameters of the radios, and the configuration is then pushed to the APs automatically. If an AP fails, the controller can be configured to adjust the transmit power on two other nearby APs to restore Wi-Fi coverage to the area previously served by the failed AP. Extra APs can be set up as monitoring devices to detect the presence of unauthorized APs, as well as to monitor the quality of the wireless signals, and even to detect possible WLAN intrusions and security attacks.

Quality-of-service (QoS) features incorporated into the wireless controllers can make it easier to deploy **Voice over WLAN** (**VoWLAN**), transmitting voice calls on WLANs. Wireless controllers can greatly simplify the deployment and continuous management of large WLANs. A new breed of controllers, consisting of cloud-based software that is used to configure and manage the WLANs, employs APs that handle all of the MAC-layer functionality and forward traffic directly to the wired network, without involving the software-based controllers. These products make it very easy and simple to deploy and manage a WLAN.

For additional information on wireless controllers, see *www.cisco.com*, *www.arubanetworks.com*, and *meraki.cisco.com* and search for their wireless products. Meraki is among a few WLAN equipment manufacturers that do not make a hardware-based controller. Instead, its APs are managed exclusively over the Internet, using cloud-based software controllers.

WLAN Design Considerations

When designing and deploying enterprise WLANs, there are some considerations that must be taken into account. As discussed earlier, the size of the office or campus, the number of APs, security aspects, etc., must be taken into account. The design of enterprise networks usually follows a hierarchical structure including the core layer that includes servers and the main Internet connection, a distribution layer that functions as the main interconnection for all networking nodes, and finally the access layer where the switches, APs, user computers, and wireless devices reside. Figure 8-3 shows a hierarchical network design. Note the APs at the access layer, connected to switches that are also wireless controllers, and the wireless devices that communicate with the APs.

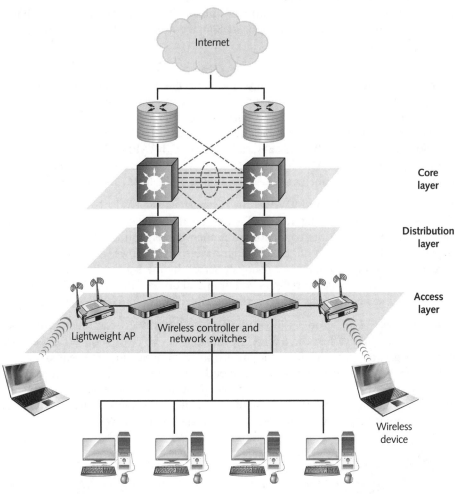

Figure 8-3 A hierarchical network design

Bridged connections between buildings are normally treated as a distribution layer technology. The limited data throughput and range of a Wi-Fi WLAN means that this technology would never be deployed at the core layer, the backbone of a network that usually employs fiber-optic technology to support very high data throughput.

The diagram in Figure 8-3 shows an example of an access layer network diagram using wireless controllers and LWAPs. Note the branch office connection, using wireless controllers and LWAPs. These are managed by the controller located at the head office, through the distribution layer. The connection to the branch offices can be made via dedicated communications lines or via the Internet using a VPN (see the section on VPN later in the chapter). Remote, branch office APs can also be managed using a cloud-based controller, if compatible.

Wi-Fi Direct

Although it has been possible to set up an ad hoc Wi-Fi network since the introduction of the 802.11 standard, configuring laptops, smartphones, printers, or other devices to connect to the WLAN has always required a certain amount of technical skill. This is true in spite of Windows Zero Configuration, Universal Plug and Play, WDS, and other methods that were created in an attempt to simplify configuration tasks for users.

Wi-Fi Direct is a Wi-Fi Alliance specification intended to make it simpler and more convenient for end users to share printers, share files, synchronize devices, play networked games, and display video and picture camera images and information without the need to join a WLAN in a home, hotspot, or office. With Wi-Fi Direct, devices can connect to each other at the press of a button, or by touching two devices that are near field communication (NFC) capable, as well as by entering a PIN number to automatically configure and connect two devices in peer-to-peer or ad hoc mode. Wi-Fi Direct employs a pre-defined set of configuration parameters, including security, and pre-defined services, depending on the type of device, that lets users "discover" other capable devices and eliminates the need to manually configure a connection between the two. With Wi-Fi Direct, a connection between two compatible devices can be established even when there is not a wireless router or AP.

Many new photo and video cameras, as well as several other types of devices, now include Wi-Fi Direct and make it quite simple for users to connect them to their smartphones or tablets, wherever they may be. In photo and video cameras, this feature allows users to view the image that the camera will produce, control the camera, and shoot remotely.

WLANs and Multimedia Distribution

The explosive growth in the WLAN market originally spawned a new range of software and equipment for media distribution in the wirelessly connected home, such as PCs that were dedicated to playing media. High-speed and higher-capacity WLAN standards, coupled with the WMM specification from the Wi-Fi Alliance, have made many of the products created specifically for distributing media or connecting computers and media projectors unnecessary. Instead of dedicated standards, media player devices like Apple TV, Western Digital WDTV, Roku, Google Chromecast, Amazon Fire, and others simply take advantage of an existing WLAN to accomplish the same task. This section looks at a previous standard and a couple of specifications developed to support multimedia distribution, compares them, and looks at what might happen as a result of the development of the recent IEEE 802.11ad standard.

IEEE 802.15.3c

IEEE 802.15.3c is an amendment to the 802.15.3-2003 personal area network standard. The original standard specified operation in the 2.4 GHz band and the amendment, introduced in 2009, was developed to support high-rate transmissions for multimedia distribution in homes, businesses, hotels, conference centers, etc. The amendment defines operation in the 60 GHz band and includes support for:

- Superframe operation
- Contention access periods to allow devices to connect and communicate on the PAN
- Guaranteed time slots that allow video and audio transmissions to be prioritized
- Omnidirectional and quasi-omnidirectional transmission using beamforming in the 60 GHz band, to increase the gain at the receiver, and enhance the range
- Frame aggregation to support high-throughput transmission in the 60 GHz band
- Channel probing to allow devices to determine the best modulation and coding (MCS) to be used under the current RF channel condition

Since 2003, two industry associations were formed by several well-known manufacturers of TVs, video, and audio equipment. These organizations created specifications for transmitting HDMI audio and video signals wirelessly to a compatible device.

The **WirelessHD** specification transmits video and audio on the 60 GHz band and has a range of 30 feet (10 meters). Some add-on equipment is available in both the business and consumer markets that support the WirelessHD and WHDI (discussed below) specifications, but although many of the same TV and audio manufacturers are members of the organizations that are behind these technologies, their market penetration has been limited, so far. To date two models of Dell Alienware laptops have been produced and sold that incorporate WirelessHD interfaces. In addition to the laptop, users must also purchase a receiver device to connect to their TV sets in order to play PC games using a wireless connection to large TV screens or monitors. Dell also offers a dock for PCs or laptops that allows wireless connection to desktop monitors. The **Wireless Home Digital Interface (WHDI)** association's specification utilizes the 5 GHz band and can transmit signals to a 1080p-compatible television from laptops or desktop PCs, game consoles, and even mobile devices with a maximum range of 100 feet (30 meters). Neither of these technologies is compatible with 802.11.

To learn more about WirelessHD, visit *www.wirelessHD.org*.

You can view videos about some WHDI devices available on the market today, on the main page of the WHDI organization website at *www.whdi.org*.

As you learned in Chapter 7, the IEEE introduced the 802.11ad amendment, along with the Wi-Fi Alliance's specifications, which make it possible for devices to switch seamlessly between 60 GHz and the 5 GHz bands using 802.11ac, when transmission at the higher-frequency band is not possible due to obstacles or distance. This feature of 802.11ad is likely to eventually make WirelessHD and WHDI equipment redundant, but this might not happen until 802.11ad is included with video monitors and business audio equipment. In the meantime, WHDI and Wireless HD equipment will likely continue to be available as upgrades to audio and video devices. In the future, it appears to make more sense for everyone to standardize on 802.11ac/ad. A few manufacturers already provide residential wireless routers and laptops with 802.11ad-compatible wireless NICs.

WLAN Security

No discussion of WLANs would be complete without considering the topic of security. Broadcasting network traffic over EM waves has created an entirely new set of issues for keeping data transmissions secure. It is no secret to IT professionals that the security provisions of the original IEEE 802.11 standard were seriously flawed and, as a result, businesses were initially reluctant to deploy WLANs. The security measures originally defined in 802.11 were "broken" within a matter of minutes. Since then, both the IEEE and Wi-Fi Alliance have done a lot of work to improve the security of WLANs, and it has improved to the point where WLANs are widely deployed in businesses everywhere today.

Because the 802.11 standard defines how data is transmitted at the PHY and MAC layers, the security implementations are similar to those used in an Ethernet network. However, because WLAN transmissions utilize a medium (EM waves) that is not confined to wires, information transmitted on a WLAN is far more exposed to intrusion, jamming, and hijacking.

No security measure can prevent all potential breaches. Security must always be viewed as a work in progress and be constantly monitored. Network administrators must check systems and logs regularly to ensure that security has not been compromised. For example, a user who frequently travels with a laptop computer often needs to configure his system to connect to other WLANs. Some types of unsecured connections, such as hotspots, can expose a company's LAN or WLAN to security attacks and breaches unless certain measures are taken to prevent this and protect the company. In addition to discussing security concepts, this section provides an introduction to some common types of network attacks as well as measures that have been engineered by the IEEE and Wi-Fi Alliance to improve WLAN security.

The IEEE 802.11 standard defines several steps for securing WLANs, along with support for keeping data private through the use of encryption.

Authentication

Authentication is the process of verifying that the devices have permission to access the WLAN or the wired network through an AP. The authentication process only verifies that the device is allowed to access the wired network via the AP. A wireless device only "knows" that it is connecting to a WLAN using the SSID and password provided by the user, but it cannot determine if the AP is actually part of the enterprise WLAN; in other words, it could be a rogue AP set up by an unscrupulous person to impersonate the correct WLAN (more on this in the 802.11i section later in the chapter).

In a BSS or ESS, a device can be configured with the SSID of the WLAN, or in most cases, a user can simply select the SSID from a list because, by default, APs automatically transmit the SSID of the WLAN in every beacon frame. The SSID of a WLAN is also included in beacon frames transmitted in an ad hoc WLAN.

An administrator can configure the APs to "hide" (not transmit) the SSID in beacon frames. However, if an AP receives a probe request frame from an active scanning device, the 802.11 standard specifies that the AP must send a probe response frame that includes the SSID of the WLAN.

Data Privacy

Privacy is different from authentication. Authentication ensures that the device has permission to be part of the network. Privacy is part of a group of processes that attempts to ensure that unauthorized persons who may be able to capture the wireless transmissions will not be able to decode and understand the data. This is accomplished with **encryption**, which scrambles the data, according to complex mathematical formulas, in a way that it cannot be read. The data can only be decoded (unencrypted) by the intended recipient device, which also has access to an encryption key and can decode the message. The strength of encryption rests not only on keeping the keys secret but also with the length of the key itself. The longer the key, the stronger the encryption, because longer keys are more difficult to break. The trade-off is that stronger encryption increases the number of bits of data transmitted, which in turn decreases the overall throughput of the WLAN.

Wired Equivalent Privacy (WEP) was the only optional encryption feature introduced in the 802.11-1997 standard. WEP was used to encrypt the data between wireless devices to prevent eavesdropping. WEP encryption is a shared key that must be entered on the AP and all devices allowed to connect to the WLAN, and WEP encryption comes in two versions: 64-bit encryption and 128-bit encryption. The former uses a 40-bit key (5 bytes or 10 hexadecimal digits) plus a 24-bit initialization vector (IV), which is part of the encryption key, but is transmitted as clear text (unencrypted) before the encrypted data. Likewise, the 128-bit encryption uses a 104-bit key plus a 24-bit IV. Some vendors offered 256-bit encryption, which was not part of the 802.11 standard, and could cause compatibility issues among equipment from different manufacturers. Even 256-bit encryption still used the same 24-bit IV.

In 2001, researchers at various universities outlined just how an attacker could collect the necessary data for breaking WEP encryption. By late 2001, they were able to "break" the 128-bit WEP key used in a WLAN transmission in less than 2 hours. In 2005, the time to break WEP encryption was reduced to less than 2 minutes when the attacker was able to capture around 200,000 frames. WEP uses a weak implementation of an encryption algorithm (RC4) that was developed by Ron Rivest for RSA Data Security, Inc.; except in the case of some older home networks, it should not be used today to secure any WLAN.

Some manufacturers designed their equipment to use up to four different WEP keys, which could be rotated regularly, based on a timer, depending on certain configuration parameters, but this was also considered very weak security.

Wi-Fi Protected Access (WPA) is a standard for encryption introduced by the Wi-Fi Alliance in response to the weaknesses of WEP. WPA uses a 128-bit **pre-shared key (PSK)**, also known as WPA Personal, which needs to be manually added to the configuration of every device that will be connected to the WLAN. Unlike WEP, WPA-PSK uses a different encryption key for each client device, for each packet, and for each communications session.

WPA-PSK is not suitable for larger companies with many client devices because the passphrase has to be created by the user and manually entered on both the AP and devices. Strong passphrases should be longer than 8 bytes and should include a mixture of letters, numbers, and non-alphanumeric characters. The passphrase is used by the hardware to generate an encryption key. This key is rotated, based on a user-configurable timer that is often set to 300 seconds (5 minutes) by manufacturers. This mode does not offer the same level of protection as enterprise-class systems that rely on an authentication server installed somewhere else on the network.

WPA employs the **temporal key integrity protocol (TKIP)**, which provides per-packet and per-session key-mixing; in other words, each packet and each webpage requested uses a different security key for encryption. In addition, TKIP also includes **message integrity check (MIC)**, which uses a combination of variable and static data items, such as the current network uptime (not based on current clock time) and other data items, to ensure that the encrypted data has not been tampered with. With WEP, it was possible to intercept a frame and tamper (or change) the encrypted data to serve the needs of an attacker, with little possibility of detection. MIC verifies that an attacker has not modified the data sent by the source device.

TKIP uses a 48-bit hashed (scrambled) initialization vector, and WPA also includes the methods necessary for the AP to change the keys and transmit the new key to all client devices.

WPA2 is an enhancement to WPA that can use much stronger encryption. The IEEE also certified WPA2 as compatible with IEEE 802.11i, which is described in the next section. Both add support for the **Advanced Encryption Standard (AES)**, established by the U.S. National Institute of Standards and Technology in 2001, to meet the U.S. government security requirements. However, because AES requires additional processing power, it often cannot be supported by older, slower WLAN hardware. When using AES encryption, TKIP is not used.

The Wi-Fi Alliance has certification programs for WPA and WPA2. Vendors use these programs to verify that their equipment complies with these security methods and to ensure that it will interoperate with equipment from other vendors.

Introduction to Enterprise WLAN Security

The IEEE 802.11i amendment, ratified in June 2004, was the result of a series of efforts by the IEEE to deal with the security weaknesses of the original WLAN standard. **802.11i** is a grouping of several security functions that protects WLAN data frames by providing mutual authentication between wireless devices and access points, controlled access to the network, establishment of security keys, and key management. Together with **802.1X**, a series of recommendations for implementation of a grouping of security functions, 802.11i defines a **Robust Security Network Association (RSNA)**, which is the end result of using the 802.1X recommendations and 802.11i amendment to secure an enterprise WLAN. Full coverage of 802.11i and 802.1X is a topic for advanced security courses and is beyond the scope of this text.

 802.1X is part of the IEEE 802.1 group of network standards and applies to wired as well as wireless networks. However, 802.1X is not an amendment to any standard; it is a set of recommendations for implementation of RSNA.

In 802.11i, a client device must be authenticated on the network by an external authentication server—such as a **Remote Authentication Dial-In User Service (RADIUS)**, a popular method of authenticating users on a network—before completing its association with an AP. Some APs offer an option to authenticate devices on the AP itself, using an internal RADIUS server, but this is not considered as secure as using an external server. All communications between the mobile device and the wired network are blocked until the authentication process is completed, after which data protection through encryption and MIC are enabled. Only then communication between the wireless devices and the wired network is allowed. Figure 8-4 shows a diagram of a typical network employing an external RADIUS authentication server.

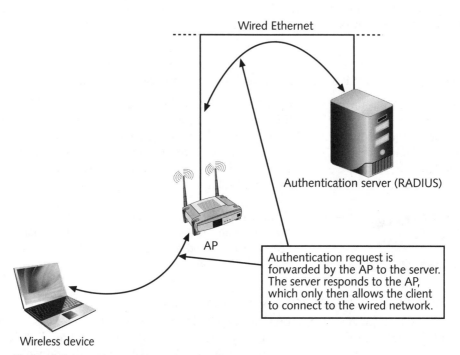

Figure 8-4   Securing a WLAN using a RADIUS server

RADIUS software is available from many different vendors and also in a free version called FreeRADIUS. The "Dial-In" portion of RADIUS is a holdover from the old telephone line modem days. RADIUS is applicable to wired as well as wireless networks. FreeRADIUS is available for download from many Internet sites and is supported by a variety of networking devices, including APs, wireless routers, and so on.

802.1X uses the **Extensible Authentication Protocol (EAP)** for relaying access requests between a wireless device, the AP, and the RADIUS server. There are several variations of EAP, each supporting a different authentication method and its associated network-security policies. For EAP to work, all three devices must support the same authentication method. When EAP is used, the network administrator does not need to configure a WPA passphrase or WEP key in each computer or device. The RADIUS server provides the key to the AP, which then provides it to the wireless devices. This saves configuration effort and time both initially and when the key is periodically changed. This method of authentication also indirectly verifies to the client device that it is communicating with an authorized AP, instead of a hacker's computer impersonating an enterprise AP.

Wi-Fi Protected Setup (Push-Button Wireless Security)

Because many home users who install wireless networks fail to set up proper security, leaving their networks exposed to potential attackers, most vendors today implement a method specified by the Wi-Fi Alliance of securely connecting mobile devices to wireless residential routers. **Wi-Fi Protected Setup (WPS)** simplifies the process of securing a WLAN for nontechnical users. Although each vendor's method may have a different name or acronym, all of them provide either a physical button on the front panel of the wireless router or a graphical software-defined button in the configuration software that can automatically configure the security settings in both the wireless router and the mobile device called WPS. Keep in mind that to take advantage of this type of push-button wireless security, both the wireless NIC and the AP or router must support the feature. The button needs to be activated once on each router, and once on each mobile device, one at a time. The feature transfers the security key to the wireless NIC, then automatically establishes a connection with the wireless device. If you are using wireless NICs and gateways from different vendors, check first to make sure this feature is compatible.

Virtual Private Networks

Virtual private networks (VPNs) use specialized protocols that create a virtual "tunnel" between two points across a public network such as the Internet. Packets from each network are encrypted and encapsulated in VPN PDUs that can only be unencapsulated and decrypted at the destination network, hence the virtual "tunnel" concept. VPNs use strong encryption algorithms such as AES and are the most secure method that can be used to access a corporate network from a remote location.

There are basically two types of VPN implementation:

- Site-to-site VPNs are used to interconnect two LANs across a public network. This type of connection is typically set up between two company routers to interconnect the main office with a branch and remains in place indefinitely. Encryption is almost always done by dedicated hardware in the routers.

- Client-to-site VPNs are temporary connections from a remote office or from a public network such as a hotspot, using mobile devices. In this type of VPN, encryption is usually done by the VPN software running on the devices.

Security specialists and VPN users must keep in mind that encryption in client-to-site VPNs tends to consume a large amount of processing resources; therefore, certain time-sensitive client-server applications might not perform acceptably in a VPN environment. Most public wireless networks are not secured at all, and using them can expose corporate data to an attacker—such as emails and application data, including customer information—if the data is not encrypted. In fact, if VPNs are not implemented properly, the entire corporate network can be exposed to attacks.

Full coverage of VPNs, protocols, and techniques is beyond the scope of this text. For more information on VPNs, start with this Wikipedia article: *en.wikipedia.org/wiki/Virtual_private_network*.

Figure 8-5 shows a diagram of the two basic types of VPNs.

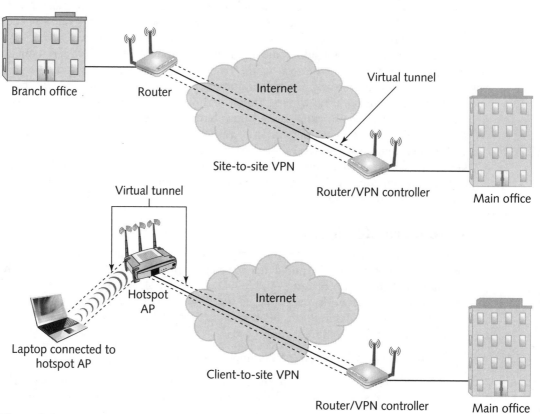

Figure 8-5   Site-to-site and client-to-site VPNs

Intrusion Detection and Intrusion Prevention

Most business networks implement one or more methods of detecting when an intruder attempts to "hack" into their wireless networks. A **Wireless Intrusion Prevention System (WIPS)** is a stand-alone wireless device or a feature of some advanced APs that can be deployed to monitor the RF spectrum and detect the presence of unauthorized APs. For example, a company employee can purchase a consumer-type wireless router and connect it to the wired network, hidden from view. Because such consumer devices cannot be set up by the employee to use the company's authentication server, they can expose the wired network to security attacks. When a WIPS detects an unauthorized wireless router, it can be configured to automatically force wireless devices to disconnect from the unauthorized router or AP, rendering it useless.

A **Wireless Intrusion Detection System (WIDS)** differs from WIPS in that it sends a notification to system administrators, instead of acting automatically when it detects an intrusion. It is then up to the WLAN administrator to locate and remove the unauthorized AP using other types of wireless networking tools.

Additional WLAN Security Tactics

In addition to the security strategies discussed in the previous section, you can increase WLAN security by reducing WLAN transmission power. However, keep in mind that an attacker equipped with a high-gain directional antenna would still be able to detect the RF signal. Changing the default security settings on the APs is probably the first and most important step in WLAN security. Don't forget antivirus and antispyware software. Mobile wireless clients are exposed to more of these threats when operating outside company offices and can introduce those threats into your corporate network once they are connected to the office wired network again.

For highly secure WLANs, administrators usually separate WLAN traffic from wired network traffic by placing a firewall between the WLAN and the wired LAN and use virtual local area networks (VLANs) to redirect traffic from the WLAN to the wired network via the firewall. This is especially important in corporate networks if you allow guest wireless devices to connect to your WLAN for Internet access.

Attacks Against WLANs

A variety of attacks can be employed against WLANs. Some of the more dangerous are hardware loss or theft, AP impersonation, passive monitoring, and denial-of-service (DoS) attacks.

The theft or loss of a mobile device is one example of a serious threat, because such devices are often configured to automatically connect to the corporate WLAN. Whoever ends up with the device might be able to use it to gain access to the corporate network and resources.

AP impersonation takes advantage of a problem with legacy 802.11 WLANs, which is that devices authenticate themselves with the APs, but unless an external authentication server is being used, devices do not know whether they are communicating with an authorized AP or not. When a rogue AP or AP impersonation software is installed on a mobile computer, it can trick clients into associating with it, allowing information from the devices to be monitored and allowing attempts to break the security keys. AP impersonation software on a laptop can spoof a corporate AP's MAC address and other parameters to make devices "think" that they are connecting to an authorized AP. This type of attack is called **man-in-the-middle**.

Passive monitoring, in which an attacker simply captures data transmissions, can also be used to acquire information, such as the MAC and IP addresses of APs and wireless clients. Over time, the attacker can build a profile of the WLAN and may be able to use this information to break into the network. An attacker can use a wireless sniffer to capture enough frames to decode the security key. Although this requires capturing perhaps several million frames (depending on the type of security key used) and can consume a huge amount of computer processing power, it can be done, especially if an attacker is targeting a particular company and has plenty of time (and computer power) to spare. Because management and control frames are not always encrypted, they can be intercepted and important data collected to help create an attack. An attacker can, for example, use this information to flood the network with transmissions directed at one or more devices. This is one example of a **denial-of-service (DoS)** attack that can effectively deny other devices access to the WLAN. DoS attacks against WLANs can take other forms as well, such as RF jamming of the frequency channel to prevent devices and APs from being able to receive frames correctly.

DoS attacks and AP impersonation can be easily detected and avoided through the use of intrusion detection and prevention equipment and software. Although this can cost thousands of dollars, it can prove a worthwhile investment if the company is subject to an attack that could end up costing a lot more in lost productivity or failure to comply with privacy laws (in cases where information is stolen).

Using MAC Filters to Enhance Security

In addition to the earlier discussions about hiding the SSID of the WLAN, APs and residential wireless routers also offer WLAN administrators the ability to limit access to the network by filtering the connections at the AP or wireless router based on the MAC address, allowing only devices with specific MAC addresses to associate and authenticate. Although this feature can be useful in large office areas to force devices to connect only with specified APs to control the maximum number of devices that connect to each AP, it is considered a weak security method because MAC addresses can be easily spoofed using an application like Technitium MAC Address Changer for Microsoft Windows, for example. Some manufacturers also allow an alternate MAC address to be configured directly in the NIC driver. Both of these methods are useful for testing and troubleshooting purposes, to enable a technician to use a single computer instead of multiple ones.

Technitium MAC Address Changer is a free utility available for download from several websites, or directly from *technitium.com /tmac/index.html*. SMAC is another example of utility software that can be used to change the MAC address on Windows computers.

Chapter Summary

- Wireless bridges are used to interconnect two-wired networks across distances of up to 16 miles (25 kilometers) using directional antennas. Multiple bridge connections on the same link can be combined to increase the data rate and effective throughput. Longer-distance connections require that the SIFS time be extended to allow the receiving bridge to acknowledge frames without generating a timeout error at the transmitting bridge.

- Wi-Fi range extenders or repeaters, sometimes erroneously called Wi-Fi signal boosters in consumer devices, can extend the range of a WLAN; however, the maximum data rate of the device or AP is effectively cut in half when communicating via a repeater, since transmissions must follow the DCF rules.

- Wireless controllers are devices designed to simplify the implementation and management of enterprise WLANs that use many APs. Using wireless controllers, administrators can also more easily deploy VoWLAN. Lightweight APs can be connected directly to Ethernet ports on the controller or remotely at OSI Layers 2 or 3, depending on the manufacturer. Cloud-based software controllers, as opposed to hardware-based, make it very easy to deploy and manage WLANs.

- WLANs are usually deployed as an access layer technology in hierarchical network designs, but bridged connections typically fall under the distribution layer.

- Wi-Fi Direct simplifies the connection between two wireless devices, without the need for an AP or wireless router. It can automatically configure a direct connection as well as security settings. Wi-Fi Direct can use near field communication to configure a direct connection to Bluetooth speakers or configure Wi-Fi between a camera and a smartphone.

- Dedicated wireless technologies and standards have been created to distribute voice, audio, and video in offices, homes, hotels, etc., in both the relatively quiet 5 GHz frequency band, as well as in the 60 GHz band. WirelessHD and WHDI have been supported by several consumer and office equipment manufacturers, but adoption by manufacturers and availability of equipment has been limited, so far. The introduction of the IEEE 802.11ac and 802.11ad amendments makes it possible to distribute multimedia using the same Wi-Fi technology that is used for home and office WLANs. The ability to switch frequency bands automatically between 802.11ac and 802.11ad could generate more interest and faster adoption.

- WLAN security in the original 802.11 standard was too weak to convince corporations to deploy Wi-Fi networks. Since then, the security of WLANs has been significantly improved and now supports authentication methods that have been in use by businesses for decades.

- Data privacy in WLANs today uses the Advanced Encryption Standard (AES), which meets the U.S. government requirements, to prevent attackers from being able to access user information.

- Wi-Fi Protected Setup (WPS) makes it easy for nontechnical users to configure strong security for residential WLANs.

- There are several types of security attacks that can create problems for WLANs. IEEE 802.11 WLANs require enhanced security measures because the signal can be captured by a would-be attacker from anywhere nearby, without access to the physical infrastructure. WLAN security has been greatly enhanced through the introduction of Wi-Fi Protected Access (WPA and WPA2).

- WLANs can also be protected against attacks through the use of VPNs, 802.11i authentication, and 802.1X security measures. Authentication is a process for verifying that the user has permission to access the network and ensuring that the client device is communicating with an authorized AP. Privacy is a collection of data-encryption processes for ensuring that unauthorized persons do not read transmissions.

- Wireless Intrusion Prevention System (WIPS) and Wireless Intrusion Detection System (WIDS) are methods that can be used to prevent the use of unauthorized APs and alert WLAN administrators to a potential breach of security.

Key Terms

802.1X   a series of IEEE recommendations for implementation of a grouping of security functions in 802.11.

802.11i   A grouping of several IEEE 802.11 security functions that protects WLAN data frames by providing mutual authentication between wireless devices and access points, controlled access to the network, establishment of security keys, and key management.

802.15.3c   An amendment to the IEEE 802.15.3 personal area network standard that specified operation in the 2.4 GHz band to support high-rate transmission for the distribution of video and audio and audio signals throughout homes, businesses, hotels, conference centers, and so on.

Advanced Encryption Standard (AES)   An encryption standard established by the U.S. National Institute of Standards and Technology that meets the security requirements of the U.S. government.

authentication   A process that verifies that a mobile device has permission to access the WLAN or the wired network through an AP.

denial-of-service (DoS)   A type of attack on a network in which an attacker performs RF jamming of the frequency channel or floods the network with frame transmissions directed at one or more devices to corrupt and block all other communications.

encryption   A process of scrambling data, usually according to complex mathematical formulas, designed to prevent anyone except the intended recipient from being able to read what is being transmitted.

Extensible Authentication Protocol (EAP)   A group of security protocols defined in IEEE 802.1X (see IEEE 802.1X) for network authentication between a wireless device, an AP, and a RADIUS server.

lightweight AP (LWAP)   A PHY-layer wireless device that also implements part of the MAC-layer functionality. These devices are used in conjunction with wireless controllers (see wireless controller).

man-in-the-middle   A network-security attack in which the attacker uses software installed in a computer to duplicate the behavior of an enterprise AP.

message integrity check (MIC)   A combination of variable and static data items that ensures encrypted data has not been altered during transmission between source and destination devices.

pre-shared key (PSK)   A 128-bit key used by WPA; it is called "pre-shared" because it is manually configured in each WLAN device before connections can be established.

privacy   Standards that ensure transmissions are not read by unauthorized users.

Remote Authentication Dial-In User Service (RADIUS)   A popular method of authenticating users on a network—before completing its association with an AP.

Robust Security Network Association (RSNA)   The end result of using 802.11i and 802.1X to secure an enterprise WLAN.

temporal key integrity protocol (TKIP)   A security protocol used in WPA that provides per-packet key-mixing.

virtual private network (VPN)   A secure, encrypted connection between two points over a public network.

voice over WLAN (VoWLAN)   A term used to describe the transmission of telephone calls on WLANs.

Wi-Fi Direct   A specification from the Wi-Fi Alliance that makes it simpler to wirelessly connect any two devices, such as a camera and a smartphone.

Wi-Fi Protected Access (WPA)   A security enhancement and interoperability certification introduced by the Wi-Fi Alliance in advance of the 802.11i standard to deal with the security flaws in WEP. *See also* WPA2.

Wi-Fi Protected Setup (WPS)   A method defined by the Wi-Fi alliance that simplifies the process of securing a WLAN for nontechnical users.

Wired Equivalent Privacy (WEP)   The IEEE 802.11-1997 specification for data encryption between wireless devices to prevent an attacker from eavesdropping.

wireless bridge   A networking component that is typically used to interconnect two-wired networks using directional antennas. Multiple bridges can be combined in a single link, to increase the data rate and throughput.

wireless controller   A device that makes it much easier to manage large WLANs by implementing most of the functions of an AP and controlling the operation of local or remotely connected Wi-Fi transceivers called lightweight APs (see lightweight AP). Some controllers are implemented in software, which allows cloud-based management of WLANs.

Wireless Distribution System (WDS)   A feature of some wireless routers and APs that enables them to be configured as a bridge or repeater.

WirelessHD   A specification by the WirelessHD organization that works in the 60 GHz band and is used for transmitting HDMI video and audio signals to televisions and display monitors. WirelessHD is not compatible with 802.11.

Wireless Home Digital Interface (WHDI)   An industry association that developed a wireless HDMI multimedia distribution specification of the same name (WHDI), which operates in the 5 GHz U-NII band. Like WirelessHD, WHDI is not compatible with 802.11.

Wireless Intrusion Detection System (WIDS) A WIDS can detect the presence of unauthorized devices, such as a computer impersonating an AP and send a notification to system administrators.

Wireless Intrusion Prevention System (WIPS) A stand-alone hardware device or feature of some advanced APs that can be deployed to monitor the RF spectrum and detect the presence of unauthorized APs.

WPA2 A security specification and interoperability certification introduced by the Wi-Fi Alliance as an enhancement to WPA that includes support for AES encryption as well as support for 802.11i and 802.1X.

Review Questions

1. What type of 802.11 wireless device is designed primarily to interconnect two-wired networks?

   a. Repeater

   b. Bridge

   c. Access point

   d. Wi-Fi booster

2. What can you do if you need to interconnect two buildings across a university campus using wireless technologies, but you need more throughput than the maximum available in any of the amendments to the 802.11 standard?

   a. Configure APs to make the frames shorter.

   b. Use a directional antenna with a very high gain.

   c. Combine multiple bridges into one link.

   d. It is not possible to increase the throughput of a WLAN.

3. What is the purpose of configuring an AP as a repeater?

   a. To increase the range of a WLAN

   b. To increase the throughput in a WLAN

   c. To reduce transmission delay

   d. APs cannot be configured as repeaters

4. What is another name for a Wi-Fi signal booster?

   a. Wi-Fi amplifier

   b. High-gain antenna

   c. Wi-Fi range enhancer

   d. Repeater

5. Using Wi-Fi bridges over long distances means that they do not comply fully with the 802.11 standard. True or False?

6. A wireless controller handles all of the functionality of an AP. True or False?

7. LWAPs can only be connected directly to a wireless controller. True or False?

8. What does an administrator need to do when an AP fails in a remote office, when using wireless controllers?

   a. Dispatch a technician to the site to replace the AP as soon as possible.

   b. Configure the controller to automatically increase power on two other APs to maintain coverage.

   c. Install a repeater on the remote site until the failed AP can be replaced.

   d. Install a bridge between the remote and local sites to continue providing coverage in the area where the AP failed.

9. What would be the approximate throughput of an 802.11n bridged link using three bridges and linking two buildings across the street from each other (disregarding possible interference issues)?

   a. 450 Mbps

   b. 300 Mbps

   c. 900 Mbps

   d. Unable to estimate

10. At which layer of a hierarchical network design are APs deployed?

    a. Layer 2

    b. Distribution

    c. Access

    d. Core

11. The Wi-Fi Alliance specification that simplifies connections between a camera and a smartphone is called _____.

    a. WPA2

    b. WIPS

    c. WCS

    d. Wi-Fi Direct

12. Which technology can enable distribution of video and audio files from a laptop to a TV, using either the 60 GHz or the 5 GHz bands, and can switch between them automatically?

    a. 802.11ad and 802.11ac

    b. 802.15.3c

    c. WHDI

    d. WirelessHD

13. The _____ encryption method is considered very weak in 802.11 and was used in WEP.

    a. AES

    b. WEM

    c. RC4

    d. None

14. Which of the following is one of the most important reasons that a company would deploy a wireless controller?

    a. It enables bridging of multiple WLANs.

    b. It enhances security.

    c. It simplifies management of the WLAN.

    d. Wireless controllers support TKIP.

15. Which of the following is the best method for enhancing WLAN security in an enterprise?

    a. Using TKIP and WEP

    b. Deploying an authentication server on the network

    c. Changing frequencies periodically

    d. Installing equipment that supports 802.11s

16. Why is WEP considered far inferior to WPA and WPA2?

    a. It transmits an unencrypted 24-bit IV.

    b. The AP cannot properly authenticate the client devices.

    c. It does not support encryption at all.

    d. It is more secure than using RADIUS.

17. Which of the following can be called a key advantage of WPA2 over WPA?

    a. It uses the much stronger AES encryption.

    b. It supports EAP.

    c. It supports TKIP and MIC.

    d. All of the above.

18. The combination of IEEE 802.11i and 802.1X defines a _____.

    a. Firewall

    b. WPA2

    c. RSNA

    d. Security configuration block

19. Using _____ helps ensure that wireless devices are allowed to connect to an AP, but it also verifies to the wireless devices that the AP they are connecting to is an authorized device.

    a. WEP

    b. Remote Authentication Dial-In User Service

    c. AES

    d. controllers

Hands-On Projects

Project 8-1

This project is intended to provide you an overview of the configuration process and management features of a web-based soft controller and APs. Configuration of a hardware-based controller is very similar, but requires the purchase of wireless controllers and APs.

1. Either you or your instructor can go to *meraki.cisco.com*, click the **DEMO** link at the top right of the page, then click **Start Demo** under Start Instant Demo.

2. Running the demo requires that you register on the site. If you do not have all of the information required to register, your instructor can register and run the demo for the class.

3. Take this opportunity to become more familiar with the available products and write a short, one-page report outlining your findings about using controllers to setup Wi-Fi in an enterprise environment.

Project 8-2

This project covers the basic security configuration of an 802.11 residential gateway. An AP would be configured in a similar way. You can do this project using any manufacturer's device. The brand of the equipment is not important, because in the real world you will likely have to configure a variety of different equipment makes and models. Although the configuration screens will be different than the ones shown in the figures, the point of this exercise is for you to explore and understand which configuration items to modify and how these will affect the security of the wireless links.

The device used to create this exercise is an ASUS RT-AC68U 802.11ac compatible wireless residential gateway. (It is a wireless router, but we will call it a gateway from now on, since routers are the gateways to other networks, which in the case of a home WLAN is usually the Internet.) The gateway supports simultaneous dual-band (2.4 and 5 GHz), and a PC running Windows 7 Professional, but virtually any type of wireless residential gateway and PC or Mac will work. The project covers only those settings that are relevant to security and assumes you already know (from Chapters 6 and 7) how to perform the basic configuration steps and connect a computer with a wireless NIC to the gateway.

1. Connect your computer to the gateway using an Ethernet cable. You should always use a wired connection to change settings on a gateway or access point. Some of the settings, such as security, will cause your computer to disconnect from the wireless link until you reconfigure it to use the new settings, which can waste a lot of time. Figure 8-6 shows a configuration page and the parameters you need to access to configure security on the 5 GHz band. The configuration steps for the 2.4 GHz are the same.

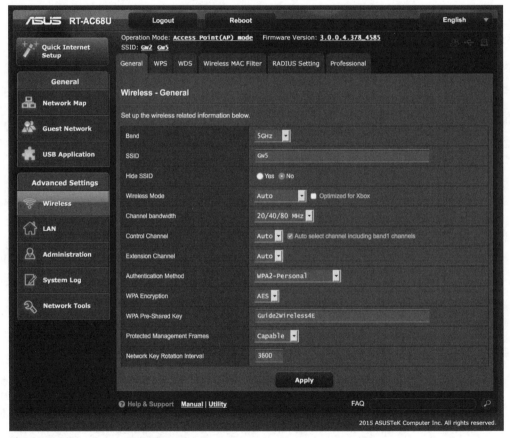

Figure 8-6   Configuring WLAN security

Source: ASUSTeK Computer Inc.

2. Ensure that you configured a unique SSID for each of the bands. You do not want to have the same SSID for both, or your devices will not know which radio to use, since they can only connect to one radio at a time. Consult with your instructor in case there are other gateways being used in the same classroom, to make sure you do not have duplicate SSIDs being used by someone else. Recall that the SSID is case sensitive.

3. The wireless security configuration can appear on a separate tab, or under a security menu setting. Each manufacturer's configuration user interface might be different than the screen shown in Figure 8-5, but it is usually not difficult navigate and find what you need.

4. Be sure to select WPA2-PSK (pre-shared key) or WPA2-Personal with AES encryption. You can use the same key, sometimes also called a password or passphrase, for both the 2.4 and 5 GHz radios, but you will need to configure two different connection profiles on your wireless devices, one for each SSID and frequency band.

5. Once you have configured your security settings, click **OK** or **Apply** to save your settings. The gateway usually reboots, which can take a minute or two, but the browser page should open automatically after the reboot and display your new settings. Now repeat Steps 1 through 5 for the other radio or frequency band. Note that sometimes you can configure both radios in a single step.

6. Configure the wireless network connection profile on one or more wireless devices to connect to the now secure WLAN.

7. Most gateways are able to display how many and which devices are connected to it. If the MAC address of the devices is displayed, compare it with the MAC address of your devices.

8. Now you can challenge yourself and experiment with other settings, such as hiding the SSID, deleting and trying to re-create the connection profile on your wireless devices, and setting up MAC filters to prevent certain devices from connecting, allowing only the devices you want to connect to the gateway.

9. Be sure to click **OK** or **Apply** to enable any of the functionality you just changed.

Real-World Exercise

Exercise 8-1

The Baypoint Group (TBG) needs your help to prepare a presentation for Academic Computing Services Inc. (ACS), a nationwide organization that assists colleges and universities with technology issues, on the advantages of using an external authentication server to protect their network. ACS would like to learn more about enterprise WLAN security so that its staff will be better prepared to explain the options to their customers.

Prepare a PowerPoint presentation that outlines the security strengths and weaknesses of WLANs and makes recommendations about the level of security that ACS should recommend to its customers in a variety of situations, such as when equipment is used in office applications and when wireless laptops or mobile devices are used by students. Your presentation should consist of at least 10, but not more than 15, slides and should cover encryption and authentication using 802.11i and 802.1X.

To assist you in preparing your presentation, search the web for "WLAN Security Best Practices."

Challenge Case Project

ACS found your presentation very useful but would like to know how someone can break into a WLAN that is configured with MAC filters. To prepare a live demonstration for ACS, you will need to download and install the Technitium MAC Address Changer software, and set up MAC filters on your gateway or AP to block a certain device. You can also use the software to hide the SSID of the WLAN, then try to capture some unprotected wireless management frames using Wireshark. Once you have identified the SSID of the WLAN and the MAC address of at least one device that is allowed to connect to the WLAN, in other words, one that is not being blocked by a MAC filter, use Technitium to manually change the MAC address of your blocked device and connect to the WLAN. Deliver a presentation to your classmates and instructor showing all of the steps you went through to spoof the MAC address and connect to the WLAN.

chapter 9

Wireless Metropolitan Area Networks

After reading this chapter and completing the exercises, you will be able to:

- Define wireless metropolitan area networks (WMANs) and explain why they are needed
- Describe various land-based fixed broadband wireless technologies, including Free Space Optics (FSO), microwave, and WiMAX
- Explain IEEE 802.16 (WiMAX) standards, applications, and protocols
- Outline the security features of WMANs

By now, you understand the tremendous impact that wireless communications have had, and will continue to have, on the world around us. Wireless networks allow users to be connected as they move about, freeing them from cables and phone lines. However, the WPANs and WLANs you have learned about thus far have restricted user mobility to homes, offices, or campuses, allowing them to roam from only a few feet to a few hundred feet from the source of the RF signal. Limits on the strength of the RF signals, mandated by the regulatory authorities and designed to prevent interference in the unlicensed bands, are the main reason for this restriction. Users have also been subject to line-of-sight limitations. Therefore, except for voice communications and data over cellular networks, user mobility has remained largely confined to homes, offices, and hotspots that offer wireless access, which include coffee shops and airports as well as the core downtown areas of a few cities that have deployed Wi-Fi networks.

In small towns and remote areas, the relatively small number of wireless network users might not make it economically viable to implement hotspots and mobile access. In fact, in areas with low user density, the cost of installing cables to provide high-speed communication channels over long distances often prevents telephone companies or small ISPs from offering high-speed Internet access at all.

In this chapter, you learn about technologies and standards that allow wireless access to expand beyond a few hundred feet—to connect buildings several miles apart, for example, or to provide Internet connectivity across an entire city, where cabling infrastructure or an extensive cellular network might not exist. The chapter begins with coverage of infrared (IR)-based short-distance and medium-distance technologies and concludes with standards for medium- and long-distance RF-based WMAN technologies.

What Is a WMAN?

As you learned in Chapter 1, a wireless metropolitan area network (WMAN) is a wireless network that covers a large geographical area such as an entire city or all its suburban areas. WMANs have two primary goals:

- To extend the reach of existing wired networks beyond a single location without the expense of deploying and maintaining high-speed copper or optical cable infrastructure.

- To extend user mobility throughout a metropolitan area. An important additional benefit of a WMAN is that it can provide high-speed connections, including Internet, to areas not serviced by any other method of connectivity. Such connectivity can encompass metropolitan areas, expanding to small towns nearby, as well as to rural areas and remote locations not usually serviced by high-speed communications lines.

Last Mile Wired Connections

A **last mile connection** is usually the link between an end-user and an Internet service provider (ISP) or telephone company, but the term is sometimes used to refer to a connection to an entire community that was not previously serviced by telecommunication lines. Even today, most last mile connections are still based on some type of copper wiring, such as telephone cable, or, more recently, optical fiber cables directly to users' homes. As of April 2016, only about 25 percent of homes in the United States were directly connected to fiber networks (See *http://broadbandnow.com/Fiber*), and only a very small number of office buildings are wired for cable TV. In spite of its exceptional reliability for data communications, fiber optics is slow and expensive to install; most important of all, it is costly to maintain, especially in regions where the ground freezes and thaws every year, which can damage buried cables. Figure 9-1 shows an example of an overhead-wire last mile connection.

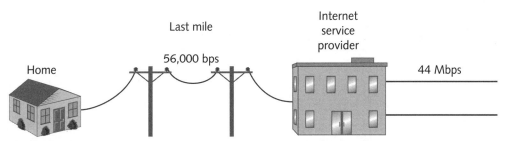

Figure 9-1   Last mile connection (wired)

Today, home users in large metropolitan areas can take advantage of both DSL at up to 100 Mbps and cable TV connections at up to 150 Mbps. However, these types of connections are usually not available in small, remote communities. Business users do have a few other options beyond basic copper wiring. However, traditional wired technologies, which offer high data rates and are widely available in larger metropolitan areas, are typically quite expensive to lease, costing several thousands of dollars per mile, per month. Table 9-1 summarizes some of the traditional and historical connection options and speeds for homes, office buildings, and Internet service providers, to provide a perspective for the remainder of this chapter.

Connection Type	Speed (or Range)	Typical Use	Approximate Cost per Month	Approximate Time to Download Full Content of a 680 MB CD-ROM (Hours:Minutes)
Dial-up modem	56 Kbps	Home	Free and up	26:53
ISDN (1 or 2 channels)	64 or 128 Kbps	Home or business	Residential: $50 setup + $29.95 Business: $49.95	24:10 or 12:50
Cable modem	100 Mbps–1 Gbps	Home	$30–$150	0:58 to less than 0:01
DSL	6–100 Mbps	Home	$15–$140	0:15 to less than 0:01
T1	1.544 Mbps	Office	$400 and up	0:58
T3	44.736 Mbps	Office, ISP	$2,500–$5,000	0:02
OC-3 (optical fiber)	155 Mbps	ISP	$10,000–$30,000	32 seconds
OC-12 (optical fiber)	622.08 Mbps	ISP	Varies greatly	8 seconds
OC-192 (optical fiber)	9.6 Gbps	Large ISP	Varies greatly	Less than 1 second

Table 9-1   Wired connection options

For long-distance connections between cities and states, copper-based digital communications lines, such as T1, require the signal to be regenerated every 6,000 feet (1.8 kilometers). In addition to the challenges of cable installation and maintenance, regenerating the signal requires electrical power at each repeater location. Maintenance costs for this type of connection are extremely high, especially where the geography or the environmental conditions (e.g., mountainous or desert areas) are challenging.

 Last mile delivery of telephone and data lines has long been a problem for the carriers (i.e., the providers and operators) of the networks, who must be able to justify the cost of installing wired connections in remote areas. In previous chapters, you learned that *carrier* refers to the RF signal that carries data. In the telecommunications field, the term **carrier** also refers to telephone, cable TV, and other communications-provider companies that own the wires and transmission towers that carry voice and data traffic.

Since the early 1980s, fiber-optic technology has largely replaced all other technologies for connections between major metropolitan centers, mainly because it has a higher capacity for carrying voice and data transmissions, lower maintenance requirements, and is much more reliable than copper wiring. However, the higher costs of the fiber-optic medium and in-ground installation often preclude its use in remote and less-populated areas. Fiber-optic cables are also used to carry voice and data traffic across the world's oceans. Submarine fiber-optic cables span the entire globe and are laid and maintained by specialized ships and crews. The cost of deploying and maintaining these cables is extremely high, but today our world is heavily dependent on them for Internet and phone connectivity. For more information, search for "submarine cable" on the web.

Last Mile Wireless Connections

Most of the technologies used in WMANs and last mile wireless connections are based on microwave signals, but they also include infrared light. **Microwaves** are higher-frequency RF waves that use the 3- to 30-GHz and 30- to 300-GHz frequency ranges of the electromagnetic spectrum. Microwaves were introduced in the early 1950s by AT&T and the technology brought about a new era in voice communications. Originally, microwaves were used to transmit in point-to-point fashion. The conventional thinking in the early days was that the lower-frequency, high-powered approach was the only way in which microwaves could be used for communication. High-frequency microwave technology was ignored for many years, and the section of the RF spectrum between 27.5 and 29.5 GHz went virtually unused.

Microwave towers today are installed between 35 miles (56 kilometers) and up to 50 miles (80 kilometers) apart from each other. A microwave link operating at 4 GHz can carry about 1,800 voice calls simultaneously. In comparison, a T1 link can carry only 24 simultaneous voice calls. Improvements in microwave technology have reduced the cost of the equipment and have made telephone and data communications services available in many remote locations worldwide that were previously out of range of high-capacity, high-speed connections.

 The first transcontinental microwave link was completed in 1951, connecting New York and San Francisco. It used 107 towers spaced about 30 miles (48 kilometers) apart, covering a distance of about 3,200 miles (5,140 kilometers). The same link using T1 digital copper-based lines would require over 2,850 repeaters to regenerate the signal.

The current alternatives for WMANs and last mile connections include Free Space Optics, microwave, cellular data (discussed in the next chapter), and WiMAX. A few legacy technologies such as Local Multipoint Distribution Service (LMDS) and Multichannel Multipoint Distribution Service (MMDS) have been replaced, or are quickly being replaced, by other technologies and are not discussed here. Instead, this chapter covers microwave links, which, although not based on standards, have been and continue to be a very popular way of interconnecting cellular communication towers, buildings, and cities. Microwave is also used in a host of other permanent and temporary communications infrastructure setups. The clear advantage of wireless connections is that they can cost less, can be installed relatively quickly, offer greater flexibility, are easier and less costly to maintain, and have better long-term reliability. Using wireless as the last mile connection or to interconnect buildings is called **fixed wireless** because these are permanent setups fixed in one location that do not normally support mobile users.

Fixed wireless networks have been used for several years for both voice and data communications in backhaul networks operated by telephone companies, cable TV companies, utilities, railways, and government agencies. A **backhaul** connection is defined as a company's internal infrastructure connection. For example, a telephone company backhaul network might be a connection from one central switching office to another. Cellular towers along highways and areas where fiber connections are not available are usually interconnected using a wireless backhaul link.

Fixed wireless systems can be used to transmit the same type of data that is sent over a wired system. However, point-to-point long-distance microwave links, such as those employed by telephone carriers, use high-power beams that are not always suitable or safe for use in crowded city skylines. In addition, high-speed microwave links often use licensed frequencies for reliability purposes, so that no one else will interfere with the connection, but the cost of licensing is high and needs to be economically justifiable. RF spectrum availability may also be very limited in crowded metropolitan areas.

In Chapter 8, you learned that WLAN equipment such as 802.11 wireless bridges can be set up to connect two buildings provided the installation does not interfere with other wireless links using the same unlicensed RF bands. Installation of longer-distance connections with this technology—beyond the range of Wi-Fi (375 feet/114 meters)—is possible but can seldom achieve the high data rates required to interconnect busy data networks. In addition to loss of speed as the distance increases, the 802.11 standard is designed to support only a single repeater link, which means that a maximum of three bridges can be used between two destination points. Achieving RF line of sight between two directional antennas in metropolitan areas is difficult or may not be possible due to tower height limitations, tall buildings, etc. Additionally, the throughput of a single 802.11 frequency channel is typically only enough to carry a limited amount of data, such as email, web browsing, and moderate file transfers, mainly due to the half-duplex characteristic of wireless bridges. Although using multiple bridge links to increase bandwidth can alleviate the problem, it tends to make antenna installation far more complex because you would have to align multiple pairs of directional antennas instead of just one.

Baseband vs. Broadband

Another point to consider when designing wireless links is that there are two ways in which digital signals can be transmitted over a wireless medium. The first is called **broadband** transmission, in which multiple signals are simultaneously sent over the medium at different frequencies. An example of broadband transmission is cable TV, in which multiple entertainment channels are sent on a single cable. When you pick a channel to watch, the TV set filters out all other frequencies and decodes and displays a single channel.

The second transmission mode is called **baseband** transmission. Baseband treats the entire transmission medium as if it were only one channel and transmits only one data signal at a time over a single frequency. An example of baseband transmission is Ethernet, in which digital signals are sent over a cable. Ethernet 100BaseT, for example, refers to 100 Mbps baseband signaling using twisted pair cabling. As you learned in Chapter 2, digital signals use a change in voltage to represent a 1 or a 0. You can change the voltage differential between two wires on a cable, but you cannot transmit this change over an analog medium such as an EM wave, which is an analog medium. To transmit digital signals over an analog medium, as you learned, you need to modulate an analog carrier wave to represent a change between a 1 and a 0.

These examples illustrate the differences between broadband and baseband transmissions over a cable, but keep in mind that transmissions over an analog medium (such as EM waves) can be sent as broadband or baseband. Purely digital signals can only be transmitted over a wire as baseband, because mixing multiple voltage changes on a cable would create different bit patterns and corrupt the data, given that there is no way to separate one signal from the other. However, if you modulate multiple digital signals over different carrier frequencies, they can be transmitted over any analog medium. The receiver can then separate each frequency using filters and decode each of the digital signals individually.

Note also that there is no predefined frequency bandwidth separating baseband from broadband. For example, the wider the bandwidth, the more frequencies are available to transmit separate channels of data using frequency division multiplexing. Alternatively, broadband transmissions can be made using time division multiplexing. Both methods can be considered broadband transmission. In comparison, a baseband transmission consists of only one data channel.

Figure 9-2 shows a rough conceptual comparison between baseband and broadband transmissions.

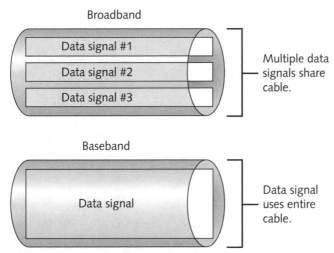

Broadband

| Data signal #1 |
| Data signal #2 |
| Data signal #3 |

Multiple data signals share cable.

Baseband

Data signal

Data signal uses entire cable.

Figure 9-2 Baseband vs. broadband transmissions

Land-Based Fixed Broadband Wireless

The data communications industry has developed a few different solutions for last mile connections over the past few decades. Some have proven too costly and were hard to justify. Others have proved to be less than totally reliable for implementation in all locations. Some RF-based solutions are proprietary, and some require licensed frequency bands. Until 2001, RF-based fixed broadband systems operated at frequencies and with modulation techniques that limited implementation to line of sight only. In addition, most fixed broadband systems could only send from one site to another—in other words, they are set up in point-to-point fashion. As a comparison, in cellular telephone systems, a single base station can communicate with several mobile devices simultaneously. However, cellular technology was originally designed to carry multiple voice conversations and not high-capacity data transmissions, although this is changing rapidly today with the latest versions of cellular standards.

Due to the high cost of land-based communications lines from telephone and cable TV carriers, many companies have chosen to deploy their own building-to-building wireless connectivity solutions. This section begins by describing an IR-based solution called Free Space Optics. Later in the chapter, you will learn about IEEE 802.16 and WiMAX wireless technologies, which are in use in many fixed wireless networks and are also used for Internet connectivity applications. Enhancements to the 802.16 standards also promise to help solve the challenges of user mobility and compete with DSL, cable TV, and even telephone carriers where cabling infrastructure is not available, such as in Africa.

Free Space Optics

Free Space Optics (FSO) is an optical, wireless, point-to-point, line-of-sight broadband technology. Although it was originally developed over 30 years ago by the military, FSO has become an excellent alternative to high-speed fiber-optic cable for shorter distances. Currently, FSO can transmit at speeds comparable to lower-end fiber-optic transmissions, reaching up to

1.25 Gbps at a distance of 4 miles (6.4 kilometers) in full-duplex mode. Future improvements in the technology will likely push the top speed to 10 Gbps and possibly beyond.

FSO uses infrared (IR) light transmission instead of RF. The light technology is similar to that used with a fiber-optic cable system. A fiber-optic cable contains a very thin strand of glass called the core, which is only as thick as a human hair. Instead of transmitting electrical signals, fiber-optic cables use light impulses. A light source, usually created by a laser or light-emitting diodes (LEDs), flashes a light at one end of the cable that is detected at the receiving end. Light travels at 186,000 miles (300,000 kilometers) per second, so fiber-optic cable systems can transmit large amounts of data at high speeds. In addition, these transmissions are immune to electromagnetic interference and cannot be easily intercepted without breaking the cable, which makes them relatively secure.

FSO is an alternative to fiber-optic cables. Sometimes called "fiberless optical," FSO does not use a medium, like a fiber-optic cable, to send and receive signals. Instead, low-powered invisible infrared beams carry the data. These beams, which do not harm the human eye, are generated by transceivers, as shown in Figure 9-3. Because FSO is a line-of-sight technology, the transceivers are mounted in the middle or upper floors of office buildings to provide a clear transmission path. However, unlike other technologies that require the units to be located on an open roof (which sometimes requires leasing roof space from the building's owner), FSO transceivers can even be mounted behind a window in an existing office.

Figure 9-3   FSO transceiver (transmitter/receiver)

Source: Courtesy of fSONA Networks Corp.

Under perfect conditions, such as environments free of fog, dust, and high heat and humidity, FSO can transmit at distances of up to 6.2 miles (10 kilometers).

Recall that the lower-frequency portion of the electromagnetic spectrum is the area in which RF EM waves travel. IR waves fall into the area above 300 GHz. FSO uses the invisible light part of this spectrum region. The only limitation on its use is that the radiated power must not exceed specific limits in order to avoid harming the human eye.

FSO equipment works at either of two wavelengths. A single worldwide wavelength will likely be standardized for these devices.

Advantages of FSO The advantages of FSO include lower cost, speed of installation, transmission rate, and security.

FSO installations cost significantly less than installing new fiber-optic cables or even leasing lines from a local carrier. One recent project compared the costs of installing fiber-optic cables to FSO to interconnect three buildings. The cost to install the fiber-optic cables was almost $400,000, compared to less than $60,000 for FSO.

FSO can be installed in days, compared to months—or sometimes years—for fiber-optic cables, which require a series of permits from city authorities, whether installed underground or strung along lampposts. In some instances, installers can set up FSO systems over a weekend without disrupting the users.

The transmission speed for FSO can be scaled to meet users' needs—anywhere from 10 Mbps to 1.25 Gbps.

Security is a key advantage in an FSO system. IR transmissions cannot be as easily intercepted and decoded as some RF transmissions.

Disadvantages of FSO The primary disadvantage of FSO is that atmospheric conditions can have an impact on FSO transmissions. **Scintillation** is the temporal and spatial variation in light intensity caused by atmospheric turbulence. Turbulence caused by wind and temperature variations can create pockets of air with rapidly changing densities. These air pockets can act like prisms and lenses that distort an FSO signal. Inclement weather is also a threat. Although rain and snow can distort a signal, fog does the most damage to light-based transmissions. Fog is composed of extremely small moisture particles that act like prisms, scattering and breaking up the light beams.

Scintillation is readily observed in the twinkling of stars in the night sky and the shimmering "mirage" effect that you see in the distance on the surface of a road on a hot sunny day.

FSO overcomes scintillation by sending the data in parallel streams from several separate laser transmitters. These transmitters are all mounted in the same transceiver but are separated from one another in such a way it is unlikely that while traveling between the transmitter and the receiver, all the parallel beams will encounter the same pocket of turbulence, given that scintillation pockets are usually quite small. At least one of the beams will arrive at the target node with adequate strength to be properly received. This solution is called **spatial diversity** because it exploits multiple regions of air space. An example of spatial diversity is shown in Figure 9-4, with parallel light beams coming from an FSO transmitter.

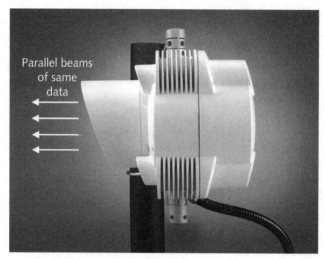

Transceiver

Figure 9-4   Spatial diversity

Source: Courtesy of fSONA Networks Corp.

In dealing with fog, there are several potential solutions. One solution is simply to increase the transmit power of the signal (the intensity of the light). In regions of heavy and frequent fog, it may be necessary to choose FSO systems that transmit at the highest available frequency because these devices can also emit light at higher power levels. Several vendors also claim to customize their distance and product recommendations based on weather statistics for particular cities. Some vendors use a backup connection with FSO to ensure that transmissions go through in foggy weather.

In order to prove that FSO can send transmissions through fog, one vendor ran trials in some of the foggiest cities in the United States. In San Francisco, one of the worst cities in the country for fog, one vendor has proven that FSO can maintain carrier-class transmission speeds (1.25 Gbps) over 90 percent of the time.

Some experts recommend that the distance between FSO transceivers in regions of heavy and frequent fog should be limited to 650 to 1,640 feet (200 to 500 meters).

Signal interference can also be a problem for FSO, such as when birds fly through the IR beam and block it. If the signal is temporarily blocked, the beam automatically reduces its power, then raises itself to full power when the obstruction clears the beam's path.

Another potential problem is that storms and earthquakes can cause tall buildings to move enough to affect the aim of the beam. This problem can be handled in two ways. In the first method, known as "beam divergence," the transmitted beam is purposely allowed to spread, or diverge, so that by the time it arrives at the receiving device, it forms a fairly large optical cone. If the receiver is initially positioned at the center of the beam, divergence can compensate for any movement of the building. The second method, known as "active tracking," is based on movable mirrors that are controlled by gyroscopes that, in turn, control the direction in which the beams are sent. A feedback mechanism continuously adjusts the mirrors so that the beams stay on target.

FSO Applications There are a variety of applications for FSO. More common ones include:

- *Last mile connections*—FSO can be used in high-speed links that connect end-users with Internet service providers or other networks.
- *LAN connections*—FSO devices are easily installed, making them a natural solution for interconnecting LAN segments that are housed in buildings separated by public streets or other obstacles, such as in a university campus spanning several city blocks.
- *Fiber-optic backup*—FSO can be deployed in redundant links to back up fiber-optic cables in case of a break in the cable.
- *Backhaul*—FSO can be used to carry cellular telephone traffic from antenna towers back to facilities wired to carrier-provided high-speed communications lines.

Most experts agree that FSO holds great potential for fixed wireless communications as well as for other wireless applications. In spite of other technology advances, FSO has remained a stable player in the wireless field to this day.

Microwave Wireless Links

As indicated at the beginning of this chapter, microwave is a group of wireless technologies that, although not based on standards such as those from IEEE, is a very common way of interconnecting buildings, cellular towers, intercity telephone networks, and so on. Microwaves are essentially EM waves, but the "micro" in microwave is not meant to imply that the wavelength is in the micrometer range. It is simply meant to suggest that the wavelength is smaller than the wavelength of radio waves that were common at the time microwave technology began to be installed. AM broadcast radio stations at the time operated, and still do, mostly in the 535- to 1,605-KHz range, which have wavelengths varying from approximately 1,839 feet (561 meters) to 613 feet (187 meters), respectively. Microwaves have been used to transmit telephone calls (voice), since the mid- to late 1950s across North America and can operate in the range of 300 MHz to 300 GHz, which have wavelengths ranging from 3.28 feet (1 meter) to 0.00328 feet (0.001 meters or 1 millimeter). Microwave transceivers today operate on a variety of frequency bands, from the ISM 5.8 GHz up to 80 GHz.

Permanent Microwave Links Most microwave links installed by carriers today are point-to-point line-of-sight, permanent links that typically operate in the 18 GHz licensed frequency band. This helps carriers to avoid potential interference and ensure the reliability of their networks. Because of the lack of standardization and interoperability testing, such as the ones conducted by the Wi-Fi Alliance, each carrier's link must use equipment from the same vendor. Data rates can range up to 2 Gbps for single transmitters to 4 Gbps for aggregated transmitter setups (two transmitters) and use between 256- and 1,024-QAM modulation with parabolic dish antennas, which are highly directional and very high gain, as you learned in Chapter 4. Carrier microwave links use **frequency division duplexing** (FDD), transmitting on one frequency and receiving on another, for full-duplex operation, and practically all microwave links in use today carry 100 percent IP traffic. Orthogonal frequency division multiplexing (OFDM) encoding is also used to transmit more than one data channel simultaneously, which means that these links are broadband communications channels. Non-carrier, private microwave links typically transmit in many different frequency bands from 24 to 80 GHz.

In the past, microwave transmitters were large and needed to be installed on the ground at the base of communications towers, with **waveguides**, rectangular cavity metal tubes that carried the transmitter signal from the ground to the antennas installed high up in the transmission towers. With either copper antenna cables or waveguides, the main issue was the signal loss between the transmitters and antennas. Today the transmitters are very compact and are installed on the towers right next to the antennas, which minimizes or eliminates signal loss, and some products are available with integrated dish antennas. Figure 9-5 shows an example of a compact microwave transmitter. Some products are also available

Figure 9-5 Compact microwave transmitter

as a split-architecture with the data circuits installed at the bottom of the tower and the radios installed on the tower, next to the antenna.

Many businesses also use compact microwave equipment working in the unlicensed 60 and 80 GHz bands to deploy private high-speed links. In one example, a college campus wanted to interconnect five buildings, two of which were across a public street. The college originally leased fiber-optic lines from a local utility, but because of the location, the optical lines ran from one side of the street to the downtown core and back from the downtown core to the other side of the street. The total length of the leased fiber-optic lines was approximately 5 miles (8 kilometers) and the cost of the 1 Gbps link was about $8,000 per month. The college looked at the maximum data rates required to interconnect the buildings, then decided to install two separate 66 Mbps links, one to each building across the street, at a cost of approximately $60,000 to link the wired and Wi-Fi networks in the two buildings across the street to the main data center, to support both data and VoIP. This meant that the cost of the wireless links was paid for in just over seven months when compared to the leased optical lines.

Gas and oil companies frequently deploy private links from drilling and production sites to the head offices of companies to provide real-time, high-speed access to information. These sites are often located in remote areas where the environment is quite harsh or on ocean platforms where wired infrastructure is not available and the data rates provided by satellite links or other means are simply not good enough.

You can watch some videos about wireless technology in oilfields and other remote locations at this link: *http://rdlcom.com/videos.*

Temporary Links Microwave equipment is currently available to support temporary installations in, for example, sports venues such as the Olympic Games or the Pan American Games. These mobile links typically use the 5.8 GHz ISM band and create small microwave "cells" that can be used to transmit multiple 100 to 200 Mbps, non-line of sight to each of three other points (point-to-multipoint), or to a single point with an aggregate data rate of up to 600 Mbps. These links use smart antennas, beamforming, time division duplexing (defined below), and OFDM with subcarrier modulations of 128- and 256-QAM.

IEEE 802.16 (WiMAX)

IEEE 802.16 is an open-standard, broadband MAN technology that can work in either line-of-sight or non-line-of-sight mode, depending on the frequency used, and is designed to support a large variety of fixed or mobile digital data communications services for MANs. The term *WiMAX* stands for Worldwide Interoperability for Microwave Access. The IEEE introduced 802.16 in 2000, with the goal of standardizing fixed broadband wireless connections as an alternative to wired access networks such as fiber-optic links, cable TV modems, and DSL. IEEE 802.16 supports enhancements and extensions to the MAC protocols so that it is possible for a **base station (BS)** (the transmitter connected to the carrier network or to the Internet) to communicate with another BS as well as directly with **subscriber stations (SSs)**, which can be either a laptop computer or a device that attaches to a LAN. FSO cannot support mobile communications because of its directional requirements.

Figure 9-6 shows a WiMAX lab setup that includes two BS controllers (top) and four SSs (bottom). Each two SSs in the photo are connected to one of the BS radios (middle, vertical). The flat areas in the front of the SSs are integrated antennas. The SSs in the photo are normally installed on the outside wall of a house or building facing the antenna of the nearest BS. For safety reasons, the lab equipment is interconnected using cables and attenuators, instead of antennas, because of the high-power RF signals.

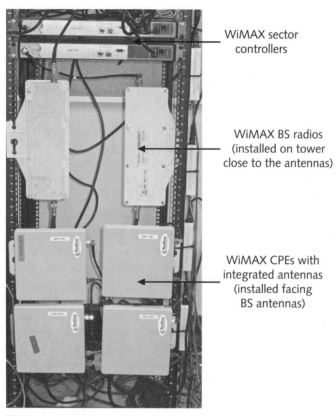

WiMAX sector controllers

WiMAX BS radios (installed on tower close to the antennas)

WiMAX CPEs with integrated antennas (installed facing BS antennas)

Figure 9-6 WiMAX equipment (lab setup)

In January 2006, Samsung introduced a laptop computer and mobile telephone handset that were both 802.16-compliant. Several other PC manufacturers followed shortly after by offering built-in WiMAX connectivity options in their mobile device product lines.

A group of manufacturers established the **WiMAX Forum** (see *www.wimaxforum.org*) in June 2001 to promote the implementation of 802.16 by testing and certifying equipment for compatibility and interoperability. The IEEE 802.16 standard offers multiple RF interfaces (PHY layers), depending on the frequencies used and associated regulations for different countries, but they are all based on a common MAC protocol.

Just as the 802.11 standards became popularly known as Wi-Fi based on the name of the industry organization, so the 802.16 standard has become popularly known as WiMAX based on the forum name.

South Korea was one of the first countries to implement wireless broadband networks based on the nation's WiBro standard. The IEEE subsequently made the 802.16 standard fully compatible with the Korean standard.

WiMAX Applications

With data rates of up to 70 Mbps in the 2 to 11 GHz bands and up to 120 Mbps at short distances in the 10 to 66 GHz bands, WiMAX is suitable for backhaul business applications as well as last mile delivery applications that replace T1, DSL, and cable TV modems for Internet connectivity. WiMAX can support simultaneous voice, video, and data transmission with QoS. This makes it particularly suitable for voice-over-IP (VoIP) connections, which has enabled small companies to enter the telecommunications market and compete with major carriers in providing telephone services to consumers in infrastructure-poor areas of the world. The convergence of voice, video, and data on IP networks is what the industry calls **triple play**.

WiMAX enables vendors to create many different types of products, including various configurations of base stations and **customer premises equipment** (CPE), which are the devices that are installed in a customer's office or home. In addition to supporting the point-to-multipoint applications just mentioned, WiMAX can be deployed as a point-to-point network to provide broadband access to rural and remote areas.

Search for "WiMAX CPE" and "WiMAX base station" to locate WiMAX product manufacturers' websites.

Manufacturers can design and build standards-based equipment that can be employed by wireless operators using licensed frequencies and also by business users using both licensed and unlicensed frequencies. Compared to other technologies, the cost of WiMAX equipment is very attractive. For example, the cost of WiMAX CPEs has dropped to below $100 each. Some CPE devices can support TV (video), telephone (voice), and data (Internet) simultaneously.

The WiMAX MAC layer includes features designed to make it easy for carriers to deploy the network. Once the BSs are in place, an end-user can connect to a WiMAX network by simply taking the CPE device out of the box, placing the antenna near a window or mounting the CPE on an outside wall facing the nearest BS, and turning it on. In contrast to configuring a Wi-Fi wireless residential gateway, for example, little or no configuration is required by the customer to install a WiMAX CPE. This process also has the effect of dramatically reducing the installation costs for the service provider, who will no longer have to send a technician to the customer's site for installation. By remotely managing the device, the provider also reduces ongoing maintenance costs. The range of a WiMAX network is measured in miles or kilometers, unlike Wi-Fi, which is measured in hundreds of feet or meters.

 In December 2005, Nortel deployed the first commercial WiMAX network, which covers 8,000 square miles (20,720 square kilometers) in the southeast region of Alberta, Canada. The network, which began serving both the public and the provincial government in 2006, operates in the 3.5 GHz band and provides Internet access to a large rural area at speeds between 1 and 3 Mbps. This article on Wikipedia lists a number of WiMAX networks deployed worldwide: *en.wikipedia.org/wiki/List_of_WiMAX_networks.*

WiMAX Standards Family

IEEE 802.16 covers a wide range of functionality and has a number of variations that address specific applications. It defines the interface specification for fixed, point-to-multipoint broadband wireless metropolitan area networks. The 802.16-2001 standard includes a PHY-layer specification for systems operating in the 10- to 66-GHz range and forms the basis for all the other standards in the family. IEEE 802.16-2004 is a revised version of the initial standard that adds support for systems operating in the 2- to 11-GHz range.

The **802.16e** amendment to the standard, ratified in December 2005, defines the specifications for a mobile version of WiMAX. This enhancement can enable data rates of up to 2 Mbps for portable devices that are slow moving or stationary, and speeds of up to 320 Kbps in fast-moving vehicles. IEEE **802.16m**, an amendment that the WiMAX Forum calls Release 2, raises the data rate to 100 Mbps and makes it possible to combine MIMO, multiple frequency channels, and spatial multiplexing to achieve rates of up to 1 Gbps. The 802.16m amendment has been incorporated in the IEEE 802.16-2012 standard document.

WiMAX Protocol Stack

As with many of the technologies you have learned about in this book, the PHY and MAC layers are the only ones that change between different networking standards. WiMAX is unique in that, in addition to the PHY layer supporting multiple frequency bands, its PHY layer is able to adapt on the fly. The modulation techniques and access mechanisms can change dynamically from a BS to the SSs as well as to other BSs, depending on distance, the existence of any interference, or the requirements of the particular device itself.

Unlike Ethernet, the MAC layer for WiMAX is connection oriented and includes service-specific convergence sublayers that interface to the upper OSI layers. Remember that in the OSI protocol model, only the Transport layer (Layer 4) is connection oriented. The convergence sublayers of the MAC layer in WiMAX can map a particular service to a connection, which allows WiMAX to offer multiple simultaneous services through the same link and to carry a mix of communications protocols, such as IPv4, IPv6, Ethernet, VLANs, and others, all in the same link and on the same network. The MAC layer in WiMAX also includes a privacy sublayer that is used to secure the link (discussed in the security section of this chapter). The 802.16 WiMAX protocol stack is shown in Figure 9-7.

WiMAX layers   Layer function(s)

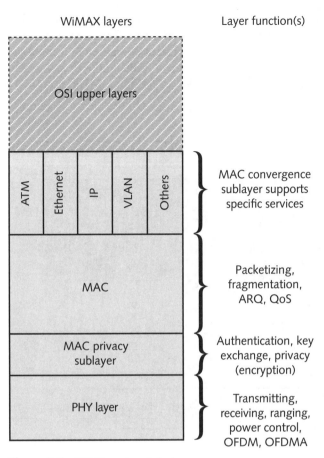

MAC convergence sublayer supports specific services

Packetizing, fragmentation, ARQ, QoS

Authentication, key exchange, privacy (encryption)

Transmitting, receiving, ranging, power control, OFDM, OFDMA

Figure 9-7   802.16 protocol stack

PHY Layer There are several variations of the PHY layer in 802.16. Determining which variation to use for a particular implementation depends on the frequency range and whether it is a point-to-point or point-to-multipoint setup. The first two are based on the modulation of a single carrier signal. Remember that when transmitting on a single frequency, all transmitters have to work in half-duplex mode because they cannot transmit and receive at the same time. In this case, each transmission is divided into fixed duration frames that are 5 milliseconds long. Each frame is subdivided into one uplink subframe and one downlink subframe. The BS transmits to the SSs during the downlink subframe, and the SSs transmit to the BS during the uplink subframe.

The PHY frames can be 0.5 milliseconds, 1 millisecond, or 2 milliseconds long and are divided into a variable uplink subframe and downlink subframe. The subframes are divided into a series of time slots. Because the uplink and downlink subframe is variable, the BS can allocate more time slots for the uplink or downlink, as required. The number of uplink or downlink time slots allocated depends on the amount of data being transmitted in either direction. A data transmission to or from a single device using multiple time slots is called a **burst**. A burst can also be a broadcast transmission from the BS to all SSs. A transmission includes commands or network management information that is sent prior to the transmission of the frame's data portion. The BS allocates time slots for specific SSs in both the downlink frame and the uplink frame. The amount of data contained in a burst depends on the number and length of the time slot as well as on the modulation and coding scheme used for that particular burst. This transmission method is called **time division duplexing (TDD)** and is shown in Figure 9-8.

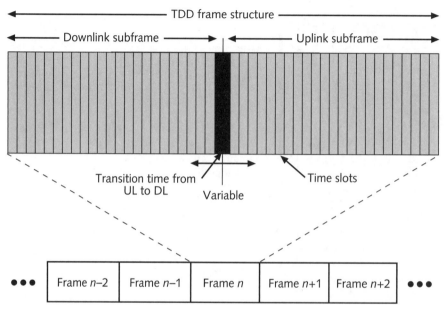

Figure 9-8 802.16 TDD frame transmission

WiMAX also allows the use of two different frequency channels (FDD). The structure of the frame in FDD is similar to that for TDD, except that one frequency is used exclusively for the downlink and the other is used exclusively for the uplink.

WiMAX can support less-expensive half-duplex equipment as well as full-duplex stations simultaneously, using different frequencies on the same network and at the same time. The adaptive characteristic of the uplink and downlink, coupled with support of both TDD and FDD, allows 802.16 to use the frequency spectrum more efficiently.

When half-duplex transmitters are connected to an FDD network, the BS needs to make sure that it does not schedule time for those devices to transmit and receive simultaneously, given that these are half-duplex-only stations.

In a point-to-multipoint architecture, the BS transmits using time division duplexing. The SSs are each allocated a time slot in sequence. Note that because only the BS transmits in the downlink direction, it does not have to be concerned with contention and can simply address information in different time slots to different SSs.

Access in the uplink direction (from the SSs to the BS) uses **time division multiple access (TDMA)**, in which one or more time slots are allocated to each SS depending on the requirements of the type of data being transmitted. Some of the time slots are also allocated for contention access, which enables SSs that are not currently members of the network to communicate with the BS for the purpose of establishing a connection to the network.

In the 10 to 66 GHz licensed bands, 802.16-2009 supports one transmission mode: **WirelessMAN-SC (single carrier)**. It is used for fixed point-to-point connections using either TDD or FDD. At these higher frequencies, line of sight to the transmitter and directional antennas are required.

All the other transmission modes in WiMAX are designed to work in the 2 to 11 GHz licensed or unlicensed bands. The 802.16 standard also supports non-line-of-sight applications. Non-line-of-sight (NLOS) occurs when the transmitter antenna cannot be "seen" (RF) from the receiver end or vice versa because of the geography of the area or obstructions such as buildings and trees that block the Fresnel zone by more than 40 percent.

Outdoor, tower-mounted antennas for homes can be expensive to purchase and install, especially in areas subject to high winds or ice accumulation, and significant multipath distortion is likely to occur. Remember that when using directional antennas in line-of-sight applications, multipath distortion can safely be ignored; however, in point-to-multipoint applications, the BS will typically use an omnidirectional antenna. Examples of LOS and NLOS are shown in Figure 9-9.

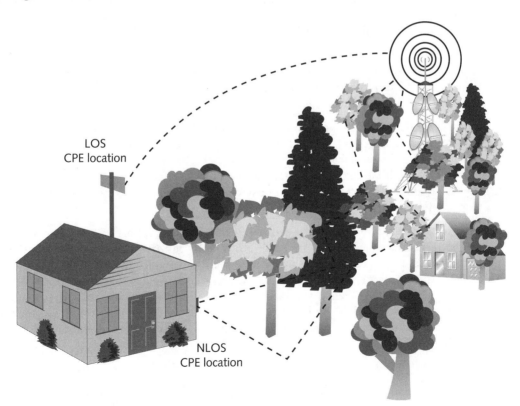

Figure 9-9 Line-of-sight (LOS) and non-line-of-sight (NLOS) CPE installation

To support NLOS applications, additional PHY-layer functionality is required. The introduction to WiMAX in this book discusses only the generic functionality because there are far too many options, and to cover all of them would require an entire chapter dedicated to WiMAX. For NLOS applications, 802.16 supports three additional PHY-layer transmission modes: WirelessMAN-OFDM, WirelessMAN-OFDMA, and WirelessHUMAN. Each of these is defined and discussed briefly in the next paragraphs.

WirelessMAN-OFDM can be used for fixed, mobile, or mesh applications. It uses TDD or FDD in licensed bands below 11 GHz. This mode divides the frequency band into a number of data subcarriers, pilot subcarriers, and null subcarriers to make it resistant to multipath problems. The radio does not transmit during null subcarriers; the null subcarriers are used as guard bands to prevent adjacent channel interference. The number of subcarriers is dependent on the bandwidth of the RF channel. For example, in a 1.25 MHz-wide channel, there can be up to 256 subcarriers, of which 192 are used for data, 8 are used as pilot subcarriers, and 55 are used for guard bands. Conversely, for a 20 MHz-wide channel, there can be up to 2,048 subcarriers.

WirelessMAN-OFDMA uses **orthogonal frequency division multiple access (OFDMA)**, a technique based on OFDM that divides the available frequency channel into 1,536 orthogonal data subcarriers and allows the transmission of frames to different destination devices and from different source devices. These subcarriers are then grouped into subchannels and each SS is allocated a subchannel, allowing multiple stations and the BS to communicate in a single transmission. Here again, the number of data subcarriers is dependent on the channel width. OFDMA is also extremely resistant to multipath problems and is used in licensed bands below 11 GHz.

A third transmission mechanism, **Wireless High-Speed Unlicensed Metro Area Network (WirelessHUMAN)**, is also based on OFDM and is specifically designed for use in the unlicensed 5 GHz U-NII band.

In 802.16, OFDMA is also scalable, meaning that the number of subcarriers allocated to an SS for the uplink can vary, depending on the QoS requirements of the transmission, the signal quality, or the distance between the SS and the BS. However, to accommodate channel aggregation (multiple contiguous channels used to increase data rates) in 802.16m, the number of UL and DL frames is fixed and asymmetric, meaning that there are more DL frames than UL frames.

Another key characteristic of the 802.16 PHY is that it supports adaptive modulation. In simple terms, this means that for each SS, 802.16 can dynamically change the modulation, increasing or decreasing the data rate based on signal quality. In addition, in order to meet the regulatory requirements in different countries as well as to optimize the use of the spectrum, the 802.16 standard allows transmitters to use frequency bandwidths of a minimum of 1.25 MHz up to a maximum of 20 MHz. Table 9-2 summarizes the WiMAX specification's nomenclature, frequencies used, applications, and duplexing alternatives.

Designation	Frequencies	Application	Duplexing
WirelessMAN-SC	10–66 GHz licensed bands	Fixed only	TDD, FDD
WirelessMAN-OFDM	Below 11 GHz licensed bands	Fixed, mobile, or mesh	TDD, FDD
WirelessMAN-OFDMA	Below 11 GHz licensed bands	Fixed or mobile	TDD, FDD
WirelessHUMAN	5 GHz U-NII band	Fixed or mesh	TDD only

Table 9-2   WiMAX specifications summary

Modulation and Error Correction In 802.16, modulation and forward error correction (FEC) are directly linked. In addition to FEC, 802.16 uses automatic repeat requests (ARQ) to ensure the reliability of the transmissions. In other words, sometimes it is necessary to resend the frame. IEEE 802.16 was designed to achieve 99.999 percent reliability—"five nines," as this level of reliability is commonly referred to in the computer industry. FEC improves the chances of receiving the data correctly and thus reduces the number of retransmissions, which increases the performance of the link. However, the additional bits add overhead to the transmissions, increasing the total amount of data and therefore reducing the overall performance of the link. By dynamically changing the modulation, 802.16 can achieve an optimum balance of speed and transmission for a given signal quality.

Table 9-3 lists the types of modulation supported in 802.16 and the associated mandatory FEC coding. The coding rates are listed here for informational purposes only; as stated before, a full explanation of the FEC is beyond the scope of this book. However, it is important to know that the different FEC coding rates are used for increasing the reliability of the transmission.

Modulation	FEC Coding Rates
BPSK	1/2, 3/4
QPSK	1/2, 2/3, 3/4, 5/6, 7/8
16-QAM	1/2, 3/4
64-QAM	2/3, 5/6
256-QAM (optional)	3/4, 7/8

Table 9-3   802.16 modulations and mandatory FEC coding

The ability of 802.16 to dynamically change modulations is also what makes it possible for WiMAX to reduce latency and improve QoS. **Latency** is the amount of time delay it takes a packet to travel from source to destination device. Figure 9-10 shows and example of how WiMAX can use different modulations. Adaptive modulation also helps WiMAX use the channel bandwidth more efficiently.

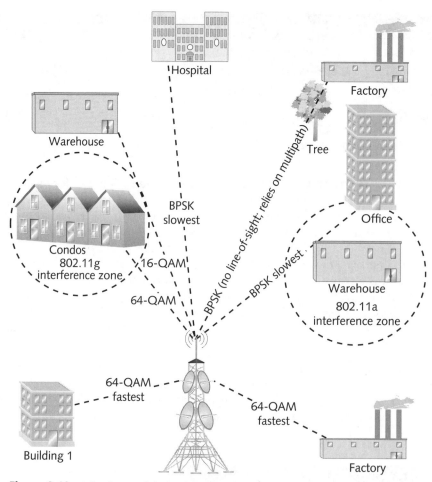

Figure 9-10   Adaptive modulation in WiMAX

The BS sends information to the SSs about which modulations it will use for a particular burst and for a particular SS in the first few data frames at the beginning of the transmission. The SSs respond by sending information to the BS at the beginning of their assigned bursts.

WiMAX Profiles IEEE 802.16 defines certain **profiles**, which are sets of predefined parameters that can include the frequency channel, bandwidth of the channel, and transmission modes (OFDM, OFDMA, etc.). These profiles also help to reduce or eliminate the need for **truck-rolls**, which are support-technician visits to the site, given that they can be changed remotely when a user signs up for a new type of service. WiMAX also specifies basic profiles: point-to-multipoint (P2MP) and point-to-point (PTP) as well as an optional mesh networking profile. A WiMAX **system profile** is a combination of the basic profile and one of the transmission profiles; it is preset on the equipment by the operator companies (carriers) before it is shipped to an end-user site. **Burst profiles** are negotiated between BSs and SSs for the allocation of time slots required to maintain QoS.

Each truck-roll to install a single broadband network device at an end-user's site can cost a carrier or communications operator up to $500.

Range and Throughput The maximum distances achievable in a WiMAX network depend on the frequency band used. Recall that the higher the frequency, the shorter the range of the signal at a given power setting. Conversely, higher-frequency signals allow for higher data rates.

In general, higher frequencies are used for metropolitan-area line-of-sight, point-to-point applications at very high data rates for carrier networks using licensed frequencies. Lower-licensed frequencies—below 11 GHz—are typically used for private, line-of-sight network connections of up to 10 miles (16 kilometers) as well as for long-distance links of up to 35 miles (56 kilometers). Frequencies below 11 GHz are also used for non-line-of-sight networks with a maximum range of up to 5 miles (8 kilometers).

WiMAX base stations and subscriber stations perform ranging (distance) calculations based on signal quality. This process occurs when a subscriber station initially joins the network and periodically thereafter, and it helps the equipment establish the modulation and FEC coding to use for data transmissions.

As you already learned, the maximum achievable data rates in WiMAX depend on the modulation, channel bandwidth, and FEC coding used. Table 9-4 shows a summary of some of the data-rate combinations that are possible.

	Modulation/ FEC Coding	QPSK 1/2	QPSK 3/4	16-QAM 1/2	16-QAM 3/4	64-QAM 2/3	64-QAM 3/4
Channel Bandwidth	1.75 MHz	1.04	2.18	2.91	4.36	5.94	6.55
	3.5 MHz	2.08	4.37	5.82	8.73	11.88	13.09
	7.0 MHz	4.15	8.73	11.64	17.45	23.75	26.18
	10.0 MHz	8.31	12.47	16.63	24.94	33.25	37.40
	20.0 MHz	16.62	24.94	33.25	49.87	66.49	74.81

Table 9-4   Sample of WiMAX data rates in Mbps vs. channel bandwidth and FEC

Note that a wider channel bandwidth combined with more complex modulation also means that more data can be sent per signal unit (symbol), as you learned in Chapter 2, hence the higher data rates that can be achieved with wider channels. Realistic throughput will be lower than the rates shown in Table 9-4. One reason for this is that the WiMAX channel bandwidth is shared among BSs and SSs, and therefore the number of simultaneous devices actively communicating affects the maximum throughput at any given time. Another reason for the lower throughput is that some of the overhead, such as MAC layer framing, is not included in the rate calculations shown in the table.

MAC Layer WiMAX is typically implemented on a point-to-multipoint basis, with one BS and potentially hundreds of SSs, including mobile users. The 802.16 MAC dynamically allocates bandwidth to individual SSs for the uplink; this is the key to the high data rates possible in WiMAX networks. In addition to supporting a large number of SSs, the MAC convergence sublayers allow WiMAX to be implemented as an efficient transport in point-to-point systems for backhaul applications and support such line protocols as ATM and T1.

A point-to-multipoint WiMAX network usually operates with a central BS that can be equipped with either an omnidirectional or a smart antenna, which is also called an **advanced antenna system (AAS)**. An AAS can transmit multiple simultaneous signals in different directions to stations that fall within the range of each of the antennas. It also helps to maximize the amount of RF energy sent in each direction.

WiMAX can also take advantage of multiple-in and multiple-out (MIMO) antenna systems to reduce interference with other systems (see the next section on WiMAX coexistence) and the impact of multipath distortion. In addition, 802.16m enables support for multiple radios and spatial multiplexing to increase data rates for mobile devices.

To address a burst to a particular SS, the BS uses a 16-bit number called a connection identifier (CID), which is used to identify both the device and the connection after it connects to the WiMAX network. Recall that the WiMAX MAC layer is connection oriented. Each station also has a 48-bit MAC address, which is only used during connection establishment. When the stations receive a transmission from the BS, they check the CID and keep only the MAC frames that contain data addressed to them.

Stations can request additional dedicated bandwidth (for QoS) if this is required to support a particular service, such as the transmission of telephone calls or a video stream. The BS polls the SSs periodically to identify their bandwidth needs, granting bandwidth as required. Except in the case of connections that require a guaranteed bit rate, such as T1, most data connections cannot tolerate errors but can tolerate latency and jitter. **Jitter** is the maximum delay variation between two consecutive packets over a period of time. Web browsing, transmitting email messages, and downloading files are latency-tolerant and jitter-tolerant activities. Video and voice, on the other hand, can tolerate a certain amount of errors but not latency or jitter. Video streams tolerate the loss of image frames, so long as the user still sees at least 15 images per second. However, voice streams do not tolerate losses or delays greater than 50 milliseconds, which seriously degrade the quality of a call to human ears.

The WiMAX MAC protocol maintains a consistent bandwidth by using a self-correcting mechanism for granting more bandwidth to SSs. This creates less traffic on the network, given that there is no need for SSs to acknowledge the grant. Instead, if an SS does not receive the bandwidth grant or the BS does not receive the request, the SS will simply request it again. The requests from the SSs are cumulative, but they will also periodically inform the BS of their total bandwidth needs. This method is far more efficient than those used by other networking standards, which makes WiMAX a very elegantly designed technology.

The scheduling services in WiMAX that map the connections in the uplink direction for allocating channel bandwidth to the SSs are based on the scheduling services defined for cable modems in the Data Over Cable Service Interface Specification (DOCSIS) standard. For more information, go to: *http://www.cablelabs.com/specs/specification-search* and enter "DOCSIS" in the search box.

A MAC frame includes a fixed-length header, an optional and variable-length payload (data), and an optional cyclic redundancy check (CRC). Header-only MAC frames are used to send commands and requests between the BS and the SSs. The generic MAC frame format is shown in Figure 9-11.

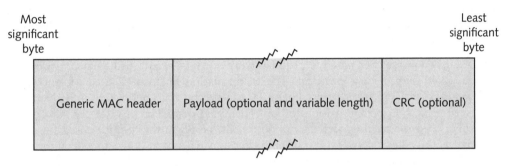

Most significant byte

Least significant byte

Generic MAC header | Payload (optional and variable length) | CRC (optional)

Figure 9-11   802.16 generic MAC frame

WMAN Security

As with other types of networks, security in WMANs is a major concern. Because FSO and microwave security for WMAN installations use proprietary technology, most of this section focuses on security measures for WiMAX.

FSO Security

Despite using multiple beam technology (which could allow an attacker to attempt to capture information by interrupting a single beam), FSO systems are generally considered secure. Anyone trying to sniff information from an FSO system would have difficulty accessing the equipment and blocking only a portion of an invisible beam. In addition, such interference would affect the performance of the network, immediately alerting the user or operator.

Microwave Security

Each microwave vendor implements its own security protocols, because most of the technology is proprietary, but 128- and 256-bit AES encryption is the norm. Using AES encryption means that systems meet not only the minimum security requirements established by the U.S. federal government but also the requirements of privacy laws.

WiMAX Security

As you learned in the section on the WiMAX protocol stack, the MAC layer includes a privacy sublayer. Unlike 802.11 and Bluetooth, the WiMAX standard was initially designed to include very powerful security measures. These features make it extremely difficult—if not impossible—for a would-be hackers to steal information from WiMAX transmissions.

The privacy sublayer provides a client/server authentication and key management protocol, with the BS controlling the distribution of security keys to the SSs. In addition, the standard encrypts all the data transmitted between the BS and SSs and makes use of **digital certificates,** which are messages digitally signed by a certification authority, as well as public-key infrastructure embedded in the BS, to ensure privacy and protect against information theft. Manufacturers install a unique digital certificate that includes a serial number in every device. The digital certificate can be verified with the manufacturer as being valid and unique by sending a copy of the certificate encrypted with the manufacturer's public key over the Internet (a connection to the Internet is required). This is a requirement of the 802.16 standard.

The privacy sublayer has two protocol components: the encapsulation protocol and the privacy key management protocol. The encapsulation protocol is used for encrypting packet data and includes a set of cryptographic suites (the encryption and authentication mechanisms) used to apply encryption to the transmitted data. The privacy key management protocol is used for securing key distribution from the BS to the SSs; it is used for synchronizing the security keys between the BS and SSs as well as for preventing unauthorized stations from associating with a WiMAX network.

Once a device is authenticated with the BS using the digital certificate, a **traffic encryption key (TEK),** which is the security key used to encrypt the data, is exchanged between the BS and SS for each service connection that's being carried over the wireless interface. Remember that the 802.16 MAC is connection oriented and can carry multiple types of service. TEKs expire, and the SS must periodically renew the keys with the BS. The default TEK lifetime is 12 hours. The minimum value is 30 minutes, and the maximum value is 7 days.

Only the headers are not encrypted in WiMAX, to allow SSs to associate with the network. All data sent across the wireless medium is encrypted using one of the following algorithms:

- *3-DES (Triple-DES)*—Data is encrypted three times with a 128-bit key, using the U.S. **Data Encryption Standard (DES).**

- *RSA with 1,024-bit key*—**RSA** was developed in 1977 by Ron Rivest, Adi Shamir, and Leonard Adleman. The algorithm uses a large integer, composed of smaller numbers that are multiplied by each other. It is based on the idea that it will be difficult to figure out each of the smaller numbers that are used to arrive at the large integer.

- *AES*—**Advanced Encryption Standard (AES)** was developed by the National Institute of Standards and Technology (NIST) to replace DES. It is still considered unbreakable and is used to protect all unclassified U.S. government material. Today, AES encryption has practically replaced all others, including the two mentioned above.

The security methods designed into WiMAX should be sufficient to allay any concerns that end-users may have.

The high reliability and high security of WiMAX, together with its long distance and NLOS characteristics, make it an excellent candidate for use by, for example, security companies providing burglar alarms for homes and businesses. WiMAX makes it viable to secure a building or home using a live video link and IP-based security cameras.

Chapter Summary

- WMANs are a group of technologies that provide wireless connectivity throughout an substantial geographical area, such as a city, without cable infrastructure. WMANs also extend user mobility throughout a metropolitan area.

- Last mile wired connections are the links between the customer's premises and an ISP. Most last mile connections today are still based on copper wiring.

- There are two ways in which a WMAN signal can be sent. The first technique, called broadband, sends multiple data signals simultaneously on the same medium. The second technique, called baseband, treats the entire transmission medium as if it were only one channel, sending only one stream of data. Until 2001, RF-based fixed broadband systems were limited to connecting with only one other device at a time and could only transmit using a line-of-sight link.

- Free Space Optics (FSO) has been an excellent alternative to costly high-speed fiber-optic connections. FSO transmissions are sent by low-powered infrared beams in point-to-point fashion. Because FSO is a line-of-sight technology, the transceivers must be mounted in high locations to provide a clear transmission path.

- Microwave is the most common way used to implement both short- and long-distance WMANs. Microwave is not based on standards, meaning that equipment is proprietary and users must purchase all of it from a single vendor to ensure interoperability.

- Microwave links can be either permanent or temporary and use frequencies ranging from 3 to 80 GHz and achieve data rates of up to 4 Gbps. This technology is used extensively by carriers to implement intercity links, as well as to link cellular telephone towers where wired infrastructure is not available. Today's microwave links carry voice, video, and data traffic over IP.

- The IEEE 802.16 (WiMAX) standard was introduced in 2000 with the goal of standardizing fixed broadband wireless services and as an alternative to wired networks. A single WiMAX base station (BS) can communicate with hundreds of subscriber stations (SSs) simultaneously in point-to-multipoint mode, or with another BS in point-to-point mode. IEEE 802.16 equipment can transmit in either the 10- to 66-GHz range or in the 2- to 11-GHz range and can use licensed or unlicensed frequency bands. A BS can also connect directly with a laptop computer equipped with a WiMAX wireless interface.

- WiMAX can transmit at speeds of up to 70 Mbps in the 2 to 11 GHz bands and can achieve 120 Mbps at short distances in the 10 to 66 GHz bands. The 802.16m amendment allows the use of multiple radios and spatial multiplexing and can potentially increase the data rates to 1 Gbps when aggregating multiple 20-MHz-wide frequency channels. QoS support makes WiMAX suitable to carry simultaneous voice, video, and data (triple play) at a much lower cost than older LMDS and MMDS networks. WiMAX equipment is relatively easy and inexpensive to install and maintain.

- The range of a WiMAX network is measured in miles or kilometers, as opposed to the range of WPAN and WLAN technologies, which is measured from inches/centimeters to a few hundred feet/meters.

- The 802.16e amendment brings full support of mobile devices to WiMAX technology. Mobile WiMAX can achieve data rates of up to 2 Mbps for portable devices that are slow moving or stationary and up to 320 Kbps in fast-moving vehicles.

- The WiMAX MAC layer is connection oriented and includes convergence sublayers that allow a WiMAX network to carry a variety of different frame formats from other technologies. There are five variations of the 802.16 PHY layer. The first two are based on the modulation of a single carrier signal. All devices work in half-duplex. The PHY frames can be 0.5 milliseconds, 1 millisecond, or 2 milliseconds long and are divided into a variable uplink subframe and downlink subframe. The subframe is divided into time slots that carry the payload. A single time slot or multiple time slots can be allocated to a specific station. The mechanism is called time division duplexing (TDD). WiMAX also supports the use of two frequency channels, one for the uplink and another for the downlink. This is called frequency division duplexing (FDD).

- The BS can support both half-duplex and full-duplex devices simultaneously on the network and is the only device transmitting on the downlink. The BS transmits using time division multiplexing (TDM). The stations transmit using time division multiple access (TDMA). The BS allocates time slots for contention access in the uplink subframe in order to allow stations to establish a connection and join the network.

- The WiMAX 802.16 standard defines three PHY layers for line-of-sight (LOS) and non-line-of-sight (NLOS) implementations in the 2 to 11 GHz licensed or unlicensed frequency bands: WirelessMAN-OFDM, WirelessMAN-OFDMA, and WirelessHU-MAN, the last which is intended for use in the 5 GHz U-NII band.

- OFDM and OFDMA in 802.16 are scalable, meaning that the number of subcarriers allocated to an SS for the uplink can vary depending on the QoS requirements of the SS, the distance between the SS and BS, and the signal quality. The WiMAX PHY layer uses adaptive modulation. It can dynamically change modulation techniques depending on the distance and signal quality. WiMAX transmitters can transmit using frequency bandwidths from 1.25 MHz up to 20 MHz. Through the use of error-correction techniques and adaptive modulation, WiMAX makes efficient use of the spectrum and achieves high performance.

- WiMAX profiles specify the frequency channel, bandwidth, and transmission mechanism. A basic profile specifies whether the network is point-to-point or point-to-multipoint. A system profile is the combination of a basic profile and transmission profile. The use of profiles helps make WiMAX installations simpler and reduces the cost of implementation for the operators.

- The MAC layer is the key to the intelligence and security behind WiMAX networks. Efficient bandwidth-saving protocols and QoS help WiMAX reduce latency and jitter and maintain a consistent bandwidth. WiMAX includes a number of features that help operators and end-users reduce interference problems.

■ The security features of WiMAX were designed to offer operators and end-users the peace of mind that other wireless technologies have failed to provide so far. WiMAX uses verifiable digital certificates, the most advanced encryption mechanisms (3-DES, RSA, and AES), and secure key exchange protocols.

Key Terms

802.16   The IEEE standard for wireless broadband metropolitan area networks.

802.16e   An amendment to IEEE 802.16 created to allow support for mobile users.

802.16m   An amendment to IEEE 802.16 that increases the data rate to 100 Mbps and beyond, depending on the method of transmission being used.

advanced antenna system (AAS)   An antenna that can transmit multiple simultaneous signals in different directions to stations that fall within the range of each of the antennas.

Advanced Encryption Standard (AES)   The latest encryption standard, developed by the National Institute of Standards and Technology (NIST) to replace the Data Encryption Standard. *See* Data Encryption Standard.

backhaul   A company's internal infrastructure connection.

baseband   A transmission technique that treats the entire transmission medium as only one channel.

base station (BS)   The transmitter connected to the carrier network or to the Internet.

broadband   A transmission technique that sends multiple data signals, at different frequencies or at different times, over a single medium or frequency channel.

burst   A transmission containing data to or from a single SS or a broadcast transmission from the BS that uses multiple time slots.

burst profile   A profile negotiated between the BS and the SSs that specifies the number of time slots allocated to the SSs to maintain QoS.

carrier   (1) The RF signal that carries data; (2) telephone, cable TV, and other communication provider that owns the wires or transmission towers that carry voice, video, and data traffic.

customer premises equipment (CPE)   WiMAX devices that are installed in a customer's office or home.

Data Encryption Standard (DES)   The encryption standard used in the United States until the adoption of AES. *See* AES.

digital certificate   A special message signed by a certification authority that is used for security and authentication.

fixed wireless   A wireless last mile connection. Fixed wireless connections are not intended to support mobile wireless communications.

Free Space Optics (FSO)   An optical, wireless, point-to-point, line-of-sight broadband technology.

frequency division duplexing (FDD)   A method of transmission that uses one frequency for uplink and another for downlink.

jitter   The delay variation between two consecutive packets over a period of time.

last mile connection   Usually, the link between an end-user and an ISP or telephone company, but the term is sometimes used to refer to a connection to an entire community that was not previously serviced by communication lines.

latency   The amount of time delay that it takes a packet to travel from source to destination device.

microwave   Higher-frequency RF wave that uses the 3- to 30-GHz and 30- to 300-GHz ranges of the electromagnetic spectrum.

orthogonal frequency division multiple access (OFDMA)   A multiple-access technique, based on OFDM, that divides the frequency channel into 1,536 orthogonal data subcarriers in WiMAX. Groups of subcarriers are then assigned to different different SSs or BSs.

profile   Set of predefined WiMAX connection parameters that include the frequency channel, bandwidth of the channel, and transmission mechanism (OFDM, OFDMA, etc.).

RSA   An encryption algorithm that uses a large integer composed of smaller numbers that are multiplied by each other. It is based on the idea that it will be difficult to figure out each of the smaller numbers that are used to arrive at the large integer. RSA encryption has been largely superceeded by the more secure AES encryption.

scintillation   The temporal and spatial variation in light intensity caused by atmospheric turbulence.

spatial diversity   Sending parallel beams of the same data during Free Space Optical transmissions.

subscriber station (SS)   In a WiMAX network, either a customer premises equipment (CPE) device that attaches to a LAN or a laptop computer.

system profile   A combination of the basic WiMAX profile and one of the transmission profiles, such as point-to-multipoint (P2MP), point-to-point (PTP), or an optional mesh networking profile.

time division duplexing (TDD)   A method of transmission that divides a single transmission into two parts: an uplink part and a downlink part.

time division multiple access (TDMA)   A method of transmission that allows multiple device communications by allocating time slots to different senders and receivers.

traffic encryption key (TEK)   The security key used to encrypt the data in a WiMAX network.

triple play   Support for transmission of video, voice, and data on the same network.

truck-roll   A visit to a site by support technicians.

waveguide   A rectangular cavity metal tube that was used to carry microwaves to and from the antennas mounted at the top of the towers, to the transmitter and receiver at the base of the tower.

WiMAX Forum   An industry organization dedicated to promoting the implementation of 802.16 (WiMAX) by testing and certifying equipment for compatibility and interoperability.

Wireless High-Speed Unlicensed Metro Area Network (WirelessHUMAN)   A WiMAX specification based on OFDM that is specifically designed for use in the 5 GHz U-NII band.

WirelessMAN-OFDM   A WiMAX specification that can be used for fixed, mobile, or mesh networking applications and uses either TDD or FDD in licensed bands below 11 GHz.

WirelessMAN-OFDMA   A method used in WiMAX to allow transmission to and from multiple source and destination devices within a single uplink or downlink frame. It divides the available frequency channel into 1,536 orthogonal data subcarriers and uses groups of subcarriers, called subchannels, to communicate with different devices simultaneously.

WirelessMAN-SC (single carrier)   A WiMAX specification that uses a single carrier and is intended for point-to-point connections in the 10 to 66 GHz bands.

Review Questions

1. The term *fixed wireless* is generally used to refer to connections between _____.

   a. buildings

   b. cars

   c. satellites

   d. cell phones

2. What is the common name for connections that begin at a service provider, go through the local neighborhood, and end at the home or office?

   a. 1 mile

   b. Last mile

   c. ISP

   d. Link

3. Which of the following terms is *not* associated with last mile connections for home users?

   a. Satellite

   b. Dial-up modem

   c. DSL

   d. Baseband

4. A leased special high-speed connection from the local telephone carrier for business users that transmits at 1.544 Mbps is called _____.

   a. T1

   b. T3

   c. DSL

   d. Ethernet

5. The technique that treats the entire transmission medium as if it were only one channel is called _____.

   a. broadband

   b. analog

   c. baseband

   d. line

6. Over short distances, WiMAX can communicate at speeds of up to _____ in the 10 to 66 GHz bands.

   a. 100 Mbps

   b. 70 Mbps

   c. 120 Mbps

   d. 30 Mbps

7. The convergence sublayers in the WiMAX MAC protocol allow it to support which of the following type(s) of transmission protocol(s)?

   a. T1

   b. ATM

   c. Voice and video

   d. All of the above

8. In the uplink direction, 802.16 transmits using _____.

   a. TDMA

   b. full-duplex

   c. TDD

   d. FDMA

9. Carrier microwave links use time division duplexing. True or False?

10. Waveguides were used because they did not cause any signal loss between the transmitter and the antenna in microwave systems. True or False?

11. Devices in a WiMAX network must transmit in half-duplex only. True or False?

12. The WiMAX base station controls all transmissions in a WiMAX network. True or False?

13. Non-line-of-sight transmissions in the 802.16 standard can only be supported in the 2 to 11 GHz bands. True or False?

14. What system, sometimes called fiberless optical, uses low-powered infrared laser beams instead of fiber-optic cable?

    a. Micro-beam

    b. Pseudo-fiber

    c. FSO

    d. WiMAX

15. The maximum distance between towers in a microwave link today is _____ miles.

    a. 80

    b. 50

    c. 35

    d. 56

16. A single WiMAX base station can communicate with potentially _____ of subscriber stations simultaneously.

    a. dozens

    b. thousands

    c. hundreds

    d. millions

17. WirelessHUMAN uses the _____ band exclusively.

    a. U-NII

    b. 2–11 GHz

    c. 10–66 GHz

    d. ISM

18. WiMAX network coverage is typically measured in _____.

    a. miles or kilometers

    b. feet

    c. hundreds of feet

    d. meters only

19. Which key factor outlines how WiMAX maximizes the use of the frequency bands?

    a. Better error correction

    b. More frequency stability

    c. Multiple frequency bands

    d. Adaptive modulation

20. How does the BS send information to the SSs about which modulations will be used for a particular burst or transmission?

    a. In the header of the frames

    b. In a burst profile

    c. In a system profile

    d. As part of the association process

Hands-On Projects

Project 9-1

As part of your job as a wireless technologist, one of your important tasks is to keep up-to-date on the hardware available. Identify a few manufacturers of FSO, microwave, and WiMAX technology discussed in this chapter and familiarize yourself with their equipment, their capabilities, and some of their customers. Prepare a brief on each technology, showing a list of manufacturer's company names what type of equipment they supply (such as transmitters, antennas, BSs, CPEs, wireless adapters). Create a one-page or two-page list that includes the frequencies that the equipment is capable of operating on, some of their existing customers and locations.

Project 9-2

Research news media websites like Forbes, Tech Republic, and others, and try to locate a current or historical article that discusses the deployment or expansion of one of the wireless technologies you have just learned about. Don't limit yourself to North America. Create a short slide presentation that shows the purpose and the extent of the deployment as well as the expectations of the project, such as what types of services are offered (i.e., Internet access, video, and telephone). How is it expected to benefit a company or the people in the area? One example of this is using WiMAX to connect oil-drilling platforms that are located near the coast.

Real-World Exercise

The Baypoint Group (TBG) is once again calling on you, their wireless expert. A customer, Advancomms Inc., plans to deploy smart (advanced) antenna systems for a mobile WiMAX network it wants to install in your area, and your task is to locate possible deployment sites. The ideal location would be a building at least eight stories high, which avoids the high cost of erecting towers and supplying power. Another important factor in selecting the site is trying to avoid other wireless antenna systems that might already be deployed in the area.

Exercise 9-1

Use Google Earth or another similar satellite and 3D map system to help you narrow down the area you want to investigate. Then drive, take public transportation, or walk around the downtown area and spot as many wireless antennas as you can, marking on a map the location and positioning of each. If there are antennas already installed on top of the buildings or in towers in your area, you will need to consider whether there is enough vertical space where Advancomm can mount smart antennas. If there are no tall buildings in your area, try to identify possible tower locations while ensuring that the antenna signals will not be blocked by any other structures or terrain, such as hills and mountains.

Use Google Maps or a similar application to display and print a map of your local downtown area, then edit the map to show all the antenna locations.

Produce a short (5–8 slides) PowerPoint presentation that includes the maps and locations of all the potential sites. Include photos of the sites if possible. Remember to indicate whether you think there might be any potential problems.

Challenge Case Project

Wheeler University's campus is spread over a remote area about the size of three city blocks to the south of Buffalo, New York. Wheeler administrators have contacted The Baypoint Group (TBG) and asked for a proposal for connecting their three student residence buildings to the university's network. The buildings are wired for Ethernet, but students currently do not have access to either the university's network or the Internet because the dorms are in a remote area without DSL or cable TV service, due to the remoteness of the campus. The university considered implementing a satellite-based system or installing fiber optics, but the cost of each option proved prohibitive. The main university buildings have access to the Internet through the computer center building. TBG has asked you to become involved, given that you are its wireless networking expert. The residence buildings have line-of-sight access to each other and to the computer center building.

Based on the research you did for Project 9-1, prepare a two-page recommendation and a 10-minute PowerPoint presentation for a specific WMAN implementation. Make sure you address the features of your WMAN and how it can provide long-term benefits for the university. Include photos and basic specifications for the equipment in your presentation. Also include similar examples that you may have located in Project 9-2.

chapter 10

Wireless Wide Area Networks

After reading this chapter and completing the exercises, you will be able to:

- Explain the basic concepts of cellular telephony and how it works
- Discuss the various generations and evolution of cellular telephony
- Discuss satellites and their application in WWANs

A wireless wide area network (WWAN) spans a geographical area as large as an entire country or even the entire world. WWANs can use the cellular phone network to span a country or an entire continent. Where cellular phone networks are not available, satellite technology can enable users to make telephone calls or access the Internet from remote areas. These two technologies complement each other in many ways and make it possible for users to enjoy connectivity to the Internet and even run business applications from almost any location on the planet.

This chapter first explores how cellular phones work and some of the issues surrounding implementation of digital cellular phone technology. It then takes a look at how satellite wireless communications work, some of the issues surrounding the use of satellites for data transmission, and how satellites complement cellular telephony to help provide a truly global wireless wide area network.

Cellular Telephony

Although the browsers on cellular phones sometimes lack the full capabilities of desktop or laptop computer browsers, a cellular phone can be connected (tethered) to a laptop using a cable or Wi-Fi, and the resulting data connection to networks like the Internet can be used to run applications that might otherwise not work from a smartphone. Practically all smartphones include a hotspot feature that enables them to act as Wi-Fi APs, allowing users to connect a laptop computer to the Internet using two different, nonconflicting wireless technologies simultaneously, Wi-Fi and digital cellular telephony.

From the user's perspective, cellular phone technology today is as ubiquitous as the wired telephone was just a decade or two ago. With some exceptions in remote areas where cellular networks are not available, people use smartphones to make and receive calls, send and receive short text messages, send and receive emails, access the web, upload and download all types of data files and pictures, and even watch TV and full-length movies. In many parts of the world, especially where the traditional wired telephone infrastructure is either outdated or nonexistent, cellular phones are making voice and data connections available to users who never before had access to a private telephone line, let alone the Internet. In fact, cellular phones are quickly replacing traditional land-based telephone lines for large groups of people.

Cellular phones literally change lives! By the time fishermen tie their boats to the dock, the catch is often already sold to the highest bidder. Farmers in remote communities can sell their products directly to retailers while on their way to the market. Cellular phones enable producers and small manufacturers to bypass middlemen and enjoy higher profits, something that in the end benefits both the producers and consumers.

From a technological point of view, there is nothing simple about digital cellular telephony. On the contrary, cellular telephony is probably one of the most complex of all wireless communications technologies. Today, cellular phone users expect their phones to perform as well for data as they do for voice calls. Over the past four decades, developments in cellular phone technology have been driven by user demand for high data rates and high-quality voice connections. Cellular phone technology is marketed by the carriers and better known by users by the generation number, such as 2G, 3G, and 4G. The cellular phone business, from the manufacturer to the carriers, is one of the most fiercely competitive businesses anywhere in the world. Governments also take advantage of the growth in the cellular business by auctioning off parts of the wireless spectrum, and in the process, they collect billions of dollars in leasing fees.

Cellular Telephone Technology

Cellular telephony technology continues to grow at what can only be described as warp speed. The ever-expanding range of uses and features that digital cellular networks can provide to mobile users is one of the main reasons for this growth. Today, practically all cellular phone networks are based on digital instead of analog transmission technology. Cellular phones transmit data at ever-increasing speeds and are no longer limited to primarily voice communications. As you no doubt know, smartphones can do much more than what a traditional telephone or the mobile phones of a decade ago could do. Today's smartphones can be used for many sophisticated applications beyond simply browsing the web or sending and receiving messages and email.

In 2013, the number of cellular phone subscriptions worldwide reached 6.8 billion. In 2015, the number of people in the world with a smartphone subscription reached 2.6 billion and it continues to grow. For more information, check some of the statistics pages available at *mobiforge.com.*

How Cellular Telephony Works

The key to understanding how cellular telephony works is that the coverage area is divided into smaller individual sections, called **cells,** as shown in Figure 10-1. A typical cell ranges from a few thousand feet in diameter to approximately 10 square miles (26 square kilometers). At the center of each cell are a transmitter and a receiver with which the mobile devices near that cell communicate, via RF signals. These transmitters are connected to a base station, and each base station is connected to a **mobile telecommunications switching office** (**MTSO**). The MTSO is the link between the cellular phone network and the wired telephone world, commonly referred to as **public switched telephone network** (**PSTN**) or sometimes **plain old telephone system (POTS).** The MTSO "controls" all transmitters and base stations in the cellular phone network. A large city may have multiple MTSOs, each controlling a group of cells.

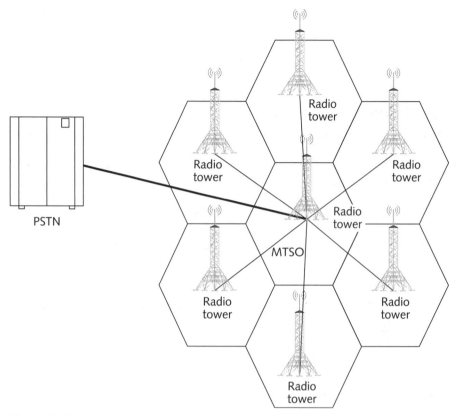

Figure 10-1 A cellular phone network

 Cells are drawn as hexagons simply because it makes it easier to show adjacent cells without the use of overlapping lines, which can be confusing. In reality, a cell's shape is closer to a circle, although buildings and other geographic features can affect the shape.

Today's digital transmitters and digital cellular phones operate at low power levels, which enables carriers to install more cells closer together and support more users. Using low-power mobile devices enables the signal from a cell transmitter or from a single phone to stay confined to a smaller area and cause little or no interference with nearby cells. Because the signal at a particular frequency does not go far beyond the cell area, that same frequency can be used in nearby cells at the same time, though not in adjacent cells. This is called frequency reuse, and a simplified example of it is shown in the diagram in Figure 10-2.

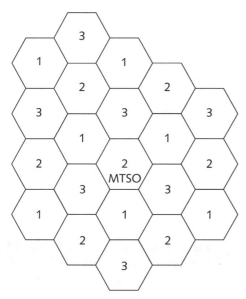

MTSO = Mobile telecommunications switching office

Figure 10-2 Frequency reuse with three frequencies

Cellular phones have special codes associated with them. These codes are used to identify the phone, the phone's owner, and the carrier or service provider (such as AT&T or Sprint). Some of these codes are preprogrammed when the phone is manufactured, whereas others are associated with the user's account. Most cellular phones today require a SIM card to be installed on the phone before they can be used. A **SIM (subscriber identity module)** card is a very small electronic card used to associate the phone with the user's account and with the carrier. Figure 10-3 shows three sizes of SIM cards used in different mobile phones today.

Figure 10-3 SIM cards

SIM cards can have between 64 KB and 512 KB of ROM, between 1 KB and 8 KB of RAM, and between 64 KB and 512 KB of EEPROM. The user's phone number is stored on the SIM card, and users have a choice of storing contact numbers on the phone's memory or on the SIM card. Users can often move the card between one phone and another and use different phones without reprogramming. An example of this is when a user is travelling in an area where the frequency bands used are different than those she uses in her home area. She may be able to rent a phone that is compatible with the local cellular phone service but still use her home account simply by moving the SIM card to a different phone.

Table 10-1 summarizes the codes used in cellular telephony along with their respective sizes and purposes. Note that although these codes are usually present on practically all cellular phones, some of them are no longer used by all carriers.

Code Name	Size	Purpose
System identification code (SID)	5 digits	A unique number that identifies the carrier
Electronic serial number (ESN)	32 bits	The cellular phone's unique serial number; not used on phones with a SIM card
International Mobile Equipment Identity (IMEI)	15 decimal digits (14 plus a check digit)	A unique number that identifies mobile phones as well as some satellite phones; also acts as the serial number
Mobile identification number (MIN)	10 digits	A unique number generated from the phone's telephone number; not used on phones with a SIM card

Table 10-1   Cellular phone codes

An ESN number is permanently assigned to a specific cellular phone when it is manufactured. The carrier or reseller programs the MIN into the phone at account-activation time. The SID code is programmed into the carrier's system and associated with the SIM card at account-activation time. The IMEI number also identifies the SIM cards. As you know, cellular phones can be "locked" to a particular carrier, in which case it cannot be used with another carrier unless it is first unlocked.

When a cellular phone user moves around within a particular cell, the transmitters at the base station for that cell handle all the communications. As the user moves toward the next cell, the cellular phone automatically communicates and associates with the base station of the cell that is closer to it, without interrupting the call or data connection. The process of the new cell taking over the user's call is called a **handoff**. However, what happens if a cellular phone user moves beyond the coverage area of the entire cellular phone network—for example, if he goes from Nashville to Boston? In this case, the cellular telephone would connect with the cellular phone network in Boston, which will then communicate with the network in Nashville to verify that the user has a valid account and can make calls. This connection to a cell outside a user's home area is known as **roaming**. A comparison between handoff and roaming is shown in Figure 10-4.

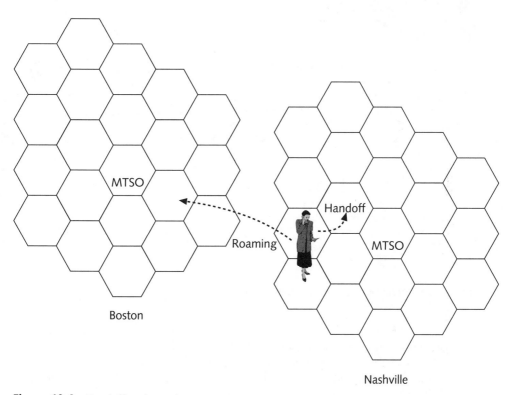

Figure 10-4 Handoff and roaming

A cellular phone user's home area is the location where he lives or works and where he has an account with the cellular phone carrier. When connected to the home area, the user pays local, per-minute call rates. When roaming, the per-minute rates tend to be higher, and a roaming fee might also apply. Per-minute rates and roaming rates depend on the carrier with which the user has an account, and some carriers have been phasing out roaming fees within their national coverage area.

The steps (shown in Figure 10-5) that a cellular phone uses to receive a call are as follows:

1. When the cellular phone is turned on, it scans the frequencies that it is programmed to use and listens for a broadcast from the nearest base station on a selected frequency known as a **control channel**. This broadcast contains information about the

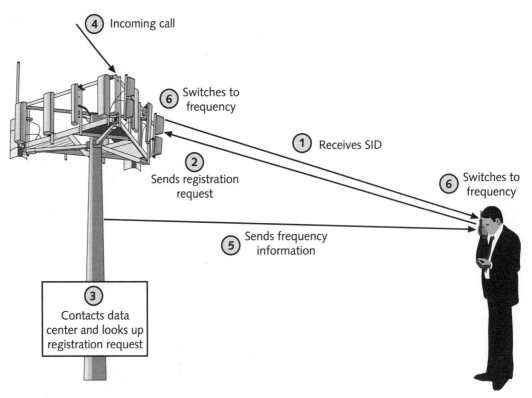

Figure 10-5 Receiving a call on a cellular phone

network, the frequencies used in a particular cell, etc. If the phone cannot detect a control channel, it might be out of range of a compatible network, in which case it displays a message to the user such as "No Service." The broadcast also contains the SID of the carrier.

2. If the cellular phone receives the broadcast information correctly, it compares it with the SID of the carrier that was programmed into the phone or the SIM card. If the information on the phone or the SIM card matches the broadcast, the cellular phone is in a network owned by its carrier. The cellular phone then transmits a registration request number to the base station that the MTSO uses for tracking the cell(s) in which the phone is located.

3. If the SID does not match, then the phone is roaming. The MTSO of the remote network contacts the MTSO of the home network, which confirms that the SID of the phone belongs to a valid account. The MTSO of the remote network then tracks the phone and sends the call information (including length of call and the call's status as a roaming connection) back to the home MTSO.

4. When a call comes in, the MTSO locates the phone through the registration request and then selects a frequency that will be used for communication.

5. The MTSO sends the frequency information to the phone over the control channel. Both the phone and the transmitter switch to that frequency, and the connection is then completed.

6. The phone and transmitter change frequencies as required.

The process of making an outgoing call is similar to the one for receiving a call.

Although the U.S. Telecommunications Act of 1996 makes it illegal to intercept cellular transmissions, callers should remember that their conversations are being broadcast across a public wireless network. The way today's cellular phones work, however, makes it extremely difficult and expensive to intercept a cellular call, but not impossible.

Evolution of Cellular Technology

Because cellular technology is available worldwide, it is useful to learn about how it evolved and where it might be going in the future. All carriers in the world today appear to be moving toward a common system. Cellular phones have been available since the early 1980s in the United States. Since that time, cellular phone technology has changed dramatically. Most industry experts talk in terms of several generations of cellular telephony. This section summarizes the evolution of cellular technologies.

1G (first generation) cellular telephony used analog transmission and modulated voice using FM. It was based on a standard called **Advanced Mobile Phone Service (AMPS)** using circuit switching, and operated in the 800 to 900 MHz frequency spectrum, using 30 KHz wide channels, with a 45 KHz passband (7.5 KHz guard bands on either side) and frequency division multiple access (FDMA, shown in Figure 10-6), allocating two frequencies to each user (one for transmit and one to receive). There were 832 frequencies available for transmission. Out of those frequencies, 790 were used for voice traffic and the remaining 42 were used for control channels. Because two frequencies were used for each full duplex cellular telephone conversation (one to transmit and one to receive), there were actually 395 voice channels, 21 of which were used for control channel functions. The total number of frequencies available might also need to be divided among multiple carriers in same area. This severely limited the maximum number of users that could make a call at any given time, and it was a common occurrence to attempt a call and get a fast busy signal indicating that there were no channels available. Although data transmission was possible, it required the use of modems and the speed was limited to 9.6 Kbps.

AMPS frequency channels provided voice quality comparable to a standard wired telephone transmission, except in the presence of interference, where voice quality degraded significantly.

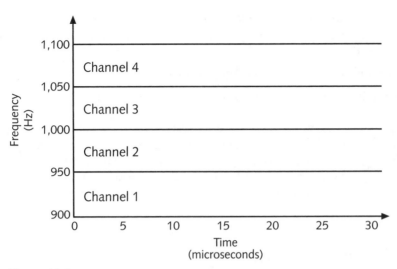

Figure 10-6 FDMA

2G (second generation) cellular telephony was first deployed in the early 1990s to replace AMPS. Most 2G networks are being or have been phased out by now. Second generation networks were capable of transmitting data at between 9.6 and 14.4 Kbps in the 800 MHz and 1.9 GHz frequency bands, but they were still circuit switched for both voice and data and so could provide only limited data services. 2G systems use digital instead of analog transmissions, which improved voice quality because digital signals can be regenerated and the interference removed. Digital transmissions use the frequency spectrum more efficiently, in a variety of ways, so the carriers are able to support a larger number of users per cell. Digital transmissions also use less power and, as a result, they enabled manufacturers to make smaller and less expensive mobile devices, tower transmitters and receivers.

Carriers deploying 2G cellular networks built their networks around various kinds of access technologies. Three technologies were used in 2G: TDMA, CDMA, and GSM. Time division multiple access (TDMA) cellular divides each 30 KHz radio frequency channel into six unique time slots, and each caller uses two time slots (one for transmitting and one for receiving). This means that TDMA could handle three times as many calls over a single frequency channel as FDMA, but it still used circuit switching for both voice and data, and it could not transmit both simultaneously. TDMA is shown in Figure 10-7.

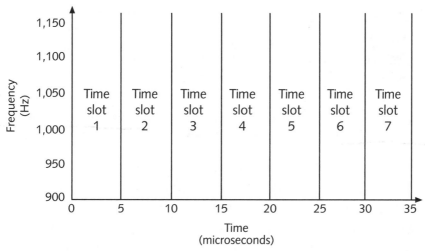

Figure 10-7   TDMA

With code division multiple access (CDMA), each user is allocated the entire spectrum all of the time, as shown in Figure 10-8. CDMA uses direct sequence spread spectrum (DSSS) and unique digital pseudo-random codes (PN codes), rather than separate RF frequencies, to differentiate between users. A CDMA transmission is spread across the frequency, and the digital codes are applied to the individual transmissions. When the signal is received, the codes are removed from the signal in the way described in Chapter 3.

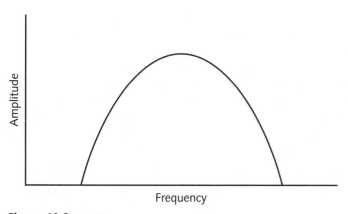

Figure 10-8   CDMA

Global System for Mobile Communications (GSM), developed in the 1980s as the European standard for public mobile communications, uses a combination of FDMA and TDMA technologies. It divides a 25 MHz wide channel into 124 frequencies of 200 KHz each. Each 200 KHz channel is then divided into eight time slots using TDMA. The modulation employed is a variation of frequency shift keying (FSK) called Gaussian minimum shift keying (GMSK), which uses filters to help reduce interference between adjacent channels. GSM systems can transmit data at speeds up to 9.6 Kbps.

In 1989, the Cellular Telecommunications Industry Association (CTIA) chose TDMA over FDMA as the technology of choice for digital cellular networks. However, with the growing technology competition posed by CDMA and the fact that Europe was using GSM for mobile communications, the CTIA reconsidered and decided to let carriers make their own technology choices.

Until the migration to the next generation technology (3G) was completed, an interim step known as **2.5G (2.5 generation)** cellular telephony was widely deployed throughout North America. 2.5G can transmit data at a theoretical maximum data rate of 384 Kbps, and it was also widely deployed in many nations, such as China, Japan, and Korea.

The primary difference between 2G and 2.5G networks is that in 2.5G networks data was transmitted over a packet-switched connection, while voice still used circuit switching.

Packet switching allows always-on data connections, and it becomes practical to keep the data connection at all times. Each packet is transmitted independently through the network to the destination and only uses the channel for the time required to transmit it, so other devices can use the channel to send and receive data, with each device taking turns sending packets, in each cell.

The ability to maintain a data connection on at all times, along with higher transmission speeds, also made digital cable modems and DSL connections more popular than dial-up connections for home use. You can watch TV, talk on the phone, and access the Internet all at the same time, and you don't have to wait for a connection to be reestablished when you want to browse the web, send or check your emails, chat, etc.

There were three 2.5G network technologies. Which one was used by a carrier depends on which 2G-network technology the carrier was migrating from. From TDMA or GSM 2G networks, the upgrade path was a 2.5G technology known as **general packet radio service (GPRS)**. GPRS uses eight time slots in a 200 KHz spectrum and four different coding techniques to transmit data at theoretical maximum speeds of 114 Kbps. The next upgrade step beyond GPRS was **Enhanced Data rates for GSM Evolution (EDGE)**, which boosts data transmission speeds up to 384 Kbps. It is based on **8-PSK** modulation, in which the phase of the carrier is shifted in 45-degree increments and 3 bits can be transmitted per phase change. EDGE-based networks can coexist with standard GSM networks.

For carriers migrating from a 2G CDMA network, the transition was to **CDMA2000 1xRTT** ("1xRTT" stands for "1-times Radio Transmission Technology"), which operates on a pair of 1.25-MHzwide frequency channels and is designed to support up to 144 Kbps packet data transmission as well as to double the voice capacity of CDMA networks.

3G (third generation) cellular telephony was designed to be a uniform and global standard for cellular wireless communication. The International Telecommunications Union (ITU) listed the following maximum data rates for a wireless cellular digital network:

- 144 Kbps for a mobile user
- 386 Kbps for a slowly moving user
- 2 Mbps for a stationary user

Converting from a 2.5G network to a 3G network depends on the 2.5G technology that was employed by the carrier. If the transition is being made from CDMA2000 1xRTT, the path would be to **CDMA2000 1xEVDO** ("EVDO" is short for "Evolution Data Optimized"). This technology can transmit at up to 2.4 Mbps. However, EVDO can only send data and must be coupled with 1xRTT to handle both voice and data. EVDO uses a pair of separate dedicated channels for data, often in new frequency bands being added to the bands available for use with CDMA2000 technologies. EVDO radios measure the signal-to-noise ratio (SNR) in each channel pair every 1.667 milliseconds to determine which cellular phone device to service next. By using dedicated data channels and continually optimizing transmissions to the devices that have the best signal at any given time, EVDO can achieve higher data rates. The successor to CDMA2000 1xEVDO was **CDMA2000 1xEVDV** ("EVDV" is short for "Evolution Data and Voice"), which can send both data and voice transmissions simultaneously over a packet-switched network. EVDV can reach data transfer speeds of up to 3.09 Mbps downstream. Release D of EVDV supports up to 1.0 Mbps upstream.

In 2005, Verizon Wireless and Sprint Nextel Corporation in the United States as well as Bell Canada and TELUS in Canada initiated nationwide deployment of 1xEVDO. Alaska Communications Systems (ACS) deployed 1xEVDO in Alaska's main population centers.

If a network is transitioning from EDGE 2.5G technology, **Wideband CDMA (W-CDMA)** is the migration path to 3G. W-CDMA adds a packet-switched data channel to a circuit-switched voice channel. It can send at up to 2 Mbps to a stationary user and 384 Kbps when mobile.

The upgrade path from W-CDMA is to **High-Speed Downlink Packet Access (HSDPA)**, another interim technology that can transmit at 8 to 10 Mbps downstream. HSDPA uses a 5 MHz W-CDMA channel along with a variety of adaptive modulations, multiple-input multiple-output (MIMO) antennas, and hybrid automatic repeat request (HARQ) techniques, all grouped together to potentially achieve very high data rates. Several carriers in North America that were supporting GSM moved quickly to update their equipment to HSDPA.

But the changes do not end there. As the number of subscribers increases, carriers are under pressure to support more users with a limited amount of frequency bandwidth. Most, if not all, of the carriers that had deployed CDMA found themselves under pressure to move to a technology that was proposed in 2005 and could support theoretical peak download data rates as high as 300 Mbps and upload rates of 75 Mbps. CDMA carriers needed to match these speeds, which could not be accomplished with EVDV, so they began deploying and testing the immediate successor to HSDPA, which is **HSPA+** (Evolved High-Speed Packet Access). This technical standard provides theoretical data rates of up to 168 Mbps on the downlink (a realistic maximum is around 42 Mbps) and 22 Mbps on the uplink and combines two HSDPA transmitters into one, using MIMO, 64-QAM modulation (downlink; 6 bits per symbol) and 16-QAM modulation (uplink; 4 bits per symbol). Two parallel transmission channels form a spatially multiplexed channel, but keep in mind that higher data rates are also dependent on the processing capacity of the cellular phones themselves.

HSPA+ allows the carriers to move to an all-IP, packet-only architecture in which the base stations can bypass the legacy infrastructure of cellular networks, connecting directly to a gateway and using IP routing technology to forward packets to and from a mobile user. HSPA+ can handle up to five times more users per cell on the downlink and twice the number of users on the uplink than previous-generation systems. All of this reduces the cost per bit for the carrier, and the savings eventually flow through to the end users.

HSPA+ also provides an upgrade path to the latest-generation technology, **Long Term Evolution (LTE)**, also known as **4G (fourth generation)**, which many carriers worldwide have adopted or moved toward. LTE expands the MIMO/Spatial Multiplexing beyond the 2 × 2 radio configuration of HSPA+ and allows the use of wider bandwidth RF transmission channels, up to 20 MHz to achieve maximum data rates of up to 100 Mbps on the downlink. Carriers have the option of using narrower channels, 1.4, 3, 5, 10, and 15 MHz, which, of course, reduces the maximum achievable data rates.

LTE uses OFDM on the downlink (tower to mobile device) and a technique called **orthogonal frequency division multiple access (OFDMA)**. The tower equipment can transmit an OFDM signal with up to 2048 subcarriers (only 72 are used by each mobile device), which enables the tower to connect to multiple devices at the same time. Each of the subcarriers is then modulated using QPSK (2 bits per symbol), 16-QAM (4 bits per symbol), or 64-QAM (6 bits per symbol). Which modulation is chosen by the transmitters depends on the SNR at any given time.

For the uplink (mobile to tower) LTE uses **single-carrier FDMA (SC-FDMA)**, which essentially assigns a single subcarrier in the same OFDM stream to each user communicating with the same tower. This not only allows carriers to increase the number of simultaneous users on the uplink and reduce peak RF traffic issues, but it also reduces the power requirements for mobile devices to help the battery charge last longer. The tower still uses at least two antennas per receiver, so the design of system is still essentially MIMO based.

LTE simplifies the cellular network infrastructure for the carriers and makes deployment easier. This is one of the reasons why a large number of cellular networks worldwide have been upgraded or are being upgraded to LTE as well as to the latest evolutions of cellular technology, LTE Advanced and **Voice over LTE (VoLTE)**. The original version of LTE was introduced by the **3rd Generation Partnership Project (3GPP)** in 2009 (see *http://www.3gpp.org /about-3gpp/partners*). 3GPP is a group of six standards organizations from Asia, Europe, and North America that proposed standards for GSM, GPRS/EDGE, HSDPA, HSPA+, and LTE. **LTE Advanced** expands on LTE by allowing carriers to combine up to five 20-MHz-wide frequency channels and raise the maximum downlink data rate possible for mobile cellular devices to 1 Gbps, albeit realistically a lot lower in urban centers, due to the shared access nature of the technology. In addition, LTE Advanced standardizes the use of very small, low-power cells called microcells and femtocells to further optimize frequency reuse and allow more carriers to share the available frequency spectrum.

NOTE   LTE was marketed as 4G, but was not originally considered a "true 4G" technology. Only LTE Advanced (LTE-A) is considered "true 4G." However, the ITU bowed to pressure from North American carriers and now classifies LTE as 4G, but only when the definition includes WiMAX and HSPA+ as well.

With the implementation of VoLTE, carriers will finally move from circuit-switched voice calls and packet-switched data to a totally packet-switched network, further simplifying infrastructure deployment for the carriers. Once this happens, all cellular traffic will be IP based, similar to VoIP, and the quality of voice calls will also improve dramatically, due mainly to more efficient use of the available frequency bandwidth.

NOTE LTE itself was designed and developed for digital data transmission only. VoLTE encapsulates digitized voice in an IP datagram in the same way that VoIP does.

New frequency bands such as 3.5 GHz are also being made available in China and Japan. In North America, the upper and lower portions of the 700 MHz band, originally used for over-the-air television, is now dedicated to LTE with approximately 450 MHz of total bandwidth available. The 500 to 800 MHz band is used in Europe. Figure 10-9 summarizes the technology paths to 4G and beyond.

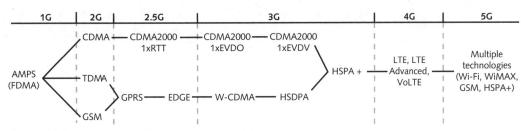

Figure 10-9 Cellular technology migration paths

5G (fifth generation) cellular technology, while still not fully approved, is already being tested by some carriers, as of this writing. The drive behind 5G is, once again, to enable carriers to support an ever-increasing number of users per cell, and the first deployments are expected to be as early as in 2020.

NOTE The FCC in combination with the ITU-R as well as other regulatory organizations around the world are currently working to make more frequency spectrum available for LTE and the upcoming 5G standard.

5G technology employs a blend of GSM, HSPA+, WiMAX, and Wi-Fi to make use of as much spectrum as possible and in the most efficient way. This also means that 5G will be able to offer a wider diversity of services to cellular subscribers and use higher frequency bands that are not currently available to cellular carriers.

Current RF systems are limited to certain parts of the EM spectrum, and parts of it are only used infrequently, so the designers of 5G are working with the ITU and several other organizations, which in turn work with the regulatory authorities of all countries, to develop radios that can take advantage of these additional seldom used parts of the spectrum by unlicensed users, when the licensed users are not using their allocated frequencies.

One way to accomplish this is to use a new breed of software-defined radios, called **cognitive radios**, that can "learn" and adapt to the RF environment; change their mode of operation and frequency bands dynamically, dramatically increasing their spectral efficiency; and take advantage of the flexibility and interoperability of the various wireless communication systems they are able to use. Another key point in the design of 5G cellular networks is the ability of many devices to communicate with each other, distributing the responsibility for processing information and decision-making around the RF environment. The use of a much larger number of antennas, MU-MIMO, 256-QAM in small cells to ensure reliability, and the ability of the radios to differentiate between indoor and outdoor environments by detecting signal strength, along with integration of different technologies, will also help increase the efficient use of the spectrum. As a result, 5G systems will be able to support a much larger number of users per area, and is expected to support 4K and even 8K video in the future. When using the cellular network, data rates should be comparable to those of LTE Advanced and VoLTE but, of course, data rates will vary depending on which wireless system the mobile devices are using at any given time. Table 10-2 summarizes the evolution of cellular technologies.

Name	Generation	Technology	Maximum Peak Data Rate (Downlink)
AMPS	1G	Analog, circuit switched	9.6 Kbps
GSM	2G	Digital, circuit switched	9.6 Kbps
TDMA	2G	Digital, circuit switched	14.4 Kbps
CDMA	2G	Digital, circuit switched	14.4 Kbps
GPRS	2.5G	Digital, packet switched for data only; circuit switched for voice calls	114 Kbps
CDMA2000 1xRTT	2.5G	Same as GPRS	144 Kbps
EDGE	3G	Same as GPRS	384 Kbps
CDMA2000 1xEVDO	3G	Digital, packet switched for both voice and data	2 Mbps
W-CDMA	3G	Digital, packet switched for data; optionally circuit switched or packet switched for voice calls	2 Mbps
CDMA 1xEVDV	3G	Digital, packet switched for data, circuit switched for voice	3.09 Mbps
HSDPA	3G	Same as CDMA2000 1xEVDV	21 Mbps
HSPA+	3G	Digital, packet switched for both voice and data (IP-based)	42 Mbps
LTE	4G	Same as HSPA+	300 Mbps
LTE Advanced/ VoLTE	4G	Same as LTE	1 Gbps
5G	5G	Multiple (Wi-Fi, WiMAX, GSM, HSPA+)	1 Gbps, but varies depending on technology being used

Table 10-2 Digital cellular technologies

Digital Cellular Challenges and Outlook

Having one standard available worldwide and the steady growth in the number of users eventually will lower costs for carriers, allowing them to deliver more competitive pricing and services.

For more information on 3G, 4G, and 5G cellular technologies, visit *www.3gpp.org* and *www.umts-forum.org*.

Carriers spend billions of dollars to build and continually upgrade their cellular networks. The cost of leasing the necessary RF spectrum alone can be astronomical. In early 2001, for example, carriers in Germany paid over $46 billion for licenses to use the spectrum. Carriers in other nations face similar costs, and that's just one element in building a modern cellular network. Networks must be deployed, tested, managed, and maintained to keep customers satisfied with the service. In addition, the cost associated with high-volume data connections to the Internet runs into the millions of dollars per month. If 5G's ambitious design is successful, it might reduce the need for the wired telephone infrastructure, thereby saving carriers the cost of deploying and maintaining much of the cable infrastructure. The integration of technologies will likely change the landscape for telephone and data users worldwide yet again. The technologies you have learned about in previous chapters are definitely worth keeping a close eye on in the upcoming years.

Satellite Broadband Wireless

Another WWAN technology that has been around for several decades is satellite communications. Satellites provide the world with global positioning systems (GPS), communications to the remotest of areas on the planet, and radio transmissions and TV signals that can reach virtually anyone anywhere on the planet in real time. Satellites have also played an important role in WWAN data networks because they can deliver signals to any point on the oceans that cover most of Earth's surface, to the Arctic and Antarctic continents, and to remote and mountainous areas where electricity and cellular phone transmission tower infrastructure might not yet exist. Because of the complexity and cost of launching satellites into space and placing them in the correct orbit, this is the most expensive of all wireless communications technologies.

Although the use of satellites for personal wireless communications is fairly recent, satellites have been used for worldwide communications for the past 50 years. Satellite use falls into three broad categories. The first use is acquiring scientific data (e.g., measuring the radiation from the sun) and performing research in space (e.g., gathering data from space telescopes). The second use is looking at Earth from space. This includes weather and surface mapping satellites as well as military satellites. The third category of satellites are those that are used as reflectors to relay signals from one point on the surface of the Earth to another. This includes communications satellites that reflect telephone and data transmissions, broadcast satellites that reflect television signals, as well as navigation satellites. The three types of satellites are compared in Figure 10-10.

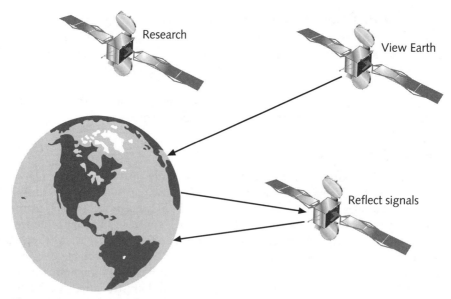

Figure 10-10   Three types of satellites

Wireless communications falls under the third use of satellites.

Satellite Transmissions

Satellites generally send and receive on one of four frequency bands, which are known as the L band, the C band, the Ku band, and the Ka band. These bands are summarized in Table 10-3.

Band	Frequency
L band	1.53–2.7 GHz
C band	3.6–7 GHz
Ku band	11.7–12.7 GHz for downlink; 14–17.8 GHz for uplink
Ka band	17.3–31 GHz

Table 10-3   Satellite frequencies

As you already know, frequency band affects the size of the antenna. Figure 10-11 compares the typical sizes of antennas used for the four satellite bands. Note that in addition to the frequency band, the size of the antenna would depend on the footprint of the satellite and its signal strength at the sending/receiving location.

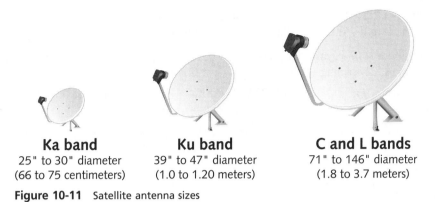

Ka band
25" to 30" diameter
(66 to 75 centimeters)

Ku band
39" to 47" diameter
(1.0 to 1.20 meters)

C and L bands
71" to 146" diameter
(1.8 to 3.7 meters)

Figure 10-11   Satellite antenna sizes

Class and Type of Service   Satellites provide two classes of service: consumer class and business class. Consumer class service shares the available bandwidth among the users; business class service, the more expensive of the two, offers dedicated channels with dedicated bandwidth.

Satellites that reflect signals back to Earth offer different types of service. They may be designed for point-to-point, point-to-multipoint, or even multipoint-to-multipoint communications, as shown in Figure 10-12.

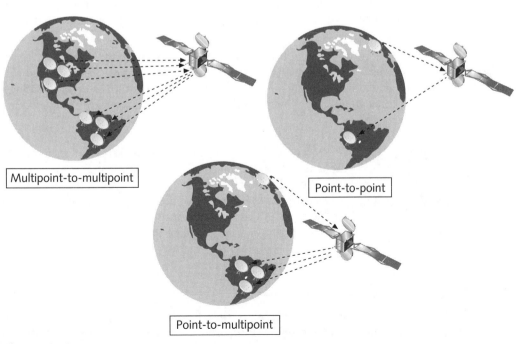

Multipoint-to-multipoint

Point-to-point

Point-to-multipoint

Figure 10-12   Types of satellite service

Modulation Techniques Satellites use a variety of common modulation techniques, most of which were discussed in Chapter 2. Here are brief descriptions of them:

- *Binary phase shift keying (BPSK)*—Shifts the starting point of a carrier wave by 180 degrees, depending on whether a 1 or a 0 is being transmitted

- *Quadrature phase shift keying (QPSK)*—Shifts the starting point of the carrier wave by 90 degrees; transmits 2 bits per symbol

- *Eight-phase shift keying (8-PSK)*—Like QPSK but transmits 3 bits per symbol

- *16-level quadrature amplitude modulation (16-QAM)*—Primarily used for sending data downstream; considered very efficient but less reliable, so it is not generally used for upstream transmissions

Multiplexing Techniques Satellite systems employ two common multiplexing techniques, FDMA and TDMA, along with some specialized techniques designed to maximize utilization of these very expensive communications channels. Detailed coverage of these specialized techniques is beyond the scope of this book, but here are brief descriptions of them:

- *Permanently Assigned Multiple Access (PAMA)*—One of the oldest techniques, in which a frequency channel is permanently assigned to a user

- *Single channel per carrier (SCPC)*—Assigns a frequency channel to a single source; used for broadcasting radio stations, which are always transmitting

- *Multiple channel per carrier (MCPC)*—Uses time division multiplexing (TDM) to consolidate traffic from different users on to each carrier frequency; it is used for the European digital video broadcasting standard and typically used in point-to-multipoint applications

- *Demand Assigned Multiple Access (DAMA)*—Allocates bandwidth on a per-call or per-transmission session between two or more Earth stations; can efficiently share the pool of available frequency and time resources and permits full mesh routing, similar to how a telephone company's switch works, but requires more complex and costly hardware

NOTE For TV broadcasting directly to the user (satellite TV), the set-top box at the user's home or office includes a utility that enables the installation technician to align the dish antenna with the satellite antenna. The antenna needs to be initially positioned in a certain direction and at a certain angle, then the technician uses the TV set and set-top box and fine-tunes the antenna position until the strongest possible signal is achieved.

Satellite Classification

Satellite systems are classified according to their type of orbit. The three orbits are low earth orbit (LEO), medium earth orbit (MEO), and a class of high orbit satellites known as geosynchronous or GEO. MEO satellites also include the subclass of highly elliptical orbit (HEO) satellites.

Low Earth Orbit Low earth orbit (LEO) satellites circle the Earth at altitudes between 200 and 900 miles (321 and 1,448 kilometers). Because they orbit so close to Earth, LEO satellites must travel at high speeds so that the Earth's gravity does not pull them back into the atmosphere. Satellites in LEO travel at an average of 17,000 miles (27,359 kilometers) per hour, circling the Earth in about 90 minutes.

Because LEOs are in such a low orbit, their area of coverage (called the footprint) is small, as shown in Figure 10-13. This means that more LEO satellites are needed to provide coverage to larger areas, compared with MEO and GEO satellites. One LEO system calls for over 225 satellites for total coverage of the Earth.

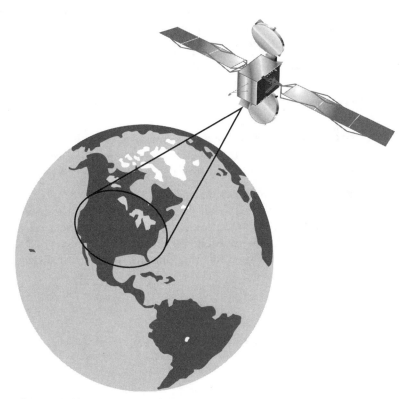

Figure 10-13   LEO satellite footprint

LEO systems have a low latency (delays caused by signals that must travel over a long distance) and use low-powered terrestrial devices (RF transmitters). It takes 20 to

40 milliseconds for a signal to bounce from a station on Earthbound station to a LEO, then back to another Earth station.

LEO satellites can be further divided into Little LEO and Big LEO groups. Little LEO satellites usually provide pager, satellite telephone, and some navigation. Using a Little LEO satellite, a user can make a satellite phone call from anywhere on Earth. In contrast, cellular telephone services require the user to be within RF range of a transmission tower. Big LEOs usually carry voice and data broadband services, such as wireless Internet access. Some satellite Internet services provide shared downstream data rates of up to 400 Kbps but require a telephone connection for upstream data to an ISP. Another LEO wireless Internet service provides two-way data services with speeds of up to 500 Kbps. Two-way satellite Internet users need a two-foot by three-foot dish antenna and two modems (one each for uplink and downlink).

In the future, LEOs are expected to be in demand for three markets: remote rural conventional telephone service, global mobile digital cellular service, and international broadband service. The speeds for wireless access are expected to exceed 100 Mbps.

Today, many companies use satellite technology to reduce line costs. National drugstore and supermarket chains, which usually have stores located in remote towns, sometimes use LEO satellites to link remote stores with the head office and download sales and inventory information at the end of each day.

Medium Earth Orbit   Medium earth orbit (MEO) satellites orbit the Earth at altitudes between 1,500 and 10,000 miles (2,413 to 16,090 kilometers). Some MEO satellites orbit in near-perfect circles, have a constant altitude, and travel at a constant speed.

Because they are farther from the Earth, MEOs have two advantages over LEOs. First, they do not have to travel as fast; a MEO can take up to 12 hours to circle the Earth. Second, MEOs have a bigger Earth footprint; thus, fewer satellites are needed, as shown in Figure 10-14. On the other hand, the higher orbit also increases the latency, which means that the signal takes from 50 to 150 milliseconds to make the round trip between Earth to the satellite and back down to the surface.

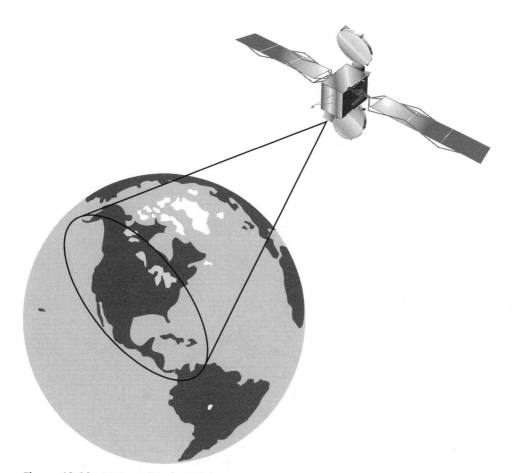

Figure 10-14   MEO satellite footprint

Highly Elliptical Orbit Highly elliptical orbit (HEO) **satellites** are a type of MEO satellite, but with elongated orbits. The average orbit characteristics of a HEO satellite are about the same as other MEOs; however, HEO satellites have a high apogee (maximum altitude) and a low perigee (minimum altitude). In addition, HEO orbits can provide good coverage for extreme latitudes. The orbits also typically have a 24-hour period, which means the satellites dwell for a long time at a fixed point over the Earth. This means that with just two satellites in the same orbit, one is always "visible" from any point on the ground.

Geosynchronous Earth Orbit These high-orbit satellites are stationed at an altitude of 22,282 miles (35,860 kilometers). When a satellite reaches this altitude at a given speed, it enters a kind of "sweet spot" and its orbit matches the rotation of the planet. This means that it remains virtually fixed over a given location on the surface of the Earth and appears to "hang" motionless in space. A few somewhat rare satellites orbit the planet above 63,333 miles (101,925 kilometers). Because of their great distance from the surface of the Earth, **geosynchronous Earth orbit (GEO) satellites** can provide continuous service to a very large footprint. In fact, only three GEO satellites are needed to cover the entire Earth (except for the polar regions). Their high altitude causes GEO satellites to have high latencies of about 250 milliseconds and require high-powered terrestrial transmitting devices along with very sensitive receiving equipment. GEO satellites are typically used for global communications —such as TV broadcasting and weather forecasting. However, today GEO satellites are not normally used for telephony or computer communications because of the one-quarter second delay in round-trip transmissions, which is unacceptable to users. The distance of the satellite from the surface of the planet causes this delay, and it affects the performance of computer communications protocols like TCP/IP. However, GEO satellites can be used as backup communication links in case major disasters affect the undersea optical cable communications infrastructure anywhere on the surface of the planet. Figure 10-15 shows how three GEO satellites can cover the entire planet. GEO satellites have also been used to monitor compliance with the nuclear test ban agreements; they are also used by Russia to provide satellite services to the polar regions.

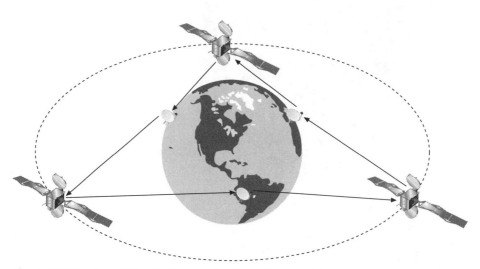

Figure 10-15   Three GEO satellites covering the entire planet (except for polar regions)

Although GEO satellites are much more expensive to launch, they are an attractive option because of their lifespan of 12 to 15 years. (The average lifespan of a LEO satellite is only 5 years.) Also, because their footprints are so large, they are much more efficient compared to LEO satellites. LEO satellites spend a portion of their orbit over sparsely populated areas where continuous coverage might not be needed. The ITU regulates GEO usage.

Some satellites, like the ones used for Sirius satellite radio (Radiosat), follow a highly elliptical orbit called Tundra. This orbit is chosen because it allows the satellites to provide better coverage at higher latitudes. Geostationary orbits are only possible around the equator, which would make it difficult to provide service across Canada and the northern part of the United States.

Table 10-4 summarizes the advantages and disadvantages of the various satellite orbits.

Satellite Orbit	Advantages	Disadvantages
LEO	Low latency (20–40 milliseconds) Low power High-speed communications (500 Kbps or higher, depending on application)	Very high orbital speed Average of 225 satellites to cover the entire Earth Small footprint Short life span (average 5 years)
MEO	Medium latency (50–150 milliseconds) Larger footprint than LEO; 24 satellites required to cover the Earth Slower orbital speed; dwells over an area longer; 12-hour orbit Longer life span than LEO (10+ years)	Higher latency than LEO More expensive to replace than LEO
HEO	Similar speed and latency characteristics to MEO; can dwell over an area longer Footprint similar to MEO Can provide good coverage at extreme latitudes (polar regions)	Fewer satellites required to cover the Earth than other MEOs At apogee (high point of orbit), latency increases Highly elliptical orbit, which requires great accuracy and increases cost
GEO	Very large footprint; only three satellites required to cover entire Earth Synchronized with Earth's rotation, allowing for permanent, fixed antennas Very high speeds used for broadcasting Long life span (15+ years)	Very high latency (250 milliseconds); not efficient for two-way IP communications Very expensive to replace Higher power required by greater distance from Earth; more subject to interference Does not provide good coverage at very high latitudes

Table 10-4   Satellites and their orbits

Experimental Technologies

Satellites are vulnerable to disturbances on the surface of our sun and other outer-space phenomena such as meteorites that can cause interruptions in communications or incapacitate a very expensive satellite. The U.S. National Aeronautics and Space Administration (NASA) has experimented with solar-powered aircraft flying at extremely high altitudes, Google (Project Loon) has launched experimental balloons that travel around the planet on the jet stream (a weather phenomenon), and Facebook is experimenting with solar-powered drones. The Google and Facebook projects are an effort to bring Internet connectivity to as many people around the world as possible, at little or no cost to the users.

Search the web to find out more about experimental projects by Google and Facebook.

TIP

Satellite Technology Outlook

The fact that satellites can provide wireless communication service in areas not covered by other WWAN technologies means that end-users and companies will continue to rely on this technology, probably indefinitely. Today's satellites enable airlines, merchant shipping companies, and tourism operators to offer Internet access and voice calls to passengers and crews across large oceans as well as near the poles and remote corners of the Earth where a communications infrastructure does not exist. As with other wireless technologies, it is likely that satellite technology will evolve, along with the experimental technologies just discussed, to increase reliability and lower costs.

Chapter Summary

- The two main wireless wide area network (WWAN) technologies are cellular telephony and satellite communications. These two technologies complement each other in many ways and make it possible for users and businesses to connect to the Internet and other networks from almost any location on the planet.

- In cellular telephone networks, the coverage area is divided into sections called cells. Each cell includes one or more transmitters with which the mobile devices communicate.

- The transmitters and cellular phones operate at a low level of power, which allows the signals to stay confined to one cell and not interfere with other cells. This means the same frequency can be used in other, nonadjacent cells at the same time. Cellular phones have special codes associated with them that identify the phone, the phone's owner, and the carrier or service provider.

- Some cellular phones use SIM cards to store the user account information and sometimes other information such as the user's contacts. SIM cards can be moved among different cellular phones, and the phones do not have to be reprogrammed to use the same account and phone number.

- When a cellular phone user moves from a cell to an adjacent cell, the cellular phone automatically associates with the base station of that cell. This is called a handoff. If a cellular user moves beyond the coverage area of his cellular network, the cellular phone automatically connects with whatever cellular network is in place in the remote area. The cellular network in the remote area communicates with the one in the home area and verifies that the user has a valid account and can make calls. This connection to a cell outside a user's home area is known as roaming.

- 1G (first generation) cellular technology uses analog signals, is based on the AMPS standard, operates in the 800 to 900 MHz frequency spectrum, and uses FDMA. 1G networks use circuit-switching technology and can transmit data at a maximum speed of 9.6 Kbps.

- 2G (second generation) cellular technology can transmit data between 9.6 and 14.4 Kbps in the 800 MHz and the 1.9 GHz frequency bands and uses circuit-switched networks. 2G systems use digital instead of analog transmissions. 2G systems employ three different multiple-access technologies: TDMA, CDMA, and GSM. GSM, developed in Europe, uses a combination of FDMA and TDMA technologies.

- 2.5G (2.5 generation) cellular networks transmit data at a maximum speed of 384 Kbps. The primary difference between 2G and 2.5G networks is that 2.5G networks use a packet-switched technique to transmit data instead of a circuit-switched technique. Voice calls still use circuit switching. Circuit switching is ideal for voice communications but is not efficient for transmitting data.

■ 3G (third generation) cellular networks provide new and expanded capabilities and data applications features to mobile users. Because 3G networks are based on purely digital rather than analog technology and can transmit data at much higher speeds, they allow always-on data connections.

■ 4G (fourth generation) cellular networks achieve data rates that are competitive with wired communications. Long Term Evolution (LTE) technology can achieve data rates as high as 1 Gbps. Many carriers worldwide are upgrading their networks to LTE and beyond at an accelerated pace.

■ 5G (fifth generation) cellular technology is currently under development and is slated to be approved in 2018. 5G is expected to be able to take advantage of multiple technologies, such as Wi-Fi and WiMAX, to support a significantly larger number of users and higher realistic data rates. 5G is also expected to be able to support 4K and even 8K video over wireless links.

■ Satellites used for wireless data connectivity employ simple modulation and multiplexing techniques. Satellite systems can transmit point-to-point, point-to-multipoint, and multipoint-to-multipoint.

■ LEO satellites orbit the Earth at a low altitude and at high speeds. They have a limited footprint and low latency and use low-powered terrestrial transceivers.

■ MEO satellites orbit the Earth at higher altitudes than LEOs but do not travel as fast as LEOs and have a bigger Earth footprint, requiring fewer satellites. MEOs have higher latency than LEOs.

■ HEO satellites are a type of MEO satellite with a highly elliptical orbit, with a high apogee and low perigee, and can provide good coverage in extreme latitudes. A HEO satellite takes approximately the same amount of time to orbit the planet as other MEOs.

■ GEO satellites orbit at much higher altitudes than MEOs, and their orbits match the rotation of the Earth, so they stay in the same position with reference to a point on the ground. GEO satellites have high latencies and require high-powered terrestrial transceivers. GEO satellites are used for global communications.

Key Terms

1G (first generation)   The first generation of wireless cellular telephony, which transmitted data at up to at 9.6 Kbps using analog circuit-switched transmission technology.

2G (second generation)   The second generation of cellular telephony, which uses circuit-switched digital transmission technology.

2.5G (2.5 generation)   An interim technology stage between 2G and 3G digital cellular networks in which data is transmitted using packet-switched technology.

3G (third generation)   Digital cellular wireless generation of cellular telephony, with speeds up to 2 Mbps.

3rd Generation Partnership Project (3GPP)   A group of six standards organizations from Asia, Europe, and North America that proposed standards for GSM, GPRS/EDGE, HSDPA, HSPA+, and LTE.

4G (fourth generation)   The latest active standard for cellular communications, currently deployed or being deployed by cellular carriers worldwide, also commonly marketed by carriers as LTE. According to the ITU, only LTE Advanced qualifies as "true 4G" cellular, but the term *4G* can be used if WiMAX and HSPA+ are included in the definition as well.

5G (fifth generation)   A new cellular standard currently under development. 5G is currently expected to be ratified in 2018 and the technology does not yet have an acronym like LTE, which is another designation for 4G.

8-PSK   A modulation technique in which the phase of the carrier is shifted in 45-degree increments and 3 bits can be transmitted per phase change.

Advanced Mobile Phone Service (AMPS)   The standard used for 1G analog cellular transmissions, based on FDMA. 1G is often simply called AMPS.

CDMA2000 1xEVDO   The 3G digital cellular technology that is a migration from CDMA2000 1xRTT.

CDMA2000 1xEVDV   The 3G digital cellular technology that is a migration from CDMA2000 1xEVDO.

CDMA2000 1xRTT   A 2.5G digital cellular network technology that is a migration from CDMA. ("1xRTT" stands for "1-times Radio Transmission Technology.")

cell   The coverage area of one transmission tower in a mobile telephone network.

cognitive radio   Software-controlled radio that can adapt to the environment by changing frequency channels, bandwidth, modulation, and encoding, depending on the RF environment. These RF characteristics can also be preconfigured by the carriers.

control channel   A special frequency that cellular phones use for communication with a base station.

Enhanced Data rates for GSM Evolution (EDGE)   A 2.5G digital cellular network technology that boosts GPRS transmissions.

general packet radio service (GPRS)   A 2.5G network technology that can transmit at up to 114 Kbps.

geosynchronous earth orbit (GEO) satellite   Satellite stationed at an altitude of 22,282 miles (35,860 kilometers) that matches the rotation of the planet and therefore appears to be in a fixed position in the sky with reference to a point on the ground.

Global System for Mobile Communications (GSM)   One of three multiple-access cellular technologies that make up the 2G digital cellular system; it uses a combination of FDMA and TDMA.

handoff   In cellular technology, the process of a cell taking over an ongoing call from another cell, as the user moves about within his or her home area's cellular coverage area.

High-Speed Downlink Packet Access (HSDPA)   A packet-switched digital transmission cellular technology that uses 5 MHz W-CDMA (wideband CDMA) channels together with adaptive modulation, MIMO, and hybrid automatic repeat request (HARQ) to achieve data rates between 8 and 10 Mbps.

highly elliptical orbit (HEO) satellite   Satellite that circles the planet in an elliptical orbit, having a high apogee (maximum altitude) and a low perigee (minimum altitude). This type of satellite can provide good coverage at extreme latitudes, such as the polar regions.

HSPA+   Also called "evolved HSPA," a technical cellular standard that provides theoretical data rates of up to 168 Mbps (realistically, around 42 Mbps) by combining two HSDPA transmitters, MIMO, and 64 QAM modulation.

Long Term Evolution (LTE)   A 4G digital packet-switched cellular technology that expands on HSPA+ beyond two spatially multiplexed channels, uses OFDM modulation, and also uses 20-MHz-wide channels to achieve data rates of up to 100 Mbps.

LTE Advanced   A proposed standard for broadband cellular communications that expands on LTE by allowing carriers to combine up to five 20-MHz-wide OFDM channels to achieve data rates of up to 1 Gbps.

low earth orbit (LEO) satellite   Satellite that orbits the Earth at an altitude of 200 to 900 miles (321 to 1,448 kilometers).

medium earth orbit (MEO) satellite   Satellite that orbits the Earth at altitudes of 1,500 to 10,000 miles (2,413 to 16,090 kilometers).

mobile telecommunications switching office (MTSO)   The connection between a cellular network and wired telephones.

orthogonal frequency division multiple access (OFDMA)   A method based on OFDM that assigns groups of subcarriers to different users.

plain old telephone system (POTS)   *See* public switched telephone network.

public switched telephone network (PSTN)   The wired telephone network. Sometimes referred to as the plain old telephone system (POTS).

roaming   What happens when a cellular user connects to a network outside of her home area.

SIM (subscriber identity module) card   Small electronic card used to associate a phone with a user's account.

single-carrier FDMA (SC-FDMA)   The technology used in LTE for mobile phones to communicate back to the tower transceivers. SC-FDMA assigns a single subcarrier to the same OFDM uplink stream to each mobile user communicating with the same tower.

Voice over LTE (VoLTE)   VoLTE enables carriers to move from circuit-switched voice and packet-switched data to a totally IP-based network, carrying both digitized voice encapsulated in IP datagrams, as well as data.

Wideband CDMA (W-CDMA)   The 3G digital cellular technology that is a migration from EDGE.

Review Questions

1. What is the purpose of the SID on a cellular phone or SIM card?

    a. To identify the user

    b. To identify the carrier

    c. To identify the phone

    d. To identify the area in which the user is located

2. Which element of a cellular network connects a base station with a wired telephone network?

   a. Transmitter

   b. Cellular phone

   c. MTSO

   d. CDMA

3. Which of the following is not a valid cellular telephone code?

   a. System identification code (SID)

   b. Electronic serial number (ESN)

   c. Digital serial code (DSC)

   d. Mobile identification number (MIN)

4. What is it called when a user begins moving toward another cell and the cellular phone automatically associates with the base station of that cell during a call?

   a. Roaming

   b. Handoff

   c. Hunting

   d. Multiplexing

5. What is the name given to the special frequency that a cellular phone and base station use for exchanging call-setup information?

   a. W-CDMA

   b. Cell tunnel

   c. Control channel

   d. GB line

6. What is the main advantage of transmitting voice calls using packet switching vs. circuit switching?

   a. There is no advantage; voice must always be transmitted using circuit switching.

   b. Call setup is faster using packet switching.

   c. The amount of bandwidth used is much larger with packet switching.

   d. The voice call does not tie up the channel 100 percent of the time using packet switching.

7. LTE Advanced achieves its increase in data rates due to being able to combine multiple 20 MHz channels. True or False?

8. Division by frequency, so that each caller is allocated part of the spectrum for all of the time, is the basis of TDMA. True or False?

9. LTE still uses circuit-switching for voice calls. True or False?

10. 5G can support more users simultaneously than LTE, but it may not provide any improvements in terms of data rates. True or False?

11. The primary difference between 2G and 2.5G networks is that 2.5G networks transmit data using _____.

    a. packets

    b. capsules

    c. DTR

    d. FDMA

12. Which of the following cellular technologies supports MIMO?

    a. CDMA

    b. AMPS

    c. LTE

    d. EDGE

13. In addition to MIMO, what enables HSPA+ to achieve data rates of up to 42 Mbps?

    a. AAS

    b. HARQ

    c. Backhauling

    d. Spatial multiplexing

14. When does roaming occur in cellular telephony?

    a. When a user is away from his or her home Wi-Fi network

    b. When a user connects to another carrier in his or her home area

    c. When a user is away from his or her home area

    d. When a user turns off his or her cellular phone

15. Control information is transmitted as _____ by the _____.

    a. individual frames; MTSO

    b. unicasts; MTSO

    c. TDMA packets; base station

    d. broadcasts; base station

16. What is a femtocell?

    a. A very large cellular area

    b. A small cell supported by LTE Advanced

    c. A GPRS cell

    d. A transmission technique used with OFDM

17. Why are some GEO satellites not usually used for transmitting TCP/IP information?

    a. They cannot transmit a strong enough signal.

    b. Their transmissions do not have a large enough footprint.

    c. They only transmit point-to-point.

    d. The round-trip delay of 250 milliseconds causes IP protocol problems.

18. Of the following types of satellite, which travels at the highest orbital speed?

    a. LEO

    b. GEO

    c. HEO

    d. MEO

19. Of the following types of satellite, which has the smallest signal footprint?

    a. HEO

    b. MEO

    c. LEO

    d. GEO

20. Of the following types of satellites, which typically has the longest lifespan?

    a. LEO

    b. MEO

    c. Big LEO

    d. GEO

Hands-On Projects

Project 10-1

Research on the Internet to determine where 4G (LTE, LTE Advanced, VoLTE) has been deployed. Include information on what types of technology have been deployed in Asia and South America in addition to the United States and Canada. Write a one-page report on your findings.

Project 10-2

There are several new techniques to increase data transmission speed in satellite technology. Use the Internet to locate information on these new techniques. Discuss their strengths, weaknesses, and the applications on which they are most often found. How are they implemented if we cannot retrieve the satellites and modify their radios? Write a one-page report on your findings.

Project 10-3

Visit and take some time to explore SpaceBook at *apps.agi.com/satelliteviewer* to see a graphical representation of the Earth and real-time motion graphic showing all of the satellites. Use the Help feature (the ? at the top right) to learn how to control the display, then write down the total number of satellites that are currently orbiting our planet, how many are nonoperational, how many are operational, and how many are used for communications. Locate the International Space Station (ISS) under Owner. Double-click ISS to zoom in and get an idea of how fast it moves over the surface of the planet.

Real-World Exercises

The Baypoint Group (TBG), a company of 50 consultants who assist organizations and businesses with issues involving network planning and design, has again requested your services as a consultant. Telecom Argentina is a company that is licensed to provide wired telecommunications services in the northern part of Argentina. The company has contracted TBG to assist it with the selection and implementation of a new field service system. The goal is to provide service technicians with wireless access to the corporate network and a vast electronic library of technical manuals and schematic diagrams, which would reduce or eliminate the need for staff to carry a large number of books and drawings, especially while servicing equipment underground or when climbing on transmission towers. In addition, this means that the technicians would be able to immediately read and update the records for all the equipment, thereby avoiding massive amounts of paperwork as well as potential errors and omissions. However, the company is having trouble deciding on which technology to adopt—handheld cellular, tablets with 3G or 4G access, or laptops equipped with cellular cards. Provide a one-page report outlining your recommendations for TBG.

Exercise 10-1

Create a presentation outlining the advantages for Telecom Argentina of using digital cellular handsets or cellular wireless cards. Determine the ability of the smaller cellular handsets (as opposed to notebook computers, which may be difficult to carry everywhere) to display standard documents such as Word, Excel, and PDF files, and evaluate how this could help the company. Because the group you will be presenting to is composed of nontechnical managers, be sure your presentation is not too technical. Limit yourself to a maximum of 15 PowerPoint slides.

Exercise 10-2

Jose Riveras, one of the senior executives at Telecom Argentina, was convinced by your presentation. However, he recently heard about 4G cellular and wants to know how this technology will affect the company's plans to purchase equipment now. TBG has asked you to create another presentation for Jose that explains the different generations of cellular technology. Use the information you obtained in the Hands-On Projects above and also visit *mobiforge.com* and search for "mobile user behavior statistics" to help you gather more data to prepare your presentation.

Challenge Case Project

Telecom Argentina is unsure about investing in cellular phones, so it is considering alternatives, including Wi-Fi tablets and laptop computers with the data preloaded onto the devices. Working with three other students, form two teams of two people, with each team selecting one of these technologies. Research in depth the advantages and disadvantages of these respective technologies and how they work. Hold a friendly debate in which each two-person team gives a 5-minute talk about the advantages of its technology. After the talk, allow time for the others to ask questions.

chapter 11

Radio Frequency Identification and Near Field Communication

After reading this chapter and completing the exercises, you will be able to:

- Define radio frequency identification (RFID) and near field communication (NFC)
- List the components of an RFID or NFC system
- Describe how RFID and NFC work
- Explain the challenges and security considerations of RFID and NFC

Imagine that you are just making a quick stop at a local supermarket to pick up a few grocery items. As you enter the store, you obtain a bag near the door. Then you walk through the aisles and load the bag with the products you need. When you are finished, you simply walk through an arch-like structure where the cash register should have been, and then you exit the store. There's no need to stop and pay for the products or even to show anyone which products you purchased. You reach for your smartphone when it beeps, and find that the grocery store just sent you a receipt by email.

While driving back home, you stop at a self-serve gas station to fill up the tank. You reach for your smartphone again, activate an app, and bring the phone near the front of the pump. The gas pump beeps and authorizes your purchase. When you are finished pumping and replace the gas nozzle, your smartphone beeps again and displays the receipt for the fuel.

Arriving home, you put your purchases in the refrigerator. A display screen outside the refrigerator door is automatically updated with the contents, the expiration date of each individual product, and the quantities of each product.

Although this example might sound like a futuristic dream, the standards and technology that make it work are already in use. In fact, there is a huge number of potential applications for this technology in our everyday lives. In this chapter, you learn about how radio frequency identification and near field communications work. You also learn about some of the challenges related to the implementation of such systems.

What Is RFID?

As you learned in Chapter 1, radio frequency identification (RFID) is a technology developed to identify "things" in a similar way that barcode labels are used to identify almost every single off-the-shelf product anywhere in the world today. The difference between barcodes and RFID is that RFID uses RF waves instead of laser light to read the product code. RFID stores product information in electronic **tags**, which are devices that contain an antenna and an integrated circuit chip. RFID tags can store significantly more information than the barcode system. This data, held in read-write or read-only memory, can include the date, time, and location where the product was manufactured; the manufacturer name; and product serial number. In comparison, barcode labels typically include only an item's stock-keeping unit or product number. Any additional data about the product must be stored in a computer.

RFID technology is not new; it has been in use around the world, in one form or another, for many years. In the late 1930s, the U.S. Army and U.S. Navy introduced a system designated IFF (Identification Friend-or-Foe), which was implemented and used for the first time in the Second World War, to distinguish Allied forces aircraft from enemy aircraft by use of special codes that could be read by a friendly aircraft at a distance. Likewise, for many years, microchips and antennas inside tiny capsules have been implanted under the skin of household pets. These tags contain a numeric code that is registered in a centralized database by the company that supplies the tags.

You might also be familiar with another type of RFID that is frequently used in retail stores to prevent theft. After you pay for an item, a small tag attached to the product is run through a powerful magnet at the checkout; the magnet disables the tag, preventing it from activating the alarm as you pass near an antenna located at the store entrance.

What is new about RFID has to do with the standardization efforts of the International Organization for Standardization (ISO) and EPCglobal Inc. **EPCglobalInc.** is an organization entrusted by industries worldwide to establish RFID standards and services for real-time, automatic identification of products in the supply chain of any company anywhere in the world. By publishing a single worldwide set of standards, it is possible for RFID to be implemented and utilized in a global context. EPCglobal adopts the ISO 18000 series of standards for RFID; these define the operating frequencies of the equipment and tags and include all of the other relevant PHY and MAC layer specifications. The EPCglobal specifications concentrate on defining services and higher-layer functions of the standards. In this section, you learn about the hardware, software, and services that are required to implement RFID. For more information about EPCglobal, visit *www.gs1.org/epcglobal*.

RFID System Components

Several components are required to implement an RFID system, connect it with a corporate network, enable integration with existing business software, and ultimately connect with the services that enable worldwide integration of a company's suppliers, manufacturers, distributors, and transportation providers, that is, the supply chain. This section describes the most common components required to implement an RFID system—the tags, antennas, readers, software, and the EPCglobal network services.

Electronic Product Code (EPC) RFID systems make use of product codes and data formats standardized by EPCglobal. The mission of EPCglobal is to make organizations more efficient by making information about any kind of product available anytime and anywhere. The standards published by GS1 enable users to track products from manufacturing through to the end-user and beyond—in some cases products can be tracked all the way to the recycling depot or trash heap, at the end of their usable life. The **Electronic Product Code (EPC)** is a standardized numbering scheme that can be programmed in a tag, which in turn can be attached to any physical product. Think of EPC as the evolution of the barcode or Universal Product Code (UPC), which you can find today on most products.

Each EPC is a unique number or code that is associated with an individual product—a case, box, or pallet, depending on how the owner or the customer wishes to identify products, so that the items can be identified electronically. EPCs are usually represented in hexadecimal notation. A sample EPC is shown in Figure 11-1.

01 • 0001B6F • 0000F3 • 00002A9C3

| Header | Domain manager | Object class | Serial number |
| 8 bits | 28 bits | 24 bits | 36 bits |

Figure 11-1   96-bit Electronic Product Code (EPC)

The EPC is either 64 or 96 bits long. The 96-bit tags, the most common type, include the following fields:

- *Header*—This 8-bit field identifies the EPC version number.
- *Domain manager*—This 28-bit field identifies the manufacturer of the product; it can represent almost 268.5 million different companies.
- *Object class*—This 24-bit field identifies a product's stock keeping unit (SKU); it can represent over 16 million different products for each company (e.g., each brand or size of shampoo bottle produced by the same company as a different product).
- *Serial number*—This 36-bit field identifies each instance of a product; it can represent over 68.7 billion unique serial numbers.

A 256-bit version of the EPC might be defined in the future. All the EPCglobal specifications for the PHY layer allow for the EPC to be expanded without any changes in the protocol.

The structure of 64-bit and 96-bit EPCs is shown in Figure 11-2. Whether a manufacturer elects to use a 64-bit or a 96-bit EPC code is dependent on the company's individual needs and that of its clients, but most tags produced today are 96-bit. The Header field identifies which EPC format is being used, and the software (discussed later in this chapter) reformats the tag's data so that it will be compatible with the end-user's business applications. Please note that the diagram in Figure 11-2 is only intended to show that there can be different formats; it does not go into specific details. Also, these illustrations are not drawn in the correct scale based on the number of bits in each field.

64-bit Type I	2	21	17	24

64-bit Type II	2	15	13	34

64-bit Type III	2	26	13	23

96-bit	8	28	24	36

Note: Not to scale

Figure 11-2   Structure of the EPC codes

RFID Tags RFID tags are also commonly known as **transponders**. The word is a combination of *transmitter* and *responder*. A typical RFID tag includes an integrated circuit that contains some nonvolatile memory and a simple microprocessor. These tags can store data that is transmitted in response to an interrogation (a transmission) from a **reader** or interrogator, the device that actually captures the data transmitted by the RFID tags.

There are two basic types of tags: passive and active. **Passive tags** are the most common type; they are small, can be produced in large quantities at low cost, and do not require battery power. Passive tags use the electromagnetic energy in the RF waves transmitted by the reader's antenna to power the built-in chip so that it can transmit the information stored in its internal memory back to the reader. Animal-tracking microchip implants, tags for asset management, and access cards for security controlled doors and parking lots are examples of passive tag applications. Figure 11-3 shows an example of a passive tag.

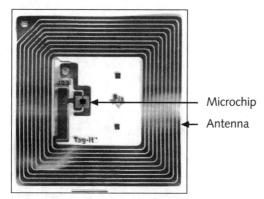

Microchip
Antenna

Figure 11-3 A typical passive RFID tag

Active tags are equipped with a battery to power the microprocessor chip and memory. Having their own power source means that these tags can transmit the signal farther away than passive tags can; however, active tags have a limited life because of the battery. They are also far more expensive than passive tags and therefore are used to track only high-value items, such as an entire pallet, a vehicle, or a shipping container. An example of the application of active tags is to track military supplies shipped around the world; they can also be used for commercial applications. Some active tags are called **beacons** because they can transmit on a periodic basis without receiving an interrogation from a reader.

A variation of active tags is the **semi-active tag**. This type of tag, also called a semi-passive tag, uses a built-in battery to power the circuit only when a reader first energizes or excites (powers) the tag. The energy transmitted by the reader activates the tag, which then uses the internal battery to power its circuits and respond to the reader. The best example of this type of tag is the device mounted in vehicles and used for electronic highway toll collection. The batteries in semi-active tags usually last several years, given that they are only used when the tag is activated by the reader's electromagnetic field.

The size of the memory in a tag varies with the manufacturer and application, but is usually between 16 bits (for storing temporary operation parameters) and hundreds of kilobits. The tags are initially programmed with a unique identification code obtained from EPCglobal. Any extra memory space in the tags can be used to record historical information about the product to which the tag is attached, such as the health and vaccination records of cattle, the temperatures that a product has been exposed to during shipping (using a sensor attached or built in to the tag), manufacturing and testing dates, and calibration records for test equipment.

Passive tags can be produced in flexible packages, also called smart labels. **Smart labels** include an adhesive backing and can be attached to a box, the underside of a product casing, or a pallet. Smart labels can be used to track luggage in airports and trains, for example. Because they use RF, the tags are not limited to being placed in a visible area or on the outside packaging of a product. They can be read regardless of their position or orientation, which is one of the major advantages of RFID over barcodes. The ability to read the tags in any position avoids the difficulty store clerks sometimes have of getting the equipment at the counter to read the barcode labels on products.

Yet another type of tag, called **1-bit tags,** are passive devices used in some retail stores. They do not contain a unique identification code, a chip, or any memory. They are simply used to activate an alarm to prevent theft. Figure 11-4 shows a 1-bit tag and a passive tag applied to the inside of a product package. These can be used for anti-theft or security, but the passive tag can also be used for inventory control.

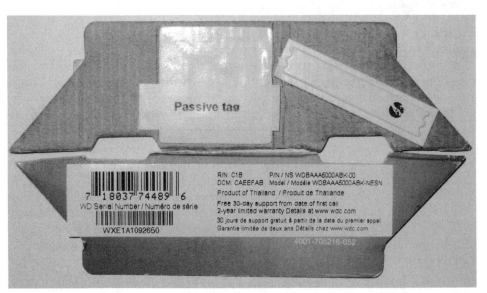

Figure 11-4 A passive and a 1-bit tag affixed to inside of the bottom flap of a product package (label shows barcode on the opposite flap for the same product)

An emerging form of RFID is **chipless tags,** also known as RF fibers. Chipless tags do not contain an integrated circuit or memory. Instead, they use fibers or other types of materials that reflect a portion of the reader's transmission signal back; the unique return signal can be used as an identifier. The fibers are made of thin threads, fine wires, or laminates that affect the propagation of RF waves. Chipless tags are typically used in applications in which the tag needs to be hidden and very difficult to reproduce. One sample use is the card invitations used for high-end events such as the Academy Awards (Oscars).

Chipless tags can be used to identify specific paper-based documents inconspicuously, which means that a person handling the document is not necessarily aware that it is "tagged." Chipless tags also perform better than other types of tags when attached to a metal surface or to a container of liquid. Both cans and bottles present significant problems for most RFID systems because metal surfaces can affect the propagation of RF waves and because most liquids attenuate the signal. Chipless tags can be read at greater distances than 1-bit or passive tags.

Sensory tags, as their name indicates, can be equipped with thermal, gas, smoke, pressure, temperature, and a variety of other kinds of sensors to monitor and record environmental conditions, liquid volume levels, or attempts to tamper with a product. Most sensory tags are considerably more expensive than other types of passive tags, come in larger packages, and are usually equipped with replaceable batteries that allow them to be used for longer periods of time.

To learn more about RFID and its applications, including sensory tags, search YouTube for "RFID applications."

The cost of a tag can vary greatly, depending on the type and number of tags purchased over a period of time. In general, passive tag prices range between about $0.07 and $0.25 each. As the technology develops and the volumes increase, RFID manufacturers and users expect the cost to fall well below $0.05 per tag. Sensory tags can cost between $25.00 and $100.00 each, depending on the battery life and tag capabilities.

Table 11-1 compares the tag classes specified by EPCglobal.

Tag Class	Type	Characteristics and Options
Class-1	Passive; identity tags	Includes EPC, tag identifier (ID), and a destroy password (discussed later in the chapter); may include optional password-protected access control and user memory
Class-2	Passive; higher functionality	Includes all features of Class-1 plus: extended tag ID, extended user memory, authenticated access control, and additional features to be defined in Class-2 specification (see GS1/EPCglobal)
Class-3	Battery-assisted passive (also called semi-active or semi-passive)	Includes all features of Class-2 plus: a power source; may include sensors with optional data-logging capabilities
Class-4	Active	Includes EPC, extended tag ID, authenticated access control, power source, and autonomous transmitter (can initiate communications with a reader if the protocol in use permits, but must not interfere with Class-1, Class-2, and Class-3 communication protocols); can optionally include user memory and optional sensors with or without data logging

Table 11-1   **EPCglobal basic tag specifications**

Class-0 tags, which are not mentioned in the table, may still be in use in a few locations around the world, but are generally considered obsolete. Class-0 tag communication protocols are not compatible with the tag classes listed in Table 11-1, and not all tag classes can be mixed and used in the same system.

Readers In addition to interfacing with the tags, RFID readers (or interrogators) connect to the company's network and transfer the data obtained from the tags to a computer. Some readers can also write data onto tags. Readers that work with passive tags also provide the energy that activates the tags. The read distance is determined by the size and location of the tag and the reader antennas as well as the amount of power transmitted. The reader specifications are generally limited by regulations in different countries that specify how much power can be transmitted in each frequency. Variations in regulations can result in incompatibilities between the equipment manufactured and licensed for use in different countries.

It is important to keep international standards and regulations in mind when designing and implementing an RFID system that will be used to identify products worldwide; these are generally available from the ISO and EPCglobal.

The frequency ranges and common applications of RFID systems are shown in Table 11-2.

Frequency Band	Common Applications
Low Frequency (LF)—135 KHz	Animal identification, access control, industrial automation
High Frequency (HF)—13.56 MHz	Smart cards, books, clothing, luggage, and various other individual-item-racking applications
Ultra-High Frequency (UHF)—433 MHz and 860–930 MHz	Asset tracking, inventory control, warehouse management
Microwaves—2.45 and 5.8 GHz (ISM band)	Electronic toll collection, access control, industrial automation

Table 11-2   **RFID frequencies and common applications**

Figure 11-5 shows an LF RFID reader used to scan cattle and an LF tag applied to the mock-up of a cattle ear.

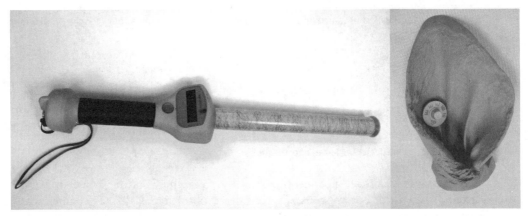

Figure 11-5   LF RFID wand reader and tag used in animals for tracking

RFID readers come in as many sizes and types as there are applications for this technology. From left to right, Figure 11-6 shows three examples of RFID readers, each with its own antennas. There is a fixed reader designed to be installed at a retail store entrance, a handheld reader designed to be plugged into a computer's USB port, and a self-contained, computer-based RFID reader (top right) with tag examples.

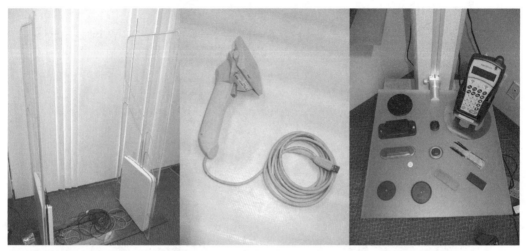

Figure 11-6   RFID equipment: readers, antennas, and sample tags

Antennas In Chapter 4, you learned that antennas are responsible for converting the RF energy from the transmitter into electromagnetic waves. The design and location of an antenna can significantly affect the range of the signal and the reliability of the communications. RFID antennas used in tags are limited in size due to the dimensions of the tag itself. Most tags are small, which allows them to be placed in a variety of different products and packaging.

There are two main types of tag antennas: linear and circular. Linear antennas offer greater range but less accurate reads. Circular antennas have greater read accuracy, especially in applications in which the orientation of the antenna varies due to positioning of the products, but have a more limited range.

Larger antennas allow the tags to be read at greater distances than smaller antennas. However, remember that, as the frequency increases, the wavelength gets smaller and, consequently, so does the antenna. Higher-frequency antennas can be made relatively small and still allow the tags to be read at greater distances than lower-frequency tags with the same antenna size. Conversely, to detect a higher-frequency signal and minimize attenuation, the tag antenna needs to be approximately 10 to 20 microns thick (10 microns = 0.0003937 inches). Lower-frequency antennas can be 2 microns thick. RFID tag design can be quite complex, due to antenna size and thickness, and this can significantly affect read performance. In passive tags, the antenna itself acts as the energy storage device, which supplies electricity to the tag and allows it to respond to a reader. Figure 11-7 shows additional examples of RFID tags.

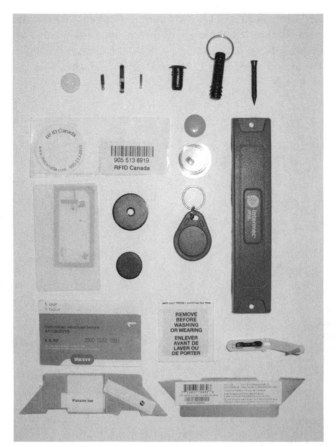

Figure 11-7   RFID tags are available in many shapes and sizes, for different applications

Reader antennas have to be designed for the specific type of application. Whether the antenna will be located at a retail store entrance for security reasons, near a warehouse shelf, or on a refrigerator door, the type, size, shape, and location of the antenna are critically important to ensure good readability and accuracy. No "typical" style of RFID antenna exists; the variety is huge. For many applications, RFID antennas are custom designed and built.

To see examples of different RFID reader antenna types, visit *www .intermec.com/products/rfid/antennas/index.aspx* or search the web for "RFID antennas."

Software   The type of software used in an RFID implementation depends on the specific application. Nevertheless, there are three basic categories of software components present in every RFID system: system software, middleware, and business application software.

System software is usually stored in read-only memory (ROM) or flash memory and is present in both the tag and the reader. It is executed by the microprocessor in each device and is used to control hardware functions, implement communication protocols (including collision control, error detection and correction, authorization, authentication, and encryption), and control the flow of data between tags and readers.

Middleware is responsible for reformatting the data from the readers to comply with the format required by the business applications used by the customer. It usually runs on a computer that is implemented as a gateway between the readers and the other data-processing equipment at the end-user company. Because each company likely uses different types of business software, RFID middleware allows users to ensure that they can communicate with the RFID equipment. Keep in mind that middleware is not usually sold as prepackaged software, like Microsoft Office or Adobe Acrobat, for example. Instead, each company in the business of providing RFID solutions usually writes its own middleware application software or uses a customizable software package provided by the reader manufacturer.

Business application software is responsible for processing orders, inventory, shipments, invoices, and so on. These types of applications usually rely on database software to store and manage all the transaction records in a typical business.

EPCglobal Network Services

To use barcodes, every retail business has to record in a database the item's UPC (barcode), the company's internal product number (SKU) for inventory management, a product description, the manufacturer's name, the price, and the quantity of items in stock. It then has to cross-reference the barcode and SKU so that this information can be accessed by the barcode readers at the cash register. With RFID, because the EPC already contains a reference to the manufacturer along with a product code, the need for manually entering data for cross-referencing is reduced; the potential for human beings introducing errors when manually entering this information into the database is lessened as well.

The manufacturer name is used to reorder products when the stock is low or depleted. With EPCs, companies are able to acquire the manufacturer's name over the Internet using a service from EPCglobal called **Object Name Service (ONS)**. Modeled after the Internet's Domain Name System (DNS), ONS is a mechanism for discovering information about a product and related services. When a reader gets the EPC from a tag, it passes it to the company's servers, which send it to ONS via the Internet. Upon identifying the manufacturer, ONS responds with the URL of the Internet server where the product information is stored. The company's servers can then retrieve all the information about that particular product and can use this for additional data processing.

If you are not familiar with how the Domain Name System (DNS) works, read the information at *http://computer.howstuffworks.com /dns.htm.*

Eventually, trillions of products from millions of companies will likely be included in the ONS database. Like DNS, ONS is a worldwide-distributed database.

An additional component that enables companies around the world to exchange information regarding their trade transactions is EPC Information Services (EPCIS). Similar to the Electronic Data Interchange (EDI) specifications that many large companies used to complete paperless transactions, EPCIS will eventually enable large organizations to purchase, invoice, and track product orders over the Internet, eliminating the need to send paper documents by mail or fax. Figure 11-8 shows the five fundamental components of an EPCglobal RFID system—tags, readers, middleware, business applications, and EPCglobal services—and how they are logically connected.

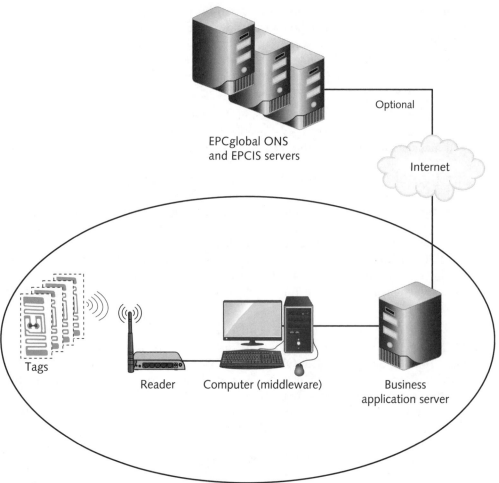

Figure 11-8   EPCglobal system components

How RFID Works

Describing how the different RFID tags and readers work would require an entire book, given that these devices use different transmission techniques in each frequency band. This section introduces you to the technical details of how two of the most common types of passive tags and readers transmit and communicate with each other at the PHY and MAC layers: UHF (400 to 900 MHz) and HF (13.56 MHz).

PHY Layer

A passive tag, the most common type, transmits only when it receives a signal from the reader. The connection between a tag and a reader is called a **coupling**. RFID primarily uses two types of coupling, depending on the application:

- *Inductive or magnetic coupling*—This type is designed for tags that either touch the surface of the antenna or are inserted in a slot in the reader's case. In these systems, the tags are typically used at a maximum distance of half an inch (just over 1 centimeter) from the antenna. The basic difference between inductive and magnetic coupling is the shape of the antennas.

- *Backscatter coupling*—This type is designed for tags that can be read at distances greater than 3.3 feet (1 meter) and up to 330 feet (100 meters) in some cases.

Backscatter is a reflection of radiation. Recall that passive tags are powered by an RF signal sent by the reader. After the reader transmits data (the reader transmission itself supplies power to the tag, so it can receive and decode the reader's transmission), it then begins to transmit a continuous wave (CW), which is an unmodulated sine wave. The CW is captured by the passive tag's antenna, and the tag uses the energy from the CW to supply power to the chip so that the tag can respond to the interrogator. The tag essentially reproduces (reflects) the same wave it receives from the reader, but it modulates this signal with the data by changing the electrical properties and consequently the reflection coefficient of its own antenna. This means that the antenna will transmit with more or less power, affecting the amplitude of the signal reflected.

Backscatter modulation is based on variations of amplitude shift keying (ASK) or a combination of ASK and phase shift keying (PSK), both of which you learned about in Chapter 2. The data is also digitally encoded to ensure that there will be enough transitions between 0 and 1 and vice versa to assist the devices in maintaining synchronization during transmission. (In Chapter 2, see the section titled "Binary Signals.")

The reader has separate transmitter and receiver circuits and antennas; and because it is a powered device, it transmits a much stronger (higher-amplitude) signal than the tags. In order to detect the modulated signal from the tag, the receiver in the reader compares its own strong CW signal with the backscatter. The difference between the two is the data sent by the tag.

Both reader and tag modulate the signal in amplitude by as much as 100 percent or by as little as 10 percent. Ten percent modulation is more sensitive to interference and noise, but the signal can travel farther. One hundred percent modulation is easier for the reader to detect; but during the periods without a CW, the tags are not being powered, so the distance between tag and reader must be significantly reduced. In practice, the signal is modulated somewhere between 10 percent and 100 percent, given that neither of the extremes is very usable. The modulated signal is a result of the amount of power generated by the reader and the size of the antenna. Figure 11-9 shows a signal modulated at 10 percent and at 100 percent. Note that the signals in the figure are not drawn to scale, in amplitude or in frequency.

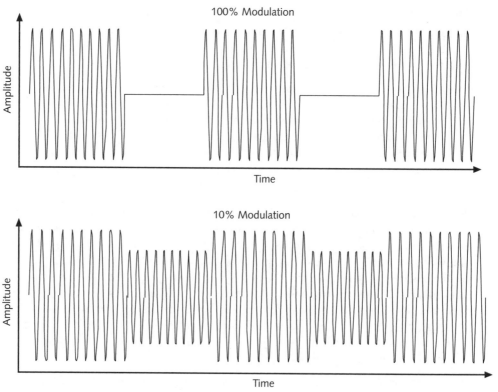

Figure 11-9 ASK modulation

Communications between tag and reader are always half-duplex. Interrogators and tags do not transmit and receive data simultaneously. To prevent interference issues from affecting the reliability of RFID systems, and to allow for environments in which multiple readers are installed in the same area (also called dense interrogator environments), the EPCglobal standards also specify the use of frequency hopping spread spectrum (FHSS) and direct sequence spread spectrum (DSSS) transmission. The latter systems are generally only used for advanced active tags.

HF Tag Communication

HF RFID passive tag communication uses a protocol called **Slotted Terminating Adaptive Collection (STAC)**, in which the tags reply within randomly selected positions or time intervals, referred to as slots, which are the reply intervals used in the STAC protocol. The interrogator transmits signals to mark the beginning and end of each slot, depending on the amount of data requested from each tag. Figure 11-10 shows the concept of slots. Note that the slots are not equal in size (the figure is not to scale). The number of slots is regulated by the interrogator and is always a power of two. Some shorter slots may exist when there is no reply from any tags, in which case the interrogator terminates the slot. The maximum number of slots available is 512. The STAC protocol is used to prevent tag collisions in HF, and it is described further in the section titled "Tag Collision Handling in HF." Note that slot F is always present and signals the beginning of the reply intervals. Slot F is the only one with a fixed size. It also ends automatically, meaning that the interrogator does not signal the end of slot F.

| Slot F | Slot 1 | Slot 2 | Slot 3 | Slot 4 | ---- | Slot N |

Figure 11-10 Reply intervals (slots) in the STAC protocol

UHF Tag Communication

UHF readers today support what is called Generation 2 (Gen2) protocols. Generation 1 (Gen1) protocols might still be used for tags and readers, but support for Gen1 RFID technology is quickly being discontinued.

The Gen2 protocol defines three techniques for communication between tags and readers. In the first technique, a reader can select tags by transmitting a bit mask that isolates a tag or group of tags. The bit mask works very similarly to the way network masks work in IP addressing, by isolating subnets. In the second technique, a reader can inventory tags by isolating them using a repetitive process (described later in this chapter). In the third technique, once the EPC for a particular tag is known to the system, a reader can alternatively access each tag individually. Gen2 readers can transmit with a lot more power and UHF systems are designed to work at greater distances than HF.

Tag Identification Layer

When an interrogator initiates communication in an RFID system, there must be a way to prevent every tag within range of the reader's signal from responding at the same time. The tag identification layer defines three methods that allow an interrogator to manage the population of tags within reach of its signal: select, inventory, and access.

With the select method, an interrogator sends a series of commands to select a particular segment of the population of tags within its reach. This is done in preparation for an inventory or for the purpose of accessing a specific tag. The selection is based on user-specified criteria, such as a particular category of products from one manufacturer. Tags do not respond to these commands. They simply set internal flags (bits) for responding to later transmissions. In UHF, with the inventory method, an interrogator sends out a series of query commands to get information from one tag at a time. As each tag receives an acknowledgment from the interrogator, it resets the inventory flag and does not respond to further inventory commands in the same round. In HF, the interrogator simply waits for each tag to reply in a different slot. With the access method, the interrogator sends one or more commands to multiple tags or exchanges data with a single tag at a time after uniquely identifying the tag with a command.

The minimum amount of information contained in a tag's memory is the EPC, a 16-bit cyclic redundancy check (CRC), and a destroy password. The **destroy password** is a code programmed into the tag during manufacturing. After the destroy password is transmitted by the reader, the tag is permanently disabled and can never be read or written to again. This tag information structure is shown in Figure 11-11.

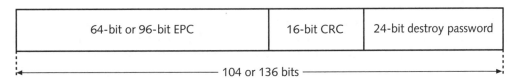

| 64-bit or 96-bit EPC | 16-bit CRC | 24-bit destroy password |

←————————— 104 or 136 bits —————————→

Figure 11-11 Structure of tag information

Tag and Reader Collisions

With a potentially very large population of tags, all tags could respond to a reader at the same time. Depending on whether each product is tagged or not (in warehouses, only boxes or pallets may be tagged), this would result in collisions and would prevent the reader from identifying individual tags. LF tags and readers do not support any collision-handling mechanism; therefore, LF systems can only read one tag at a time. This is not an issue when the application is reading an access card used to open a door or reading cattle tags as the animals pass through a narrow corridor one at a time. However, for RFID to work in a warehouse, in a store, or inside a refrigerator, the ability to read multiple tags is required, hence the use of the following tag anticollision mechanisms.

Tag Collision Handling in UHF Because the reader initially might not know which tags are present within the range of its signal, and because new tags could enter the reader's signal field from time to time, the reader can send a VerifyID command. However, if you consider how shelves in a store or warehouse are typically organized, the tags within a certain reader's field belong to certain groups of products. All tags within the reader's field that are the intended recipients of the verification command will reply with their EPC, CRC, and destroy password. If the reader can identify at least one of these tags, it can proceed to select a range of tags by sending a series of commands that instruct the tags about an upcoming inventory. The process repeats until the reader has identified every group of tags within range of its signal. The reader can also tell a tag or a group of tags to be quiet by sending a special command.

This selection process can be compared to a teacher that meets her class for the first time at the beginning of a semester and does not have a list with the names of all the students. To identify each student, the teacher might begin by asking all students to call out their full names. Initially, several students might reply at the same time. The teacher can then ask the students whose last names begin with the letter A to call out their names. Again, she might get more than one reply and not be able to single out a student. Next, she can request that only those students whose last names begin with the letters AA call out their names. This time, the chances of getting multiple simultaneous replies will be much smaller.

By repeating this process and refining the query, eventually the reader will have enough information to be able to communicate with all the tags within a group. It then sends a command to an entire group to set an inventory flag. The next command instructs the tags that the reader will begin an inventory round. During the inventory round, the reader sends an inquiry to each individual tag. Once a tag has replied to an inventory query, it resets its inventory flag and does not reply again until the reader announces the next inventory round.

Tag Collision Handling in HF In HF systems, the reader selects groups of tags based on the STAC protocol. Each tag uses its EPC, CRC, and destroy password to calculate a number that becomes the slot number in which each particular tag will reply. The calculation uses the above parameters along with a random number generator in each tag. The reader then begins an inventory round and waits for each tag to reply in its own time slot, which prevents collisions. The ISO standard assumes that the number of potential collisions in these cases will be less than 0.1 percent. If a collision does occur, thereby preventing the inventory process from finishing correctly, the reader selects a smaller group of tags using the process described earlier, under HF tag communication, and repeats the inventory process.

Reader Collisions Reader collisions can also happen in dense reader environments. If a reader does not receive any replies, it assumes a reader collision has occurred, which means that the tags could not understand the last reader transmission, and backs off for a random period of time before listening for network traffic and attempting to transmit again. In the meantime, the tags can communicate with another reader.

MAC Layer

The RFID MAC layer is responsible for establishing and communicating the transmission parameters—such as transmission bit rate, modulation type, operating frequency range, and frequency hop channel sequence—that are used for communications at the PHY layer. The reader sends commands to the tags establishing the communication parameters for each communications session. The MAC layer parameters for different types of tags—HF, UHF, and others—differ. These variances usually don't pose a problem because it is unlikely that an end-user company will use multiple types of tags in a single environment or application.

Data Rates

As you learned earlier, the amount of data stored in a typical passive RFID tag is relatively small. The lack of a power supply along with low processing power, both of which help keep the tag cost low, means that the resulting data transmission rates for the tags are also low. Some of the EPCglobal standards specify a minimum number of tags per second that a reader should be able to access rather than a specific data rate.

The specifications for HF tags call for readers to be capable of reading 200 tags per second. For tags containing just an EPC, the actual rates will likely be between 500 and 800 tags per second.

The UHF specifications define the tag-to-reader data rate as twice that of the reader-to-tag rate. In North America, the allowed tag-to-reader data rate can be up to 140.35 Kbps. In Europe, due to the RF signal power limitations, the maximum data rate is only 30 Kbps. Conversely, reader-to-tag data rates are 70.18 Kbps in North America and 15 Kbps in Europe. The Gen2 protocol specifications support much faster tag isolation, which results in tag read rates as fast as 1,600 per minute in North America and 600 per minute in Europe.

Near Field Communication

Now that you have a pretty good understanding of RFID, it's time to find out about near field communication technology. Near field communication (NFC), as you learned in Chapter 1, is a technology that provides short-range wireless connectivity between devices such as smartphones and tablet computers. NFC is based on the ISO 18092 RFID technology standard and ISO 21481, also called NFCIP-2, which was prepared by **Ecma International**, a not-for-profit standards organization for information and communication systems, such as the Ecma-352 standard.

Ecma International was originally called the European Computer Manufacturers Association. In 1994 it changed its name to Ecma International to reflect its global scope and activities, and "Ecma" is no longer considered an acronym.

As an introductory text, this book aims to discuss only the most well-known protocols used in NFC communications. There are several other ISO standards that apply to the wireless interface and protocols. For more information, visit *www.iso.org* and search for "NFC." You may also wish to visit the NFC Forum at *nfc-forum.org*.

NFC requires little or no configuration by users, and devices connect automatically as soon as they are brought to within a minimum of 1.6 inches (4 centimeters) of each other. This technology is able to transfer data between devices or read passive NFC tags at rates of between 106 and 424 Kbps.

NFC originated from and is compatible with FeliCa, a smart card protocol created by Sony that is still in use in parts of Asia, and the MIFARE protocol developed by Philips; both protocols were designed for payment systems. The NFC Forum, founded in 2004 by Nokia, Philips, and Sony, created a set of specifications that builds on HF RFID and also enables contactless two-way data transfer between two powered devices—beyond the typical one-way communication that happens between a smart card and a reader.

NFC can be used with a handheld device or card, for the following purposes:

- MasterCard PayPass transactions, Visa payWave, and other types of payment card transactions
- Electronic discount coupons and prepaid or gift cards
- Exchanging business cards, schedules, and maps between handheld devices
- Transferring images, videos, and other types of files between devices or between a device and a printer
- Debit card or prepaid card transactions
- Electronic public transport system tickets
- Airline tickets
- Automatic pairing of Bluetooth devices without entering a PIN number
- Automatic Wi-Fi and Wi-Fi Direct configuration
- Storing and using secure, encrypted identification numbers, electronic signatures, access codes, and passwords
- Apple Pay, Google Wallet (Android Pay), and similar smartphone applications

You can search for "ISO/IEC standard 1443" on Wikipedia, as well as on the web for additional information on NFC operating modes, protocols, and security and other notable implementations of NFC.

NFC Operation Modes

Many different models of Android smartphones and tablets today are NFC-capable and are typically equipped with a low-power interrogator that can read tags. Some Android devices, such as Google Nexus tablets, are also able to write to NFC tags. Apple iPhone 6 and newer models require an NFC-compatible SIM card to enable the use of Apple Pay. The technology uses inductive coupling between two loop antennas. An NFC-capable device can operate in the following modes:

- *Listen mode*—The initial mode of an NFC device, in which the device essentially acts as a passive tag.

- *Poll mode*—When an NFC device generates a CW and probes for other devices within its communication range of 1.6 inches (4 centimeters).

- *Reader/writer mode*—When an NFC device in Poll mode behaves like an interrogator. In this mode, devices can transmit commands to other devices.

- *Card emulator mode*—When an NFC device in Listen mode behaves like a smart card.

- *Initiator mode*—When an NFC device in Poll mode changes the communication protocol to talk to another device that only supports half-duplex communications, using the NFC-Data Exchange Protocol (NFC-DEP).

- *Target mode*—When an NFC device is the target of an initiator that can only communicate in half-duplex mode, using NFC-DEP.

The Initiator and Target modes are unique characteristics of NFC that differentiates it from RFID in the sense that NFC-capable devices are able to exchange many different types of information with other NFC-capable devices. RFID, on the other hand, is limited to communications between readers and tags.

NFC Tags and Devices

The NFC specifications currently define four types of tags. Each type of tag is designed for a different purpose and has slightly different capabilities, including the amount of memory. Different tag types also communicate using slightly different frame formats, at different speeds, and use different digital encoding (NRZ, NRZ-I, etc.) and different synchronization and modulation methods. Thus, the first thing an NFC-capable device in Poll mode needs to do is identify the type of tags or devices that are within range of its magnetic field.

Some tags can be written to only once; others can be protected by a password so that they cannot be written to again unless they are unlocked. The memory on the tag can be used to store URLs, business cards, pictures, brochures in PDF files, etc. This makes NFC far more flexible, useful, and accurate than the Quick Response (QR) codes that are very popular today. Depending on the type, NFC tags can store anywhere from 48 bytes to 32 KB of information. Virtually everyone can purchase NFC tags and, with the right type of app loaded on their phones or tablets, might be able to program the tags using a smartphone or a tablet (see *www.tagstand.com*). You can find more information about NFC tags at *kimtag .com/s/nfc_tags*.

The best way to stay up-to-date with which smartphones and tablets currently support NFC, along with the latest news of the industry, is to browse the NFC World website at *www.nfcworld.com*.

NFC Communications

NFC-capable devices transmit in the 13.56 MHz unlicensed frequency band (the same as for HF RFID) and modulate the signal using ASK or a combination of ASK and PSK over a range of approximately 7 to 14 KHz of RF bandwidth. Modulation varies between 10 percent and 100 percent, depending on the type of tag. The digital signal is encoded using a method similar to the return-to-zero (RZ) technique you learned about in Chapter 2, which provides enough signal transitions to help ensure good synchronization between wireless devices and between devices and tags.

To transfer data between two smartphones or tablet computers, NFC employs the **Data Exchange Protocol (NFC-DEP)**. A DEP message consists of one or more records. Each record is encapsulated in an RF frame that contains a header and a payload. The header includes the following fields:

- *Identifier*—This optional field is used to define the type of payload carried by the record.

- *Length*—This field can be one octet long for short records but is normally four octets long. A payload length of 0 is used to indicate an empty message (no payload field) and signals the end of the current NFC-DEP communication session.

- *Type*—This field indicates what type of data is carried within the payload and will be used by the receiving device to decide which application will process the data.

For example, pictures are automatically stored in the photo app and URLs are sent to the browser app on the receiving device. An error is generated if the device cannot support the data type specified in this field.

Because data transfer between two smart devices like a digital camera, tablet, or smartphone using NFC-DEP is limited to a few hundred Kbps, when transferring large amounts of data such as pictures or music, NFC is used only to configure and initiate a Bluetooth or Wi-Fi Direct connection, which is then used to transfer the data.

Figure 11-12 shows the components of a DEP message and how they relate to one another.

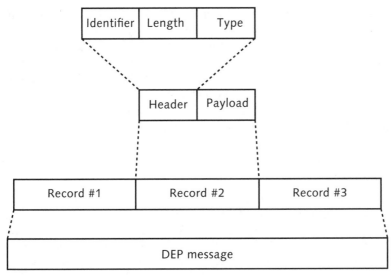

Figure 11-12   Structure of a DEP message

RFID and NFC Challenges

It is easy to imagine a thousand other applications for RFID that have the potential for making life and business easier, safer, and simpler. However, the technology does face some challenges, as you learn in this section.

RFID Impact on Corporate Networks

One of the major challenges for the implementation of RFID systems is the impact of the volume of data on a company's network. With manual or barcode-based inventory control systems, the amount of data that is collected and transmitted across a company's network is usually limited to the on-hand quantities of particular products along with the UPC code for each product. However, RFID systems are usually implemented so that inventory can be counted by simply activating the readers. To ensure that the shelves in a large retail store are always fully stocked with products, for example, the system can direct the readers to interrogate all of the RFID tags every 5 minutes or so. This scanning can add a lot of traffic to an organization's network.

To get a sense of the amount of increased traffic on a company's network, consider a scenario in which a large national retailer tags each of the 10,000 individual items in each of its 1,000 stores and then interrogates all of its readers from a central head-office location every 15 minutes. At 17 bytes per EPC code alone (remember that with the 96-bit EPC, the minimum information from a tag is about 136 bytes), this would generate 170 MB of data for a single read. It would fill a CD-ROM in 1 hour and create 5.44 gigabytes of network traffic in a typical 8-hour business day. In only 1 month, the total volume of traffic would swell to 1.632 terabytes of data. Although most of this data will be processed and the duplicate data discarded, we are still talking about a significant increase in the volume of data on the network.

Network Availability in RFID Assume that such a system is eventually implemented and that a company relies on it to replenish inventory automatically. In this case, network availability becomes a serious factor in the store's ability to serve its customers. As retailers become dependent on RFID systems to enhance service and reduce costs, greater network bandwidth must be available. The retailer's network must also be reliable—that is, it must remain functional. (Recall that 99 percent availability means that the network is expected to be down for about 80 hours per year, which is usually an unacceptable amount of time for most businesses.) Any downtime that occurs during business hours can quickly become a serious problem. For most companies, these demands will translate to expanding and adding redundant equipment and communications capabilities to their existing networks, a costly undertaking at best.

In grocery stores and large retail establishments, products are out of stock 7 percent of the time, and some popular items are unavailable 17 percent of the time. This inventory shortfall can represent significant losses for retailers. To combat this problem, many retailers order more products than they need or can sell out of one location. As a result, supermarkets in particular often are forced to discard perishable products, which leads to higher costs for consumers. Item-level tagging for product tracking is a means to reduce or eliminate these types of problems.

Storage Requirements for RFID Large banks and corporations already are saddled with archiving tremendous amounts of historical data—potentially, tens or even hundreds of terabytes of data for each company. In addition, new laws designed to protect consumers and investors, such as the Sarbanes–Oxley Act, require companies to accumulate and securely store even more information, in some cases indefinitely. The huge volume of data that can be generated by RFID systems significantly increases the need to store information accurately and reliably.

Since 2003, cattle producers in Canada and Europe have been using RFID to track their animals' histories. As of January 1, 2005, each head of cattle in Canada must have an RFID tag that stores such information as any health issues, vaccinations, movement (locally or to a new herd), and production of milk and offspring. Records must be kept, even on slaughtered cattle, for many years afterward.

RFID Device Management Even without RFID in place, businesses are finding it a challenge to manage the huge numbers of devices on their networks. Network management software does not come at a low price. Even for small networks with fewer than 1,000 devices, the cost of network management software can easily escalate to well over half a million dollars. As networks expand, the need to remotely monitor and manage servers, routers, switches, and RFID readers from a central location becomes a critical factor in a company's ability to ensure greater network availability. Add to this the task of managing and tracking hundreds, thousands, or even millions of RFID tags, and you can imagine the security issues related to wireless RFID transmissions. Managing RFID systems can quickly become a very complex and costly job.

Security Considerations for RFID and NFC

The growth of RFID and the development of relevant worldwide standards have given rise to a large number of security and privacy concerns. There are solutions for RFID-related security issues, but they are not perfect fixes, and challenges still exist. For example, the growth of NFC is still being driven by its application as an electronic wallet that can be used in place of credit and debit cards as well as by its applications in public transportation tickets, passwords, and so forth, and concerns from users are increasing. Recent developments in multicore processors will no doubt enable the use of more sophisticated encryption algorithms that can help ensure the security and privacy of device users. NFC transmissions are harder to interfere with or capture, due to the short distance between devices; nevertheless, it is theoretically possible to access information from a user's smartphone or tablet if you have a reader that is sensitive enough to capture information from a greater distance.

To see how an attacker could exploit security flaws in RFID, search YouTube for "RFID hacking."

It is possible to read the information from a tag or RFID/NFC-enabled credit card, but financial organizations would not allow these systems to be used by their customers unless there were enough security mechanisms in place to prevent financial loss. Ultimately it is the financial organizations and the retailers that have to absorb any losses that might result from someone stealing your credit card number and name. The financial organizations employ a large variety of tactics to prevent theft. Users are not made aware of these tactics for the simple reason that making this information available would invite additional attempts to defeat the security measures.

Debit and credit card agreements clearly state that customers are not responsible for the charges if their card information is stolen. No personal information other than the person's name and credit card number, which are already displayed on the front of the card, is stored in the RFID chip. Keep in mind that additional personal information may be stored in a tablet or NFC-enabled cellular phone. This is one of the reasons why when using a smartphone app such as Google Wallet or Apple Pay for payment, the user must first verify who she is, either by entering a password or fingerprint scan. Financial institutions worldwide have deemed RFID and NFC safe enough to be used by the general public, and we should remember that these institutions are not in the business of losing money. Nevertheless, it remains the responsibility of the users to monitor their bank accounts for suspicious transactions, even though it is likely that your bank will block your cards and call you before you have a chance to notice anything wrong.

In the United States, some of the concerns about RFID are centered on privacy. Tag data used for a product after it is purchased could be linked to the consumer and used for targeted marketing. Businesses could collect that data about a person's purchases and use it for a number of applications that would potentially interfere with the consumer's privacy. This is not that different from data being captured from the use of debit and credit cards; the difference is that RFID-generated data could possibly be captured without the user being aware of it. However, to associate this data with a particular person would require obtaining information from debit and credit cards or by following the user home. Most of the privacy concerns that people have regarding RFID are due to not having enough information about the technology.

Security related to RFID readers falls under the wired network security policy. Reader-to-tag and tag-to-reader communications have the same vulnerabilities as any wireless network, the only exception being that capturing the tag-to-reader communications can be very difficult. Tag transmissions occur at very low power levels; readers are also transmitting a CW during tag-to-reader communications. Once a tag is installed on a product or packaging, it usually cannot be removed without permanently damaging the tag; however, it is still possible to tamper with the *data* in a Class-1 (read/write) tag by recording over the existing tag data or by adding new data. Powering a mobile reader capable of emitting a high-power signal would require heavy batteries. This could be done from inside a vehicle, but then the mobility of the reader would be severely limited.

Most passive tags do not support authorization or encryption security methods because they lack their own power supply, use chips with low processing power, and are low in cost. Shielding stores and warehouses to prevent RF signals from coming in or going out might solve some of the problems associated with unauthorized access from outside the building, but that can be a very expensive proposition. In addition, once consumers take the products to their homes or workplaces, someone using an interrogator nearby could still expose them to privacy violations.

RFID tags do not carry the type of information that would be so critical and useful as to require drastic measures to prevent anyone from capturing the information contained in the tags' memory storage. In the case of credit and debit cards, there are far easier, but no less criminal, ways to capture the information contained in RFID/NFC chips, so the use of remote sensing equipment, which requires a very complex setup, is unlikely. Nevertheless, both financial institutions and users should continue to be aware of the need to protect against losses and identity theft.

Data in tags can be locked and require a password for the tag to be used again. By using a combination of the EPC, CRC, and built-in destroy password, tags can also be permanently disabled. Locking the tags would make it very difficult to use the information from the tag throughout the distribution channels. Permanently destroying the tag, either by issuing a kill command or by physically damaging it, would prevent a retailer from using the tag again if the customer returned the product, limiting the functionality of the RFID system. Physically destroying tags would also prevent the consumer from taking advantage of features like the smart refrigerator application described at the beginning of this chapter.

A **blocker tag** is a device that can be used to simulate the presence of a virtually infinite number of tags. Blocker tags can be used to disable unauthorized readers from accessing the information from a selective group of tags by sending so many responses that an unauthorized reader cannot differentiate between the blocker tag and a legitimate tag. Blocker tags also offer an alternative solution that minimizes some of the issues described earlier in this section, and at a much lower cost. After getting his purchase home, the consumer can optionally destroy the blocker tag so he can continue to use the legitimate tags in, say, his smart refrigerator.

Security for RFID and NFC systems is a complex topic, and there is no single solution that addresses all possible situations. Applications of RFID and NFC far outweigh the potential problems, however. RFID and NFC usage will continue to expand, and eventually these technologies will be present in nearly every aspect of our lives. Educating users and implementing legislation related to data collection and privacy will play a big part in raising consumers' comfort level with the technology, just as similar measures have increased their comfort with the Internet.

Chapter Summary

- Radio frequency identification (RFID) stores information about an item's manufacturer and the date and location of production in electronic tags that include an antenna and a chip.

- Standards being published by EPCglobal Inc. allow RFID to be used worldwide.

- RFID systems are composed of electronic tags, readers, antennas, software, and EPCglobal network services. The format of the Electronic Product Code (EPC) is defined by the EPCglobal standards. The EPC is either 64 or 96 bits long and includes a code that refers to the manufacturer, a stock-keeping unit number, and a serial number.

- RFID tags are also known as transponders. Typical tags include a microprocessor and memory. Tags are accessed by a reader device that captures and processes the data. There are two basic types of tags: passive and active. Passive tags are the most common type. They do not have a power source and rely on the electromagnetic energy in the RF waves transmitted by the reader to power their microprocessors. Active tags are equipped with a battery and can cost upward of $20 per tag. The battery usually limits the life span of active tags. Semi-active tags also include a battery. However, the battery is used only when the tag is activated by a transmission, which helps the battery last many years.

- Tags can be produced in flexible packages called smart labels with an adhesive backing. They can be affixed to product packaging, pallets, or to the product itself. They are also used to track passenger baggage. Tags are not limited to being placed in a visible area and can be read in virtually any position.

- Retail stores sometimes use 1-bit tags to prevent theft. These tags do not include a unique identification, a chip, or any memory; they are only used to activate an alarm. Chipless tags use fibers or materials that reflect a portion of the reader's signal with a unique pattern that can be used as an identifier.

- Sensory tags are equipped with thermal, smoke, or other type of sensors used to monitor environmental conditions to which a product may have been exposed during shipping and storage. The cost of a tag can vary, depending on the type. Most passive tags cost between $0.07 and $0.25. Class-1 tags are read/write. Some tags can be written to, whereas others are read-only.

- A reader, also called an interrogator, communicates with both the tags and the corporate network. Some readers have the ability to write data to the tags. Readers also provide the energy to activate and power passive tags. Readers and tags operate in one of four frequency bands: 135 KHz (LF); 13.56 MHz (HF); 433 MHz and 860–930 MHz (UHF); and 2.5 and 5.8 GHz (ISM).

- There are two types of tag antennas: linear and circular. Linear antennas have a better range, but circular antennas achieve more reliable reads.

- RFID software includes system software, which controls the functions of the tag and reader hardware; middleware, which is responsible for reformatting the data to meet the requirements of the business applications; and the programs that companies use to process business transactions.

- The connection between a reader and a tag is called a coupling. Inductive coupling tags need to be placed within a half-inch of the antenna. Backscatter coupling allows tags to be read at distances of 3.3 to 330 feet (1 to 100 meters). Backscatter is a reflection of the reader's signal modulated with the tag data. In order to power the tags, the reader, when not transmitting, sends out a continuous wave. Backscatter modulation is based on variations of ASK and PSK. Communication between tags and readers is always half-duplex.

- In HF RFID, the tags use time slots to communicate with the reader. The number of slots is always a power of two, and the communication is always controlled by the reader. Most RFID tags are passive and are not able to initiate communications with the reader.

- RFID has the potential for significantly increasing the amount of traffic and storage requirements in the corporate network. With the implementation of RFID systems, network availability and device management become even more critical.

- NFC is a wireless communication technology, based on RFID, that allows enabled devices to communicate at short distances. Unlike RFID, NFC allows devices to transfer files, pictures, videos, URLs, and business cards between smartphones and tablet computers. NFC-enabled devices can also read and write to passive tags. NFC tags typically have greater storage capacity than RFID tags.

- With the implementation of wireless technologies such as RFID and NFC, there are many security and privacy concerns. A tag can be locked or destroyed (electronically or physically), but doing so can limit its functionality. Blocker tags may offer an alternative solution. User and consumer education, along with government legislation, should help raise the comfort level and allow RFID usage to expand.

Key Terms

1-bit tag   RFID device that does not include a chip or memory and cannot store an EPC; these tags are used only to activate an alarm at retail store entrances as a means of preventing theft.

active tag   RFID tag that includes a battery.

backscatter   A reflection of radiation in which the RFID tag reflects the signal sent by an interrogator while modulating it with the data to be transmitted, used in passive RFID tags.

beacon   RFID tag that is battery powered and transmits on a periodic basis.

blocker tag   A type of Class-1 passive tag that can be used to disable unauthorized readers from accessing the information from a selective group of tags by sending so many responses that a reader cannot differentiate between the blocker tag and a legitimate tag.

chipless tag   RFID device that uses embedded fibers to reflect a portion of the RF waves emitted by a reader; the reflected portion of the RF waves is unique and can be used as an identifier.

coupling   A connection between an RFID reader and a tag.

Data Exchange Protocol (NFC-DEP)   A protocol used by smart NFC devices to transfer data such as pictures, URLs, and many other items, between devices.

destroy password   A code programmed into an RFID tag during manufacturing that can be used to permanently disable the tag.

Ecma International   A not-for-profit standards organization for information and communication systems, such as the Ecma-352 standard.

Electronic Product Code (EPC)   A standardized numbering scheme that can be programmed in a tag and attached to any physical product.

EPCglobal Inc.   An organization entrusted by industry worldwide to establish RFID standards and services for real-time, automatic identification of information in the supply chain of any company anywhere in the world.

Object Name Service (ONS)   An EPCglobal Inc. service, modeled after DNS, that can assist in locating information about a product over the Internet.

passive tag   The most common type of RFID tag. It does not include a battery and is powered by the electromagnetic energy in the RF waves transmitted by the reader. Passive tags never initiate a transmission and must wait for a reader to interrogate them.

reader   The RFID device that captures and processes the data received from the tags. Also called an interrogator.

semi-active tag   RFID tag that includes a battery that is only used when the tag is interrogated. The batteries in semi-active tags usually last for several years. Also referred to as a semi-passive tag.

sensory tag   RFID tag that includes a thermal or other kind of sensor and can record information about the environmental conditions to which a product has been exposed during transportation or storage.

Slotted Terminating Adaptive Collection (STAC)   The communications protocol used by passive RFID tags that work in the 13.56 MHz HF band.

smart label   Another name for a flexible RFID tag that includes a microprocessor chip, memory, and antenna.

tag   Device that includes an antenna and a chip containing memory and can store information about products, such as the manufacturer, product category, and serial number along with date and time of manufacturing.

transponder   Another name for RFID tags.

Review Questions

   1. The protocol used to handle collisions in HF RFID is called _____.

     a.   STAC

     b.   recurrent

     c.   CS

     d.   blocker

2. Which of the following is true about 1-bit tags?

   a. They store a unique identification code.

   b. They can only be read by a passive reader.

   c. They do not carry any information about the product.

   d. They are also known as RF fibers.

3. One of the characteristics of sensory tags is that _____.

   a. they can sense the presence of other tags

   b. they can block the signal from other tags

   c. they only respond to the reader if a password is sent first

   d. they can capture information about environmental conditions

4. What is the purpose of an interrogator?

   a. To read information from the tags

   b. To prevent unauthorized access to the tags

   c. To increase the read distance

   d. To store a charge that powers passive tags

5. The function of RFID middleware is to _____.

   a. store information about the types of tags used

   b. convert the data read from the tags into a format that is compatible with that of the business application

   c. control the functions of the reader hardware

   d. control the functions of the tag hardware

6. Reader antennas are sometimes designed for a specific application. True or False?

7. The orientation of the tag's antenna usually does not affect readability. True or False?

8. RFID is not expected to have a major impact on network traffic. True or False?

9. Which of the following is an important characteristic of UHF passive tags?

   a. They have a shorter read distance.

   b. They require less power to be read.

   c. They work at greater distances than most other tags.

   d. They only support very slow communications.

10. What kind of modulation is used with most NFC tags?

   a. OFDM

   b. DSSS

   c. ASK

   d. NRZ-I

11. What type of coupling is used in NFC between a smartphone and a tablet computer?

    a. Backscatter

    b. Capacitive

    c. Physical

    d. Inductive

12. To modulate a response signal using backscatter, a tag has to _____.

    a. change the polarity of the incoming signal from the reader

    b. deflect the signal from the transponder

    c. change the characteristics of its own antenna

    d. store the energy from the interrogator before using it

13. Interrogators and tags communicate using _____ communications.

    a. half-duplex

    b. full-duplex

    c. simplex

    d. complex

14. What is the largest amount of memory in a typical NFC passive tag?

    a. 2 KB

    b. 8 KB

    c. 16 KB

    d. 32 KB

15. Before an NFC-enabled smartphone can communicate with a tag or another device, what must it do?

    a. Read the serial number of the other device

    b. Identify the capabilities of the device or tag

    c. Receive a reply from all devices within its range

    d. Transmit its clock speed

16. One of the ways used by the Gen2 protocol to select tags is by transmitting _____.

    a. a quiet command

    b. a null CW

    c. a bit mask

    d. a higher or lower intensity signal

17. What is one of the most critical challenges associated with RFID system implementation?

    a. The cost of the tags

    b. The fact that tags can be read by anyone with a smartphone

    c. The large amount of storage required

    d. The encryption protocols

18. Which of the following methods can be used to temporarily or permanently disable a tag? (Select two.)

    a. A blocker tag

    b. An authentication password

    c. A very-high-power pulse

    d. The destroy password

19. Which mode must an NFC-capable device be in to behave like a smart card?

    a. Poll

    b. Listen

    c. Initiator

    d. Smart card

20. Which of the following RFID technologies does not support reading more than one tag at a time?

    a. Readers

    b. UHF

    c. Smart labels

    d. LF

Hands-On Projects

Project 11-1

Using the Internet, locate suppliers of tags that can be used to track animals. What types and classes of tags are available? What kinds of animals are the tags being used on, other than for tracking herds of cattle? Write a report on your findings.

Project 11-2

As you know, security is an extremely important aspect of any wireless network. There are many security-related issues surrounding RFID, especially with the U.S. government now promoting the use of RFID tags in passports. Using the Internet, research some of these issues and the organizations involved in creating possible solutions. Focus in particular on what is being done about increasing security and privacy protection. Write a report focused on one of the issues you have identified.

Project 11-3

Many manufacturers and retailers of nonperishable goods already use RFID technology. Several products come already tagged, and if you have recently purchased a high-value product in a computer store, you may find some tags in the box. Go to several large stores located in a local shopping area and ask the stores' staff whether they are currently using RFID to protect against theft. Do they use it for security only or do they also use it for inventory control? Be conscious of some of the security issues with RFID and identify yourself as a wireless communications student before you ask any questions regarding their use of RFID. Keep in mind that some job opportunities might be available through contacts that you initiate through this project; therefore, be sure to present yourself in a professional manner. If possible, make a list of the types of tags used, such as passive semi-active, etc. Write a report on your findings.

Real-World Exercises

Exercise 11-1

Instrument Rentals Inc. (IRI) rents electronic test instruments to a variety of heavy industries. The instruments are usually rented for a period of 1 week to 1 year. IRI offers a customer guarantee that its instruments will always be available and calibrated to factory specifications. With 120 locations across the country, the company ships the instruments, checks their calibration upon arrival, and recalibrates them if necessary. It also often services the instruments at the customer's site, which can be in an oil field or inside a mine, to maintain them in top working condition. Finally, it checks every instrument when it is returned at the end of its rental period.

To prevent delays, minimize errors, and avoid Internet access problems, IRI would like to store each instrument's calibration records, its technicians' names, the rental/travel log, and other relevant information stored with the instrument itself. Toward this end, the service-call software that the technicians have in their notebook computers needs to be able to automatically read a record, display it on the screen, and update it on the instrument record storage device. All the instruments are leased by IRI from the manufacturers for a period of 3 years. When a lease expires, IRI wants to be able to look at the records for that particular instrument and make a decision whether to replace it with a new model or extend the lease to prevent interruption of service to its customers. As a well-known RFID and NFC expert, you have been asked to recommend which of these two technologies would be the right solution for its needs.

Prepare a PowerPoint presentation (consisting of 10 to 15 slides) that lists the advantages and disadvantages of RFID and NFC for this type of application, and specify the type of tags and devices that IRI should acquire, should it decide to go ahead with this project.

Exercise 11-2

IRI has decided to go ahead with the project and has asked you to provide a proposal (five pages maximum) specifying all the equipment that will be required to add this technology to 1,000 of its most expensive test instruments. There are two technicians per location, but only one will be equipped to service the equipment in the field. The other technician will be servicing equipment in the office.

Your proposal should include pricing for the tags (including about 100 replacement tags), a portable reader, a fixed reader, middleware, and other equipment. If required, IRI's IT staff will be in charge of reprogramming the middleware to interface with the company's in-house database. Keep in mind that if the project is successful, it may be expanded within 6 months to a year to cover IRI's entire instrument asset base, which consists of more than 10,000 instruments.

Challenge Case Project

CASE PROJECTS

The trade union to which the technicians at IRI belong has sent a letter to the company expressing concerns about the privacy of its members, given that the company intends to include the name of the technician who last serviced a particular instrument in its RFID tag. Now, the company has asked you to become involved. A team of three people from IRI will research the union's concern, including checking state regulations. It will then organize a meeting so that all the parties can discuss the matter.

In groups of six, form two teams of three members each—one team representing the union and the other representing IRI. Research the issues just outlined and engage in a friendly debate regarding the union's concerns. The union team may need to do added research so that it is prepared to defend its members' rights.

TIP

If you are taking an online course with this text, you can take advantage of collaboration tools such as Google Docs, Google Hangouts, Wiggio, or Skype to participate in an online group. Your school may also have its own Learning Management System that allows you to participate in online collaboration groups.

chapter 12

Wireless Communications Everywhere

After reading this chapter and completing the exercises, you will be able to:

- Describe the Internet of Things (IoT)
- Explain the relationship of the IoT to wireless technologies
- Explore current applications of wireless technologies
- Consider future applications of wireless technologies

Predicting how an idea or technology can be used requires vision, but it is not without its challenges. When Alexander Graham Bell made the first-ever telephone call between two Canadian cities about 22 miles apart, many people dismissed it as an interesting yet useless technology, because the regular post office worked so well at the time. Likewise, when the first handheld cellular phone call was made, some people questioned who would want to make and receive calls while moving around. We all know what happened to both of these technologies, as well as others that did not "make it."

Even with vision, predicting how technologies might be used is a challenging task. Many wireless technologies are being used today in ways that surprise even the original developers. Wireless communications have grown so much and so fast that frequency bands are becoming overcrowded and the standards organizations are always looking to develop new ways to solve these challenges. There is an ever-growing demand for technologists and RF engineers with solid knowledge, who can design, install, troubleshoot, and find solutions for wireless issues, regardless of how technically advanced and automated the hardware and software might be. Wireless data communication continues to expand into new areas, creating new challenges, users are constantly demanding more wireless freedom and mobility, and standards organizations continue to work on creating new open wireless standards.

Short-range technologies like Bluetooth for headsets and portable speakers, and ZigBee for lighting and environmental control, can be relatively simple to install and operate and require little user intervention or technical support after initial setup and configuration. Cellular and WiMAX demand a higher level of involvement from designers and field technologists to ensure users enjoy a reliable, secure, and stable environment. Although residential Wi-Fi installations usually do not require specialized skills, deployment in large-business environments is often far more complex. For example, wireless signal propagation presents specific challenges to office buildings, sports stadiums, cruise and merchant ships, passenger aircraft, and manufacturing environments. Security can also be a constant challenge.

This chapter begins with an introduction to the Internet of Things (IoT), and then provides an overview of the ever-expanding ways wireless technologies are being deployed and used in different fields. Although it does not attempt to predict future uses for wireless data communications, the aim of this chapter is to provide a broad perspective of where wireless is today and a glimpse of where it might go from here.

The Internet of Things

Wireless technologies coupled with powerful single-board computers (SBCs) and microcontrollers the size of a credit card (and often smaller), are enabling a large number and variety of sensors to be installed in a multitude of devices and locations and connected to the Internet via WLANs or cellular technology. This Internet of Things has actually been around for some time, and its expansion to cover a larger variety of sensors and devices is probably inevitable. Wireless technologies are set to become one of the major enablers of this phenomenon.

Contrary to what some people believe, the **Internet of Things (IoT)** does not refer solely to small "smart devices." It is really about the type and amount of data that can be collected from a multitude of smart sensors, transmitted to servers, and analyzed in real time or saved for historical analysis. The IoT has the potential of providing us with far more in-depth knowledge of the world around us, so we can better manage it and take any necessary or corrective actions sooner. IoT applies to virtually all the topics discussed in this chapter.

Estimates vary, but between 50 and 100 billion "things" could be connected to the Internet by the year 2020. Consider the simple case that most water, electrical, and natural gas meters in homes today still need to be read once a month by a person physically accessing the meters in each house. Data on total electricity consumption for a particular distribution area can be easily obtained at the utility company, but more detailed information requires individual meter readings. If these meters can be read in real time and the information transmitted and updated automatically, the power utility companies would have a much better idea of where and when consumption is changing, and this would lead to better planning, as well as potentially lowering costs and benefitting everyone. Utility companies in many cities are already upgrading to wireless systems that transmit the readings automatically, but widespread deployment will probably wait until the industry selects one standard and wireless IoT network connections are more widely available.

Check out the wide assortment of tiny, low-power SBCs, microcontrollers, and sensors available today. Start at *www.adafruit.com*, and search for "IoT," then you can expand your search to explore microcontrollers at *www.arduino.cc* and SBCs at *www.raspberrypi.org* and search the web for "Intel Edison." The assortment is so large that this book would have to devote an entire chapter to list all of the available choices.

Recent IoT Developments

LoRa is a wireless technology that enables low-power wide-area networks (LPWANs) for **machine-to-machine (M2M) communications**, that is, devices that communicate with other devices instead of with human beings. LoRa consists of a mix of long-range, low-power consumption and secure data transmission devices and gateways. Due to the low duty cycle of sensors, meaning that most collect data at lower rates, LoRa gateway devices that receive transmissions from multiple sensors can be powered by batteries that last between 5 and 10 years. LPWAN equipment can be added much like a new IP network switch to a carrier's cellular network, but LoRa alone is not expected to be able to handle all IoT applications and the volume of data. For example, within a home, Wi-Fi and ZigBee might be used instead, and in remote areas, WiMAX, satellite, and cellular networks can cover a much wider range. For reliability reasons, sensors can also connect to multiple LoRa gateway devices and the servers that manage the network can filter redundant transmissions. LoRa devices can also be bidirectional and incorporate actuators to control devices such as traffic lights and parking lot gates, for example.

To learn about LoRa equipment that is already available, start at *www.semtech.com* or check the products page at *www.lora-alliance.org*.

LoRa networks operate at lower, usually license-exempt, frequencies. In North America, LoRa transmits in the 902 to 928 MHz ISM band using sixty-four 200 KHz downlink channels and eight 500 KHz uplink channels, plus an additional eight 500 KHz downlink channels. In Europe LoRa uses the 867 to 869 MHz band with a total of 10 channels. The LoRa specification covers OSI Layer 1 only and currently specifies the use of **chirp spread spectrum (CSS)** modulation, which has been used in military applications for several decades, because CSS supports long-range communications, as well as being resistant to interference and to multipath distortion.

Chirp spread spectrum modulation is based on FSK. Each bit is transmitted as a frequency that sweeps from the lowest to the highest in the allocated channel. CSS supports data rates from 0.3 to 50 Kbps in LoRa, which should be enough for the majority of IoT devices. Figure 12-1 shows a typical LPWAN.

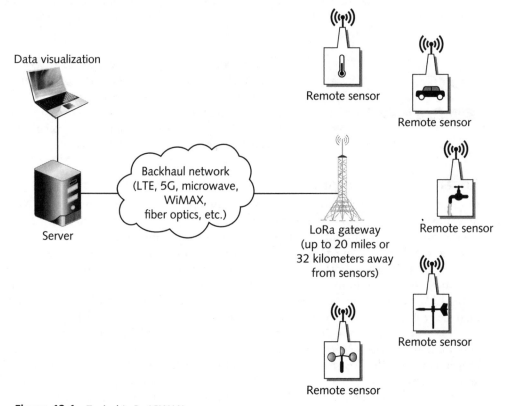

Figure 12-1   Typical LoRa LPWAN

Although Cisco, IBM, HP, and others are members of the LoRa Alliance (*www.lora-alliance.org*), which was founded in early 2015 and is a promising technology, a more detailed discussion of this technology is beyond the scope of this book. For more information, check the white papers available at the Alliance's website and on the web.

Applications of Wireless Data Communications

Because of the well-known advantages of using wireless technologies, such as productivity increases in corporate networks and Internet access from virtually anywhere and at any time, and in spite of the challenges of RF interference and security, wireless communication is now a part of almost every aspect of our daily lives. It is helping to improve access to services provided by practically all types of businesses and areas of endeavor, so let's look at some of them in more detail.

Healthcare

Wireless technologies are being used to enhance the ability of healthcare providers to monitor patients, as well as vastly improving the quality of life of the patients themselves.

Administering the correct medication is a major concern in the healthcare industry. It is estimated that incorrectly administered medication results in hundreds of thousands of medical emergencies annually. Typically, printouts of prescriptions are posted in the pharmacy area of a healthcare facility. As the medications are dispensed for delivery to a patient, they are crossed off the list. However, because the paper record cannot always be updated immediately, there is a possibility that a patient could get an extra dose of medication before an order for a new or changed medication has been processed. This potential problem necessitates duplicate documentation, with nurses first checking the printout to determine the medication and dosage to be given, then noting on paper that the medication was actually given, and later entering the data into the hospital's database.

Wireless point-of-care computer systems based on smartphones, tablet computers, or wireless-equipped computers mounted on movable carts allow medical staff to access and update patient records immediately. Hospitals are using portable devices with barcode scanners or RFID and a wireless connection. Healthcare professionals can immediately document a patient's medication administration in the computer while moving from room to room. The patient's barcoded or RFID-enabled armband is scanned, and all medications that are currently due for that patient are brought up on the screen. The medications to be administered are sealed in pouches that can be read by a barcode or RFID device connected to the computer. Nurses identify the medications before opening the package. An alert immediately appears on the screen if the wrong medication or incorrect amount is selected. After administration, the nurse indicates through the wireless network that the medication has been given, electronically signing the distribution form.

The system immediately verifies that medication is being administered to the correct patient in the correct dosage, which eliminates potential errors and documentation inefficiencies. The documentation process now takes place at the bedside, where care is delivered, which improves accuracy. In addition, all hospital personnel have real-time access to the latest medication and patient status information.

Gone are the days when doctors and patients had to wait for photographic X-ray film to be developed and sent to the right office or patient room. Doctors can view full patient diagnostic tests and results while at a patient's bedside, using a mobile device.

In 2004, Baycrest, a center for geriatric care in Toronto, Canada, was one of the first hospitals in North America to implement a computerized physician order entry system. The system lets doctors order tests, exams, and medications directly from a patient's bedside using the WLAN from a handheld device and has helped dramatically reduce errors and omissions. Physicians can also check the patient's records and charts in the hospital's health information system, in addition to viewing MRIs, X-rays, etc.

Mental health patients can be fitted with Wi-Fi monitoring devices or RFID tags, and their movements can be tracked within the healthcare center, increasing patient safety. A **real-time location system (RTLS)** can be used to detect if a patient wanders outdoors or falls on the floor and alert the hospital staff immediately. In addition, RTLS can be used to monitor the location of doctors and nurses, as well as medical equipment, such as blood pressure and heart rate monitors, making access to everyone and everything much quicker, especially in case of an emergency, in addition to tracking assets and preventing equipment theft. RTLS systems can also be used to monitor staff and patient movement throughout a hospital to monitor and help prevent the spread of infectious diseases, one of the most serious problems faced by hospitals. Doctors and nurses no longer have to be paged over a PA system, nor do they have to be in an office or nursing station to access lab results. Doctors can also consult with specialists while at a patient's bedside, and the specialists can be more easily reached, no matter where they are in the hospital or elsewhere. Figure 12-2 shows examples of patient and staff RTLS tags.

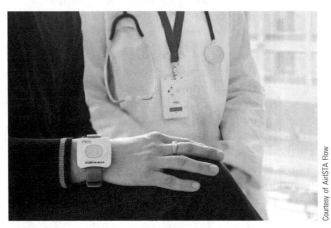

Figure 12-2   Patient and staff RTLS tags

For more information on RTLS systems, see *www.airistaflow.com*, *www.sonitor.com*, and *www.aeroscout.com* or search the web for other companies.

At the Pan American games in Toronto in 2015, a Cisco Telepresence system was deployed to allow specialists to examine injured athletes remotely, while another doctor was present on location to assist. This dramatically reduced the amount of time it would take if the patient had to wait for the specialist to travel sometimes dozens of miles to reach the venue where the athlete was injured during competition. Although the system installed was not wireless, similar deployments can use an 802.11ac wireless connection.

Patients can also be outfitted with monitoring devices and their vital stats can be accessed by a doctor from a mobile phone or tablet, regardless of the time of day or location of the patient or doctor. The data can be transmitted via the cellular network or Wi-Fi. Non-critical-care patients who need to be checked periodically are then free to move around a hospital or even go home and resume their daily activities, or maybe even travel, while being remotely monitored by their own healthcare provider. For an example, see *www.airstrip.com*.

The elderly or patients who have vision challenges can use mobile devices or their own smartphones equipped with RFID readers to identify medications fitted with RFID tags. This might also prevent people from taking the wrong medicine or incorrect dosage, which is a frequent challenge. When a patient simply touches the medication package with a reading device, the device reads the tag and tells the patient (using simulated speech) the name, dosage, and time when the medication should be taken.

People who are at risk for falls and living on their own can wear devices that are activated if they fall or if they simply press a button. The device connects to a gateway attached to the WLAN in the home, which immediately notifies emergency services via the Internet or telephone. The emergency services attendant can then attempt to speak directly with the client before sending help, if necessary.

For tracking a patient's critical medication intake, pills are being fitted with wireless transmitters that send a signal to a home wireless router to notify a healthcare provider when the pill has been swallowed by the patient. Tiny cameras fitted inside a pill can wirelessly transmit images from inside the patient's body, helping doctors diagnose some types of health problems and avoid exploratory surgery. Although the cost of some of these items may be high, it is still significantly lower than the cost of exploratory surgery and hospital stays for the patients.

Visually challenged individuals can use a cane that is equipped with GPS, cellular, and Wi-Fi connectivity. This has the potential to assist these folks in gaining more independence and freedom to move around; more easily locate transit stops, offices, and retail locations; these smart canes can also notify relatives of their location at any given time, via cellular networks.

Disposable surgery supplies and medication containers are also tracked using RFID. The item is scanned when used during surgery and a "smart" disposal container reads the tags when the supplies or tools, such as needles, are disposed.

Education

Wireless technology is ideal for schools. An instructor can create a classroom presentation on a laptop at home, then carry it right into the classroom. The instructor does not necessarily have to plug and unplug cables to attach to the campus network. Instead, the device connects to the school's WLAN and can even connect to multimedia display projectors wirelessly, using 802.11ac or WiGig. Teachers can also distribute handouts directly to students' wireless devices and conduct pop quizzes in which students submit their answers directly on their devices. This can reduce or eliminate the need for paper tests and enable instant results for both students and teachers.

The wireless connection also frees students from having to go to a specific computer lab or the library to get on the school's computer network. They can access the school network wirelessly from practically any location on campus or from anywhere they can connect to the Internet.

Wireless technology translates into a cost savings for colleges. Traditional classrooms become fully accessible computer labs without the expense of additional wiring and infrastructure. Colleges no longer have to consider the expense of adding open computer labs for students because everyone can access the resources from any building on campus, indoors or out-doors. Collaboration tools are also being used to allow students to attend live lectures remotely, using a mobile device. Students can attend classes and even interact with the tea-chers from virtually anywhere in the world, at any time, via the Internet.

The Connected North project is a very good example of a remote classroom application. Working with Cisco Canada and satellite com-munication providers, Connected North provides isolated northern communities in Canada with access to classroom resources and tea-chers that students in these communities would seldom, if ever, have access to, using Cisco's Telepresence. For more information, visit *www.connectednorth .org* and explore the site and video about its work.

Much more can and will be done with wireless technologies in schools. For example, large campuses can be difficult to navigate. Bluetooth devices such as Apple's iBeacon can be used to direct students to the right location on campus. Small, inconspicuous, low-power iBeacon devices installed throughout the campus transmit information to Bluetooth-equipped smart-phones, which is then used by an app to display the right location map and directions, via the campus WLAN. The app on the smartphone provides the location and directions as the person passes near each iBeacon device.

Search YouTube for "Classroom of the Future" to watch a few videos and get a new perspective on some of the technology ideas being envisioned for education. Note that some of the collaboration technology shown in the videos for sharing files and documents is already a reality today from Cisco and other vendors.

Government

Many cities have deployed broadband and Wi-Fi wireless networks to let residents, city employees, contractors, visitors, and utility staff access the Internet, as well as collect and transmit data to central databases. For example, building inspectors can look up drawings and update permits and other data from the construction sites. City employees can locate and monitor municipal vehicles. Visitors to the city can access the Internet in key areas, which promotes tourism and stimulates the local economy.

Allegany County in western Maryland saved millions of dollars by deploying an IEEE 802.16 network instead of fiber optics. The county's AllCoNet2 project uses 16 radio towers to pro-vide Internet connectivity to schools, libraries, and government buildings in remote county areas where a cable infrastructure was not readily available. To avoid conflict with Internet service providers, the excess capacity of the county's broadband network is sold at a reduced rate to commercial users, which further stimulates economic development in the region.

The city of Fredericton in New Brunswick, Canada, deployed a system called "Fred-eZone" that covers the entire downtown business district and uses a mix of technologies. An IEEE 802.16 wireless broadband backhaul network connects all the major points, and an IEEE 802.11 WLAN is available in the major downtown streets as well as in restaurants, bars, and many other retail businesses. These options provide free Internet access from laptops, tablets, and smartphones. In 2005, the city won a major award for innovation as a result of this project.

Similar city-wide 802.11 deployment projects have been decommissioned and abandoned due mainly to the high cost of keeping the technology up-to-date. However, other cities are beginning to deploy wireless mesh networks to interconnect cameras, public transportation systems, and other services.

Search YouTube for "City of Mississauga: Transforming with the Internet of Everything" for a perspective on how this town is using wireless networks to improve services to its residents.

In Lima, the capital of Peru, city authorities are using an innovative method to deal with problems of illegal dumping of garbage. They are equipping vultures with GPS tracking devices and GoPro cameras. The birds are attracted to garbage; when they fly over an area where garbage should not be dumped, the GPS identifies the location and the GoPro cameras are used to attempt to identify the culprits. The program is being partially funded by USAID.

Home Automation

Several manufacturers today offer wireless products that enable control of lighting, heating, ventilation, air conditioning, drapes, security systems, door locks, and a variety of home appliances from a smartphone or tablet while in the home or from anywhere in the world where a Wi-Fi or cellular connection to the Internet is available. The newer systems use ZigBee or Wi-Fi to enable remote control of light switches, wall sockets, as well as environmental controls such as the Nest system. Lighting and alarm controls can help keep the home secure by turning lights on and off at preset times to make the home look "lived-in." Door locks connected via ZigBee or Wi-Fi networks can be opened, locked, and monitored from anywhere via the cellular network. Family members or contractors can be given temporary or permanent access to the home and eliminate the potential dangers of a lost key. No need to leave a spare key under the carpet, the flower pot, or in a lock box.

Home control systems are also more "green," given that lights, etc., can be automatically or remotely turned off and the environment can be adjusted even when no one is home. Appliances such as ovens, slow-cookers, pool heaters, and others are already available that can be controlled from your smartphone. Other wireless devices are available that can display your energy consumption and enable utility meters to be read remotely, saving carbon emissions by eliminating the need for a person to go from house to house to read the meters. What the future will bring in this area is dependent upon consumer demand, but it will certainly be interesting to follow.

Check out the websites of lock manufacturers such as Schlage (see *www.schlage.com*) and Weiser (see *www.weiserlock.com*) to learn more about smart electronic locks.

Home Entertainment

A number of manufacturers have introduced wireless products designed to enhance the home entertainment experience. From wireless speakers to media players, game consoles, DVD players, televisions, digital video recorders (DVRs), and multimedia personal computers, wireless networking capability is enabling people to distribute all forms of digital media throughout the home. It is now possible to locate a TV set anywhere and stream video and audio from other locations around the house. Current and upcoming wireless technologies such as 802.11ad have the potential to eliminate the cables required to interconnect multimedia devices. If movies or music are stored in your mobile devices, it is possible to transmit them wirelessly to your audio system or TV using Apple AirPlay, Google Chromecast, and other similar systems. Many devices like the Amazon Echo are voice-enabled, allowing you to use voice control for entertainment functions as well as home automation.

IEEE 802.11ad promises to bring many more innovations in connectivity for home entertainment devices. It is the only technology able to support 4K and the future 8K video casting between devices and, even though its maximum distance is limited to 30 feet (10 meters) or less, its compatibility with 802.11ac makes it the ideal technology for video and audio casting applications within a room in the home or school.

IEEE 802.11ay, which you learned about in Chapter 8, could provide even greater support for wireless TV broadcasting and might even eventually reduce or eliminate the need for fiber to the home, which is very expensive to install. 5G cellular and the latest microwave technology supporting 2 Gbps or higher will also play a significant part in this wireless ultra-high definition TV availability, particularly in areas where fiber infrastructure does not yet exist.

Search the web for more information about devices like Google Chromecast, Amazon Fire, Apple TV, Roku, and similar devices.

Transportation

Private passenger cars, buses, trains, and commercial airlines already offer Wi-Fi connectivity using the cellular networks and satellite communications. Transport trucks using GPS are now being monitored using cellular and satellite technologies, increasing safety and reducing losses. The next technology frontier, currently under research and development, is vehicle-to-vehicle communications. Tesla cars are already using cellular networks and Wi-Fi to connect and update the software used to control all the car systems. Vehicle-to-vehicle communications is expected to make transportation safer. Vehicles will be able to communicate with other nearby vehicles, detect and communicate road and driving conditions, and warn nearby vehicles to prevent accidents and even to help save fuel and reduce carbon emissions. Research on these technological advances is currently being conducted at several universities and companies around the world.

Visit the *www.rfidjournal.com* website and search for "Transit" to read about how RFID is being used to track vehicle maintenance as well as for electronic fare collection.

Cities are beginning to deploy systems that can warn drivers about traffic conditions and suggest alternative routes that can reduce congestion for passenger cars, buses, and transport vehicles. The system can also suggest alternate routes for public transit riders.

In the recent past airlines moved from a few displays along the passenger cabin to individual flat screens offering on-demand content. More recently, many airlines are modifying their equipment and offering on-demand content over Wi-Fi on a passenger's own tablet or smartphone, via dedicated free apps. Tablets can be rented by passengers who do not have or carry their own devices. This has the added benefit of saving a significant amount of weight and complexity of wiring in each aircraft, which, in turn, saves the airlines money.

You can check out the details of the in-flight entertainment system at *www.westjet.com* as an example.

Smartphones are quickly becoming an integral part of automobiles and light trucks. Manufacturers are replacing CD drives, which are mechanical and prone to failures, with Bluetooth connections to smartphones, because a large percentage of people today carry their media library on their mobile devices. Vehicles equipped with rear-seat entertainment systems also offer owners the ability to simply connect their own iPads and Android tablets. GPS and maps on smartphones are more powerful and frequently more up-to-date than dedicated GPS systems, so maps and favorite locations saved on the owner's smartphone can also be displayed in the vehicle's console screen.

A Bluetooth adapter can be plugged into the vehicle's On Board Diagnostic II (OBD II) connector to display diagnostic and performance information the vehicle's engine and other sensors. Connected vehicles with Internet access can transmit information about location, how much fuel you have, and if the car is locked. An OBD II system can also be used instead of a key or remote key fob to open the vehicle's doors. Industry experts expect that your smartphone will be able to detect a distracted pedestrian's smartphone and warn the driver to prevent accidents. Smartphones will also assist in vehicle-to-vehicle communications to help increase safety.

Many cities now provide vehicle owners with the ability to pay for parking spots via a dedicated app. If your parking time is about to expire, the app will send you a warning, so if necessary you can pay again, to extend your time.

Office Environments

Thanks to wireless technologies, employees in all lines of work today have access to the data they need to help them be productive and make decisions from anywhere around the office. In addition to data accessibility, wireless technologies allow businesses to create an office where the traditional infrastructure doesn't exist. Typically, an office space must be wired with computer cables for network connections and telephone wires. With wireless technologies such as Wi-Fi, that expensive cabling infrastructure, which is expensive to install and difficult to troubleshoot and modify, is no longer required. This means that an office can be created in a very short period of time with minimum expense. For example, a hotel conference room that might not have the infrastructure to support a wired network can be quickly turned into a wireless networked environment. During office renovations or reorganization, employees can move to another location in the building or to a completely different place and can be connected immediately, saving businesses the expense of rewiring the entire office.

Online collaboration is one of the keys to office productivity today. Many vendors now offer a range of sophisticated collaboration tools that allow people to share documents or their device screens, as well as a nearby video display, easily and simply. Meeting rooms can detect the presence of a participant's mobile device and automatically turn on displays and voice links to initiate a meeting, greatly simplifying and speeding up the connection.

Search the web for "Cisco Intelligent Proximity" to learn about what can be done with collaboration technology today.

TIP

Event Management

Managing spectators attending a sporting event or concert can be a daunting task. Each attendee has a ticket, and there are special passes for the press and team officials. However, tickets can be lost, stolen, or counterfeited. Attempting to identify a stolen or counterfeit ticket as thousands of spectators are waiting to be admitted has until now been almost impossible. But several large arenas and stadiums are now turning to wireless systems to facilitate this process.

Event tickets are printed with a unique barcode and have an RFID tag embedded that is then scanned at the venue's point of entry using handheld or integrated turnstile hardware, which in turn is connected to a wireless network. The network instantly validates the ticket and then sends a signal back to the turnstile that permits the patron to have access to the venue. This technology is made very difficult to reproduce, can prevent the use of counterfeit tickets, and can also be used to identify stolen or duplicated tickets.

The wireless point-of-entry turnstiles can provide organizers with a real-time look at traffic flow, thus helping a venue to more effectively manage its staff and determine where additional people might be needed. Advertisers can also tailor their marketing based on who is entering at which gate on wireless display screens installed near the entry points. Figure 12-3 shows an example of a concert attendee scanning an RFID-enabled ticket.

Figure 12-3   Scanning an RFID-enabled event ticket

In addition, wireless technologies are changing the entertainment experience itself. In several major stadiums, wireless transmissions of in-progress game statistics are available to fans in the stadium with a smartphone or tablet computer. Fans can also view instant replays of the event they are attending or watch segments and results from other games around the country. In the Arizona Cardinals' football stadium, fans can use their wireless devices to play fantasy football or order concessions and have them delivered to right to their seats.

Event tickets can often also be loaded on to Apple Wallet and, as of the release of the iPhone 6, together with an NFC-enabled SIM card, be used to scan at turnstiles to access certain events. Industry shows and conferences are making almost exclusive use of RFID-enabled passes for attendees. These passes can be scanned by a wireless device at each exhibitor's booth so you can receive more information via email, instead of carrying paper brochures.

Travel

Because wireless technology creates mobility, the travel industry was one of the first to embrace it widely. Wireless global positioning systems (GPS) that tie into emergency roadside assistance have become standard features on many automobiles sold today. Satellite radio transmission of over 150 music and talk stations solves the problem of losing a station outside its transmission range. Satellite radio is a subscription service, meaning that users pay a monthly fee for the privilege of listening to the stations without any commercial interruptions. The OnStar roadside assistance service uses GPS and cellular technology to link the vehicle and driver to a central service center. Users can also use the system to make phone calls using the cellular network. The OnStar system was originally available only for GM vehicles, but electronics and auto accessory retailers now sell it to the general public as OnStar FMV (For My Vehicle), with a user interface built into the rearview mirror (see Figure 12-4).

Figure 12-4 OnStar FMV user interface embedded in rear-view mirror
Source: Courtesy of General Motors

 Verizon and other carriers, as well as some automobile associations, also offer roadside assistance plans supported by cellular networks. See *www.verizonwireless.com/solutions-and-services/roadside-assistance/*.

Airport terminals are likewise turning to wireless technologies. Most large airport terminals in North America are equipped with Wi-Fi that passengers can use while waiting for their flights. For a nominal fee (or at no cost in some airports, such as Pearson International in Toronto, Canada), they can also surf the Internet or read email as well as check in or view flight schedules.

Many airlines have installed WLANs on their planes, offering wireless Internet capabilities to passengers on cross-country or long-haul flights, supported by satellite communications and even on short-haul flights, using 4G cellular networks. Like their Earth-bound counterparts, these passengers can access the Internet or view their corporate data and email from their seats while in flight.

City transit systems are also "going wireless." People in Finland can purchase bus, train, and movie tickets (not to mention a can of soda) without ever needing to show a piece of paper or any cash money. They can pay for the ticket from their phones and the cost is debited automatically from their bank accounts or credit cards, and in most cases they simply present a two-dimensional barcode or QR code on their phone screens when entering a cinema or bus. Tram tickets in Amsterdam, Holland, and monthly passes in Toronto, Canada, are other examples. To use them you simply wave the ticket by a box placed near the doors when you board and when you exit the vehicle. The units make a sound to indicate that your ticket is still valid or to let you know that you need to purchase a new one if your current one has expired.

Passports are currently being issued with embedded RFID tags, which speeds up the trip through immigration. You can also now check in via smartphone, before arriving at the airport, especially if you only have carry-on luggage, which helps save time standing in-line at airline check-in counters. The boarding pass, including the departure gate and seat number, along with its associated QR code can be displayed on the smartphone screen and read by desktop or wireless handheld devices at security checkpoints and prior to boarding the airplane. Most people can usually find their smartphones but might more easily misplace a paper or card boarding pass.

Delta Airlines recently spent $50 Million US Dollars to install 4,600 RFID readers and 3,800 bag tag printers to better handle and track the 120 million items of passenger luggage it checks each year at airports around the world. In addition, for frequent flyers, Delta has also issued an estimated 1.5 million permanent tags in the past two years. These tags can be programmed with the passenger's flight destination at the check-in counters.

Sports and Fitness

Sports equipment such as baseball bats, golf clubs, basketballs, and soccer balls are now being outfitted with sensors that can help players improve the way they play the game and help coaches analyze the motion and effectiveness of a bat swing, for example. This equipment can provide immediate feedback to the player through a smartphone or nearby computer. Apps and attachments are readily available in Google Play and the Apple store.

You are, no doubt, familiar with the large number of smart fitness tracking bracelets, apps, and gizmos that people can purchase to track their exercise routines, prompt them to exercise more, track sleep patterns, etc. Most of the apps communicate with smartphones and upload the data via cellular or Wi-Fi to a website. If you choose, you can then compare your performance with that of your friends.

Many sports and fitness devices today are based on an ultra-low-power 2.4-GHz wireless technology that is proprietary, supported by a special interest group, and openly accessible to manufacturers, called ANT. Originally created in 2003, the ANT protocol is currently used in hundreds of cycling and fitness devices and has also been incorporated in medical equipment and IoT devices. ANT-compatible devices are typically designed for a maximum range of about 100 feet (30 meters), but this can be easily extended by combining ANT with other technologies such as 4G.

For more information about ANT-compatible technology, check *www.thisisant.com.*

People who practice yoga now have a tool to help them achieve the correct form and alignment by wearing smart fitness pants. The pants guide the person by providing gentle vibrations, as well as transmitting data to a smartphone that displays an image of the body position along with an indication of which areas of the body need to be adjusted to achieve the perfect results. The clothing can be machine washed several times before it needs to be replaced.

Construction

Although at first glance the construction industry might not seem to be a prime candidate for wireless technologies, in reality it benefits greatly. Special rugged tablet computers allow engineers and architects to review drawings and plans at the job site. One challenge for builders is that each construction phase must be completed before the next one can begin. For example, if the concrete footings for a new building cannot be poured, then the entire project must be put on hold. This series of events often means idle construction employees and last-minute schedule adjustments. Information from the job site, such as a tardy subcontractor or a problem with materials, could be relayed back to the main office for rescheduling of workers to other sites to prevent idle time.

Because foremen are often at multiple sites during a day's work, filing daily payroll paperwork can be a challenge. Payroll clerks often wrestle with scrawled or illegible notes and are unable to contact the foreman on the job for clarification. The paperwork problems can be eliminated when foremen enter time sheet information on a tablet computer and transmit it to the main office.

Construction equipment such as bulldozers and earth graders also participate in wireless networks by being fitted with wireless terminals, turning them into "smart" equipment. A GPS on a bulldozer or digger can provide very accurate location information. The exact location of the dig coordinates can be transmitted to a terminal on the bulldozer, which displays a color-coded map to guide the operator. Smart equipment can be connected through wireless transmissions back to the home office, which tracks engine hours and equipment location. Wireless terminals in the engine's diagnostic system can send an alert when the oil needs to be changed or other maintenance operations are due.

Site engineers can consult drawings, make any necessary adjustments, and have access to updated plans without having to wait until new drawings are copied and shipped to the site. In addition to building construction on land, undersea pipeline and bridge construction, as well as ocean-based wind generator farms, were among the first businesses to take full advantage of wireless technologies to ensure accuracy and reduce problems.

RFID and Wi-Fi is also being used on construction sites to check contractors in and out, as well as to direct them where and what work to do at different locations. Engineers no longer need to check with contractors on a day-to-day basis. An RFID tag at the location where the work needs to be done is read by an app and the specifications for the work, drawings, and any special instructions are displayed right from the app. This process can improve speed and accuracy and prevent errors, which can be costly and require work to be redone. It can also improve safety.

Warehouse Management

Managing a warehouse stocked with inventory can be a nightmare. New products arrive continually and must be counted and stored. When products are shipped out of the warehouse, they must be located and then transferred to the correct loading dock so they can be placed on the right truck. Then, employees must update the stock database to reflect the outgoing shipment. A mistake in any one of these steps can result in a warehouse stocked with products that it cannot locate, irate customers receiving the wrong items, or a store running out of goods to sell.

Implementing wireless technology is essential in many warehouse operations. By equipping all of the warehouse's machinery and personnel with wireless networking devices, managers can use warehouse management system (WMS) software to supervise all the activities, from receiving through shipping. And because this network is tied into the front-office computer system, managers can have statistics that are always current.

Pallet loads arriving from locations outside the receiving warehouse come with barcoded labels or RFID tags. The RFID tags can include product identification numbers, product code dates or expiration dates, manufacturing location, and sequentially assigned serial numbers. As pallets arrive at a warehouse, RFID or barcode readers can identify it and the documentation can be matched to the database. A forklift operator scans the RFID or barcode with his portable wireless device. This device sends the data to the wireless network, where the warehouse software immediately designates a storage location for the pallet and relays the information back to the computer on the forklift. The forklift operator then transports the pallet to the designated storage location. The operator scans the pallet again, as it is placed on a shelf, to confirm that it is the correct location before depositing the load.

In the front office, orders for merchandise to ship out are received and entered into the computer that connects to the WLAN in the warehouse. The WMS software manages order picking, balances workloads, and selects pick sequences for forklift operators. The dock control module of the WMS then releases orders for picking. A forklift operator locates the correct storage location, scans the barcode of the pallet, and then ferries it to the shipping dock to be loaded onto a truck. Some highly sophisticated warehouses are operating with fully automated pallet machines and forklifts that can process the storing and retrieving of products completely without human intervention.

Checkout how RFID can improve the accuracy and speed of shipping on YouTube. Search for a video called "RFID Shipping with FedEx."

Retail Stores

In the near future, most barcode functions, including inventory counting, will be replaced by RFID tags. Large retailers already have instructed their suppliers to implement RFID in all the products they purchase, some at the pallet level and some at the individual item level. RFID will greatly simplify inventory counting and it will eventually benefit the customers as well. Some stores, like clothing retailer Old Navy in Canada, already tag each item. RFID is used mainly to prevent losses due to theft at these stores.

Apple retail stores and several others are making use of iBeacon technology to promote their products and increase sales by offering specials and discounts to loyal customers. As you enter the store or while you are looking at products on a particular shelf, a dedicated store app on your smartphone or tablet is activated by an iBeacon device. The app can generate a sound and provide you with more information, discount coupons, etc., via the store's Wi-Fi WLAN. iBeacon is a short-distance, one-way transmission technology.

Checkout lines at supermarkets and other large retailers can become far more efficient or can even be completely automated by the use of RFID tags at the individual item level. As you learned in Chapter 11, you may soon be able to simply walk out of the store with your purchases and smartphone without ever stopping at a cash register. Many stores already have self-checkout machines. In the small town of Viken, Sweden (population, 4,200), the first unstaffed grocery store opened its doors recently. Customers register for the service and then use their smartphones to open the door, pick items from the shelves and scan them, and then receive an invoice once a month for their purchases.

Apple Pay and Android Pay, which use NFC, are considered much more secure than using credit or debit cards. When you scan your credit or debit card at a retail store, your card information is stored, albeit temporarily, on the retailer's system. With Apple Pay and similar systems, the retailer does not have access to your card information at all. A number is generated by the phone and used as confirmation of the purchase. Only Apple has a record of your actual card information, which it uses to transmit to your financial institution, and this helps keep your card information safer than ever before.

Environmental Research

One of the most challenging aspects of documenting research while in the field is that it is difficult and dangerous to extend long cables or install heavy equipment inside, say, deep caves or at the tops of trees. Earthquake and Tsunami monitoring on land or at sea also benefits from real-time data collection. Today, in places that were previously difficult to access and monitor, scientists are using small, battery-powered or solar-cell-powered sensors that can connect to satellites and cellular networks. For example, small wireless sensors located at the tops of tall trees monitor the effects that ultraviolet rays are having on our forests due to holes in the ozone layer. The heavier computer equipment that records the sensor readings can be installed in a much more accessible location nearby, along with large, heavy batteries or generators, and it can communicate with the sensors using a WLAN. The data collected can then be transmitted to a research or monitoring facility via cellular or satellite. This capability has proven to be a major breakthrough in many scientific fields and has helped collect data that, until recently, was very difficult—if not impossible—to record.

Drones are also being used extensively to survey crops, examine fauna and flora, survey ground features and stability in areas such as vertical cliffs or under bridges or other places difficult for a human being to reach. Small, highly maneuverable remote-controlled drone airplanes or multi-rotor helicopters can be equipped with cameras that can transmit live video over Wi-Fi to a computer, tablet, or smartphone, as well as recording both video and still images, for later analysis.

In the past, scientists had to be content with placing a radio collar on wild animals to learn more about their movements and habits, and they often had to spend time in the environment and track the animals from a distance. Today they can attach a GPS-enabled collar and cameras to mammals, birds, and even insects and monitor them from a remote location. Scientists are also monitoring the health of flora and fauna in the oceans by placing sensors deep below the water surface as well as sensors and cameras on the sea creatures themselves. The sensors record a variety of data for a specified period of time, then detach themselves automatically, float to the surface, and can either transmit their GPS location to be collected by boat or transmit the data via satellite. Figure 12-5 shows an example of an animal with a GPS tracking collar.

Figure 12-5 Animal with GPS tracking collar

Visit *www.lotek.com* to explore their full range of GPS animal-tracking collars.

Industrial Control

Because of their size and complexity, large manufacturing facilities often find that it is a challenge to install a full-featured network using very long cables, such as in automotive assembly plants. If machines need to be monitored, it can take hours or even days for a technician to access every machine and record or download the status of each piece of equipment. Wireless networking solves the problem. Remote sensors can connect to a WLAN, then collect data and transmit it to a central location, via the Internet or the enterprise network. Manufacturing managers can monitor their equipment from an office or from any location, detecting potential problems instantly. Technicians in a control room can monitor the status of every machine or device and dispatch a technician to perform maintenance work on the equipment when necessary. Components and tools used in the manufacturing process can also be tracked using RFID.

Learn more about RFID tags for challenging manufacturing applications, search YouTube for "Confidex" and watch the videos about two of their tag products, X-Bolt and Corona.

Industrial applications can be very demanding. The environment can be corrosive, dusty, damp, too hot or too cold, etc. Specialized sensors and systems have been available for some time, but recent advances in size and cost of sensors, together with low-cost, low-power, and compact wireless devices is set to revolutionize industrial control applications.

Chapter Summary

- In addition to computers, smartphones, tablets, and servers connected to the Internet, today we have a large number and variety of devices equipped with sensors, actuators, and built-in single-board computers and microcontrollers that are able to collect and relay data to a central database. This Internet of Things (IoT) is expected to grow by a staggering amount within the next decade or two, and is already on its way to being as much a part of our lives as the Internet itself. Technologies such as LoRa may give a boost to the IoT.

- Every day wireless technologies are being applied in new and creative ways. The demand for technicians, technologists, and RF engineers is growing and will likely continue to grow as new technologies are invented and standardized. The need is for skilled people who can design, implement, manage, and support wireless networks. Each technology requires a different set of skills.

- Healthcare is one area in which the use of wireless technologies is expanding dramatically. From monitoring the movements of patients in a hospital to tracking their intake of medication with wireless transmitter-equipped pills, to saving the lives of elderly people who live alone, or allowing a doctor to monitor the vital signs of a patient from the other side of the world using a smartphone, wireless health applications have seen tremendous growth in the recent past.

- Students in remote areas of the world can now have interactive access to teachers from many other parts of the world via satellite. Teachers can connect to wireless displays and share lecture slides or display video from a tablet. Students can find any location on campus with the aid of iBeacons, a Bluetooth technology.

- Cities are taking advantage of Wi-Fi and broadband to attract visitors and business-people and to let residents, city employees, contractors, and utility staff access the Internet, as well as collect and transmit data to central databases.

- Home owners can increase the safety, security, and convenience of their properties using Wi-Fi, ZigBee, and cellular networks to control lighting, heating, and air conditioning. Wireless door locks connected to the Internet can be monitored, opened, and closed from any remote location with access to Wi-Fi or cellular. Using a smartphone, children and trusted contractors can have a temporary key to access the home when necessary.

- Devices attached to a TV can be used to send music or video to any location in the home, from a smartphone, tablet, or computer. Wireless ultra-high definition TV might make a comeback with the introduction of the IEEE 802.11ay standard in the future. IEEE 802.11ad can support wireless transmission of 4K TV, and in the future, even 8K TV.

- RFID-enabled fare tickets are used to pay for public transit, and Wi-Fi Internet access is available from passenger cars to airplanes. Airlines are saving a lot of weight and complexity by moving to the delivery of in-flight entertainment via Wi-Fi on the passengers' own devices.

- RFID is being used to manage access to entertainment events. RFID-enabled tickets that are very hard to reproduce have to be scanned at the entrance so that turnstiles will allow attendees into the venue. This can prevent fake and duplicate tickets from being used to access the events and provides management with real-time information on the number and location of people entering the venues.

- Transportation systems also benefit from wireless. The safety of trucks and drivers increases with the use of real-time tracking using GPS technology. The OnStar system can detect accidents, open vehicle doors when the owner locks the keys inside, and allow the vehicle owner to make cellular phone calls.

- Athletes and coaches make use of smart equipment to monitor and improve their performance. Wireless transmitters installed in golf clubs, baseball bats, clothing, and other types of sports gear transmit information in real time to an app on a smartphone or to a computer nearby that helps the athlete or coach analyze their movements and performance.

- Construction sites are being made safer and the jobs more accurate through the use of RFID and Wi-Fi. Contractors can check in and out using a wireless device and RFID and can be also more accurately directed to the place where the work is to be done. Engineers can update drawings from the job site, and changed drawings can be accessed faster using tablets without having to wait for updated drawings to be shipped to the site.

- RFID and Wi-Fi are being used for inventory counting and to improve accuracy for warehouse management. Readers installed at the loading docks can check the shipments against orders and can also help place items on the correct shelves in warehouses.

- Retail stores can increase sales using apps and iBeacon devices to offer coupons and discounts to loyal customers when they visit the store. RFID is also used to increase security and prevent theft.

- Scientists can track animals remotely, on a map, instead of following them physically. The health and habits of sea animals and the ocean flora can be monitored and tracked with GPS and camera-equipped devices that collect data for a period of time and then float to the surface, transmitting the data via satellite or their GPS location so they can be picked up.

- Factories use wireless devices to monitor machines and RFID to track parts and tools. Managers can monitor all machines, tools, and components used from a central location instead of having to send a technician to collect the data from each machine on the factory floor. Wireless technology also solves the challenges of installing long cable connections in large plants.

Key Terms

chirp spread spectrum (CSS)   A type of modulation consisting of a sweep starting from the lower frequency in a channel to the highest frequency in the same channel. CSS has been used by the military for decades due to its resiliency to interference and multipath signals and is now being employed in IoT devices using LoRa because of its greater range, up to 20 miles (32 kilometers). *See also* LoRa.

Internet of Things (IoT)   A term used to describe a large variety of sensors and actuators that are built with single-board computers and microcontrollers and can be equipped with many different wireless communications interfaces. IoT is about the data that can be collected by these sensors and what can be learned from our environment by analyzing this data in real time or from a historical perspective.

LoRa   A wireless technology specification published by the LoRa Alliance. The specification defines classes of IoT devices, communication protocols, etc., for gateways and sensors used in IoT networks that use very low power and have a range of up to 20 miles (32 kilometers).

machine-to-machine (M2M) communication   A term used to describe devices that are intended to communicate with other devices, not with human beings.

real-time location system (RTLS)   A technology that makes use of wireless transmitters (tags) worn by people or permanently attached to movable assets to track their location and activity. Through the use of multiple receivers installed throughout a building, RTLS can display the location of a wireless tag on a central computer screen. RTLS is widely deployed in hospitals to enable doctors, nurses, and equipment to be located quickly and efficiently.

Review Questions

1. What is the most important thing to mention when trying to explain the Internet of Things to other people?

    a.   That the devices are low-cost and small in size

    b.   The variety of sensors

    c.   The data

    d.   The amount of Internet traffic it creates

2. What type of modulation was initially specified for LoRa?

    a.   DSSS

    b.   FHSS

    c.   CSS

    d.   ASK

3. What is the highest transmission speed of LoRa currently?

    a.   50 Kbps

    b.   500 Kpbs

    c.   300 Kbps

    d.   144 Kbps

4. What is the acronym used for indoor systems used to locate people and equipment?

    a.   GPS

    b.   LOC

    c.   BTFD

    d.   RTLS

5. Which IEEE standard will most likely be used to support wireless 4K television?

    a.   802.11ax

    b.   802.11ad

    c.   802.11ay

    d.   802.11ae

6. Which Wi-Fi specification is the most applicable for casting video signals to a classroom display?

   a. 802.11ac and WiGig

   b. WirelessHD

   c. Wireless HDMI

   d. WiMAX

7. All wireless technologies are clearly based on approved industry standards. True or False?

8. Long-distance Wi-Fi has been deployed in many cities to replace other backhaul technologies. True or False?

9. Even though enterprise-class Access Points can cost about $1,000 each, deploying Wi-Fi can make it much less expensive and quicker for a business to relocate people around the office. True or False?

10. LoRa alone will not likely be able to handle of the requirements of IoT. True or False?

11. Using RFID instead of barcode can improve the speed and accuracy of shipments from a warehouse. True or False?

12. In addition to LoRa and Wi-Fi, _____ technology will also most likely be used to communicate with IoT sensors.

    a. Bluetooth LE

    b. microwave

    c. Internet

    d. satellite

13. iBeacon is a(n) _____ technology.

    a. short-distance

    b. two-way transmission

    c. non-RF

    d. RFID

14. Apple Pay and Android Pay use _____ technology.

    a. RFID

    b. NFC

    c. Bluetooth

    d. iBeacon

15. One of the advantages of using wireless technology for environmental research is that
    _____.

    a. it is based on Bluetooth

    b. it can use RFID or NFC

    c. multiple sensors can be located at a distance from the transmission equipment

    d. it is not dependent on satellite technology

16. Large factories can benefit from WLANs because it reduces the need to install
    _____.

    a. iBeacon devices

    b. Access Points

    c. additional machines

    d. long network cables

17. The explosive growth of wireless data communications increases the need for
    _____.

    a. wireless problem solving skills

    b. iBeacon

    c. IoT devices

    d. smart users

18. Which other wireless technology is ideal for, and will most likely be deployed in, home applications of IoT?

    a. 802.11ad

    b. Bluetooth

    c. LoRa

    d. ZigBee

Hands-On Projects

Project 12-1

Do some research on the Internet and write a one-page report that explains the differences between single-board computers and microcontrollers. List the capabilities of each, and provide a few examples.

Project 12-2

Pick one of the wireless application topics in this chapter and research it thoroughly on the web. Write a two- to five-page report that will educate the reader on the wireless technologies available and how a business or the general population can benefit from this wireless technology application. Provide your own conclusions, insights, and your vision in the report and be sure to use as many images and graphics as you can find.

Real-World Exercises

The Baypoint Group (TBG) needs your help with a proposal. General Sports Health is a chain of medical clinics that specialize in treating athletes injured in competitive sports. GSH's reputation has grown across the country and the organization is planning to expand its services to provide live monitoring of athletes during training, as well as during competition, and data analysis that can also be used to advise coaches on potential ways to prevent future injuries.

Exercise 12-1

TBG has asked you to research the availability of sports equipment, including clothing, that is or can be equipped with wireless sensors to collect real-time data on the activities of the athletes. Your task is to prepare a two- to five-page report for TBG on your findings. Be sure to include links to the equipment and clothing manufacturers' webpages at the bottom of your report. Your instructor may choose a specific sport or a list of sports for you to work on.

Exercise 12-2

After reviewing your report, TBG would like you to expand it to explore the possibility of offering a similar report to other kinds of medical organizations. Research the use of connected sensors and devices, including Bluetooth, RFID, and other technologies that can provide either live real-time data or that can record medical data to assist doctors in tracking a patient's condition. Create another two- to five-page report and a slide presentation showing the benefits of using these wireless devices to people in the medical profession.

Challenge Case Project

CASE PROJECTS

Many countries have laws designed to protect the privacy of data related to people. Some of these laws are specific to health data, whereas others are related to RFID tagging of products, IoT, and wireless technologies. Search the web and locate information on one of these privacy laws that cover the use of a wireless technology. Prepare a slide presentation that describes the law and what needs to be done to prevent breach of privacy. Be sure to include your own conclusions at the end of the presentation.

Completing Hands-On Projects Using Windows 10

This appendix contains instructions on how to complete Hands-On Projects in Chapters 5, 6, and 7 using Microsoft Windows 10. Note that these instructions assume that you have installed the Windows 10 Anniversary update that was released on August 2, 2016 (see the cautionary note below).

These instructions were created using Windows 10 Professional Edition, version 1607 or higher, as a minimum. If you are using a different version or edition of Windows 10, you might need to adjust the instructions. To perform the exercises in this book, Windows 10 Home Edition is not recommended.

To check your Windows 10 edition and version, click **Start**, click **Settings**, click **System**, and then click **About** to display a dialog that shows you the Windows 10 Edition and version, along with other information.

For all other Hands-On Projects throughout the book, specific Windows 10 instructions are not required. Please follow the project instructions listed in each chapter.

Chapter 5—Configuring Bluetooth

Project 5-1

1. In the Notification area at the bottom right of the Home screen, click the Show hidden icons **up arrow,** then click the **Bluetooth** icon. The context menu that appears is very similar to the one in Windows 7. Refer to Figure 5-18, if necessary. If you do not see a Bluetooth icon, in the Notifications area click the **Action Center** icon to the left of the time and date display, then click **Bluetooth** to turn Bluetooth on. The Bluetooth icon should then appear when you click the Show hidden icons up arrow.

2. Click **Open Settings** and if necessary select the **Options** tab.

3. Ensure that all options are selected (checked) in this dialog, especially the **Allow Bluetooth devices to find this PC,** then click **OK.** Do this on both computers.

4. Now you will pair the two computers. On one of the computers, click the **up arrow** in the Notification area again, click **Bluetooth,** then click **Add a Bluetooth Device** on one of the computers. The **Manage Bluetooth devices** dialog opens, and after a few seconds it displays all devices and computers that are available for pairing. See Figure A-1.

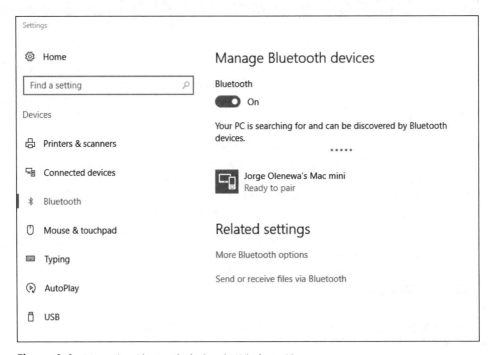

Figure A-1   Managing Bluetooth devices in Windows 10

5. Once you see the other computer listed, click its icon, then click the **Pair** button.

6. A dialog appears asking you to compare the pairing codes on both computers. On the other computer, compare the pairing code to the one displayed on the first computer, as per the instructions. If the codes match, accept the pairing request by clicking **Pair.** In some cases, you might not see a code on the second computer, but you will see a dialog asking you to allow the pairing of the two. If you have just installed a Bluetooth adapter, Windows might need to install a few more drivers first. This might take a few minutes.

7. To verify that the two computers are connected via Bluetooth, in the **Manage Bluetooth devices** dialog, look under the computer name. You should see Connected as the status.

8. Click the **up arrow** in the Notification area again. Click the **Bluetooth** icon, then point to and click **Send a File**. Click the icon with the name of the other computer you connected to via Bluetooth, then click **Next**.

9. The **Bluetooth File Transfer** dialog opens, asking you for the name of the file to send. Click **Browse**, and locate a file that is 2 or more megabytes in size, but preferably not larger than about 5 megabytes, then click **Next**.

10. You may need to enable the file transfer on the receiving computer. To do so, click the **up arrow** in the Notification area again, click the **Bluetooth** icon, and click **Receive a File**.

11. Depending on which version of Bluetooth hardware you have, data will be transmitted at a maximum of 3 Mbps for Bluetooth 4.0 when there is little or no interference. Most other Bluetooth file transfers will happen at the maximum speed of a little more than 700 Kbps. You can check the progress of the file transfer by monitoring the progress bar in the file transfer dialog.

12. If the transfer is successful, you will see a confirmation in the dialog when it is finished. Click **Finish** to terminate this file transfer. On the receiving computer, the file will be located in the **Bluetooth Exchange Folder**, under Libraries\Documents.

Chapter 6—Configuring an Ad Hoc WLAN

Project 6-1

Microsoft has removed the ability for users to create an ad hoc WLAN in Windows 10, except for (currently) a very limited number of WLAN adapters that can be used for Internet Connection Sharing (ICS). To find out if you have one of the adapters that still support ad hoc networks perform the following steps.

1. Right-click the **Start** button and click **Command Prompt (Admin)**. Note that you will need to be logged in to an account that has system administrator privileges. Type the following command at the CMD window prompt: **netsh wlan show drivers** and press **Enter**.

2. Click **Yes** if the system asks you if you wish to allow this program to make changes to your system.

3. Look for the line "Hosted network supported." If you see **No** after the colon, then skip to the next project, because you will not be able to create an ad hoc WLAN.

4. If you see **Yes** after the colon, then search the web for "*How to create an ad hoc WLAN in Windows 10*" and follow the instructions to create a hosted network. Note that you will need to have a second network adapter connected to the Internet, since this process will create a shared Internet connection.

If you find that your adapter supports this feature, search for instructions on how to configure ICS at the following website: *answers.microsoft.com*

Chapter 7—Configuring a Wireless Router or Gateway

Project 7-1

1. Follow the instructions in Project 7-1 up to step number 6.

2. Right-click the network connection icon in the notification area, at the bottom right of your Windows home screen, the click **Open Network and Sharing Center**.

3. To see the status and connection speed of your network in Network and Sharing Center, click the name of your wireless network listed to the right of **Connections:** in the Wireless Network Connection status dialog.

4. See Figure 7-19 and follow the remaining steps in Project 7-1.

1/3 rate Forward Error Correction (FEC) An error correction scheme that repeats each bit three times for redundancy.

1-bit tag RFID device that does not include a chip or memory and cannot store an EPC; these tags are used only to activate an alarm at retail store entrances as a means of preventing theft.

1G (first generation) The first generation of wireless cellular telephony, which transmitted data at up to at 9.6 Kbps using analog circuit-switched transmission technology.

2.5G (2.5 generation) An interim technology stage between 2G and 3G digital cellular networks in which data is transmitted using packet-switched technology.

2/3 rate Forward Error Correction (FEC) An error correction scheme that uses a mathematical formula to add extra error correction bits to the data sent.

2G (second generation) The second generation of cellular telephony, which uses circuit-switched digital transmission technology.

3G (third generation) A digital cellular technology that can send data at up to 21 Mbps over the cellular network.

3rd Generation Partnership Project (3GPP) A group of six standards organizations from Asia, Europe, and North America that proposed standards for GSM, GPRS/EDGE, HSDPA, HSPA+, and LTE.

4G (fourth generation) The latest active standard for cellular communications, currently deployed or being deployed by cellular carriers worldwide, also commonly marketed by carriers as LTE. According to the ITU, only LTE Advanced qualifies as "true 4G" cellular, but the term *4G* can be used if WiMAX and HSPA+ are included in the definition as well.

5G (fifth generation) A new cellular standard currently under development. 5G is currently expected to be ratified in 2018 and the technology does not yet have an acronym like LTE, which is another designation for 4G.

6LoWPAN The protocol that implements IPv6 on WPANs. Also the name of an IETF working group that defines how the Internet protocols—IPv6 in particular—are applied to the smallest devices so that they can participate in the "Internet of Things."

802.11 standard An IEEE standard released in 1997 that defines wireless local area networks at a rate of either 1 or 2 Mbps. All WLAN features are confined to the PHY and MAC layers. This is the original IEEE standard for WLANs and the basis for later 802.11b, a, g, n, and ac/ad amendments.

802.11a An IEEE 802.11 amendment developed in 1999, a standard for WLAN transmissions at speeds of up to 54 Mbps.

802.11ac An IEEE 802.11 amendment that works exclusively in the 5 GHz band and can achieve data rates of up to 6.9 Gbps by supporting channel bandwidths of 80 and 160 MHz.

802.11ad An IEEE 802.11 amendment that expands the standard to work in the 60 GHz portion of the ISM band and can reach speeds of up to 10 Gbps at distances of no more than 2 meters, due to signal attenuation that can be caused by molecules of oxygen in the air.

802.11ax An IEEE 802.11 amendment currently under development that enhances MU-MIMO by allowing the AP to communicate with different devices by using different subcarriers within the same PHY frame.

802.11ay An IEEE 802.11 amendment under development that will enable communications in the 60 GHz band to transmit between 20 and 40 Gbps at distances between 300 and 500 meters.

802.11b An amendment to the IEEE 802.11 standard for WLANs that added two higher speeds, 5.5 and 11 Mbps, and is also known as Wi-Fi, a name given by the Wi-Fi Alliance to technology that has been certified for interoperability with equipment from different manufacturers.

802.11e An IEEE 802.11 amendment for WLAN applications that implements QoS for WLANs and provides for improvements in their capabilities and efficiency.

802.11g An IEEE 802.11 amendment that allows for WLAN transmissions at speeds of up to 54 Mbps using the ISM band.

802.11i A grouping of several IEEE 802.11 security functions that protects WLAN data frames by providing mutual authentication between wireless devices and access points, controlled access to the network, establishment of security keys, and key management.

802.11n An IEEE 802.11 amendment that increases the theoretical data rate up to 600 Mbps. Note that no 802.11n compatible equipment has ever been manufactured that achieves this rate. The maximum data rate achievable with 802.11n today is 450 Mbps.

802.11r An IEEE 802.11 amendment aimed primarily at reducing the reassociation time in an ESS to less than 50 ms, to prevent breaks that reduce the quality of voice calls. It also enables mobile devices to communicate with APs within range, on different channels, ahead of reassociating with one of them, to determine whether they have enough processing resources to handle an ongoing voice call over the WLAN.

802.11s An IEEE 802.11 amendment that enables APs to communicate with each other over the wireless medium. Prior to 802.11s, the standard only allowed APs to communicate with each other over the Ethernet medium and only for the purpose of disassociation of roaming mobile devices.

802.15.3c An amendment to the IEEE 802.15.3 personal area network standard that specified operation in the 2.4 GHz band to support high-rate transmission for the distribution of video and audio and audio signals throughout homes, businesses, hotels, conference centers, and so on.

802.16 (WiMAX) A set of IEEE standards for fixed and mobile broadband wireless communications that allows computers to communicate at up to 75 Mbps and at distances of up to 35 miles (56 kilometers) in a point-to-point configuration, used in metropolitan area networks. This set of standards also allows the use of both licensed and unlicensed frequencies.

802.16e An amendment to IEEE 802.16 created to allow support for mobile users.

802.16m An amendment to IEEE 802.16 that increases the data rate to 100 Mbps and beyond, depending on the method of transmission being used.

802.1X a series of IEEE recommendations for implementation of a grouping of security functions in 802.11.

8-DPSK A simple method of phase shift keying introduced in Bluetooth version 2 that uses eight degrees of phase to encode tribits. This method of modulation is very sensitive to cochannel and intersymbol interference.

8-PSK A modulation technique in which the phase of the carrier is shifted in 45-degree increments and 3 bits can be transmitted per phase change.

A

access control list (ACL) A list of addresses of other devices from which the device that maintains the list expects to receive frames.

acknowledgment (ACK) A procedure used to reduce collisions by requiring the receiving station to send an explicit packet back to the sending station, provided that the received transmission had no errors.

active antenna A passive antenna with an amplifier built-in.

active mode A state in which the Bluetooth device actively participates on the channel.

active scanning The process of sending frames to gather information.

active tag RFID tag that includes a battery.

ad hoc mode A WLAN mode in which wireless devices communicate directly among themselves without going through an AP.

adaptive array processing A radio transmission technique that replaces a traditional antenna with an array of antenna elements.

adaptive frequency hopping (AFH) A feature added by Bluetooth version 1.2 that further improves compatibility with 802.11b by allowing the master in a piconet to change the hopping sequence so that it will not use the frequency channel occupied by 802.11b in the piconet area.

advanced antenna system (AAS) An antenna that can transmit multiple simultaneous signals in different directions to stations that fall within the range of each of the antennas.

Advanced Encryption Standard (AES) The latest encryption standard developed by the National Institute of Standards and Technology (NIST) to replace the Data Encryption Standard. *See* Data Encryption Standard.

Advanced Mobile Phone Service (AMPS) The standard used for 1G analog cellular transmissions, based on FDMA. 1G is often simply called AMPS.

alternate MAC/PHY (AMP) A feature added in version 3 of the Bluetooth specification that makes it possible for Bluetooth radio manufacturers to add a second radio that uses 802.11 to transmit data at speeds of up to 24 Mbps. Compatible Bluetooth devices use FHSS to establish communications with each other and exchange commands and control information, while using the secondary radio for data transfers only.

American National Standards Institute (ANSI) A clearinghouse for standards development in the United States.

American Standard Code for Information Interchange (ASCII) An arbitrary coding scheme that uses the numbers from 0 to 127 to represent alphanumeric characters and symbols.

amplifier A component that increases a signal's intensity.

amplitude The height of a carrier wave.

amplitude modulation (AM) A technique that changes the height of a carrier wave in response to a change in the height of the input signal.

amplitude shift keying (ASK) A digital modulation technique whereby a 1 bit is represented by the existence of a carrier signal, whereas a 0 bit is represented by the absence of a carrier signal.

analog modulation A method of encoding an analog signal onto a carrier wave.

analog signal A signal in which the intensity (amplitude or voltage) varies continuously and smoothly over a period of time.

antenna A copper wire, rod, or similar device used to send and receive radio signals that has one end up in the air and the other end connected to the ground through a receiver.

antenna diversity A technique that uses two antennas to improve the range of 802.11 and transmits a signal through the antenna that received the strongest signal during the last transmission.

antenna pattern A graphic that shows how a signal radiates out of an antenna.

antenna polarization An indication of the horizontal or vertical orientation of the sine waves leaving an antenna.

associate request frame A frame sent by a device to an AP that contains the device's capabilities and supported rates.

associate response frame A frame returned to a device from the AP that contains a status code and device ID number.

association A procedure for a device to join a network.

asynchronous connectionless (ACL) link A packet-switched link that is used for data transmissions.

attenuation A loss of signal strength.

authentication The process of verifying that the device asking to join a piconet, WLAN, or wired network should be allowed to join.

automatic retransmission request (ARQ) An error-correction scheme that continuously retransmits until an acknowledgment is received or a timeout value is exceeded.

B

backhaul A company's internal infrastructure connection.

backscatter A reflection of radiation in which the RFID tag reflects the signal sent by an interrogator while modulating it with the data to be transmitted, used in passive RFID tags.

band A range of radio frequencies. Frequency bands are defined by each country's regulatory agencies, such as the FCC in the United States, and each range is allocated for a specific radio communications purpose.

bandpass filter A filter that passes all signals that are between the maximum and minimum threshold, that is, within the passband.

bandwidth The range of frequencies that can be transmitted.

Barker code (or chipping code) A bit pattern used in a DSSS transmission. The term *chipping code* is used because a single radio bit is commonly referred to as a chip. A data bit in DSSS is composed of a specific pattern containing multiple *chips*.

base station (BS) The transmitter connected to the carrier network or to the Internet.

baseband A transmission technique that treats the entire transmission medium as only one channel.

Basic Service Set (BSS) A WLAN mode that consists of at least one wireless device and one AP. *Also called* infrastructure mode.

baud A change in a carrier signal.

baud rate The number of times that a carrier signal changes per second.

beacon (1) A frame that signals the beginning of a superframe and contains information about the type and number of time slots contained in the superframe. (2) RFID tag that is battery powered and transmits on a periodic basis.

beamforming A technique employed by 802.11n devices that uses multiple radios and antennas to virtually direct the transmission to the location of a device, similar to the way that phased array antennas work (*see* "Phased array antennas" in Chapter 4).

binary phase shift keying (BPSK) A simple digital modulation technique that uses four phase changes to represent 2 bits per signal change.

binding The process of establishing a relationship between endpoints in a ZigBee network.

bits per second (bps) The number of bits that can be transmitted per second.

blocker tag A type of Class-1 passive tag that can be used to disable unauthorized readers from accessing the information from a selective group of tags by sending so many responses that a reader cannot differentiate between the blocker tag and a legitimate tag.

Bluetooth A wireless standard that enables devices to transmit data at an effective rate of 721.2 Kbps over short distances of up to 33 feet (10 meters). Bluetooth is popular for shortdistance communications between wireless devices such as smartphones, laptops, speakers, headsets, printers, smartwatches, and keyboards.

Bluetooth Low Energy (BLE) An amendment to the Bluetooth specification designed to save energy by sending transmissions at a maximum rate of 270 Kbps or lower.

Bluetooth radio module A single radio transmitter/receiver (transceiver) that performs all the necessary transmission functions.

broadband A transmission technique that sends multiple data signals, at different frequencies or at different times, over a single medium or frequency channel.

BSSID In an infrastructure WLAN, the BSSID is the MAC address of the AP. In a peer-to-peer network, the BSSID is the

MAC address of the first station to be turned on and configured to establish the ad hoc WLAN.

buffering The process that the AP uses to temporarily store frames for devices that are in sleep mode.

burst A transmission containing data to or from a single SS or a broadcast transmission from the BS that uses multiple time slots.

burst profile A profile negotiated between the BS and the SSs that specifies the number of time slots allocated to the SSs to maintain QoS.

C

cable modem A technology used to transmit data as well as video signals over a television cable connection.

carrier (1) The RF signal that carries data; (2) telephone, cable TV, and other communication provider that owns the wires or transmission towers that carry voice, video, and data traffic.

carrier sense multiple access with collision avoidance (CSMA/CA) A device-access mechanism in which, before transmitting, a device must listen to the medium to determine if the channel is free.

carrier wave An analog wave having a frequency that a receiver is tuned to. Although the term is commonly used to refer to any wave at a particular frequency that is used to transmit a wireless signal, technically speaking, a wave is only a carrier if some kind of data is encoded into it. Until data is encoded onto the wave, it is more correct to refer to it as a continuous wave (CW).

CDMA2000 1xEVDO The 3G digital cellular technology that is a migration from CDMA2000 1xRTT.

CDMA2000 1xEVDV The 3G digital cellular technology that is a migration from CDMA2000 1xEVDO.

CDMA2000 1xRTT A 2.5G digital cellular network technology that is a migration from CDMA. ("1xRTT" stands for "1-times Radio Transmission Technology.")

cell The coverage area of one transmission tower in a mobile telephone network.

certificate authority An organization that supplies security keys and authenticates users.

challenge-response strategy A process used to check if the other device knows a shared identical secret key.

channel The frequency or range of frequencies used by a particular technology to transmit and receive data. In Bluetooth, a channel consists of all the frequencies in a hop sequence.

channel access methods The different ways of sharing resources in a network environment.

chipless tag RFID device that uses embedded fibers to reflect a portion of the RF waves emitted by a reader; the reflected portion of the RF waves is unique and can be used as an identifier.

chirp spread spectrum (CSS) A type of modulation consisting of a sweep starting from the lower frequency in a channel to the highest frequency in the same channel. CSS has been used by the military for decades due to its resiliency to interference and multipath signals and is now being employed in IoT devices using LoRa because of its greater range, up to 20 miles (32 kilometers). See also LoRa.

circuit switching A switching technique in which a dedicated and direct physical connection is made between two transmitting devices—for example, between two telephones during a call.

co-channel interference Interference between two devices configured to use the same frequency channel.

Code Division Multiple Access (CDMA) A technique that uses spread spectrum technology and unique digital codes to send and receive radio transmissions.

cognitive radio Software-controlled radio that can adapt to the environment by changing frequency channels, bandwidth, modulation, and encoding, depending on the RF environment. These RF characteristics can also be preconfigured by the carriers.

collision The scrambling of data that occurs when two computers start sending messages at the same time in a shared medium.

Complementary Code Keying (CCK) A table containing 64 8-bit code words used for transmitting at speeds above 2 Mbps. This table of codes is used instead of the process of adding a Barker code to the bit to be transmitted.

consortia Industry-sponsored organizations that have the goal of promoting a specific technology.

constellation diagram A graphical representation that makes it easier to visualize signals using complex modulation techniques such as QAM. It is generally used in laboratory and field diagnostic instruments and analyzers to aid in design and troubleshooting of wireless communications devices.

continuous wave (CW) An analog or sine wave that is modulated to eventually carry information, becoming a carrier wave.

control channel A special frequency that cellular phones use for communication with a base station.

control frame MAC frame that assists in delivering the frames that contain data.

coupling A connection between an RFID reader and a tag.

crosstalk Signals from close frequencies that may interfere with other signals.

CTS-to-Self Short for "clear-to-send-to-self," a coordination method used by 802.11g devices that prevents 802.11 and 802.11b devices that do not "understand" OFDM from attempting to initiate a transmission while the 802.11g device is transmitting data.

customer premises equipment (CPE) WiMAX devices that are installed in a customer's office or home.

cycle An oscillating sine wave that completes one full series of movements.

D

Data Encryption Standard (DES) The encryption standard used in the United States until the adoption of AES. *See* AES.

Data Exchange Protocol (NFC-DEP) A protocol used by smart NFC devices to transfer data such as pictures, URLs, and many other items, between devices.

data frame MAC frame that carries the user information to be transmitted to a device.

data link layer The OSI layer responsible for the transfer of data between nodes in the same network segment; it also provides for error detection.

dB dipole (dBd) The relative measurement of the gain of an antenna when compared to a dipole antenna at the same frequency.

dB isotropic (dBi) The relative measurement of the gain of an antenna when compared to a theoretical isotropic radiator.

dBm A relative way to indicate an absolute power level in the linear watt scale.

DCF Interframe Space (DIFS) The standard interval between the transmission of data frames.

de facto standard A common practice that the industry follows for various reasons.

de jure standard A standard that is controlled by an organization or body.

decibel (dB) A ratio between two signal levels.

denial-of-service (DoS) A type of attack on a network in which an attacker performs RF jamming of the frequency channel or floods the network with frame transmissions directed at one or more devices to corrupt and block all other communications.

destroy password A code programmed into an RFID tag during manufacturing that can be used to permanently disable the tag.

detector A diode that receives a light-based transmission signal.

device discovery The process of querying other devices on the network to identify their locations and how many of them there are.

dibit A signal unit that represents 2 bits.

diffused transmission A light-based transmission that relies on reflected light.

digital certificate A special message signed by a certification authority that is used for security and authentication.

digital convergence The power of digital devices such as desktop computers and wireless handhelds to combine voice, video, and data, as well as to be connected to business and home networks and to the Internet.

digital modulation A method of encoding a digital signal onto an analog carrier wave for transmission over media that does not support direct digital signal transmission.

digital signal Data that is discrete or separate.

digital subscriber line (DSL) A technology used to transmit data at high speeds over a telephone line.

dipole An antenna that has a fixed amount of gain over that of an isotropic radiator.

directed transmission A light-based transmission that requires the emitter and detector to be directly aimed at one another.

directional antenna An antenna that radiates the electromagnetic waves in one direction only. As a result, it can help reduce or eliminate the effect of multipath distortion if there is a clear line of sight between the two antennas.

directional gain The effective gain that a directional antenna achieves by focusing RF energy in one direction.

direct sequence spread spectrum (DSSS) A spread spectrum technique that uses an expanded, redundant code to transmit each data bit.

disassociate frame A frame sent by the new AP to the old AP in an ESS to terminate the old AP's association with a device. Disassociation frames are transmitted from one AP to another over the wired network only, not via the wireless medium.

disassociation A procedure used by devices to leave (i.e., disconnect from) a network.

distributed coordination function (DCF) The default channel access method in IEEE 802.11 WLANs, designed to avoid collisions and grant all devices on the WLAN a reasonably equal chance to transmit on the selected channel.

dynamic rate selection (DRS) A function of an AP that allows it to automatically select the highest transmission speed based on the strength and quality of the signal received from a device WNIC.

E

Ecma International A not-for-profit standards organization for information and communication systems, such as the Ecma-352 standard.

eighth-wave antenna An antenna that is one-eighth of the wavelength of the signal it is designed to transmit or receive.

electromagnetic (EM) wave A signal composed of electrical and magnetic forces that in radio transmission usually propagates from an antenna and can be modulated to carry information.

electromagnetic interference (EMI) Interference with a radio signal; also called noise.

Electronic Product Code (EPC) A standardized numbering scheme that can be programmed in a tag and attached to any physical product.

emitter A laser diode or a light-emitting diode that transmits a light-based signal.

encryption A process of scrambling data, usually according to complex mathematical formulas, designed to prevent anyone except the intended recipient from being able to read what is being transmitted.

energy detection (ED) One of two types of procedures used by IEEE 802.15.4 compatible devices to detect the presence of RF waves from another transmission in the medium.

enhanced data rate (EDR) A feature of the Bluetooth version 2.0 specification that allows it to support data rates of 2 and 3 Mbps (by adding two modulations) while remaining fully backward compatible with Bluetooth versions 1.1 and 1.2.

Enhanced Data rates for GSM Evolution (EDGE) A 2.5G digital cellular network technology that boosts GPRS transmissions.

enhanced DCF (EDCF) An enhancement to the MAC protocol layer defined in 802.11e that enables prioritization of traffic, so that a station with higher priority frames, such as voice traffic, waits less time to transmit.

EPCglobal Inc. An organization entrusted by industry worldwide to establish RFID standards and services for real-time, automatic identification of information in the supply chain of any company anywhere in the world.

European Telecommunications Standards Institute (ETSI) A standards body that develops telecommunications standards for use throughout Europe.

exabytes One exabyte is equal to a one followed by 18 zeroes or 1 billion GB (1,000,000,000,000,000,000).

Extended Rate PHY (ERP) The generic name given by the IEEE to refer to the 802.11g amendment.

Extended Service Set (ESS) A WLAN mode that consists of wireless devices and multiple APs using the same SSID, extending a WLAN seamlessly beyond the maximum range of an 802.11 transmission.

extended synchronous connection-oriented link (eSCO) A Bluetooth SCO link that can be either asymmetric or symmetric. eSCO links are used to send point-to-point constant-rate data with limited retransmissions in case of errors.

Extensible Authentication Protocol (EAP) A group of security protocols defined in IEEE 802.1X (see IEEE 802.1X) for network authentication between a wireless device, an AP, and a RADIUS server.

F

Federal Communications Commission (FCC) The primary U.S. regulatory agency for telecommunications.

filter A component that is used to either accept or block a radio frequency signal.

fixed broadband wireless A group of wireless technologies intended for communications between fixed points such as buildings or communication towers.

fixed wireless A wireless last mile connection. Fixed wireless connections are not intended to support mobile wireless communications.

forward error correction (FEC) A technique that is used to correct bit errors in transmissions by sending extra redundant bits that are used to calculate which bit was lost or changed during transmission, so the receiving equipment can correct the error. This saves time in the case of single-bit errors because no retransmission is required.

fragmentation The division of data to be transmitted from one large frame into several smaller frames.

frame A data link layer container that includes physical addresses in the header and a trailer required for transmission in the medium (wireless or wired), but does not include any synchronization bits.

frame aggregation In the 802.11n and 802.11ac amendments, MAC (layer 2) frames can be combined in a data frame to further increase throughput on the WLAN.

free space loss The signal loss that occurs as a result of the tendency of RF waves to spread, resulting in less energy at any given point, as the signal moves away from the transmitting antenna.

Free Space Optics (FSO) An optical, wireless, point-to-point, line-of-sight broadband technology.

frequency A measurement of radio waves that is determined by how frequently a cycle occurs.

frequency division duplexing (FDD) A method of transmission that uses one frequency for uplink and another for downlink.

Frequency Division Multiple Access (FDMA) A radio transmission technique that divides the bandwidth of the frequency into several smaller frequency bands.

frequency hopping spread spectrum (FHSS) A spread spectrum technique that uses a range of frequencies and changes frequencies during the transmission.

frequency modulation (FM) A technique that changes the number of wave cycles in response to a change in the amplitude of the input signal.

frequency shift keying (FSK) A digital modulation technique that changes the frequency of the carrier signal in response to a change in the binary input signal.

Fresnel zone An elliptical region spanning the distance between two directional antennas that must not be blocked more than 40 percent to prevent interference with the RF signal.

full-duplex transmission Transmissions in which data flows in either direction simultaneously.

full-function device (FFD) A device used in 802.15.4 (ZigBee) networks that can connect to other full-function devices and has the capability of routing frames to other devices in a ZigBee network. It can also connect to endpoint or child devices. Full-function devices can maintain a connection to multiple devices and can become coordinators.

full-wave antenna An antenna that is as long as the length of the wave it is designed to transmit or receive.

G

gain A relative measure of increase in a signal's power level.

general packet radio service (GPRS) A 2.5G network technology that can transmit at up to 114 Kbps.

geosynchronous earth orbit (GEO) satellite Satellite stationed at an altitude of 22,282 miles (35,860 kilometers) that matches the rotation of the planet and therefore appears to be in a fixed position in the sky with reference to a point on the ground.

gigahertz (GHz) 1,000,000,000 (1 billion) hertz.

Global System for Mobile Communications (GSM) One of three multiple-access cellular technologies that make up the 2G digital cellular system; it uses a combination of FDMA and TDMA.

greenfield A mode of operation of 802.11n in which only HT-capable devices are supported, unless a legacy station joins the WLAN or a legacy AP is within range.

ground-plane A metal disc or two straight wires assembled at 90 degrees, used to provide a reflection point for monopole antennas that are not mounted on or near the surface of the ground.

guaranteed time slot (GTS) A reserved period for critical devices to transmit priority data.

guard band Frequency space in which no signal is transmitted. Intended to prevent interference between two transmitters using adjacent channels.

guard interval (GI) An added 800-nanosecond delay at the end of each 802.11 that allows all reflected signals to arrive at the receiver's antennas before another symbol is transmitted.

H

half-duplex transmission Transmission that occurs in both directions but only one way at a time.

half-wave antenna An antenna that is half as long as the wavelength of the signal it is designed to transmit or receive.

handoff (1) In an ESS, when a WLAN device reassociates with an AP on the network and disassociates with the one to which it was previously connected. (2) In cellular technology, the process of a cell taking over an ongoing call from another cell, as the user moves about within his or her home area's cellular coverage area.

harmonics Stray oscillations that result from the process of modulating a wave and that fall outside the range of frequencies used for transmission. Harmonics also occur when a signal goes through a mixer and must be filtered out at several points before the signal is finally fed to the antenna for transmission.

hertz (Hz) The number of cycles per second.

high throughput (HT) The generic name given to the 802.11n amendment.

highly elliptical orbit (HEO) satellite Satellite that circles the planet in an elliptical orbit, having a high apogee (maximum altitude) and a low perigee (minimum altitude). This type of satellite can provide good coverage at extreme latitudes, such as the polar regions.

high-pass filter A filter that passes all signals that are above a maximum threshold.

High-Speed Downlink Packet Access (HSDPA) A packet-switched digital transmission cellular technology that uses 5 MHz W-CDMA (wideband CDMA) channels together with adaptive modulation, MIMO, and hybrid automatic repeat request (HARQ) to achieve data rates between 8 and 10 Mbps.

hold mode A state in which the Bluetooth device can put slave units into a mode in which only the slave's internal timer is running.

hopping code The sequence of changing frequencies used in FHSS.

horn antenna A two-dimensional directional antenna typically used for microwave transmission; it resembles a large horn with the wide end bent to one side.

HSPA+ Also called "evolved HSPA," a technical cellular standard that provides theoretical data rates of up to 168 Mbps (realistically, around 42 Mbps) by combining two HSDPA transmitters, MIMO, and 64 QAM modulation.

hybrid coordination function (HCF) A combination of DCF and PCF that enhances performance, with the AP assigning both contention and contention-free periods in the beacons. The AP can allocate more contention-free periods to a device with higher-priority traffic.

I

impedance The opposition to the flow of alternating current in a circuit. Represented by the letter Z and measured in ohms, impedance is the combination of a circuit's resistance, inductance, and capacitance.

Independent Basic Service Set (IBSS) A WLAN mode in which wireless devices communicate directly among themselves without using an AP. Also called ad hoc mode and peer-to-peer mode.

Industrial, Scientific and Medical (ISM) band An unregulated radio frequency band approved by the FCC in 1985.

infrared light Light that is next to visible light on the light spectrum and that has many of the same characteristics as visible light.

infrastructure mode *See* Basic Service Set.

inquiry procedure A process that enables a Bluetooth device to discover which other Bluetooth devices are in range and determine the addresses and clocks for the devices.

Institute of Electrical and Electronics Engineers (IEEE) A nonprofit organization that creates standards related to electrical and electronics products and devices that are adopted by manufacturers worldwide. IEEE's core purpose is to foster technological innovation and excellence for the benefit of humanity.

interframe spaces (IFS) Time gaps used in CSMA/CA to allow devices to finish receiving a transmission and checking for errors before any other device is allowed to transmit.

intermediate frequency (IF) The output signal that results from the modulation process.

International Organization for Standardization (ISO) An organization to promote international cooperation and standards in the areas of science, technology, and economics.

International Telecommunication Union (ITU) An agency of the United Nations that sets international telecommunications standards and coordinates global telecommunications networks and services.

Internet Architecture Board (IAB) The organization responsible for defining the overall architecture of the Internet, providing guidance and broad direction to the IETF. The IAB also serves as the technology advisory group to the Internet Society and oversees a number of critical activities in support of the Internet.

Internet Engineering Task Force (IETF) A standards body that focuses on the upper levels of telecommunications protocols and Internet technologies.

Internet of Things (IoT) A term used to describe a large variety of sensors and actuators that are built with single-board computers and microcontrollers and can be equipped with many different wireless communications interfaces. IoT is about the data that can be collected by these sensors and what can be learned from our environment by analyzing this data in real time or from a historical perspective.

Internet Society (ISOC) A professional-membership organization of Internet experts that comments on policies and practices and oversees a number of other boards and task forces dealing with network policy issues.

intersymbol interference (ISI) Interference caused when delayed multipath signals arrive at the receiver antenna while a later, different symbol taking a more direct path is already arriving at the antenna.

isotropic radiator A theoretically perfect sphere that radiates power equally in all directions; it is impossible to construct one.

J

jitter The delay variation between two consecutive packets over a period of time.

K

kilohertz (KHz) 1,000 hertz.

L

last mile connection Usually, the link between an end-user and an ISP or telephone company, but the term is sometimes used to refer to a connection to an entire community that was not previously serviced by communication lines.

latency The amount of time delay that it takes a packet to travel from source to destination device.

license exempt spectrum Unregulated radio frequency bands that are available in the United States to any users without a license.

light spectrum All the different types of light that travel from the Sun to the Earth.

lightweight AP (LWAP) A PHY-layer wireless device that also implements part of the MAC-layer functionality. These devices are used in conjunction with wireless controllers (see wireless controller).

line of sight The direct alignment as required in a directed transmission.

link budget The process of calculating the signal strength between the transmitter and receiver antennas to ensure that the link can meet the receiver's minimum signal strength requirements.

link manager Special software in Bluetooth devices that helps identify other Bluetooth devices, creates the links between them, and sends and receives data.

Logical Link Control (LLC) One of the two sublayers of the IEEE Project 802 data link layer.

Long Term Evolution (LTE) A 4G digital packet-switched cellular technology that expands on HSPA+ beyond two spatially multiplexed channels, uses OFDM modulation, and also uses 20-MHz-wide channels to achieve data rates of up to 100 Mbps.

LoRa A wireless technology specification published by the LoRa Alliance. The specification defines classes of IoT devices, communication protocols, etc. for gateways and sensors used in IoT networks that use very low power and have a range of up to 20 miles (32 kilometers).

loss A relative measure of decrease in a signal's power level.

low earth orbit (LEO) satellite Satellite that orbits the Earth at an altitude of 200 to 900 miles (321 to 1,448 kilometers).

low-pass filter A filter that passes all signals that are below a maximum threshold.

LTE Advanced A proposed standard for broadband cellular communications that expands on LTE by allowing carriers to combine up to five 20-MHz-wide OFDM channels to achieve data rates of up to 1 Gbps.

M

machine-to-machine (M2M) communication A term used to describe devices that are intended to communicate with other devices, not with human beings.

management frame MAC frame that is used, for example, to set up the initial communications between a device and the AP.

man-in-the-middle A network-security attack in which the attacker uses software installed in a computer to duplicate the behavior of an enterprise AP.

master A device on a Bluetooth piconet that controls all the wireless traffic.

Media Access Control (MAC) One of the two sublayers of the IEEE Project 802 data link layer.

medium earth orbit (MEO) satellite Satellite that orbits the Earth at altitudes of 1,500 to 10,000 miles (2,413 to 16,090 kilometers).

megahertz (MHz) 1,000,000 (1 million) hertz.

message integrity check (MIC) A combination of variable and static data items that ensures encrypted data has not been altered during transmission between source and destination devices.

message integrity code (MIC) A code composed of a subset of the data, the length of the data, and the symmetric key; used by the receiving device to verify that the data has not been tampered with during transmission.

microwave Higher-frequency RF wave that uses the 3- to 30-GHz and 30- to 300-GHz ranges of the electromagnetic spectrum.

Mini PCI A small card that is functionally equivalent to a standard PCI expansion card used for integrating communications peripherals onto a laptop computer but that is much smaller.

mixer A component that combines two inputs to create a single output.

mobile telecommunications switching office (MTSO) The connection between a cellular network and wired telephones.

modem (MOdulator/DEModulator) A device used to convert digital signals into an analog format and vice versa.

modulation The process of changing a carrier signal.

modulation and coding sets (MCSs) A combination of modulation, guard interval, and FEC coding that defines the data rates in 802.11n/ac.

monopole antenna An antenna built of a straight piece of wire, usually a quarter of the wavelength with no ground point or reflecting element.

multipath distortion What occurs when the same signal reflects and arrives at the receiver's antenna from several different directions and at different times.

multiple-input and multiple-output (MIMO) A technology that uses multiple antennas (usually three or four) and reflected signals (multipath reflections) to extend the range of the WLAN by attempting to correctly decode a frame from multiple copies of it received at different times.

multi-user MIMO (MU-MIMO) A feature of 802.11ac that enables an AP with multiple radios to communicate with different devices simultaneously using different groups of radios and different spatial streams.

N

narrow-band transmission Transmission that uses one radio frequency or a very narrow portion of the frequency spectrum.

near field communication (NFC) A technology similar and sometimes compatible with RFID that can store data that can be used to configure and activate a connection between two devices over Bluetooth or Wi-Fi. NFC tags are similar to RFID tags and can also store web addresses and may contain commands to be executed by a smartphone or tablet, such as opening a web browser and automatically entering an address.

noise *See* electromagnetic interference (EMI).

nomadic user A user who moves frequently but does not use the equipment while in motion.

non-return-to-zero (NRZ) A binary signaling technique that increases the voltage to represent a 1 bit but provides no voltage for a 0 bit.

non-return-to-zero, invert-on-ones (NRZ-I) A binary signaling technique that changes the voltage level only when the bit to be represented is a 1; a variation of NRZ-L.

non-return-to-zero-level (NRZ-L) *See* polar non-return-to-zero.

null data frame The response that a device sends back to the AP to indicate that the device has no transmissions to make in PCF.

O

Object Name Service (ONS) An EPCglobal Inc. service, modeled after DNS, that can assist in locating information about a product over the Internet.

official standards *See* de jure standards.

offset quadrature phase shift keying (O-QPSK) A transmission technique in 802.15.4 that uses two carrier waves of the same frequency but with a phase difference of 90 degrees between them. This technique modulates even-numbered chips in the in-phase wave and odd-numbered chips in the other phase (Q-Phase), using quadrature amplitude modulation, before combining the waves for transmission.

omnidirectional antenna An antenna that sends out the signal in a uniform pattern in all directions.

one-dimensional antenna A straight length of wire or metal connected to a transmitter at one end.

optical fiber A glass strand, about the thickness of a human hair, that carries data signals encoded in a laser beam.

orthogonal frequency division multiplexing (OFDM) A transmission technology that divides the available frequency bandwidth into multiple orthogonal subcarriers, then modulates bits onto different subcarriers, and transmits multiple bits at the same time in each.

orthogonal frequency division multiple access (OFDMA) A method based on OFDM that assigns groups of subcarriers to different users.

oscillating signal A wave that illustrates the change in a carrier signal.

P

packet switching Data transmission that is broken into smaller units.

packet A smaller segment of the transmitted signal.

paging procedure A process that enables a device to make an actual connection to a piconet.

pairing A two-step process for establishing a connection between a Bluetooth master and slave devices.

PAN coordinator The 802.15.4 device that controls access to the piconet and optionally the timing as well.

parabolic dish antenna A high-gain directional antenna that emits a narrow, focused beam of energy and is used for long-distance outdoor links.

park mode A state in which the Bluetooth device is still synchronized to the piconet but does not participate in the traffic.

passband A minimum and maximum threshold that spells out which range of frequencies will pass through a filter.

passive antenna The most common type of antenna. Passive antennas can only radiate a signal with the same amount of energy that appears at the antenna connector.

passive scanning The process of listening to each available channel for a set period of time.

passive tag The most common type of RFID tag. It does not include a battery and is powered by the electromagnetic energy in the RF waves transmitted by the reader. Passive tags never initiate a transmission and must wait for a reader to interrogate them.

patch antenna A semidirectional antenna that emits a wide horizontal beam and an even wider vertical beam.

PBCC (packet binary convolutional coding) An optional transmission mode of 802.11 that can send data at rates of 22 or 33 Mbps using either QPSK or 8PSK, respectively.

peer-to-peer mode *See* ad hoc mode.

phase The relative starting point of a wave, in degrees, beginning at 0 degrees.

phase modulation (PM) A technique that changes the starting point of a wave cycle in response to a change in the amplitude of the input signal. This technique is not used in analog modulation.

phase shift keying (PSK) A digital modulation technique that changes the starting point of a wave cycle in response to a change in the binary input signal.

physical layer (PHY) The OSI layer that is responsible for converting the data bits into an electromagnetic signal and transmitting it on the medium.

Physical Layer Convergence Procedure (PLCP) The IEEE 802.15 sublayer that formats the data received from the MAC for transmission by adding a header and a trailer appropriate to the medium to be used, creating what is called a frame.

Physical Medium Dependent (PMD) The IEEE 802.15 sublayer that is responsible for converting the bits into a modulated carrier wave and transmitting it on the medium.

pi/4-DQPSK A method of modulation introduced in Bluetooth version 2 that uses two different frequencies exactly 90 degrees apart and that therefore do not interfere with each other.

piconet A Bluetooth network that contains one master and at least one slave that use the same channel.

plain old telephone system (POTS) *See* public switched telephone network.

PN code Pseudo random code; a code that appears to be a random sequence of 1s and 0s but actually repeats itself. Used in CDMA cellular telephone technology.

point coordination function (PCF) The 802.11 optional polling function.

point-to-multipoint wireless link A link in which one central site uses an omnidirectional antenna to transmit to multiple remote sites, which may use omnidirectional antennas or directional antennas to maximize the distance and the quality of the signal.

point-to-point The most reliable link between two antenna sites using directional antennas to maximize the distance and the signal quality.

polar non-return-to-zero (polar NRZ) A binary signaling technique that increases the voltage to represent a 1 bit but drops to negative voltage to represent a 0 bit.

polling A channel access method in which each computer is asked in sequence whether it wants to transmit.

power management An 802.11 standard that allows the mobile device to be off as much as possible to conserve battery life but still not miss out on data transmissions.

power over Ethernet (PoE) A technology that provides power over an Ethernet cable.

Power Save Multi-Poll (PSMP) An alternate method of reducing power consumption defined in 802.11n that allows devices to switch off all but one radio.

pre-shared key (PSK) A 128-bit key used by WPA; it is called "pre-shared" because it is manually configured in each WLAN device before connections can be established.

privacy Standards that ensure transmissions are not read by unauthorized users.

probe A frame sent by a device when performing active scanning.

probe response A frame sent by an AP when responding to a device's active scanning probe.

profile Set of predefined WiMAX connection parameters that include the frequency channel, bandwidth of the channel, and transmission mechanism (OFDM, OFDMA, etc.).

protection mechanism A protocol feature used to allow devices to participate in an 802.11 WLAN without interfering with transmissions and causing data corruption due to collisions because they are not able to "understand" the modulation and coding.

pseudo-random code A code that is usually derived through a number of mathematical calculations as well as practical experimentation.

public key infrastructure (PKI) A unique security code that can verify the authenticity of a user.

public switched telephone network (PSTN) The wired telephone network. Sometimes referred to as the plain old telephone system (POTS).

Q

QoS (quality-of-service) A resource reservation enhancement to the 802.11 MAC layer that enables prioritization of traffic and is most often used to support delivery of voice, video, and audio frames between WLAN devices.

quadbit A signal unit that represents 4 bits.

quadrature amplitude modulation (QAM) A combination of phase modulation with amplitude modulation to produce 16 different signals.

quadrature phase shift keying (QPSK) A digital modulation technique that combines quadrature amplitude modulation with phase shift keying.

quarter-wave antenna An antenna that is one-quarter of the wavelength of the signal it is designed to transmit or receive.

R

radio chains The name given in the 802.11 standard to devices that have multiple radios.

radio frequency (RF) communications All types of radio communications that use radio frequency waves.

radio frequency identification (RFID) A technology developed to replace barcodes that uses small tags placed on product packaging and boxes that can be remotely activated and read by sensors. The data about the product is then transferred directly to an information-processing system for inventory control, location tracking, and item counting.

radio frequency spectrum The entire range of all radio frequencies that exist.

radio module Small radio transceiver built onto micropro-cessor chips and embedded into Bluetooth devices, which enable them to communicate.

radio wave (sometimes called radiotelephony) An electromagnetic wave created when an electric current passes through a wire and creates a magnetic field in the space around the wire.

reader The RFID device that captures and processes the data received from the tags. Also called an interrogator.

real-time location system (RTLS) A technology that makes use of wireless transmitters (tags) worn by people or permanently attached to movable assets to track their location and activity. Through the use of multiple receivers installed throughout a building, RTLS can display the location of a wireless tag at a central computer display. RTLS is widely deployed in hospitals to enable doctors, nurses, and equipment to be located quickly and efficiently.

reassociate request frame A frame sent from a device to a new AP asking whether it can associate with the AP.

reassociate response frame A frame sent by an AP to a station indicating that it will accept its reassociation with that AP.

reassociation The process of a device disconnecting from one AP and reestablishing a connection with another AP.

Reduced Interframe Space (RIFS) A 2-microsecond inter-frame space that can be used in 802.11n networks working in greenfield mode to help reduce overhead and increase throughput.

reduced-function device (RFD) In ZigBee networks, a device (such as a light switch or lamp) that can only connect to one full-function device at a time and can only join the network as a child device.

Remote Authentication Dial-In User Service (RADIUS) A popular method of authenticating users on a network—before completing its association with an AP.

repeater A device commonly used in satellite communica-tions that simply "repeats" the signal to another location.

request-to-send/clear-to-send (RTS/CTS) An 802.11 protocol option that allows a station to reserve the network for transmissions.

return-to-zero (RZ) A binary signaling technique that increases the voltage to represent a 1 bit, but the voltage is reduced to 0 before the end of the period for transmitting the 1 bit, and there is no voltage for a 0 bit.

RFID reader or RFID interrogator A device that emits electromagnectic energy to power a typical RFID tag and can transmit to and read the data stored in the tag's memory.

RFID tag Device embedded in or attached to an object that contains a chip and antenna. The chip is powered by the energy emitted by an RFID reader and can then transmit information contained in its memory back to the reader.

roaming What happens when a cellular user connects to a network outside of her home area.

Robust Security Network Association (RSNA) The end result of using 802.11i and 802.1X to secure an enterprise WLAN.

RSA An encryption algorithm that uses a large integer composed of smaller numbers that are multiplied by each other. It is based on the idea that it will be difficult to figure out each of the smaller numbers that are used to arrive at the large integer. RSA encryption has been largely superceeded by the more secure AES encryption.

S

scatternet A group of piconets in which connections exist between different piconets.

scintillation The temporal and spatial variation in light intensity caused by atmospheric turbulence.

semi-active tag RFID tag that includes a battery that is only used when the tag is interrogated. The batteries in semi-active tags usually last for several years. Also referred to as a semi-passive tag.

sensory tag RFID tag that includes a thermal or other kind of sensor and can record information about the environmen-tal conditions to which a product has been exposed during transportation or storage.

sequential freshness A security service available in 802.15.4 and used by the receiving device; it ensures that the same frames will not be transmitted more than once.

service discovery The process of sending a query to other devices on the network to identify their capabilities.

Service Set Identifier (SSID) A unique network identifier assigned to an AP during configuration. In an Extended Ser-vice Set (ESS), all APs will be configured with the same SSID.

Short Interframe Space (SIFS) A time period used to allow a receiving station to finish receiving all signals, decode them, and check for errors.

sidebands The range of frequencies, above and below the carrier frequency of the transmitted signal, in which a signal is transmitted.

signal-to-noise ratio (SNR) The measure of signal strength relative to the background noise.

SIM (subscriber identity module) card Small electronic card used to associate a phone with a user's account.

simplex transmission Transmission that occurs in only one direction.

sine wave A wave that illustrates the change in a carrier signal.

single-carrier FDMA (SC-FDMA) The technology used in LTE for mobile phones to communicate back to the tower transceivers. SC-FDMA assigns a single subcarrier to the same OFDM uplink stream to each mobile user communicating with the same tower.

slave A device on a Bluetooth piconet that takes commands from the master.

sleep mode A power-conserving mode used by portable, battery-powered devices in a WLAN.

Slotted Terminating Adaptive Collection (STAC) The communications protocol used by passive RFID tags that work in the 13.56 MHz HF band.

smart antenna A new type of antenna that uses a signal processor and an array of narrow beam elements to track the user and send most of the RF energy in the direction of the mobile receiver in order to prevent interference and avoid wasting RF energy. There are two types of smart antennas, switched-beam and adaptive or phased array antenna.

smart label Another name for a flexible RFID tag that includes a microprocessor chip, memory, and antenna.

smartphone A device that combines a cellular phone with the capabilities of a personal digital assistant (PDA). These devices provide the user with the ability to enter appointments in a calendar, write notes, send and receive email, play games, watch videos, and browse websites, among other functions.

smartwatch Device that functions as a regular watch but also connects via Bluetooth to the owner's smartphone. Some of these devices can run applications that link directly to the same app on the smartphone, while others only display email messages, notifications, and calls from the smartphone. A few models are equipped with speakers and microphones that allow you to answer a call without having to use the smartphone and others give you the ability to respond to text messages using your voice, directly from the watch.

sniff mode A state in which the Bluetooth device listens to the piconet master at a reduced rate so that it uses less power.

spatial diversity Sending parallel beams of the same data during Free Space Optical transmissions.

spatial multiplexing A transmission technique that uses multiple radios and multiple antennas to send different parts of the same message simultaneously, thus increasing the data rate.

Spatial Multiplexing Power Save (SMPS) A power-saving mode defined in 802.11n in which devices can switch off all except one radio to reduce power consumption.

spread spectrum transmission A technique that takes a narrow signal and spreads it over a broader portion of the radio frequency band.

subnets Subsets of a large network that use a different group of IP addresses belonging to the same domain IP address. Subnets are separated from other subnets by routers.

subscriber station (SS) In a WiMAX network, either a customer premises equipment (CPE) device that attaches to a LAN or a laptop computer.

superframe A mechanism for managing transmissions in a piconet. The superframe is a continually repeating frame containing a beacon, contention access periods, channel time allocation periods, and management time allocation periods. Using the superframe is optional in 802.15.4 WPANs.

switching Moving a signal from one wire or frequency to another.

symbol A data unit that can represent one or more bits.

symmetric key A sequence of numbers and letters, much like a password, that must be entered by the authorized user on all devices.

synchronous connection-oriented (SCO) link A symmetric point-to-point link between a master and a single slave in the piconet; it functions like a circuit-switched link by using reserved slots at regular intervals.

system profile A combination of the basic WiMAX profile and one of the transmission profiles, such as point-to-multipoint (P2MP), point-to-point (PTP), or an optional mesh networking profile.

T

T1 An older wired technology used to transmit data over special telephone lines at 1.544 Mbps.

tag Device that includes an antenna and a chip containing memory and can store information about products, such as the manufacturer, product category, and serial number along with date and time of manufacturing.

Telecommunications Industries Association (TIA) A group of more than 600 companies that manufacture or supply the products and services used in global communications.

temporal key integrity protocol (TKIP) A security protocol used in WPA that provides perpacket key-mixing.

time division duplexing (TDD) A method of transmission that divides a single transmission into two parts: an uplink part and a downlink part.

time division multiple access (TDMA) A method of transmission that allows multiple device communications by allocating time slots to different senders and receivers.

time slots The measurement unit in a PLCP frame.

traffic encryption key (TEK) The security key used to encrypt the data in aWiMAX network.

traffic indication map (TIM) A list of the stations that have buffered frames waiting at the AP. The TIM is sent in the beacons by the AP.

transponder Another name for RFID tag.

tribit A signal unit that represents 3 bits.

triple play Support for transmission of video, voice, and data on the same network.

truck-roll A visit to a site by support technicians.

two-dimensional antenna An antenna, such as a dish or patch, that has both height and width. In omnidirectional antennas, the thickness of the pole or wire is not considered a second dimension.

two-level Gaussian frequency shift keying (2-GFSK) A binary signaling technique that uses two different frequencies to indicate whether a 1 or a 0 is being transmitted.

U

Ultra Wide Band (UWB) A wireless communications technology that allows devices to transmit data at hundreds of megabits or even gigabits per second at short distances—up to 6 feet (2 meters) at the higher speeds and up to 150 feet (50 meters) at lower speeds.

Unicode An international encoding standard that is capable of supporting numeric character codes to represent all the different languages and scripts in the world, such as Arabic, Hebrew, multiple Chinese and Japanese scripts, Sanskrit, etc.

Unlicensed National Information Infrastructure (U-NII) An unregulated band approved by the FCC in 1996 to provide for short-range, high-speed wireless digital communications.

unregulated bands *See* license exempt spectrum.

USB A common way of connecting peripherals such as flash drives, Wi-Fi NICs, printers, and other peripherals to a computer. Stands for Universal Serial Bus.

V

very high throughput (VHT) The generic name given to the 802.11ac amendment by the IEEE.

virtual private network (VPN) A secure, encrypted connection between two points over a public network.

Voice over Internet Protocol (VoIP) A technology that allows voice telephone calls to be carried over the same network used to carry computer data.

Voice over LTE (VoLTE) VoLTE enables carriers to move from circuit-switched voice and packet-switched data to a totally IP-based network, carrying both digitized voice encapsulated in IP datagrams, as well as data.

Voice over WLAN (VoWLAN) A term used to describe the transmission of telephone calls on WLANs.

voltage Electrical pressure.

W

war driving The practice of discovering and recording information about WLANs in a neighborhood or around a city while driving or walking.

waveguide A rectangular cavity metal tube that was used to carry microwaves to and from the antennas mounted at the top of the towers, to the transmitter and receiver at the base of the tower.

wavelength The length of a wave as measured between two positive or negative peaks or between the starting point of one wave and the starting point of the next wave.

Wideband CDMA (W-CDMA) The 3G digital cellular technology that is a migration from EDGE.

Wi-Fi A trademark of the Wi-Fi Alliance, used to refer to 802.11b and later WLANs that pass the organization's interoperability tests. The acronym is often thought to stand for Wireless Fidelity, but this is a common misconception. The name was chosen by the alliance purely for marketing reasons and is not an acronym at all.

Wi-Fi Direct A specification from the Wi-Fi Alliance that makes it simpler to wirelessly connect any two devices, such as a camera and a smartphone.

Wi-Fi hotspot A public Wi-Fi network that is available at many stores, coffee shops, auto repair shops, fast-food outlets, etc., for use by its customers. Individuals can also use some smartphones to create a private Wi-Fi hotspot.

Wi-Fi Protected Access (WPA) A security enhancement and interoperability certification introduced by the Wi-Fi Alliance in advance of the 802.11i standard to deal with the security flaws in WEP. *See also* WPA2.

Wi-Fi Protected Setup (WPS) A method defined by the Wi-Fi alliance that simplifies the process of securing a WLAN for nontechnical users.

WiGig A specification for connecting computers, communication, and entertainment devices over short ranges, using the 60 GHz band at multi-gigabit speeds, developed by an alliance of companies.

WiMAX Forum An industry organization dedicated to promoting the implementation of 802.16 (WiMAX) by testing and certifying equipment for compatibility and interoperability.

Wired Equivalent Privacy (WEP) The IEEE 802.11-1997 specification for data encryption between wireless devices to prevent an attacker from eavesdropping.

wireless access point (wireless AP or just AP) A device that receives the signals and transmits signals back to wireless network interface cards (NICs), typically in a WLAN. APs connect wireless devices to a wired network such as the Internet.

wireless bridge A networking component that is typically used to interconnect two-wired networks using directional antennas. Multiple bridges can be combined in a single link, to increase the data rate and throughput.

wireless communications Generally refers to any type of communications that does not require the use of wires or cables. In this sense, smoke signals and police radio may be understood as forms of wireless communications, but for the purpose of this book, wireless communications is defined as the wireless transmission of digital data while connected to some type of network.

wireless controller A device that makes it much easier to manage large WLANs by implementing most of the functions of an AP and controlling the operation of local or remotely connected Wi-Fi transceivers called lightweight APs (see lightweight AP). Some controllers are implemented in software, which allows cloud-based management of WLANs.

Wireless Distribution System (WDS) A feature of some wireless routers and APs that enables them to be configured as a bridge or repeater.

WirelessHART A wireless sensor network protocol based on the highway addressable remote transducer protocol (HART), designed for interfacing manufacturing equipment and machines.

WirelessHD A specification by the WirelessHD organization that works in the 60 GHz band and is used for transmitting HDMI video and audio signals to televisions and display monitors. WirelessHD is not compatible with 802.11.

Wireless High-Speed Unlicensed Metro Area Network (WirelessHUMAN) A WiMAX specification based on OFDM that is specifically designed for use in the 5 GHz U-NII band.

Wireless Home Digital Interface (WHDI) An industry association that developed a wireless HDMI multimedia distribution specification of the same name (WHDI), which operates in the 5 GHz U-NII band. Like WirelessHD, WHDI is not compatible with 802.11.

Wireless Intrusion Detection System (WIDS) A WIDS can detect the presence of unauthorized devices, such as a

computer impersonating an AP and send a notification to system administrators.

Wireless Intrusion Prevention System (WIPS) A stand-alone hardware device or feature of some advanced APs that can be deployed to monitor the RF spectrum and detect the presence of unauthorized APs.

wireless local area network (WLAN) A local area network that is not connected by wires but instead uses wireless technology. Its range extends to approximately 330 feet (100 meters) and has a data rate of 600 Mbps and higher. Today's WLANs are based on IEEE 802.11a/b/g/n/ac/ad standards.

WirelessMAN-OFDM A WiMAX specification that can be used for fixed, mobile, or mesh networking applications and uses either TDD or FDD in licensed bands below 11 GHz.

WirelessMAN-OFDMA A method used in WiMAX to allow transmission to and from multiple source and destination devices within a single uplink or downlink frame. It divides the available frequency channel into 1,536 orthogonal data subcarriers and uses groups of subcarriers, called subchannels, to communicate with different devices simultaneously.

WirelessMAN-SC (single carrier) A WiMAX specification that uses a single carrier and is intended for point-to-point connections in the 10 to 66 GHz bands.

wireless metropolitan area network (WMAN) A wireless network that covers a large geographical area such as a city or suburb. The technology is usually based on the IEEE 802.16 (WiMAX) set of standards and can span an entire city, covering distances of up to 35 miles (56 kilometers) between transmitters and receivers or repeaters.

wireless network interface card (wireless NIC) A device that connects to a computer or other digital device to transmit and receive network data over radio waves. It includes an antenna for wireless communication between networked devices.

wireless personal area network (WPAN) A very small network that typically extends to 33 feet (10 meters) or less. Due to its limited range, WPAN technology is used mainly as a replacement for cables. See also piconet and Ultra Wide Band.

wireless residential gateway (often called a wireless router) Device used to set up a Wi-Fi network in a home or small office. These devices are used to connect a home or small office to the Internet and are often supplied by the service provider, integrated with a cable modem.

wireless site survey A test that is conducted before deployment of a WLAN to determine the best location for APs and antennas, in order to provide maximum coverage.

wireless wide area network (WWAN) A WAN that uses cellular phone technologies and encompasses any geographical region, including the entire globe.

WPA2 A security specification and interoperability certification introduced by the Wi-Fi Alliance as an enhancement to WPA that includes support for AES encryption as well as support for 802.11i and 802.1X.

Y

yagi antenna A directional antenna that emits a wide, less-focused beam and is used for medium-distance outdoor applications.

Z

ZigBee A specification based on IEEE 802.15.4 developed by the ZigBee Alliance, an organization that creates protocols and specifications for devices used for home automation that can wirelessly control lighting, as well as security and energy systems, in homes and industries.

ZigBee Alliance An association of manufacturers and interested organizations formed to promote the creation of a global standard for wireless devices used in monitoring and control applications.